795

croeconomic Stabilization and Adjustment

For Shubha
— MJMR

For my mother Sulochana and
the loving memory of my
father Krishna Naidu
— RN

Macroeconomic Stabilization and Adjustment

M.J. Manohar Rao
Raj Nallari

OXFORD
UNIVERSITY PRESS

OXFORD

UNIVERSITY PRESS

YMCA Library Building, Jai Singh Road, New Delhi 110001

Oxford University Press is a department of the University of Oxford. It furthers
the University's objective of excellence in research, scholarship, and education
by publishing worldwide in

Oxford   New York

Athens   Auckland   Bangkok   Bogota   Buenos Aires
Cape Town   Chennai   Dar es Salaam   Delhi   Florence   Hong Kong   Istanbul
Karachi   Kolkata   Kuala Lumpur   Madrid   Melbourne   Mexico City   Mumbai
Nairobi   Paris   Sao Paolo   Shanghai   Singapore   Taipei   Tokyo   Toronto   Warsaw

with associated companies in   Berlin   Ibadan
Oxford is a registered trade mark of Oxford University Press
in the UK and in certain other countries

Published in India
By Oxford University Press, New Delhi

ISBN 019 565548 6

Typeset by Inosoft Systems, Delhi 110 092.
Printed at Saurabh Print-O-Pack, NOIDA, UP.
Published by Manzar Khan, Oxford University Press
YMCA Library Building, Jai Singh Road, New Delhi 110 001

Acknowledgements

The fact that we were able to conceptualize and complete the first draft of this work within five months (July–November 1996) is indeed a tribute to the intellectually stimulating environment provided by the Research Department of the International Monetary Fund (IMF), as well as to the help and encouragement of several individuals at that institution and elsewhere.

More than anyone else, we are grateful to P.R. Narvekar, without whose help and encouragement, this book could never have even been contemplated, let alone completed. To him, we owe the greatest debt of all.

We would also like to express our heartfelt appreciation to Mohsin Khan for providing us with his technical expertise on the subject of merged Bank–Fund modelling in which he is the undisputed authority. Special thanks are also due to Paul Masson and Donald Mathieson for sharing their insights on macroeconomic policy formulation, thereby helping to sharpen the focus of the study.

We are also deeply indebted to Jayanta Roy and R. Kannan for providing extremely valuable comments on the technical formulation of the financial programming approach to stabilization and adjustment.

We wish to thank Hazel Vargas, Usha Pitts, and Cynthia Galang for all the assistance they provided in putting together the initial draft of the manuscript.

Last, but not the least, our deepest gratitude to Nina Asher who, after assiduously carrying out the laborious task of checking and correcting the final draft, gave finishing touches to the manuscript with her word-processing expertise.

While writing this book, we have, as far as possible, attempted to derive most of the theoretical results by strictly adhering to macroeconomic 'first principles' and trying to avoid, what has been aptly termed by Jean Waelbroeck as, 'John Wayne Econometrics' in which 'the valiant econometrician strides through his sample, his trusted OLS colt at his hip, ignoring dangerous outliers, avoiding concealed residuals, pursuing elusive theories, and finally riding off into the sunset with the beautiful regression at his side'. In trying to do so, and considering the extent of territory we had to cover, it is possible that we could have stumbled into analytical pitfalls which have very often surprised even the most wary of economic researchers and, in this context, we alone are responsible for the resulting application errors, design flaws, or theoretical inconsistencies (and we sincerely hope that these are in descending order of magnitude) that could have cropped up in the study.

M.J. Manohar Rao
Raj Nallari*

*The findings, interpretations, and conclusions are the author's own and should not be attributed to the World Bank, its Executive Board of Directors, or any of its member countries.

Contents

Tables

Figures

Notations and Model Versions

A	Domestic absorption
b	Internal debt–income ratio
B	Stock of internal debt
ΔB	Total domestic borrowings
c	Government consumption–income ratio
Cg	Government non-interest consumption expenditure
Cp	Private consumption
d	Depreciation rate of capital stock
ΔDC	Change in domestic credit
ΔDCg	Change in domestic credit to the government sector
ΔDCp	Change in domestic credit to the private sector
e	Rate of change in the nominal exchange rate
E	Nominal exchange rate
$fg*$	External debt–income ratio (fcu)[1]
ΔF	Total foreign borrowings/capital flows (dcu)[2]
$\Delta F*$	Total foreign borrowings/capital flows (fcu)
FD	Gross fiscal deficit
$Fg*$	Stock of external debt (fcu)
$\Delta Fp*$	Private sector external borrowings/private capital flows (fcu)
g	Real growth rate
G	Total government expenditure
GI	Gini index

[1]fcu: foreign currency units
[2]dcu: domestic currency units

i	Domestic rate of interest
i_f	Foreign rate of interest
I	Total investment
Ig	Public sector investment
Ip	Private sector investment
I^t	Inflation tax revenue
k	Output–capital ratio
m	Real money stock
ΔM	Change in money supply
Md	Nominal money demand
NW	Banking sector net worth
P	Domestic price level
P_f	Foreign price level
Qz	Volume of imports
r	Real domestic interest rate
r_f	Real foreign interest rate
ΔR	Change in foreign exchange reserves (dcu)
ΔR^*	Change in foreign exchange reserves (fcu)
RER	Real exchange rate
s	Savings rate
S	Domestic savings
S^*	Seignorage revenue
Sg	Public sector savings
Sp	Private sector savings
t	Average tax rate
T	Total tax revenue
v	Income velocity of money
X	Exports of goods and net services (dcu)
X^*	Exports of goods and net services (fcu)
y	Real output
Y	Nominal income (in currency units)
Y^*	Nominal income (fcu)
Yg	Public sector income
Yp	Private sector income
Z	Imports of goods
Z^*	Imports of goods
Γ	Rate of growth of domestic borrowings
μ	Growth rate of money supply
π	Domestic inflation rate
π_f	Foreign inflation rate
τ	Growth rate of tax revenue

MODEL VERSIONS

Chapter	Model Version	Target Variables	Policy Variables	Comments
4	RM1	ΔR, π	ΔDC, ΔE	• the original Fund model solved to obtain forecasts for 1995–6
6	RM2	ΔR, π, g	ΔDC, ΔE	used for stabilization and financial programming analysis • the basic merged Bank–Fund model. solved to obtain forecasts for 1995–6
6	RM3	ΔR^*, π, g	ΔDC, e, ΔF^*	used to explain the concept of Fund–Bank equilibrium • foreign exchange reserves specified in foreign currency units additional instrument (ΔF^*) added solved to obtain forecasts for 1996–7
7	RM4	ΔR^*, π, g, i	ΔDC, e, ΔF^*	used to obtain stabilization policy options • the rate of interest endogenized and related to growth and inflation solved to obtain forecasts for 1996–7
8	RM5	ΔR^*, π, g, i	ΔDC, e, ΔF^*, τ	used to design a consistent interest rate policy • the fiscal deficit is implicitly endogenized additional instrument (τ) is included in the model used to obtain forecasts for 1996–7
9	RM6	ΔR^*, π, g, i, FD, Fg^*	ΔDCg, ΔDCp, e, τ, Ig, Γ	to design fiscally consistent options • fiscal deficit and external debt are explicitly endogenized additional instruments (Ig, Γ) included used to obtain forecasts for 1996–7
10	RM7	ΔR^*, π, g, i, FD, Fg^*, GI	ΔDCg, ΔDCp, e, τ, Ig, Γ	to derive policy coordination options • income distribution is endogenized and the impact of policy variables on income distribution is estimated used to establish the concept of joint Bank–Fund–UNICEF equilibrium

1

Introduction

1.1 OVERVIEW

This book is a technical introduction to the theory and design of stabilization and growth-oriented structural adjustment programmes. As the ongoing debate over such programmes has often been very confused due to the inherent unfamiliarity with the basic macroeconomic logic underlying these programmes, the objective of this book is to provide an analytical framework essential for understanding certain key aspects related to the structure and transformation of open economies, so as to facilitate discussions on these issues amongst students, researchers, academicians, as well as policy makers.

The existing teaching material has largely ignored these concepts which relate development economics to macroeconomic analysis. Consequently, economic growth, rather than short-run stabilization policy, remains the dominant concern in existing texts in development economics; while inflation, rather than long-run structural adjustment policy, remains the recurrent theme in standard texts on macroeconomics. Consequently, when issues related to both stabilization as well as structural adjustment need to be jointly discussed within the context of developing economies, there is no analytical framework readily available to fall back upon. This book attempts to bridge this gap between macroeconomics and development economics by adapting the existing theory of short-run macroeconomic stabilization to the particular conditions and structural characteristics of developing economies.

Considering the fact that the framework of most stabilization and structural adjustment programmes is a blend of two extremely influential approaches to macroeconomic analysis, that is the financial programming approach developed by the International Monetary Fund (IMF) and the financial requirements approach developed by the World Bank, it is essential to consider our analysis on broadly similar lines if one has to fully grasp the overall implications of any reform process. It is primarily with this view in mind that we have made every possible effort to present the fairly rigorous analytical underpinnings behind these two approaches in as simple a manner as possible without loss of generality or precision in the process.

In doing so, and subsequently extending these results, this book attempts to present a more coherent approach to the macroeconomics of developing countries. Moreover, by providing empirical evidence, with special reference to the Indian economy, to highlight the predictions of the analytical models, it illustrates the applicability and robustness of such an integrated approach towards 'development macroeconomics'. This book's level of theoretical rigour makes it suitable for teaching graduate students in macroeconomics as well as development economics; while its empirical content should make it interesting enough for policy makers and their advisers in developing countries.

1.2 Interest in Structural Adjustment Programmes

There are several reasons for the current interest in macroeconomic adjustment throughout the developing world. Macroeconomic adjustment, which broadly comprises stabilization and structural reform policies, is required whenever imbalances persist between aggregate domestic demand and aggregate domestic supply. This imbalance could be generated by exogenous shocks, such as adverse changes in the terms of trade or natural events. Disequilibria could also be generated due to distortions on account of unsustainable domestic policies. However, as long as foreign resources are available, such a situation of excess demand can be sustained, albeit at severe economic costs, such as rising external debt, high inflation, and stagnant growth. Eventually, however, macroeconomic adjustment, in terms of reducing absorption as well as improving the balance of payments (BOP) situation, would be needed in order to rectify the deteriorating situation.

As a result of the second oil price shock in 1980, the external debt crises in 1982, and the economic failure of centrally-planned economic systems in the mid-1980s, most developing countries faced severe foreign exchange constraints, resulting in protracted stagnation. In response to these and related problems, including the increase in real interest rates and weaknesses in domestic policy management, the IMF and the World Bank embarked on structural adjustment programmes in the 1980s. The objective of these adjustment programmes was to put the economy on to a path of sustainable development with improved prospects of economic growth and income distribution while, at the same time, ensuring a balance in the external and internal accounts. However, reaching a sustainable BOP and simultaneously achieving high growth is proving to be more difficult than previously anticipated. Except for the once high performing East Asian economies, growth has been elusive in most other countries despite the implementation of moderate to intensive economic reforms. Even after over five years of 'shock therapy', several countries of Eastern Europe, sub-Saharan Africa, and Latin America have yet to show signs of satisfactory growth, leading development economists to dub the 1980s as the 'lost decade'. Although, in response, adjustment programmes have widened their scope to include policy-based investment projects and sector adjustment programmes, Burki and Edwards (1996) note that what most countries essentially require are 'second generation reforms' aimed at modernizing the state and reforming the institutions, including moving towards independent central banks, the judiciary, regulatory bodies, and budgetary processes. Some, if not most, of these aspects are part of the reform agenda of most developing countries, including India.

Adjustment is, thus, now seen as an ongoing process with reforms impacting upon all aspects of economic life. Broader issues include not only sustainable development and poverty reduction but also a major shift in the economic systems of the developing countries towards a market-friendly orientation. There is now a consensus that over-centralized planning and overt-protectionism are fundamentally wrong. There is also a near convergence on the efficacy of competitive markets in economic development. The debatable issues currently are not state versus market, or intervention versus laissez-faire, but the speed of reform, the complementarity between markets and governments, and the appropriate transition to the correct macroeconomic balance that would determine a less rocky road to reform and a more effective path of development.

1.3 A TYPICAL REFORM PROGRAMME

Countries undertaking adjustment programmes generally suffer from a broad range of economic problems. These include: (i) external imbalances as reflected in unsustainable current account deficits, capital flight, and rising levels of external debt; (ii) high and sometimes accelerating inflation, often accompanied by declining private investment levels and low or negative gross domestic product (GDP) growth; and (iii) increasing reliance on rationing and control (for credit, imports, prices, and foreign exchange) with consequent reductions in capacity utilization.

In response, the design of a typical structural adjustment programme, which has evolved over the past fifteen years in response to the changing economic and political scenarios of countries, usually comprises the following reforms:

(i)   Fiscal reforms to reduce deficits in the public sector through tax reform (Indonesia, Mexico), civil service reform, rationalization of public investment (Pakistan, Turkey), privatization of public enterprises and/or reduction in their losses (Argentina), cost recovery in the provision of public services, and strengthening of public sector management (Trinidad and Tobago);

(ii)   Monetary and financial sector reforms to enhance control over money supply (Chile), liberalization of interest rates, elimination of interest rate subsidies, phasing out of directed credit (Jamaica), and strengthening prudential regulations and bank supervision (Mexico, Colombia);

(iii) Trade reforms to reduce protection through flexible exchange rates (Jamaica), elimination of quantitative restrictions (South Korea, Turkey), and uniform but low tariffs (Caribbean and Central American countries);

(iv)   External debt management policies to limit external foreign borrowing if the external accounts are likely to be unsustainable and to ensure consistency of foreign financing with public sector investment requirements;

(v)   Agricultural sector reforms to increase production through improvements in pricing policies, reform of parastatals and marketing boards, coupled with investments in irrigation and extension services;

(vi)   Industrial sector reforms to make manufacturing firms more competitive internationally through changes in trade and exchange rate policies, investment incentives and redirecting public investment from manufacturing to encourage private investment (India, China);

(vii)   Labour market reforms to improve the quality of the workforce and labour productivity through changes in wage-negotiation frameworks (Chile, Malaysia);

(viii) Anti-poverty policies to mitigate the social cost of adjustment through social funds/programmes to protect the most vulnerable groups and by replacing generalized subsidies with more effective and better-targeted public expenditures (Mexico, Morocco).

In addition, policy-induced lending for private sector development, human resource development, infrastructural development, and environmental management have also been part of most reform programmes in developing countries.

1.3.1   Reform of the Transition Economies

The Eastern European countries, the former Soviet Union, China, and Vietnam are some of the transition economies moving from a centrally planned economy to a market economy. These economies have posed difficult challenges to economic policy making in recent years, and newer conditionalities on specific policies have had to be introduced in adjustment programmes in order to effect the transformation as costlessly as possible.

Under command planning and given fixed prices, central directives, apart from directing credit to enterprises taking into account investment targets, also regulated wages and incomes in order to balance output and demand. The enterprises faced 'soft budget constraints' because transfers from the Centre could always be counted on to fill the budgetary gaps. In order to move from this situation to a market economy, prices have had to be set right and enterprises have had to be restructured with hard budget constraints, while simultaneously eliminating the inter-sectoral backlog of arrears. Liberalization in transition economies has involved abolishing state orders and procurement, state production and trading monopolies, and the centralized allocation of foreign exchange. By deliberate policy decisions, implicit prices of certain services, such as housing, energy, transport, education, and health care, were kept low or near zero in many command economies. A better pricing system for these services is now improving microeconomic efficiency and moving the macroeconomy towards its production possibility frontier. Recent experience has, however, shown that these reforms have led to a sharp increase in inflation accompanied by macroeconomic destabilization and a drastic fall in output. This has implied that stabilization must be the necessary first step for the resumption of growth.

Output, in particular, industrial production, and manpower planning were crucial under centralized planning. However, the introduction of market mechanisms disrupted this coordination, and output growth declined sharply as a result of the structural transformation. Moreover, under central planning, state ownership of all assets was predominant and there was no profit motive due to an absence of private incentives. Consequently, economic efficiency was seriously affected. The recent legalization of private ownership, establishment of property rights, and free entry of businesses have led to the setting up of several small firms, bringing in its wake an efficiency in resource allocation along with the potential of a growth spurt. However, the restoration of sustained growth would largely depend on the credibility of the reform programme and the speed of the transformation process.

Thus, the transformation has involved a complex process of restructuring existing systems, institutions, policies, and behaviour because the initial conditions, including income, the nature and extent of economic distortions, and the levels of institutional development, have been substantially different in the transition countries than in other developing countries. However, the long-term goal of transition is the same as elsewhere—to develop a market economy capable of generating sustained growth. What distinguishes the transition economies is the profound social, political, and economic changes that have to occur during the move from the plan to the market. The reforms must fundamentally alter the rules of the game as well as the institutions that shape behaviour and guide organizations. The scale and intensity of reform programmes is what distinguishes the transitional economies from other countries.

1.4   CONVERGENCE OF VIEWS ON POLICY PRIORITIES

1.4.1   *The Washington Consensus*
The processes driving economic development are by no means fully understood. Consequently, in an effort to design adjustment programmes, the Washington-based international financial institutions—the World Bank and the IMF—invoked many development paradigms as a first step to put economies on a development path that could improve the quality of life for its people.

The first adjustment lending by the World Bank was initiated in 1980. Since then, along with the IMF, the World Bank has supported the adjustment programmes of many developing countries. Based upon these efforts, the 1980s witnessed a gradual convergence of views among economists and policy makers in favour of a market friendly approach to development. As pointed out, '. . . on every continent, countries have moved to open their economies, free up prices, and reduce the role of the state in managing and regulating economic activity' (Summers and Pritchett 1993, p. 383). The convergence of views regarding the factors conducive for rapid and sustained economic development as well as the use of macroeconomic policy instruments in effecting structural changes was described by Williamson (1990) as the 'the Washington Consensus'.

It is now recognized that human capital is as important a factor of production as physical and natural capital, and that economic policies, institutions, and technological developments play a more crucial role than external factors in the economic development of a country. Equally true, a stable macroeconomic foundation is now considered as a prerequisite public good that governments can, and should, provide. There is also a common understanding in economic management that large and sustained fiscal deficits result in excessive domestic and external borrowings or monetary expansion, with concomitant problems for the domestic financial sector, including inflation, low growth, chronic overvaluation of the local currency, loss of competitiveness leading to large current account deficits, and, ultimately, capital flight. Fiscal discipline is therefore considered a crucial element in prudential economic policy making. By fiscal discipline is meant generating adequate fiscal surpluses or sustainably low deficits such that the above scenario, or any of its variations, can be avoided.

Similarly, there is a broad agreement that clear priorities need to be established for public expenditures, including public investment projects. When a fiscal deficit needs to be shrunk, it is preferable that this is done by reducing expenditures, especially by pruning generalized subsidies (for example food subsidies) and by phasing out transfers to loss-making state-owned enterprises, rather than by raising new and distortionary taxes. However, this does not preclude tax reforms in the form of lower tax rates, control of tax evasion, strengthening of the tax administration, and the elimination of tax and duty concessions as well as exemptions. All these reforms, if implemented successfully, could bring in adequate revenues on a consistent basis. Equally important, targeted subsidies to the most vulnerable groups of the society and outlays to education, health, and basic infrastructure need to be protected. The size of public sector employment, if typically large, needs to be trimmed while certain public services need to be privatized in order to bring in the discipline of market forces.

Getting the prices right is another set of measures to improve the efficiency of resource use. Deregulation increases competition, while the decontrol of prices enables the market to reflect the forces of supply and demand. Similarly, positive, but moderate, real interest rates, implying low inflation, are conducive for savings and investment, and help to discourage capital flight. Openness or an outward orientation is preferable and, in this context, a competitive real exchange rate would help to promote export growth, especially that of non-traditional exports. Protection, except for infant industries, needs to be dismantled speedily through trade policy reform by discouraging import licensing systems, eliminating quantitative restrictions, and limiting tariff dispersion. Foreign direct investment needs to be encouraged, partly because of the limited domestic private sector in most developing countries and partly because it brings in new investment and technology. However, the deregulation of investment would increase competition only if controls on investment, foreign capital inflows, and profit remittance outflows are reduced. The so-called 'one-stop shops' need to be encouraged to further facilitate investment and to unshackle the private sector.

The role of the state is to do less in those areas where market forces work or can be made to work reasonably well, and to do more in those areas where markets alone cannot be relied upon. This essentially implies that governments need to ensure a sound macroeconomic framework by investing in education, health, nutrition, family planning, and poverty alleviation; by building social and physical infrastructure, by strengthening administrative and legal institutions; and by setting up clear rules of the game (including regulatory frameworks and enforcement mechanisms) to support private sector development. The remaining challenge is to determine the conditions under which government intervention is likely to be conducive rather than a hindrance to the private sector. This is a logical corollary of the familiar 'crowding-in' versus 'crowding-out' argument. The achievements of the East Asian economies and Japan in this regard indicate that interventions are likely to 'crowd-in' the private sector, provided they are market friendly. In such a setting, public spending policies in critical areas are more likely to succeed than alternative measures like state-directed production. However, for intervention to be successful, it should be limited in duration, transparent to the public, and subject to the rules of the game rather than to official discretion.

Experience also suggests that, during periods of reform, the protection of the poor through temporary labour-intensive activities, sufficient spending on primary education and preventive health care, and adequate social safety nets (SSNs), as well as through attempts to ensure a more equitable distribution of income and assets, broadens the base of political support which is essential during such difficult times.

The quality of life encompasses access to education, higher standards of health and nutrition, lower incidence of poverty, a cleaner environment, more equality of opportunity, greater individual freedom, and a richer cultural life. In several of these areas, government intervention is essential for development. There is also, by now, a realization that protection of the environment is necessary for sustainable development. In this regard, appropriate policies include the proper pricing of resources, cost recovery for public facilities, clearer property rights and resource ownership, enforcement of the polluter-pays principle, and investment in production alternatives.

The intensity, timing, and sequencing of all the different components of an adjustment programme is an important consideration. Should stabilization, liberalization, and privatization be pursued simultaneously, or should a country first try and achieve low inflation and then move towards external balance and finally on to trade and financial market liberalization? In this context, there has been a continuing debate on whether countries should go in for a shock therapy (the so-called 'cold turkey' approach) of liberalizing all prices and simultaneously adopting fundamental reforms or follow a sequential approach (the so-called 'gradualist' strategy) to reform. In the former, the macroeconomy is stabilized in a radical manner through demand contraction, currency devaluation, price decontrols, and a simultaneous liberalization of trade, financial and labour markets in order to increase economic efficiency, obtain an adequate supply response, and move on to a higher growth path. In the latter, the same broad strategy is invoked but, as the name suggests, in a more gradual and sequential manner. A mixed approach can also be adopted wherein the macroeconomic system is more-or-less continuously 'perturbed' by mild shocks emanating from gradual market liberalization and financial sector reforms, against the backdrop of an overall planning blueprint. Shock therapies were adopted by Poland (1989), Argentina (1990), and Russia (1991); gradualist approaches were followed by China (1978), Hungary (1989), and Czechoslovakia (1989); while the mixed approach was followed by India (1991).

In principle, the speed and sequencing of policy reforms are often the most decisive elements determining the success of adjustment programmes, because swift and comprehensive reforms with measures to safeguard the poor tend to neutralize the resistance of vested-interest groups opposed to change. This proposition seems to have been corroborated by the recent experience in the transition economies which has indicated that, due to the collapse of the planning apparatus and the strong links between economic liberalization and political changes, rapid reform is better than slow reform. Although countries that reformed faster have experienced a more rapid initial decline in output than those that reformed slowly, the cumulative output loss for the rapid reformers over a period of three to five years has been smaller than that for the slow reformers (see De Melo, Denizer, and Gelb 1996). However, the rapid reformers have suffered higher inflation because they have had to liberalize prices typically in the context of a substantial monetary overhang. Thus, the evidence indicates that, by and large, gradually reforming countries have recorded lower inflation and larger output losses than the rapidly liberalizing ones. However, on the fiscal front, the evidence is more clear: neither slow nor rapid reformers have fared any better as far as balancing the consolidated public sector accounts is concerned.

By early 1995, only 15 of the 26 transition economies that had gone in for stabilization had their growth revived suggesting that stabilization is a necessary but not a sufficient condition for growth. In this context, the evidence for high-inflation countries indicates that growth appears to resume once inflation falls below a certain rate. This finding complements the results of Bruno and Easterly (1995) which showed that an annual inflation rate above a threshold level of 40 per cent is inimical to growth, and that only countries that initially stabilize from high inflation generally experience growth. However, it is equally true that the continuing success of any stabilization effort would depend largely on the quick resumption of growth, in the absence of which governments could find it difficult to sustain the reform programme.

1.4.2   *Long-term Structural Reforms and Sustained Growth*

Based upon the accumulated experiences of the last two decades, it is generally felt that in order to successfully generate and sustain high growth rates, countries have to transit through three stages. In Stage

I, they have to address themselves to reducing macroeconomic instability which initially manifests itself in the form of high inflation. As a result, the appreciation of the real exchange rate fuels expectations regarding devaluation which leads to increases (decreases) in imports (exports) and a consequent worsening in the BOP. Such a widening deficit in the external current account can only be sustained by drawing down international reserves in order to maintain the nominal exchange rate or by external capital inflows or by external borrowing.

In recent years, capital inflows into some developing countries have increased sharply. While these have financed higher levels of investment, they have also resulted in an increase in domestic expenditures leading to an appreciation of the real exchange rate and ultimately to a larger current account deficit. In countries that have opted for a fixed exchange rate system, such unanticipated capital inflows, also known as 'hot capital inflows', have resulted in a spurt in domestic inflation, high nominal interest rates, and an accumulation of foreign reserves which, in turn, have resulted in a rapid increase in domestic debt, as well as interest payments on the debt, on account of sterilization measures. These domestic borrowings have not only crowded out credit to the private sector but put further pressure on the interest rate which, in turn, has resulted in shifting private resources away from productive investment towards short-term financial instruments with higher returns. The high interest rates and the larger volume of resources being intermediated through the financial sector have also contributed to the fragility of this sector, given the weak supervisory system and inadequate prudential regulations in most developing countries. Rather than relying only on sterilized intervention, governments should avoid the deleterious side effects of such capital inflows through tighter fiscal policies and by conducting open market operations to mop up excess domestic liquidity. This should be accompanied by current (and then capital) account convertibility in order to accommodate capital outflows. Thus, the challenge then in Stage I is to manage the exchange rate and capital inflows in a way that will prevent inflation and lay the basis for the growth of real output.

Factors limiting long-run growth include not only the instabilities described above, but also disincentives and structural impediments with special reference to the industrial, financial, trade, and transport sectors. Therefore, Stage II should deal with measures and structural reforms that liberalize the incentive system. These should include: (i) deregulation of prices, interest rates, and directed credit; (ii) trade reforms which are incentive-neutral between export promotion and import substitution; (iii) gradually lowering reserve requirements on commercial banks and other financial institutions; (iv) eliminating barriers to entry and exit to enhance competition; (v) making capital and labour regulations more flexible; (vi) divestment of loss-making public enterprises and the introduction of cost recovery provisions from public utilities and public services; and (vii) an adequate provision of infrastructural facilities and the introduction of a transparent regulatory framework in order to entice the private sector into providing supporting infrastructure.

By the time countries reach Stage III, the preconditions for sustained growth should be established and the supporting infrastructure should be well underway. By then, the government should be:

- Modernizing the financial sector by facilitating the restructuring of failing or troubled firms by either placing them under conservatorship, effecting their merger with relatively sound commercial banks, or accelerating their liquidation; identifying the roll-over of large loans for monitoring and ensuring capitalization of 8 per cent of assets (the Basle convention); improving financial sector prudential norms and standardizing the asset/loan quality; strengthening the supervisory system, both in its structure and in its capacities; increasing staffing adequacy as well as enforcement capabilities of these supervisory agencies; upgrading the information systems used as inputs for off-site analysis; and improving the auditing standards for financial institutions.

- Improving the functioning of the labour market through labour market regulations pertaining to minimum wages, job security, and severance pay; ensuring a speedy wage-bargaining mechanism that is fair to both employers as well as employees; devising alternative mechanisms to avoid work stoppages; and enhancing the employee–employer relationship.

- Improving public policies by introducing reforms to reduce business overhead costs through one-stop shopping for registration, certification, and tax collection, supporting business development through the provision of services in planning, accounting, and packaging; improving existing credit delivery mechanisms through the simplification of credit procedures as well as through group guarantees for risk-pooling; and removing barriers to business which perpetuate a widening circle of informal markets, participants of which are often used as 'shock absorbers' during adjustment programmes.

- Increasing the human capital of the workforce by collaborating with the private sector to improve the quality of education by facilitating curriculum development as well as management training programmes, and including the use of computers in both formal and vocational training.

Moreover, institutional strengthening should be accorded top priority in any reform package given its critical role in economic performance. As there is always some investment pause by the private sector, external financing becomes crucial at this stage to ensure adequate public investment. In addition, the external financing agencies should provide some external debt relief, including debt-forgiveness, which would assure the private sector that the government would not have to resort to additional taxation or forced savings to service the external debt.

While there could be trade-offs between growth and income distribution in the short-run, in general, sustained growth is considered as a necessary as well as sufficient condition for poverty alleviation. However, while formulating medium-term growth-oriented adjustment policies, it is important to note that sustained growth should not imply indifference to the composition of output. Unless the new productive capacity enables the country to increase exports at a rate not less than that at which output itself is growing, external payments difficulties are eventually bound to reappear.

1.5 ANALYTICAL FRAMEWORK AND THE USE OF MODELS

There are three reasons for specifying the analytical framework used in reform efforts. First, policy makers need to understand the main relationships between instruments and targets so as to make judgments as to where and how fast the economy is likely to move in the short- to medium-term. Second, models ensure the consistency of policy measures and provide a framework by means of which trade-offs can be coherently discussed. Third, there is a certain symbiosis between models and policy making: in effect, the specification of models depends upon the policy makers' statement of economic problems, preferences, and priorities, and, in turn, policy makers depend upon models to provide information regarding future scenarios. Thus, in the formulation of any structural adjustment programme, political processes and technical analysis are closely related, and to the extent that there is a certain amount of discipline involved in the overall design of an adjustment programme, economic policy making generally draws upon economic models or frameworks implicitly or explicitly.

An integrated system of national accounts is necessary for the macroeconomic appraisal of any economy. Such a framework of income and flow-of-funds accounts indicates the existence of various identities amongst the recorded magnitudes in the economy which can be useful in assessing the effects of policy changes. By themselves, however, these identities are an 'empty box' and need to be supplemented by relations that indicate the typical reactions of some of the variables included in the accounting framework to changes in other variables. These behavioural relationships can then be combined with the identities in order to form a schematic quantitative representation, or model, of economic processes involving the accounts, or variables, that define the economy in question. Such economic models provide the quantitative framework required for forecasting and policy prescription. They can be used in two distinct modes: first, the positive mode which assesses the consequences of assumed changes in the exogenous variables, determined independently of the processes illustrated in the model, on the magnitudes of the endogenous variables which are determined within the model; and second, the programming mode which determines the changes in policy variables (instruments) required in order to achieve the desired changes in some of the endogenous variables of the model considered to be the objectives (targets) of economic policy. Financial programming involves the use of models in this second mode because it attempts to determine the appropriate setting of the policy instruments against the backdrop of the economic situation and the desired outcomes.

However, it should be emphasized that economic models, being mathematical representations of economic theory, do not capture all the complexity of economic reality. They often possess the underpinnings of paradigms, which manifest themselves in differences in the underlying assumptions, specification of equations, direction of causality, and manner in which the model is closed. While economic theory does provide guidelines as far as the first three aspects are concerned, there is nothing to fall back on as far as model closure, which is the specification of the binding constraint, is concerned, except the features of the economy under consideration. For example, is the economy constrained by domestic savings, credit creation, or availability of foreign exchange? Depending upon which constraint is binding, the model yields qualitatively different results. These pitfalls need to be fully grasped in the specification and design of any adjustment programme.

1.5.1 *Objectives and Instruments*

Not all structural adjustment programmes emphasize the same objectives, although it is possible to discern a set of 'core objectives' including the achievement of external and internal balance as well as adequate economic growth. However, very often, the government pursues other objectives as well that may at times conflict.

One well-known analysis (see Musgrave 1959) classifies three functions of the government from an economic standpoint: in addition to the stabilization function, there are also the functions of allocation and distribution. In such a context, the pursuit of allocational and distributional objectives may impede the adoption of stabilization measures: for example, fiscal cuts may be postponed because the government is unwilling to reduce food subsidies reflecting its distributional priority; or it may be unwilling to eliminate credit controls reflecting its allocational priority.

Be that as it may, the problem of conflicting objectives is not confined only to the trade-offs that exist between the stabilization, allocation, and distribution objectives. For example, while it is accepted that price stability is a necessary condition for achieving adequate economic growth, in certain cases, the inflationary process seems to take a life of its own and it is very difficult, even with appropriate demand-management policies, to eliminate this 'inertial inflation' without inflicting a protracted period of stagnation upon the economy. In such a context, perhaps the greatest problem is forecasting the dynamics of policy efforts to reduce inflation. This is especially true of a gradualistic approach, where the results depend crucially on expectations generated by the credibility of government policies.

In most adjustment programmes, targets set for the objectives are open-ended, that is, they are regarded as floors or ceilings rather than as point targets, since it is perceived that there is no apparent cause for concern in over-performance. Nevertheless, this is not always true. For example, greater-than-targeted output growth, if not directed towards export orientation or import-substitution, may conflict with the inflation target or result in a violation of the BOP constraint. Thus, once a targeted set of objectives has been achieved, it may be best to avoid over-performance, as there could be trade-offs amongst objectives. If, however, it is apparent that over-performance is inevitable, then it might be best to redesign the entire structural adjustment programme in order to align the revised targets appropriately.

In any model, intermediate targets link the ultimate objectives and the policy instruments. For example, the BOP could be an intermediate target linking reserve accumulation (ultimate objective) with the exchange rate (instrument). In some instances, these intermediate targets themselves are regarded as targets, and the ultimate objectives are not made explicit but are implied in the desired values of the intermediate targets. In such cases, a choice might need to be made between an intermediate target that is highly correlated with the ultimate target but bears little relationship with the policy instrument, and one which is strongly influenced by policy but has a weak association with the ultimate objective. Needless to say, the eventual choice of ultimate objectives, intermediate targets, and policy instruments, apart from being constrained by the stage of development of economic institutions and the role of planning, would be largely dictated by the circumstances under which the adjustment programme is being formulated.

1.6   THEMES FOR ANALYSIS

The rest of the book is organized into five parts. The first part focuses on macroeconomic relationships and policies. Chapter 2 initially discusses certain basic accounting concepts revolving around three key macroeconomic relationships and between four key sectors. The sectors identified for this purpose are the government sector, the private sector, the monetary (banking) sector, and the external (foreign) sector. It then presents the framework for macroeconomic management in terms of a consistency matrix which, apart from specifying the sources and uses of funds by these four sectors, serves as the analytical building block for much of the analysis on financial programming later on.

Chapter 3 discusses macroeconomic adjustment from a policy perspective. It focuses on monetary, fiscal, and exchange rate policies in developing countries. It initially specifies the dynamics of monetary policy with special reference to its transmission mechanism. It then reviews the guidelines for fiscal adjustment and examines the means of assessing the fiscal stance as well as effecting the required fiscal adjustment. Finally, it discusses various issues related to exchange-rate management—in particular, policies required to achieve a target real exchange rate, as well as the impacts of exchange rate adjustments.

The second part of the book essentially sets out the analytical framework underlying the concept of growth-oriented structural adjustment programmes. Chapter 4 initially discusses the Polak model against the background of the theory it was partly responsible for creating, viz. the monetary approach to the balance of payments. It then presents the basic analytical framework of the Fund approach to macroeconomic adjustment with its emphasis on the balance of payments and inflation. It then focuses on short-run stabilization issues and empirically discusses the methodology for arriving at alternative stabilization policy options. It then highlights the theory and practice underlying the concept of financial programming (FP) which is used by the IMF for economic policy discussions during structural adjustment in developing countries. It concludes by providing a critique of the Fund approach to macroeconomic adjustment.

Chapter 5 initially discusses the accounting framework underlying growth and resource gap models. It then presents the basic framework of the World Bank approach in terms of the Harrod–Domar and two-gap growth models which form the intellectual underpinning of the Bank's financial requirements (FR) model known as the Revised Minimum Standard Model (RMSM). It then discusses the steps involved in the Bank growth programming procedure with its focus on foreign inflow constraints. The chapter concludes with a brief critique of the Bank approach.

Chapter 6 initially relates the analytical approaches of the Fund and the Bank and integrates growth into the basic monetary model, thereby highlighting the joint determination of inflation and growth. The structural analysis of the merged model, including the derivation of robust policy options, indicates that this is a definite refinement for the analysis of structural adjustment programmes. The conceptual framework underlying growth-oriented financial programming is then developed and the model is solved in its positive and programming modes. The merged model is then used to obtain alternative options for stabilization with growth.

The third part of the book integrates monetary, fiscal, and external sector adjustments into the basic inflation-growth processes underlying the merged Bank–Fund model. Chapter 7 initially discusses the concept of financial repression and monetary sector reform which is followed by an overview of the specific features of interest rate policy. A theoretical model of interest-rate determination in the context of a semi-open economy is then presented and the results are integrated into the merged model of Chapter 6, thereby endogenizing interest rates as well. The chapter concludes by highlighting the procedures involved in designing a consistent interest rate policy.

Chapter 8 initially discusses the underlying implications of fiscal arithmetic and provides empirical evidence regarding monetary accommodation. It then specifies an analytical framework for highlighting the relationships between fiscal deficits, money creation, and debt. In this context, the concepts of seignorage, optimal inflation tax, and fiscal erosion are discussed in detail. The sustainability of fiscal policy is then examined within the framework of a consistent fiscal policy design. Fiscal deficits are then incorporated into the integrated model of Chapter 7. The macroeconomic effects of fiscal deficits, in particular, the relationship between fiscal policy, interest rates, and growth, are then evaluated.

Chapter 9 initially specifies the analytical framework for formulating an external debt strategy in terms of a sustainable debt–output ratio and the role of the exchange rate in the analysis. It then uses the framework to highlight the feedback between debt, output growth, and the current account with reference to solvency and creditworthiness. The model of Chapter 8 is then extended by incorporating external debt management into the framework of financial programming. The concept of unsustainable deficit–debt dynamics is then examined in this fully expanded framework which provides guidelines for formulating a sustainable growth-oriented adjustment programme as well as obtaining policy coordination options.

The fourth part of the book highlights areas of development macroeconomics that have been particularly active in recent years. Chapter 10 initially discusses the concept of 'adjustment with a human face' with special reference to the relationship between poverty, income distribution, and growth. The model of the previous chapter is then extended by incorporating income distribution into its framework. In the process, the impact of policy variables, associated with adjustment programmes, on income distribution is quantified.

Chapter 11 discusses several alternative approaches to adjustment with growth. It initially discusses the structuralist approach to development, and, based upon alternative model closures, a structuralist model is developed and, subsequently, the three-gap model is integrated into it. It then presents the more orthodox twin-deficits approach to growth which, by strengthening certain structuralist arguments, accentuates some of the complementarities that exist between these rival schools of thought. It concludes with a brief discussion on the heterodox concepts of inertial inflation and reciprocal conditionality. The fifth and last part of the book dwells on the lessons of the adjustment experience, in particular, the impacts of financial and economic policies on growth. Chapter 12 initially discusses the basic characteristics of financial crises, with special reference to the types, origins, identification, and signals of such crises. It then briefly deals with some of the analytical insights provided by the recent Asian crisis, in particular those related to contagion effects as well as balance sheet and transfer problems. Finally, based upon a theoretical model of financial crisis, along with the early warning signals of vulnerability to currency crises developed by the IMF, it sets out an empirical framework which highlights some of the important issues involved in designing appropriate policy coordination measures which are capable of preempting financial crises and stimulating economic growth.

Chapter 13 initially discusses the issues involved in liberalization with stabilization with special reference to the optimal sequencing of reforms and the high-inflation trap. It then discusses the political economy of stabilization and adjustment and, in the process, highlights the relationship between the form of government, role of institutions, and the long-run growth rate. Finally, the lessons of experience are briefly summarized and the chapter concludes with a few brief injunctions to policy makers in the form of specific economic policy guidelines.

1.7 SOME ISSUES

Our attempt to provide a systematic treatment underlying the design and application of stabilization theory, with special reference to growth-oriented adjustment, at an accessible level has inevitably involved simplification of what are essentially complex issues. However, it needs to be noted that, as far as possible, we have not attempted to sacrifice precision in the interests of analytical elegance. Proofs of most propositions have been presented in the Notes; in other cases, involving complicated derivations, references to the literature have been provided. The mathematical background required for this book includes only standard matrix algebra, basic econometric techniques, and, in some cases, elementary difference (differential) equation systems.

The most compelling aspect of the sequence of models developed in this book is that they have been derived from 'first principles' and that, despite their apparent simplicity, they have proved to be immensely useful in understanding many key macroeconomic issues involved in designing growth-oriented structural adjustment programmes. Although some of the equations specified and estimated towards the end can be considered as rather *ad hoc,* these have yielded important insights on certain issues that have not yet received much attention from economists but may prove particularly relevant for explaining the growth of many developing countries.

We have tried to ensure that the notation in the book is uniform and consistent; and to this extent, we have provided at the outset a list of all symbols used and the variables they represent. However, in certain instances, the same phenomena are represented by different symbols. However, differences in notation never occur within the same chapter, and hence there should be little scope for confusion. Throughout this book, the symbol 'Δ' represents the backward-difference operator, that is $\Delta y = y - y(-1)$; the derivative of a function of one variable is given by 'δ'; while the transpose of a matrix is denoted with a prime. Finally, the derivative of a variable with respect to time, in the rare cases that it appears, is denoted by a dot over the variable.

MACROECONOMIC FRAMEWORK AND POLICIES

2

Analytical Framework for Macroeconomic Management

2.1 INTRODUCTION

Planned and orderly adjustment is necessary when imbalances, such as the ones reviewed in the earlier chapter, appear. There are however various ways of interpreting the underlying economic reasons for the faltering performance, and they can lead to different policy conclusions unless these problems are viewed from the perspective of a consistent macroeconomic framework. Consistency is thus a first and basic requirement in all macroeconomic analysis. Consequently, this chapter is devoted to setting out a precise macroeconomic accounting framework and providing a general overview of what macroeconomists mean by balances. It needs to be stressed at the outset that the balances to be reviewed are not all independent and that model closure would eventually involve the specification of behavioural equations in order to come to grips with the essence of the structural adjustment issues at stake.

An integrated system of national accounts covering income and expenditure, as well as financial flows and associated stocks, lies at the heart of the macroeconomic appraisal of any economy. These economic accounts serve two basic purposes in the process of designing an adjustment programme. First, they provide a framework for specifying a macroeconomic model that gives a logical structure to any adjustment programme. Second, the accounts provide consistency checks for forecasts and policy packages.

For purposes of financial programming, it is useful to divide an economy into sectors and subdivide the transactions taking place between them into two categories: transactions arising in the course of producing or acquiring goods and services, and financial transactions. Since the two sets of accounts contain all incoming and outgoing transactions, the balance of all transactions for each sector is necessarily equal to zero, and the balance of income/expenditure transactions is thus equal and of opposite sign to the balance of financial transactions. Indeed, the complete framework of income and flow-of-funds accounts shows numerous equivalence relationships, or 'identities', among the various magnitudes recorded in the accounts.

Section 2.2 discusses the starting point of economy-wide identities which are organized around the three basic accounting concepts of production, income, and expenditure. The national income accounting concepts derived from these principles are explained in Section 2.3 with the help of a consistency matrix, and are then used in Section 2.4 to derive the necessary sectoral budget constraints. These results are extended in Section 2.5 which deals with the specification of a flow-of-funds matrix.

2.2 BASIC ACCOUNTING CONCEPTS

2.2.1 *Production, Income, and Expenditure*
Macroeconomic analysis is organized around three key accounting concepts: production, income, and expenditure. The production of goods and services is carried out by resident economic agents, such as corporate entities, unincorporated enterprises, own-account workers, producers of government goods and services, and producers of non-profit services to households and to business enterprises. The boundary of production is conventionally defined to exclude further processing of goods and services in households.

Incomes are generated through production and are in the form of wages and salaries, operating surpluses of enterprises, incomes of self-employed, and/or the imputed value of production by households for their own consumption. Property income, such as interest, dividends, royalties, and land rent, accruing to individuals for the use of their assets is also included. We assume that this is paid from the operating surpluses of enterprises and, by the national income accounting convention, all operating surpluses of enterprises accrue to households. However, the leasing of structures, equipment, machinery, and other goods is considered production of a service. Total rent received (or imputed) is part of the output (income) of the owner, and net rent is part of the operating surplus of the owner in his or her capacity as producer of a service. Total rent paid by producing units is part of intermediate consumption; while it is a final consumption expenditure in the case of households. A second form of income that accrues to households is often referred to as contractual transfers of income, which include net premiums/ contributions towards life and medical insurance, pension funds, and social security. A third form of income accruing to households is unrequited transfers, such as gifts, that an economic agent may receive from another. However, from the viewpoint of the overall economy, such transfers between residents of the same country always cancel out each other.

The value of services provided by financial institutions, comprising banks, savings and loan associations, and insurance companies, amongst others, is included in the domestic product. Because the service charges of these institutions rarely cover the costs of providing their services, it is often necessary to impute a value for the output of these institutions. This imputed value normally consists of the service charges actually paid by the clients of the financial institutions and the difference between the income received by the financial institutions on its assets and payments made on its liabilities.

The types of expenditures are normally distinguished by whether the expenditures are for final consumption of durable and non-durable goods, or for investment. In most cases, production and consumption (expenditure) are very distinct activities. In particular, production decisions are often made by producing units that are quite different from consuming units (usually households or government). In the case of subsistence production (production by households for their own consumption) and the production of government services, however, both production and consumption units coincide. Thus, the value of government services is considered to be the same as government current expenditures on goods and services.

2.2.2 Three Basic Macroeconomic Relationships

From the viewpoint of an economy or an economic agent, production, income, and expenditure (or savings) are linked together by three basic relationships: between production and income, between income and expenditure, and between savings and asset acquisition. These three notions are linked, since budget constraints must be adhered to by all sectors (or agents in the economy). This implies that for any sector, income from production plus net transfers is equal to expenditures plus savings; and that savings plus borrowings is equal to the acquisition of physical and financial assets. For the economy as a whole, the value of production must equal the value of incomes generated. These concepts are briefly explained below.

For any producing unit, the value of production must be equal to the value of income that the unit generates. A similar argument holds for the macroeconomy as a whole: the value of domestic production must be equal to the value of income—excluding transfers—that is domestically generated. This income, however, may accrue to either resident economic agents or to foreign residents. Similarly, domestic economic agents may receive factor payments from abroad. Income accruing to nationals or national income, therefore, equals gross domestic product less net factor payments from abroad.

For any economic agent, income earned (regardless of whether the source is domestic or foreign) plus transfers received finance expenditure. However, income plus transfers need not be equal to expenditure. Savings, which may be positive or negative, is the balancing item. The basic relationship linking income and expenditure is, therefore, as follows: For any economic agent, income plus transfers must be equal to expenditure plus savings.

A third basic relationship links savings and asset acquisition: for an economic agent, savings plus borrowings must equal asset acquisition. These assets may be either physical assets (excluding consumer durables) or financial assets. There is no presumption about savings or borrowings being positive or negative. Specifically, either or both can be negative, and the relationship will still hold.

2.3   NATIONAL INCOME: CONSISTENCY ACCOUNTING MATRIX

Production decisions are made in business enterprises, households, and government agencies. Incomes earned from production accrues to households, whereas expenditure decisions are made by households, business enterprises (on behalf of households), and government agencies. Thus, for the production, consumption expenditure, and capital formation accounts of an economy, the relevant decision-making units are households, businesses, and the government. In addition, financial institutions, such as the banking system, play an important role in channelling savings for the acquisition of financial assets and physical capital. The central bank issues currencies and holds the foreign exchange reserves of a country. It would have liabilities in the form of deposits of commercial banks and often of the government. On the other hand, commercial banks take deposits (liabilities) and make loans (assets). All such principal economic transactions of economic agents can be incorporated into the national accounts of an economy in the form of a consistency matrix.

2.3.1   Current Account Transactions

Table 2.1 presents the principal transactions in an economy in the form of a consistency accounting matrix (see Easterly 1989) which essentially describes the sources and uses of funds. The four sectors distinguished for this purpose are the government sector, the private non-financial sector, the monetary (banking) sector, and the external (foreign) sector. The government is defined as the general government, thereby comprising all levels of government (central, state, and local) as well as public sector corporations funded through the government budget. The non-government (private) sector includes the household sector as well as the private corporate sector. The monetary system includes both the central bank and all other scheduled commercial banks, as well as private savings banks and other public savings institutions. As we are interested only in the role of the monetary system as an intermediary for channelling savings from one sector to the other, such an aggregation is preferable. However, any study that attempts to analyse how the operations of the central bank would affect money supply through commercial bank regulations, such as cash reserve ratios, statutory liquidity ratios, and bank rates, amongst others, would require further disaggregation. The external sector includes all transactions of non-residents with residents, and the consolidated accounts of this sector thus become an abbreviated balance of payments (BOP) account.

   The first row and first column (the national accounts) depict the production account of the economy. As presented, the national accounts group the activities of all producing units together. Thus, they include the production of all incorporated enterprises (including financial institutions), unincorporated enterprises, producers of government services, and production by households, regardless of the type of good or service produced. Across row 1, the table describes how goods and services that are produced domestically (Y) or imported (Z), in the

TABLE 2.1 CONSISTENCY ACCOUNTING MATRIX

Sources (Across) and Uses (Down)	Current Account of:					Capital Account of:					Total
	(C1) National Accounts Sector	(C2) Government Sector	(C3) Monetary Sector	(C4) Private Sector	(C5) External Sector	(C6) Government Sector	(C7) Monetary Sector	(C8) Private Sector	(C9) External Sector	(C10) Total Investment	
National Accounts (R1)		Government Consumption (Cg)		Private Consumption (Cp)	Exports of Goods and Services (X)	Gross Government Investment (Ig)		Gross Private Investment (Ip)		Gross Total Investment (I)	Gross Domestic Product at Market Prices plus Imports $(Y + Z) = Cg + Cp + X + I$
Government Sector (R2)	Operating Surplus of G plus Indirect Taxes less Subsidies $= OSg + (Ti - Sb)$			Direct Taxes (Td)	Net Transfers E to G $(NTReg)$						Total Government Revenue $(Yg) = OSg + (Ti - Sb) + Td + NTReg$
Monetary Sector (R3)											
Private Sector (R4)	Wages plus Profits $= W + II + Ifs$	Net transfers and interest payments from G to P $= NTRgp + INTgp$			Net transfers and Factor Payments from E to P $= NTRep + NFPep$						Total Private Sector Income $(Yp) = (W + II + Ifs) + NTRgp + INTgp + NTRep + NFPep$

Table 2.1 contd.

Table 2.1 contd.

Sources (Across) and Uses (Down)	(C1) National Accounts	(C2) Government Sector	(C3) Monetary Sector	(C4) Private Sector	(C5) External Sector	(C6) Government Sector	(C7) Monetary Sector	(C8) Private Sector	(C9) External Sector	(C10) Total Investment	Total
External Sector (R5)	Imports of Goods and Services (Z)	Interest on G Debt to E sector (INTge)		Interest on P Debt to E sector (INTpe)							Current Expenditure or Payments (Abroad) = Z + INTge + INTpe
Savings and Borrowings of:											
Government Sector (R6)		Gross Government Savings (Sg)					Change in Domestic Credit to G (ΔDCg)	Net Change in G Borrowing from P (ΔB)	Net Change in Foreign Borrowing of G (ΔFg)		Govt. Savings plus Change in G Borrowings = Sg + ΔDCg + ΔB + ΔFg
Monetary Sector (R7)								Change in Broad Money (M3) plus other Liabilities (ΔM)			Change in Domestic Monetary Liabilities = ΔM
Private Sector (R8)				Gross Private Savings (Sp)			Change in Domestic Credit to P (ΔDCp)		Net Change in Foreign Borrowing of P (ΔFp)		Private Sector Savings plus Change in P Borrowings = Sp + ΔDCp + ΔFp

Table 2.1 contd.

Table 2.1 contd.

Sources (Across) and Uses (Down)	(C1) National Accounts	(C2) Government Sector	(C3) Monetary Sector	(C4) Private Sector	(C5) External Sector	(C6) Government Sector	(C7) Monetary Sector	(C8) Private Sector	(C9) External Sector	(C10) Total
External Sector (R9)					E Sector Savings or CAD of the Domestic Economy		Change in International Reserves (ΔR)			Current Account Deficit plus Change in Reserves = $CAD + \Delta R$
Total Savings (R10)		Gross Government Savings (Sg)		Gross Private Savings (Sp)	Current Account Deficit (CAD)					Savings plus Current Account Deficit = $Sg + Sp + CAD$
Total	GDP at Market Prices + Imports $(Y + Z)$ $= OSg + INTge + Sg$ $+ (Ti - Sb)$ $+ (W + \Pi$ $+ IIs) + Z$	Total Govt. Current Uses $(CEXPg + Sg)$ $= Cg + NTRgp$ $+ INTgp +$ $INTge + Sg$		Total Private Current Uses $(CEXPp +$ $Sp) = Cp +$ $Td + INTpe$ $+ Sp$	Total Current Foreign Exchange Receipts $X + NTReg$ $+ NTRep$ $+ NFFep$ $+ CAD$	Total Current Gross Government Investment (Ig)	Change in Assets of Monetary System $=$ $\Delta DCg +$ $\Delta DCp +$ ΔR	Change in Assets of Private Sector $= Ip$ $+ \Delta B$ $+ \Delta M$	Change in Total Foreign Borrowing $(\Delta F) =$ $\Delta Fg +$ ΔFp	Gross Total Investment $(I) = Ig$ $+ Ip$

Notes: (i) G, P, and E refer to Government Sector, Private Sector, and External Sector respectively;
(ii) The Δ preceding any variable indicates a one-period change in that variable, i.e., $\Delta R = R - R(-1)$.
Source: Easterly (1989).

current production period, are disposed off between government consumption (Cg), private consumption (Cp), exports (X), and government and private investment (Ig and Ip, respectively), the last two representing the acquisition of physical assets as distinct from the acquisition of financial instruments. Here, Y represents the gross domestic product (GDP) at current market prices. Column 1 breaks down this value of current domestic production at market prices by identifying the type of incomes that are generated through the sale (plus own consumption) of domestic production. These incomes are in the form of net indirect taxes, that is indirect taxes (Ti) less subsidies (Sb), the operating surpluses of government enterprises (OSg), wages and salaries (W), profits (Π), and incomes of the self-employed and own-account producers (Πs).

The sum of wages, salaries, and the incomes of own-account producers, that is compensation of employees, as these three items are referred to in the United Nations System of National Accounts (SNA), along with the operating surpluses of all enterprises (including funds set aside for depreciation by producing units), is value added at producers' prices and is referred to as GDP at factor cost (Yfc), as opposed to GDP at purchasers' or market prices (Y). By convention, value added at factor cost accrues to households (and to the government, in the case of the operating surplus of government-owned enterprises) even though a portion of the operating surplus might be retained by enterprises on behalf of households or the government to finance accumulation. Value added at market prices (that is, what purchasers' actually pay for goods and services) would therefore include net indirect taxes. Thus, such value added at market prices plus imports would then be equal to the total available goods and services for final use.

Row 2 and column 2 depict the current transactions of the government. Across row 2, the sources of government revenue (Yg) are identified. These include the operating surpluses of government-owned enterprises (OSg), net indirect taxes ($Ti - Sb$), direct taxes (Td), and the net transfers that the government receives from external sources ($NTReg$). Column 2 details all items of current government expenditures ($CEXPg$): government consumption of currently produced goods and services (Cg) which is the cost of producing government services, net transfers to domestic households from the government ($NTRgp$), interest paid to households on the domestic debt ($INTgp$), and interest payments on the external debt of the government ($INTge$). Government savings (Sg) is thus the difference between government revenue and expenditure.

Row 3 and column 3 account for the consolidated balance sheet of the monetary (banking) system. As a pure intermediary, the monetary system has no independent (own account) current revenues and expenditures. The revenues of financial institutions less their costs constitute the value added of these institutions within the monetary system as producing units. As this value added is included in the production account of the domestic economy as income to households (or to the government), row 3 and column 3 are therefore empty.

Row 4 and column 4 describe the accounts of the non-government (private) sector. Across row 4, the sources of income of the private sector (Yp) are identified: factor income including wages and salaries (W), profits (Π), and incomes of the self-employed and own-account producers (Πs); net transfers received from the government ($NTRgp$) and interest payments from the government on its domestic debt ($INTgp$); and net transfers plus net factor payments from abroad ($NTRep + NFPep$). Column 4 identifies how private sector income is disposed off: private consumption (Cp), payment of direct taxes (Td), and interest payments on the external debt of the private sector ($INTpe$). Private savings (Sp) is the balancing item and is the difference between total private sector income (Yp) and total current expenditures of the private sector ($CEXPp$). Note that property incomes paid and received by resident households do not appear as separate entries in the matrix. As mentioned earlier, such property incomes are accounted for in the operating surpluses of producing units and, in any case, they must, of necessity, cancel each other out.

Row 5 and column 5 depict the current account balance of the balance of payments. Across row 5, the sources of income accruing to foreign residents are provided: these are in the form of public and private sector interest payments on their respective external debts ($INTge + INTpe$) and the value of imports of goods and services (Z). Payments of principal on the external debt are recorded in the capital finance account, that is 'below the line' (see rows and columns 6 through 9), and are thus not included in the current account. Column 5 lists the sources of income accruing from foreign residents: these are in the form of exports of goods and services (X) and in the form of net current (as opposed to capital) transfers to the government and private sectors ($NTReg + NTRep$) as well as net factor payments to the private sector ($NFPep$). The savings of foreign residents—identical to the current account balance—is the balancing item between current external receipts and payments.

2.3.2   Capital Account Transactions

While rows and columns 1 through 5 describe the current accounts of the economy, rows and columns 6 through 9 describe the corresponding capital account transactions, that is the financing of asset acquisition by the government, the private sector, and the external sector through the intermediation of the monetary system.

In row 6, government savings (Sg), along with government borrowings from the monetary system (ΔDCg), net direct government borrowing from the private sector (ΔB), and net foreign borrowing (ΔFg), are used to finance asset accumulation by the government (Ig in column 6). Asset acquisition is usually of three forms: gross fixed investment (including physical assets, inventories and working capital, as well as intangible non-financial assets), financial assets in the form of loans to the private sector, and the acquisition of foreign assets. However, the last two items have been netted out from government borrowings from the private sector and foreign borrowings of the government, respectively, and, therefore, these items do not appear explicitly as separate entities in the matrix.

Row 7 and column 7 deal with the monetary system. Row 7 indicates that, as an intermediary, it acquires liabilities principally in the form of new domestic currency issues, demand deposits, and time deposits, as well as other liabilities including treasury bills and so on (ΔM). Column 7 implies that it, in turn, acquires assets in the form of loans to the government sector (ΔDCg) and to the private sector (ΔDCp), as well as net foreign assets or international reserves (ΔR).

Row 8 and column 8 deal with the private sector. In row 8, private sector savings (Sp), borrowings by the private sector from the domestic monetary system (ΔDCp), and net new private sector borrowings from abroad (ΔFp) are used to finance asset acquisition by the private sector. These include the items detailed in column 8, namely private investment (Ip), net lending to the government (ΔB), and new issues of money and near money (ΔM) held by the monetary system.

Row 9 and column 9 deal with the external sector. Row 9 implies that the savings of foreign residents or the current account deficit (CAD) plus the proceeds from the acquisition of net foreign exchange reserves by the monetary system (ΔR) are used to finance the items listed in column 9, namely net foreign borrowings of the government sector (ΔFg) and the private sector (ΔFp).

Finally, row 10 and column 10 deal with the overall savings–investment balance at the macroeconomic level. Row 10 shows that total domestic savings, that is the sum of government savings (Sg) and private savings (Sp), plus foreign savings, that is the current account deficit (CAD), must finance total investment (I in column 10), that is the sum of government investment (Ig) and private investment (Ip).

In effect, therefore, Table 2.1 summarizes the current and capital account transactions of the four principal transactors in an economy, and can be used to demonstrate that the national income identities are no more than a series of budget constraints.

2.4   A MACROECONOMIC CONSISTENCY FRAMEWORK

2.4.1   *The National Balance and Absorption*

Gross domestic product (GDP), or the value of goods and services that are produced by the domestic economy, can be derived from the basic macroeconomic relationship which states that the value of domestic production must be equal to the value of incomes that are domestically generated. From Table 2.1, two different approaches can be adopted for estimating GDP: the expenditure approach or the value-added approach. From row 1 and column 1, we have:

$$Cg + Cp + X + Ig + Ip = W + \Pi + \Pi s + OSg + (Ti - Sb) + Z. \tag{2.1}$$

GDP at market prices (Y) is given by the sum of private consumption (Cp), public consumption (Cg), private investment (Ip), public investment (Ig), and net exports of goods and services ($X - Z$). Therefore, we have:

$$Y = C + I + (X - Z), \tag{2.2}$$

where C ($= Cp + Cg$) is total consumption; and I ($= Ip + Ig$) is total investment.

Similarly, GDP at factor cost (Yfc) is given by the sum of factor incomes, that is wages (W), profits (Π), and own-income of self-employed (Πs), as well as the operating surpluses of government enterprises (OSg), that is:

$$Yfc = W + \Pi + \Pi s + OSg. \tag{2.3}$$

Therefore, substituting (eqn 2.2) and (eqn 2.3) into (eqn 2.1) yields:

$$Y = Yfc + (Ti - Sb), \tag{2.4}$$

which implies that GDP at market prices is equal to GDP at factor cost plus net indirect taxes, that is indirect taxes (Ti) less subsidies (Sb).

(Eqn 2.2) can be rewritten as follows:

$$Y + (Z - X) = C + I = A \qquad (2.5)$$

which indicates that the total availability of goods and services in the domestic economy, as given by the sum of output (Y) plus the excess of imports (Z) over exports (X), should equal domestic absorption (A), which is the sum of consumption plus investment. (Eqn 2.5) can be rewritten as follows to reveal the two guises of a trade deficit:

$$(Z - X) = A - Y, \qquad (2.6)$$

$$(Z - X) = I - (Y - C) = I - S. \qquad (2.7)$$

(Eqn 2.6) and (eqn 2.7) indicate that the current account deficit, $(Z - X)$, reveals itself either in the form of an excess of domestic absorption over production, or in an excess of investment over savings. Thus, in order to bring about a reduction in the current account deficit, the government should either reduce absorption (A) or alternatively, and equivalently, increase savings (S).

2.4.2 *Sectoral Budget Constraints*
2.4.2.1 The Government Budget Constraint
The basic relationship that must exist between the income and expenditure of any economic agent leads to the derivation of the government budget constraint (GBC). Equating the sum of the entries in row 2 and column 2 shows:

$$(Ti - Sb) + OSg + Td + NTReg = [Cg + NTRgp + INTge \\ + INTgp] + Sg \qquad (2.8)$$

which can be written as:

$$Yg = CEXPg + Sg, \qquad (2.9)$$

implying that the current revenue of the government ($Yg = Ti - Sb + OSg + Td + NTReg$) is equal to current government expenditure ($CEXPg = Cg + NTRgp + INTge + INTgp$) plus government savings (Sg).

Equating the sum of the entries in row 6 and column 6 shows:

$$Sg + \Delta DCg + \Delta B + \Delta Fg = Ig, \qquad (2.10)$$

which basically expresses the savings, borrowings, and asset acquisition relationship (or the savings constraint) for the government sector:

government savings plus net borrowings is identical to the (physical) assets acquired by the government during the accounting period. We recall that the government acquisition of foreign assets as well as domestic financial assets (such as loans to the private sector) are netted out from foreign borrowings and from domestic borrowings, respectively.

Substituting (eqn 2.9) into (eqn 2.10) and rewriting the result as follows reveals the sources of financing a government fiscal deficit:

$$(CEXPg + Ig) - Yg = \Delta DCg + \Delta B + \Delta Fg, \qquad (2.11)$$

where the expression on the left-hand-side of (eqn 2.11) is the overall fiscal deficit of the government. The sources of financing such a fiscal deficit are, therefore, foreign borrowings, direct borrowings from the private sector (provided there is a well-developed capital market), and borrowings from the monetary system.

(Eqn 2.11) reveals two possible sources through which excessive government borrowings as a result of high fiscal deficits can crowd out the private sector. Assuming that government borrowing from external sources is restricted in some way, for example, through an International Monetary Fund (IMF) conditionality or problems related to creditworthiness, then crowding-out can occur either through direct government borrowing from the private sector, or through government borrowing from the monetary system. The latter presumes that there is a ceiling on overall credit expansion of the monetary system, which is often the case in anti-inflationary stabilization programmes. This explains as to why, in addition to overall domestic credit ceilings, structural adjustment programmes often have sub-ceilings on bank credit to the government in order to prevent crowding out of private sector investment.

2.4.2.2　The Private Sector Budget Constraint

The private sector budget constraint can be derived in a similar fashion. Equating the sum of the entries in row 4 and column 4 shows that:

$$W + \Pi + \Pi s + NTRgp + INTgp + NTRep + NFPep = [Cp + Td \\ + INTpe] + Sp, \qquad (2.12)$$

which can be written as:

$$Yp = CEXPp + Sp, \qquad (2.13)$$

implying that total private sector income ($Yp = W + \pi + \pi s + NTRgp + INTgp + NTRep + NFPep$) equals private consumption ($CEXPp = Cp + Td + INTpe$) plus private savings (Sp).

Equating the sum of the entries in row 8 and column 8 yields:

$$Sp + \Delta DCp + \Delta Fp = Ip + \Delta B + \Delta M. \tag{2.14}$$

Substituting (eqn 2.13) into (eqn 2.14) yields the required private sector budget constraint given by:

$$(Yp - CEXPp) + \Delta DCp + \Delta Fp = Ip + \Delta B + \Delta M, \tag{2.15}$$

which states that private sector income plus borrowings less current outlays equals private sector asset acquisition in the form of money (currency plus demand and time deposits), fixed investment, and lending to the government.

2.4.2.3 The External Sector Budget Constraint

The external sector budget constraint is obtained by initially equating the sum of entries in row 5 and column 5. This yields:

$$Z + INTge + INTpe = X + NTReg + NTRep + NFPep + CAD. \tag{2.16}$$

Equating the sum of the entries in row 9 and column 9 shows:

$$CAD + \Delta R = \Delta Fg + \Delta Fp, \tag{2.17}$$

which indicates that a *CAD*—or positive savings by the external sector— must be financed either by an increase in net capital inflows (implying an increasing indebtedness of the domestic economy) or by drawing down reserves.

Substituting (eqn 2.16) into (eqn 2.17) yields:

$$\begin{aligned}(Z + INTge + INTpe) &- (X + NTReg + NTRep + NFPep) \\ &= (\Delta Fg + \Delta Fp - \Delta R),\end{aligned} \tag{2.18}$$

where the expressions in parentheses are, respectively, current receipts, current outlays (expenditures), and asset acquisition (negative asset acquisition of the domestic economy) of the external sector. This external sector budget constraint, therefore, states, as expected, that current receipts (of the external sector) less current outlays equals its asset acquisition.

(Eqn 2.18) can be simplified by adding all interest payments on the external debt into imports (gross payments by the domestic economy) and adding net transfers and net factor payments from abroad into exports (gross receipts to the domestic economy). This yields the external sector budget constraint:

$$Z - X = \Delta F - \Delta R, \tag{2.19}$$

where Z is now defined as $(Z + INTge + INTpe)$; X is now defined as $(X + NTReg + NTRep + NFPep)$; and $\Delta F = \Delta Fg + \Delta Fp$.

Note that the elements on the left-hand-side of (eqn 2.19) are in the form of goods and services, while those on the right-hand-side are in terms of foreign exchange (currencies). In particular, imports constitute a consumable or investable resource inflow, whereas exports constitute a resource outflow. This explains as to why it is argued that whenever interest payments on external debt exceed new borrowings, a resource transfer takes place from the debtor to the creditor. By the same token, it can be seen that a capital flight, which usually manifests itself in a dramatic fall in private external borrowings ($\Delta Fp < 0$), would imply reduced consumption of goods from abroad (imports), unless financed by increased external sales of goods and services (exports) or offset by a drawdown of foreign exchange reserves. Thus, there is an opportunity cost to holding foreign exchange reserves which could either be in the form of forgone consumption and/or domestic investment. Depending on the level of per capita consumption or the rate of return on domestic investment, this cost may be considerable (see Krugman 1988).

2.4.2.4   Assets and Liabilities of the Monetary System

Being an intermediary, the monetary system does not face a budget constraint *per se* but rather a balance sheet accounting identity. Equating the sum of the entries in row 7 and column 7 shows:

$$\Delta DC + \Delta R = \Delta M, \tag{2.20}$$

where:

$$\Delta DC = \Delta DCg + \Delta DCp. \tag{2.21}$$

(Eqn 2.20) states that the assets of the monetary system, in the form of foreign assets (international reserves) as well as credit to the government and private sectors, are equal to its liabilities, in the form of broad money.

(Eqn 2.20) can be rewritten as:

$$\Delta R = \Delta M - \Delta DC. \tag{2.22}$$

(Eqn 2.22) states that the change in foreign exchange reserves is equal to the demand for money (assuming that the money market is in equilibrium, in effect, that the supply of money is equal to its demand) less the change in total domestic credit. This equation suggests that if the demand for money is held constant, then increases in domestic credit are offset by decreases in reserves on a one-to-one basis. Alternatively, it implies that given a desired level of reserves, and with the demand for money exogenously determined, the required change in domestic credit can be estimated.

It needs to be noted that this type of analysis, which is characteristic of the 'Chicago version' of the monetary approach to the balance of payments (see Frenkel and Johnson 1976), applies only when the domestic price level is determined by foreign prices through the purchasing power parity (or the 'law of one price') so that the demand for money is independent of changes in domestic credit. However, in any actual formulation of adjustment programmes, the relevance of this assumption needs to be carefully analysed. In the present context, we shall treat it only as an accounting relation which establishes the equality between the assets and liabilities of the monetary system.

It has been argued that the central banks can sterilize capital inflows, that is prevent capital inflows from increasing domestic money supply, by attempting to offset the resulting expansion in reserves by a corresponding contraction of domestic credit. Sterilization may be necessary because capital inflows, by expanding money supply, increase domestic price levels, thereby causing the real exchange rate to appreciate. From (eqn 2.22), it can be seen that sterilization could help to stabilize money supply because it would have the effect of increasing foreign exchange reserves while decreasing the indebtedness of the government and private sectors to the monetary system.

With a well-developed capital market, the government would be able to compensate for its inability to borrow from the domestic monetary system by selling bonds to the private sector. Otherwise, the private sector will have to bear the entire brunt of the sterilization and the resulting credit squeeze could, unless counterbalanced by foreign capital inflows, lead to a crowding out of private sector investment.

2.4.3   *The Savings–Investment Balance*

Summing up, the budget constraints of the government and private sectors, that is (eqn 2.10) and (eqn 2.14), yields:

$$S + \Delta DC + \Delta F = I + \Delta M, \tag{2.23}$$

where $S = Sg + Sp$; $\Delta DC = \Delta DCg + \Delta DCp$; $\Delta F = \Delta Fg + \Delta Fp$; and $I = Ig + Ip$.

Substituting the external sector budget constraint, given by (eqn 2.19), into (eqn 2.23) above yields:

$$S + \Delta DC + (Z - X) + \Delta R = I + \Delta M. \tag{2.24}$$

Substituting the balance sheet of the monetary system, given by (eqn 2.20), into (eqn 2.24) above yields the savings–investment balance:

$$I = S + (Z - X), \tag{2.25}$$

which states that aggregate domestic investment (I) is financed by domestic savings (S) and foreign savings ($Z - X$), the latter being synonymous with the current account deficit (CAD). (Eqn 2.25) above is identical to the result obtained by equating the sum of the entries in row 10 and column 10, thereby indicating that the overall savings–investment balance is a macroeconomic budget constraint obtained by summing up the sectoral budget constraints.

2.4.4   *Deficits, Absorption, and Credit*

Much of the debate on structural adjustment focuses on the relationship between the fiscal deficit ($Ig - Sg$) and the external balance ($X - Z$). Equating the sum of the entries in row 10 and column 10 and rearranging terms yields:

$$(Sg - Ig) + (Sp - Ip) = X - Z, \tag{2.26}$$

implying that an improvement in the current account balance (that is the right-hand-side of the identity) can take place only if sectoral savings rise relative to sectoral investment. This explains as to why it is argued (see Dornbusch and Helmers 1988) that if policies do not have any effect in improving either government or private sector savings, the external balance cannot be expected to improve.

In a similar manner, the link between domestic credit and absorption can be obtained by combining (eqn 2.6), (eqn 2.19), and (eqn 2.20) to yield:

$$(Y + \Delta F) - A = \Delta M - \Delta DC, \tag{2.27}$$

where the expression in parentheses on the left-hand-side of (eqn 2.27) is total resources available for domestic consumption and investment. The above equation thus indicates that domestic absorption (A) will exceed total available resources ($Y + \Delta F$) by the amount that domestic credit expansion (ΔDC) exceeds the flow demand for (equal to supply of) money (ΔM). The identity also reveals that with the expression in parentheses as well as the flow demand for money fixed, any reductions in domestic credit will automatically improve the BOP, that is increase reserves, by reducing absorption.

2.5 FLOW OF FUNDS VERSUS MARKET EQUILIBRIUM

The (10 × 10) consistency matrix, presented in Table 2.1, explains all the intersectoral transactions of the four sectors identified for the purpose. However, if the main aim is to study only the intersectoral links between savings and investment, we can focus attention exclusively only on the capital account transactions which highlight the sources and uses of funds of each of these sectors. The ensuing (5 × 5) flow-of-funds matrix, presented in Table 2.2, is far more compact than the earlier (10 × 10) matrix as it excludes intersectoral current account transactions which are relevant only if one is analysing all the three relationships spelt out in Section 2.2. The logic of this flow-of-funds matrix is guided only by the savings–investment relationship: savings plus borrowings must equal asset acquisition; in effect, row totals (which equal savings plus borrowings) must equal column totals (investment) for all the four sectors. The fifth row and column sums up all these four budget constraints to obtain the overall macroeconomic savings–investment balance.

The link between savings and investment of each sector and its associated financial transactions with the other sectors must be clearly understood so that appropriate financial policies, based on reliable and consistent macroeconomic forecasts, can be formulated and executed. In this context, flow-of-funds accounts are essential prerequisites for the formulation of any financial programme as they form the basis for ensuring consistency.

TABLE 2.2   FLOW OF FUNDS MATRIX

	Government	Private	External	Monetary	Savings
Government		ΔB	ΔFg	ΔDCg	Sg
Private			ΔFp	ΔDCp	Sp
External				ΔR	$Z - X$
Monetary		ΔM			
Investment	Ig	Ip			

The procedure in formulating a financial programme is to construct flow-of-funds matrices for each year so that the transactions pattern is discernible. Based upon such patterns, it is possible to fill in the elements of a matrix for a future period, consistent with each sector's savings and investment behaviour, the monetary and fiscal policies likely to be in force, as well as the prevalent financial conditions. While doing so, certain assumptions have to be made regarding the behaviour of each variable, whether it is purely exogenous, policy controlled, or endogenous. Since the flow-of-funds matrix depends on financial conditions which can be influenced by policies and which interact with the behaviour of income and expenditure flows, the construction of such a consistency matrix often involves an iterative procedure to adjust the initial estimates until overall consistency is achieved (see Bain 1973).

In Tables 2.1 and 2.2, reading across rows provides the sources of finance for each sector while reading down columns indicates the uses of finance. *Ex post*, each sector's deficit must be financed and, as such, the sum of the rows is always equal to the sum of the columns. *Ex ante*, these sectoral balances become constraints for modelling sectoral behaviour, be it financial or non-financial. It is these constraints that will be included while specifying all versions of the financial programming models that follow in this book.

The fundamental difference between the flow-of-funds and the market equilibrium approaches while formulating a model is that sectoral balances are treated as constraints in the former while the latter treats market equilibria as constraints. In the case where market forces and instantaneous adjustments coexist, these two types of constraints are equivalent since when all sectoral accounts are balanced, all markets must be cleared. However, any market imperfections and lag adjustments would create a situation where sectoral balances are not equivalent to market equilibria. For instance, when credit rationing is in force, the money market cannot be in equilibrium by definition. The resulting disequilibrium in the money market must coexist with disequilibrium in at least one other market in the economy. In such cases, sectoral balances yield more reliable constraints.

3

Macroeconomic Adjustment: A Policy Perspective

3.1 INTRODUCTION

In recent years, many developing countries have found themselves in serious economic difficulties, including worsening BOP positions, rising rates of inflation and declining rates of growth. The continuing predicament of these countries has led to an increasing interest in the subject of macroeconomic adjustment, in general, and particularly on how to eliminate the disequilibrium dynamics that give rise to such problems *without* sacrificing growth in the process. In such a context, the basic question that is currently being asked by academicians and policy makers in the developing world and, indeed, the international economic community at large, is what kind of policies, and in what combination, can achieve the desired goals of macroeconomic adjustment.

The need for macroeconomic adjustment essentially arises when a country has a fundamental imbalance between aggregate domestic demand and aggregate supply. Whatever be the underlying reasons for this demand–supply imbalance, in principle, a country can avoid adjustment by borrowing from abroad and, consequently, the disequilibrium in the economy can be made to persist for an extended period. There are, however, costs involved with such a strategy that are well known. These include overvaluation of the domestic currency leading to unsustainable reserve depletion, increasing inflation, reduced economic growth, loss of international competitiveness leading to a widening current account deficit, as well as a higher foreign debt.

Obviously, this type of disequilibrium cannot continue indefinitely, and in the absence of appropriate policy actions to correct these underlying imbalances, the steady loss of international competitiveness and the increasing level of external debt would jeopardize the country's creditworthiness and thus its ability to obtain additional foreign financing. Naturally, a cessation of external financing would impose adjustment on the country as a result of simple accounting arithmetic and, as recent experiences in a number of countries have indicated, this forced adjustment can be extremely disruptive.

Consequently, the fundamental objective of an adjustment programme is to provide for an orderly elimination of the imbalance between aggregate domestic demand and resource availability before the point at which the economy becomes seriously distorted and external resources are exhausted. To achieve this objective, the adjustment programme has necessarily to include a variety of policies that simultaneously reduce aggregate demand and increase the availability of total resources. These policies can be broadly grouped according to whether their primary impact is on the level of absorption—*demand management policies;* on the level of current and potential output—*structural policies;* on the composition of absorption and production as between tradeable and non-tradeable goods—*exchange rate policies;* and, finally, on the level of capital flows—*external debt management policies.*

Demand management policies typically include monetary and fiscal measures designed to affect the aggregate level or rate of growth of demand relative to production. On the other hand, structural policies are intended to increase the supply of goods and services in the economy for any given level of domestic demand. Policies to improve international competitiveness and expand the supply of tradeable goods through both reduced consumption and increased production principally involves changes in the exchange rate. Therefore, exchange rate policies have both demand-side as well as structural characteristics and are, thus, treated separately. Changes in the net flow of foreign financing also affect absorption and, if they assist domestic capital formation, raise potential output as well. In such a context, guidelines on external debt management basically describe policies that would provide the country with the maximum sustainable net resource transfer over the adjustment period.

Generally speaking, comprehensive and long-term macroeconomic adjustment would involve elements of all four of these policies. Programmes aimed at growth-oriented adjustment cannot rely exclusively on demand-management policies, nor for that matter solely on structural policies. In fact, all these policies are closely interrelated. For example, the achievement of a higher long-term growth rate generally requires an increase in investment, while stabilization requires a reduction in the savings–investment gap. The resulting policy package must, therefore, be designed so as to reduce the level of aggregate domestic demand and simultaneously cause a shift in the composition of demand away from current consumption and towards capital formation. Exchange rate policies will assist in this adjustment process by damping down demand and creating incentives for investment in the tradeables sector. Debt management policies would set limits to the current and future availability of external resources which would, in turn, limit both the degree and speed of the required adjustment.

The purpose of this chapter, largely based on the guidelines set out by IMF (1987, 1995), is to describe how these policies can be expected to affect the targets towards which they are directed and thereby achieve the goal of macroeconomic adjustment, characterized by a sustainable BOP, a low rate of inflation, a stable and high rate of economic growth, and a manageable level of external debt. While an attempt is made to cover the main links between policy instruments and these ultimate objectives, the chapter does not deal with all of the possible effects of macroeconomic policy measures. For example, no attempt is made here to discuss the supply-side effects of adjustment policies, even though it is recognized that the pattern of resource allocation is often a key objective of policy makers. Such exclusions were considered necessary to limit the scope of this chapter which, nevertheless, highlights a number of important theoretical and empirical questions that need to be addressed in the course of designing macroeconomic adjustment programmes.

The remainder of this chapter proceeds as follows: Section 3.2 discusses the specification of monetary policy. The guidelines for fiscal adjustment are described in Section 3.3. The analytical aspects of exchange rate policies are specified in Section 3.4, while some of the problems associated with external debt management are discussed in Chapter 9.

3.2 SPECIFICATION OF MONETARY POLICY

One possible extension of the financial programming framework discussed in Chapter 2 is to relate the basic monetary relationship to the balance sheet of the central bank as opposed to the banking system as a whole. The policy variable in such a case would be changes in domestic credit of the central bank rather than total domestic credit expansion. To apply the exercise solely to the central bank, we have to define the balance sheet equality between changes in the liabilities of the central bank, that is reserve money, and changes in its assets, that is net domestic assets and net foreign assets:

$$\Delta H = \Delta DCB + \Delta NFA, \tag{3.1}$$

where H is reserve money (the monetary base), equal to currency in the hands of the public and reserves of commercial banks; DCB is the stock of domestic credit extended by the central bank; and NFA is its stock of foreign assets.[1]

The total supply of money (M) is related to reserve money (H) through the so-called 'money multiplier' relationship:

$$\Delta M = m\Delta H, \tag{3.2}$$

where m is the money multiplier which is partly determined by the public's preferences and partly by government policies (changes in reserve requirements or the discount rate) that affect the reserve positions of banks. These two additional equations imply that the financial programming approach can be conducted as before by merely substituting (eqn 3.1) into (eqn 3.2) to obtain:

$$\Delta M = m(\Delta DCB + \Delta NFA). \tag{3.3}$$

(Eqn 3.3) above along with a (stable) money demand function, $\Delta Md = f(.)$, and an equilibrium condition, $\Delta Md = \Delta M$, implies that:

$$\Delta NFA = (1/m)\, f(.) - \Delta DCB, \tag{3.4}$$

and the earlier analysis will carry through under fairly general assumptions.[2]

The choice between alternative forms of credit is based on a number of factors. First, it depends crucially on the manner in which the authorities conduct monetary policy. To the extent that the monetary authorities implement credit policy through controls over total bank credit, and that other financial variables are poorly developed, the obvious credit variable would be the broader one covering the overall banking system. If, on the other hand, the monetary authorities take decisions related to credit policy in the context of their own credit operations, supplemented by policies that affect the money multiplier, then the appropriate credit variable would be the one covering the domestic assets of the central bank alone. Second, the behaviour of the money multiplier is an important factor in the decision. If the money multiplier is either erratic or unstable, it would clearly be more effective to work with overall domestic credit expansion. Thus, ultimately the question of which is the more appropriate definition of domestic credit is an empirical one and will depend on the structure of the financial system and the operating procedure for monetary policy in the particular country under consideration (see Rao 1992b).

The financial programming framework described above provides a useful way of thinking about the BOP and macroeconomic policy. With some extensions, this framework can be used to handle issues relating to the determination of both the overall BOP as well as its components, and can be easily linked to monetary policy and to the fiscal accounts of the government. However, it must be stressed that this framework is only a theoretical abstraction and must be specified more precisely for policy purposes. In particular, it must be supplemented by specific information regarding the transmission mechanism relating the policy instruments to the ultimate objectives of BOP improvement and price stability. Equally important, its validity in the short run can be questioned under certain circumstances and, in its simplest form, it considers only one particular policy instrument, namely the rate of domestic credit expansion, leaving open the issue of whether it is in all circumstances more practicable to target domestic credit rather than the money supply itself. These three issues will be discussed briefly in the remainder of this section.

3.2.1 *The Transmission Mechanism*
The standard view of the transmission mechanism between monetary policy and aggregate demand emphasizes the role of interest rates. In the closed-economy case, an increase in the supply of money causes individuals to purchase real and financial assets in an effort to reduce portfolio disequilibrium. This lowers market interest rates and stimulates aggregate demand. A basic description of the way monetary policy works in a small open economy, on the other hand, is that which appears in versions of the monetary approach to the balance of payments. In such models, under fixed exchange rates, the public disposes off surplus cash balances produced by an expansion of domestic credit through purchasing foreign goods and securities, reducing the level of

international reserves but leaving domestic output and prices unchanged. Under flexible exchange rates, a similar expansion in domestic credit results in an increase in money supply, a rise in the domestic price level, and a proportional depreciation of the exchange rate via an initial 'overshooting'.

To approximate the situation in a typical developing country which, by using the exchange rate as an adjustable nominal anchor, shares the characteristics of both fixed as well as flexible exchange rate systems, it is useful to analyse the effects of monetary policy on aggregate demand and the BOP, especially in situations where financial markets are underdeveloped, interest rates are set below market-clearing rates by the government, a relatively free informal financial sector (or, the so-called 'curb market') operates and there are foreign exchange controls. If exchange controls are effective, then the authorities can control the monetary base via their control over the availability of foreign exchange and over credit extended by the central bank. In terms of the model described above, this implies that the authorities can change both net foreign assets and domestic credit. Since (eqn 3.4) must continue to hold, the change in money supply (ΔM) will adjust to preserve the balance sheet relationship. Starting from portfolio equilibrium, an increase in the supply of bank credit to the private sector will cause borrowers to shift away from the curb market, thus leading to a decrease in the curb-market interest rate. Since this rate represents the marginal cost of funds in the economy, interest-sensitive components of private demand will be stimulated, thereby resulting in an upward pressure on inflation.

Monetary policy works differently if exchange controls are ineffective. Under these circumstances, the private sector can now add foreign exchange to its portfolio of financial assets. This case approximates more closely the simple monetary model because the authorities can no longer exercise direct control over the change in international reserves. With the relaxation of the assumption of exchange controls, the power of monetary policy to affect aggregate demand is diminished. Some of the effects of an increased supply of credit on demand are dissipated as the private sector can satisfy this demand by acquiring foreign exchange reserves from the central bank in exchange for domestic money. As a result, the initial increase in the money supply is partially reabsorbed back by the central bank. Therefore, effects on the curb-market interest rate and, consequently, on the demand for real assets are weakened. The ultimate effects of such changes in aggregate demand will therefore be dispersed between a downward pressure on reserves and an upward pressure on inflation.

Therefore, for policy purposes, it is necessary to have an understanding of the manner in which the BOP is likely to be affected by changes in the rate of credit expansion. Achieving a short-run BOP target becomes especially complicated when the variables that determine the demand for money are themselves influenced by policy, and thus it becomes essential for the authorities to know how these variables will respond. While the financial programming approach does emphasize monetary relationships, it does not imply that the transmission mechanism has to be monetarist in character. What the discussion demonstrates is that this approach is equally consistent with a broad class of models that can include fixed and flexible exchange rates, and market-determined or administered interest rates, amongst others.

3.2.2 *Dynamics of Monetary Policy*

Use of the financial programming approach is relatively straightforward when applied in the long run, when all adjustments have worked themselves out, because empirically the money demand function is usually regarded as more stable over a period of a year or so, rather than over the very short term. In the short run, the demand for money may be more or less passive, operating as a buffer stock that serves to absorb changes in other variables. The evidence indicates that the stock of real money balances tends to rise initially, or that the income velocity of money falls, when there is an increase in the nominal supply of money. These excess cash balances are worked off slowly over time until the public is once again in equilibrium. Consequently, one might observe no particular relationship between increases in domestic credit and changes in reserves if the period of observation were too short.

All this implies that a monetary approach may be unsuitable for a very short-run analysis of the BOP and the period over which the theory is applicable may well be over a year. This is however an empirical question. Furthermore, there is nothing in the methodology that precludes the introduction of dynamics into the analysis. In the actual formulation of adjustment programmes, however, these considerations raise a number of specific problems. Two of these—the way that time lags are generally introduced into the formulation in order to account for short-run movements in velocity, and the 'liquidity overhang' problem—are briefly discussed below.

Within the framework of money demand models, there is a variety of ways to introduce dynamic behaviour. A common practice is to use some variant of the 'error-learning' model where it is hypothesized that because of adjustment costs and the costs of being out of equilibrium, the stock of real (or nominal) money balances adjusts proportionately to the discrepancy between the demand for money and its actual supply. In other words, whenever there is a change in the demand for money, the public is assumed to adjust only partly to it in the same period. Complete adjustment is thus achieved only slowly over time. This partial-adjustment variant of the error-learning framework allows one to empirically ascertain how long the adjustment will take. If the model indicates that all adjustment takes place within the year, then the equilibrium model can be utilized in the financial programming exercise. Contrariwise, the presence of slow adjustments would require the use of short-run money demand functions.

While error-learning models do introduce dynamics into the analysis, they are not able to capture the short-run phenomenon that an increased rate of monetary expansion results in a larger initial stock of real money balances or, equivalently, that the income velocity of money tends initially to move in the opposite direction of the change in monetary growth. This behaviour of real money balances was empirically noticed by Harberger (1963) and a theoretical rationale was provided for it by Friedman (1970). Typically, one observes that the time path of real money balances after a monetary increase appears is as shown in Figure 3.1. At time $t(0)$, there is a once-and-for-all increase in the rate of money growth and, with the rate of inflation lagging behind, initially the stock of real money balances rises, reaching a maximum point at time $t(1)$. As the price level catches up with money supply at time $t(2)$, real money balances are back to their initial level. The process however continues beyond $t(2)$ as inflation overshoots the rate of money growth, and real money balances fall below their original level, giving rise to the classic macroeconomic dictum, that *a sustained increase in money supply reduces real money stock*.

This type of behaviour has two important implications for financial programming. First, if the authorities set a credit ceiling that involves a reduction in money growth, then the observed demand for money may also fall in the short run. Therefore, while analysing the effects of monetary policy on the BOP, care must be exercised in using the short-run money demand function and an allowance must be made for shifts in the function.

The second problem has to do with the phenomenon of 'liquidity overhang'. If a contractionary monetary policy has to be implemented in situations of fundamental disequilibrium when there has been excessive monetary expansion in the past, then, in projecting the likely behaviour of velocity over the next year, the authorities have to recognize that, in all probability, there is a large build-up of cash balances; in effect, it cannot therefore proceed as if the money market was in equilibrium and use the standard money demand model. In other words, it would be an error to assume that the situation was characterized by a position like $t(0)$ in Figure 3.1. More likely, the economy is going to be somewhere between $t(0)$ and $t(2)$, if not at $t(1)$. Thus, the desired growth rate of money would have to allow for the existing excess stock of money balances, and this may entail a sharper reduction in money growth than if there were no overhang. Therefore, in the design of programmes, a judgment has to be made regarding the approximate magnitude of the liquidity overhang which can then be used as a base to project velocity over the programme period.

3.2.3   Choice Between Money and Credit as Policy Variables

Under circumstances in which the central bank is defending a fixed exchange rate, it can be argued that the inflationary effects of an overall BOP surplus could be mitigated by limiting the expansion of reserve money. Holding down the growth of reserve money would require reducing central bank domestic credit in order to sterilize the impact

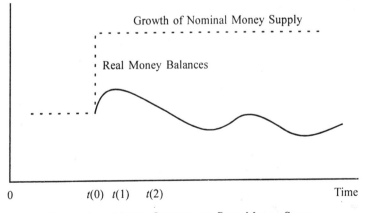

FIGURE 3.1   MONEY GROWTH AND REAL MONEY STOCK

of capital inflows on the monetary base. The sterilization of an external surplus may involve a sharp redistribution of available credit within the private sector, creating serious financing difficulties for those sectors of the economy especially dependent on domestic bank credit and not directly benefiting from the higher foreign exchange receipts. Although the feasibility of continued sterilization will eventually be determined by the nature of the BOP surplus, it would be important to limit domestic credit expansion since in the absence of a capital inflow, it would still be important to ensure that the BOP target was achieved.

The policy dilemma just analysed in the context of fixed exchange rates suggests a trade-off between price stability and exchange rate flexibility. For example, if the exchange rate has been substantially devalued in an effort to secure a favourable trade balance, then substantial unexpected capital inflows could be generated by yield differentials that partly reflect the expectation that further exchange rate depreciations are unlikely. If such flows occur, there could be substantial inflationary pressure in the economy and to contain this inflation, a greater degree of exchange rate flexibility may be required. In such a context of relatively unrestricted capital inflows, a fixed exchange rate and ceilings on reserve money may be mutually incompatible.

In general, with an exchange rate that is fixed or is adjusted only gradually (for example, to reflect inflation differentials), the ability of the authorities to control the growth of domestic monetary aggregates over extended periods is very limited. Even when the authorities limit the issuance of reserve money from domestic sources, portfolio and spending adjustments in the private sector would lead to external payments imbalances that would expand reserve money as the authorities intervene in the foreign exchange market to maintain their exchange rate policy. In contrast, a flexible exchange rate allows the authorities to control the growth of reserve money, thereby making a ceiling on a monetary aggregate an effective performance criterion.

In summary, unless the exchange rate is allowed to float without official intervention, the feasibility of the authorities controlling a reserve money aggregate depends upon their ability to sterilize inflows of foreign exchange. As pointed out earlier, this may not only entail costs arising from the contraction and redistribution of credit, but may also be limited by the lack of financial instruments available for sale by the central bank to mop up excess liquidity. This is a situation prevailing in many developing countries. Second, a 'clean float' may, in many circumstances, be ruled out, either because a country is committed to membership of a currency union or another arrangement entailing long-term fixity of the exchange rate,[3] or because some degree of official intervention is justifiable—for instance, to avoid the inflationary effects of 'overshooting'. Under these conditions, there are severe constraints on the ability of the monetary authorities to control monetary aggregates; consequently, ceilings on domestic credit rather than on such aggregates have therefore been chosen in most cases.

3.3 GUIDELINES FOR FISCAL ADJUSTMENT

Fiscal policies are a key determinant of both national and international economic developments, and guidelines for fiscal adjustment play a major role in any stabilization programme. In this section, we discuss some of the issues and concerns that underlie the approach to fiscal adjustment—namely, the ways governments can use their fiscal stabilization and structural policies to achieve macroeconomic objectives relating to growth, inflation, and the BOP. The focus here is on broad issues and practical policy options that need to be considered, although certain theoretical aspects of the literature on fiscal policy will also be discussed. In keeping with its practical emphasis, the remainder of this section is organized around four basic questions:

- Why is fiscal adjustment needed?
- How should the fiscal stance be assessed?
- How much fiscal adjustment is required?
- How should fiscal adjustment be effected?

3.3.1 *The Need for Fiscal Adjustment*

The need for fiscal adjustment may be seen in the context of the impact of fiscal policy on stabilization objectives, the sustainability of the fiscal policy stance, and the linkages between fiscal and other policy instruments.

In order to examine this issue, (eqn 2.26) can be written as:

$$(Ip - Sp) + (G - T) = (Z - X), \tag{3.5}$$

which shows the current account balance as the counterpart of the sum of the private sector's investment–savings balance and the fiscal deficit. Thus, the fiscal deficit ($FD = G - T$) must be matched by a private sector that saves more than it invests and/or by a current account deficit ($CAD = Z - X$).

Much of the theoretical debate on structural adjustment focuses on this relationship between the fiscal deficit (*FD*) and the current account deficit (*CAD*). Based upon (eqn 3.5), which shows that improvements in the *CAD* can take place only if sectoral savings rise relative to sectoral investment, Dornbusch and Helmers (1988) concluded forcefully that policies which do not have any effect on savings cannot be expected to improve the external balance.

However, (eqn 3.5) can also be written in terms of the linkages between the fiscal and external deficits as follows:

$$Ip = Sp - FD + CAD, \tag{3.6}$$

which indicates that increases in external savings, that is the *CAD*, offset public sector dissaving, thereby pre-empting the crowding out of private sector investment. Now, if the government deficit is corrected, will that eliminate the trade deficit? Based upon the results of Feldstein and Horioka (1982), the answer is 'No', because their evidence indicates, just as forcefully, that cutting the budget deficit (thereby increasing the national savings rate) will only increase investment with very little impact on the external deficit.

Thus, whether changes in the savings rate are reflected primarily in the external balance *à la* Dornbusch and Helmers or in investment levels *à la* Feldstein and Horioka becomes a policy issue of very great practical relevance and any effort to study this issue must examine the factors which caused these deficits in the first place.

The current account deficit as well as the fiscal deficit are usually linked within a general equilibrium framework because their basic proximate determinants—mainly the rates of inflation and growth—are themselves endogenous variables. Thus, any meaningful analysis of these deficits would require that their fundamental causes be specifically identified because the general equilibrium nature of the problem is not merely a theoretical fine point. The conclusions of most economists who have studied these issues (see Easterly, Rodriguez, and Schmidt-Hebbel 1994) is that the twin deficits are largely the result of the development strategies being followed by the country as well as the macroeconomic policies pursued by its major trading partners. Therefore, reducing these deficits would probably, although not necessarily, entail a reversal of these policies in order to correct the imbalances.

The literature provides three lines of approach for analysing responses towards such imbalances. The conventional method usually involves an eclectic model in which trade and fiscal flows are determined by price and income flows. Another approach is known as the dual-gap analysis which can be expanded into a three-gap model. In such a framework, one can view these imbalances as reflective of the savings–investment behaviour of a nation. A third strand of thought involves the neoclassical model of public debt (see Diamond 1965) which provides a theoretical analysis of the implications of funding a public sector deficit by borrowing from abroad. Studies based upon the open-economy characteristics of such a model (see Turnovsky 1995) have indicated that the adjustment towards a higher external debt implied by a higher public debt is shown to involve an extended period of current account deficits followed by an initial government budget deficit. This result involves the use of foreign savings (and therefore current account deficits) to supplement domestic savings both during the initial period of the government deficit as well as during subsequent periods when domestic savings are depressed by taxes which are used to service the higher debt. In fact, such an analysis of the interaction between the debt, the fiscal deficit, and the current account deficit reflects the more-or-less conventional view in academic circles of the relationship that seems to exist between the twin deficits in most developing countries.

Therefore, considerable caution is required in moving from (eqn 3.5) to the assumption that a simple causal relationship exists between fiscal and external deficits; because the manner and extent of linkages between fiscal and external deficits would depend on the impacts, if any, of fiscal policy on private sector savings and investment behaviour; moreover, fiscal deficits may respond to, as well as influence, external deficits.

In such a context, the primary responsibility of policy makers would be to ensure the long-term viability of a non-inflationary growth path that does not entail an unsustainable growth in public debt or the creation of an unfinanceable future external position. Thus, fiscal adjustment initiatives may be necessary in the short-run to prevent the occurrence of an unsustainable fiscal position in the future.

3.3.2 *Assessing the Fiscal Stance*

Given the size and complexity of most government budgets, it becomes important to develop broad indicators that convey a sense of the impact of fiscal policy on domestic demand and financial resources. The most commonly used indicator to assess the stance of fiscal policy is the overall balance between revenues and grants, and expenditure and net lending. This balance may be in surplus or deficit. As a starting point of analysis, an overall deficit (surplus) would suggest an expansionary (contractionary) fiscal stance on the basis that the negative impact of taxes and other revenues on aggregate demand is more (less) than offset by the positive effects of government spending. Intertemporal developments in this balance, particularly when related to GDP, provide an indication of the changing impact of the government sector on the economy. In this context, two other fiscal indicators which are often used to provide additional insights into the impact of a fiscal stance are the primary balance and the operational balance. While these measures offer a perspective on the aggregate demand effects of fiscal policy, they are related to special issues or circumstances and are only partial approaches and indicators for assessing complex situations. In particular, they are deficient as indicators of the impact of fiscal actions on other policy variables of concern, including growth, monetary stance, and sustainability (see Blejer and Cheasty 1993).

Moreover, they abstract from the range of items that comprise government operations, notably, the way the deficit is financed. On a cash basis, total incomings and outgoings from the budget must always balance. A deficit (or surplus) is determined by drawing a balance among a subset of receipts and payments (classified 'above the line'), which are then financed by other transactions (shown 'below the line'). Considering that a deficit may be financed from domestic (bank and non-bank) or external sources, any assessment of the fiscal policy stance would need to take account of the way the deficit is financed, since each method of financing has its own particular macroeconomic effect and cost. Such a delineation is based on the analytical needs sought from the measure of the fiscal balance.

Efforts at assessing fiscal policy lead to important questions about the institutions comprising the government. Based on a functional definition of the general government[4] and fiscal policy, the quasi-fiscal operations of public financial institutions, the most important of which is the central bank, may have a fiscal impact comparable to that of the more traditionally defined government activities. In many countries, the central bank and, indeed, the entire banking system, if it has been nationalized, play an important role in fiscal policy. By undertaking financial transactions that serve the same role as taxes and subsidies, they increase the effective size of the fiscal deficit. These so-called quasi-fiscal activities (QFAs), which often result in a quasi-fiscal deficit, can have a significant allocative and budgetary impact in many countries. The majority of these QFAs arise from the dual roles of the central bank as the regulator of the exchange rate and as the banker to the government. QFAs can involve multiple exchange rate arrangements, interest rate subsidies and sectoral credit ceilings, central bank rescue operations, and lending to the government at below-market rates. Under the circumstances, these QFAs ought to be explicitly considered in the formulation of fiscal programmes, and any quantifiable quasi-fiscal deficit should be added to the overall fiscal balance to provide a broader and more appropriate measure of the fiscal stance.

3.3.3   The Required Fiscal Adjustment

Fiscal adjustment policies should be designed within an overall methodological framework that links the implementation of a comprehensive set of policy measures to the achievement of the country's objectives. Policy setting within this framework requires decisions regarding the appropriate amount and form of fiscal adjustment, including the desired level of the fiscal deficit. Large structural deficits, rising government debt, and tightening domestic and external constraints emphasize the crucial importance of fiscal consolidation and ultimately dictate the required fiscal adjustment strategy.

In such a context, the need for fiscal adjustment and the amount of fiscal adjustment needed is usually discussed in relation to the desired reduction in the overall fiscal deficit; often, possible trade-offs are suggested between the quality and quantity of adjustment measures. One of the most important factors affecting the required amount of fiscal reduction is the need to stabilize the economy. To reduce inflation and/or the *CAD,* fiscal contraction is usually necessary and may even imply a surplus. To dampen business cycles, governments often need to smooth aggregate demand over the cycle, which may imply a surplus during a boom. A negative supply shock (such as a drought), a positive demand shock (such as a property boom), or large capital inflows also justify a fiscal contraction, amounting to a surplus.

Yet another important factor is that of debt dynamics and sustainability. A strategy for fiscal stabilization implies the targeting of a time path over which fiscal deficits will be reduced. The deficit that must be financed during this period will thus need to be serviced from future public sector resources. Although governments can borrow indefinitely, in the long run, they must have the financial capability to meet their interest costs without borrowing or, in other words, the primary balance should be in surplus. Otherwise, the level of debt as a share of GDP will rise continuously and will eventually become unsustainable. Once that happens, a primary fiscal surplus will, in general, be necessary; indeed, the debt problem may become so severe so as to warrant an overall surplus (see Hemmings and Daniel 1995). The only exception to this requirement is when the resources the government borrows are used so effectively that the economy's real growth rate persistently exceeds the real interest rate on government debt; but this is unlikely, because when the growth rate exceeds the real interest rate, the increasing level of debt will push up interest rates which, in turn, might dampen growth.

The determination of the required amount of adjustment can also be viewed by evaluating the appropriate level of financing items. Normally, adjustment programmes seek to curtail the rate of expansion of credit in order to reduce inflation. Now, given a growth in overall bank credit which is consistent with inflation and BOP objectives, a limit may then be established on the amount of bank credit that can be provided to the government. A ceiling may also be placed on government borrowings from abroad in order to ensure consistency with domestic and external debt-servicing capacities. If, simultaneously, access to non-bank borrowing is also limited, or constrained by a desire not to 'crowd out' private sector activities, then these three constraints automatically limit the overall fiscal deficit from 'below the line', that is from the financing side. The required amount of fiscal adjustment would then depend upon the excess of the projected fiscal deficit over this implied limit.

3.3.4 *Effecting the Fiscal Adjustment*

Undertaking fiscal adjustment often requires difficult decisions involving increasing government revenue and decreasing spending. Expenditure reductions often tend to be stressed in the initial stages of adjustment, with particular emphasis on cuts in capital spending and current outlays on other goods and services (excluding wages, subsidies and transfers, and interest payments). However, cutbacks in productive capital spending and essential operations and maintenance expenses can inhibit growth and need to be avoided. Equally important, effecting such types of fiscal adjustments is not independent of the quality of the measures chosen during implementation. An assessment of quality would focus on the sustainability and durability of the measures being considered and on the relative impact of alternative policy options on investment and production incentives. Specifically, short-term measures that cannot be sustained, or which may have adverse effects on growth over the medium term should be viewed critically. Consequently, countries need to move swiftly on to longer-term structural reforms affecting expenditure, revenue, and public enterprises in order to allow for a more balanced and less myopic approach to fiscal adjustment and to generate the resources necessary to support spending that addresses itself to productive and social needs.

In designing such fiscal adjustment strategies, policy makers are often faced with short-term costs and constraints. Such concerns include the output and employment losses that may be incurred in rationalizing expenditures, the possible negative effect on growth of raising taxes, and the difficulties involved in modifying implicit social contracts by altering the role of the government. Experience with adjustment in many developing countries has, however, shown the high costs of delayed or suboptimal adjustment in terms of a deteriorating BOP, rising inflation, and stagnant growth. Although attention to a proper mix and phasing of policies is essential to provide social support for adjustment programmes, nevertheless, fiscal adjustment invariably entails many adverse effects, and vulnerable groups would need to be protected through well-targeted social safety nets (SSNs).

In certain cases, revenue can be increased by raising rates within an existing system. However, the ability to generate increased revenue in this manner may be limited especially when the economy is undergoing substantial structural change, traditional tax bases are declining, and there are fundamental weaknesses in the tax system. In such a context, it needs to be noted that structural problems in the tax system could well be a major factor underlying not only fiscal deficits, but also poor growth and employment performance. Consequently, programmes of fiscal adjustment need to be often accompanied by an effort to improve and restructure the existing tax system.

Similarly, expenditure reduction measures have to be pragmatic, adequate to achieve the intended stabilization, but nevertheless economically, politically, and socially feasible. While several types of short-term expenditure measures can be adapted quickly to contain a rapidly deteriorating fiscal situation, sustainable expenditure reform, however, requires a review of the underlying government policies, the composition of spending, the coverage of activities by the public sector, and the modes of delivery of public services. Quite often, a thorough structural reform of government expenditure policies can be done only in a medium-term framework (see Tanzi 1993).

3.4 EXCHANGE RATE POLICIES

Exchange rate action to improve international competitiveness and increase the incentives to produce tradeable goods is often the centrepiece of any adjustment effort. There are several theoretical approaches to exchange rate determination although, in practice, the economic structure of the country and the institutional capacity of its central bank and financial markets would be the factors which govern the success of its exchange rate system and policy.

The *absorption approach* suggests that the excess of domestic absorption (that is gross domestic expenditure) over domestic income induces an increase in imports resulting in a deterioration of the external resource balance. To correct this situation, an exchange rate depreciation is needed. On the other hand, the *monetary approach* suggests that an expansion in domestic credit relative to changes in money demand will result in a decline in international reserves. In order to reverse this down turn, it may be necessary for the exchange rate to depreciate. The *asset market approach* is an extension of the monetary approach, and suggests that both the demand and supply of different currencies (viewed as assets) determine the exchange rate. Changes in interest rates and expectations about future exchange rates affect the demand for a particular currency leading to changes in the exchange rate. The *structural approach* is of the view that changes in productivity and efficiency which affects unit costs, as well as the introduction or elimination of import tariffs or export subsidies, all have an effect on the exchange rate.

Since devaluation, in the terminology of Johnson (1958), is simultaneously an expenditure-reducing and expenditure-switching policy, it affects domestic absorption and domestic supply, and thus contains aspects of both demand-side and structural policies. A depreciation of the currency from a fixed rate would create an excess demand for real cash balances, and this in turn would result in a decline in real absorption. Devaluation is therefore an expenditure-reducing policy in such a context. At the same time, however, exchange rate adjustment is also an expenditure-switching policy, influencing the composition of domestic expenditure—through the alteration of incentives—between foreign and domestic goods. Therefore, any analysis of exchange rate policies has to take into account the effects of devaluation both on demand (via absorption) and supply (via incentives). The basic demand-side and supply-side aspects of devaluation have been extensively discussed in the literature (see Dornbusch 1981); in effect, both the aggregate demand and aggregate supply effects of a devaluation work toward reducing the excess demand in the economy and the current account deficit. Whether total output rises or falls during this process would depend on whether the contractionary effects on aggregate demand are outweighed by the supply-stimulating aspects of this policy.

The above analysis does highlight the importance of getting the real exchange rate 'right' in the adjustment process. However, although exchange rate action may be the only obvious way to correct a misalignment of relative prices, there are still a number of difficult theoretical and empirical issues involved. This section discusses four such issues: (a) the exchange rate regime or exchange rate rules that a country should adopt; (b) achieving the target value of the real exchange rate; (c) determining the 'equilibrium' real exchange rate, and therefore the size of the real depreciation required; and (d) estimating the effects of a change in the real exchange rate.

3.4.1 Exchange Rate Systems and Regimes

Unlike the developed industrial countries, there are not many developing countries that operate a freely floating exchange rate system. Most either maintain fixed parities or follow some type of crawling peg rule. While there may be advantages to maintaining a fixed peg, such a system has the drawback that the policy leaves the country vulnerable to speculative attacks which may result in an exchange rate crisis unless the authorities are willing to alter the peg. At the other extreme from countries with fixed exchange rates are high-inflation countries where continual exchange rate adjustments are built into the system. Indeed, in many such instances, these exchange rate changes can be regarded as merely a particular type of indexation. For these countries, the key decision is the rate at which the exchange rate should be depreciated. Considering the difficulties involved in making such a decision, many writers have questioned the use of exchange rate rules, arguing that they either increase fluctuations in output or increase domestic inflation, and are therefore inconsistent with macroeconomic stability.

In this context, it needs to be noted that most of the transition economies adopted market reforms with a common set of structural imbalances. After price liberalization, fixed exchange rate regimes in Czechoslovakia, Hungary, and Poland helped bring down inflation, while flexible rates in Ukraine, Russia, and Latvia resulted in high inflation for many years. Based upon these experiences, Bruno (1995) and Sachs (1996) suggest that in the early phases of stabilization, a pegged rate ties the hands of the government and thereby enhances its credibility. It also helps price and wage setters to coordinate their medium-term actions and contracts. However, a long-run unsustainable pegged rate could turn out to be a nightmare, as in Mexico.

Confronted with persistent BOP problems, some developing countries have adopted a dual exchange rate system under which certain selected transactions take place at the official exchange rate, which is maintained by official intervention, while the remaining transactions take place at a more depreciated ('free' or 'parallel') exchange rate, which is usually determined by market forces. However, dual exchange rate systems have been unsuccessful in achieving the objectives that motivated their adoption. In particular, they have been largely ineffective in preventing speculative capital flows from affecting international reserves, as uncertainties concerning the long-run viability of the official exchange rate have produced leads and lags in imports and exports in the official market. Similarly, differentials between the free and official exchange rates have motivated the over-invoicing of imports and the under-invoicing of exports, thus contributing to a further deterioration of reserves. In addition, dual exchange rates are equivalent to a series of implicit taxes and subsidies that work against the objectives of macroeconomic stabilization. For example, commodities that receive export promotion incentives are sometimes assigned to the official market, thus implicitly taxing these exports, which could defeat the initial purpose of export promotion.

In summary, there is a need to study the workings of dual exchange rate systems in greater detail in order to determine the reasons as to why they are unlikely to survive very long. Also at issue is how and when rules that are designed to keep the real exchange rate constant, or slowly depreciate over time, should be changed when circumstances dictate.

3.4.2   *Policies to Achieve a Target Real Exchange Rate*

Adjustment is needed whenever macroeconomic disequilibria are generated due to exogenous shocks or because of linkages with the rest of the world. Macroeconomic policies leading to disequilibria are also quite common in the developing world. The effects of such unsustainable policies need to rectified by appropriate macroeconomic adjustment. The conventional response is to reduce total expenditures and to insist on a real devaluation, that is a nominal devaluation accompanied by monetary and fiscal restraints, thus attempting to avoid a domestic price rise which would negate the nominal devaluation.

Figure 3.2 is a graphic illustration of this argument. The real exchange rate (RER) is represented on the y-axis, while real output (Y) is depicted on the x-axis. The vertical line represents the internal balance schedule implying that the economy is at its full-employment level of output (*Yf*). The upward-sloping line EE represents the external balance schedule where the demand and supply of foreign exchange are assumed to be in equilibrium. An increase in income (*Y*) raises imports and worsens the trade balance. To restore trade balance equilibrium, the real exchange rate would have to be increased by increasing the nominal exchange rate and/or by decreasing the price level. This would make the economy more competitive, raise exports, and reduce imports. Consequently, the external balance equilibrium schedule is upward-sloping.

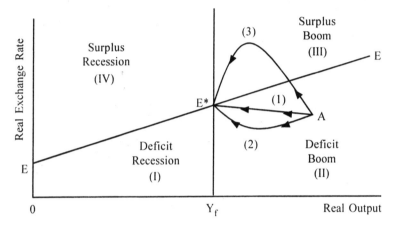

FIGURE 3.2   OPEN ECONOMY EQUILIBRIUM WITH SHORT-RUN ADJUSTMENTS

Thus, the diagram has four regions corresponding to booms and recessions, surpluses and deficits. Assume now that the economy is at point A in Region II (deficit and boom) and that the government wants to achieve not only internal balance but also external balance. This implies that the objective would be to reach the equilibrium point E*. In such a framework, we have two targets (internal and external balance) and adjustment can take place by manipulating the two instruments (demand-management and exchange rate policies). The interaction of these alternative sets of policies effect the economy through a number of different linkages (see Taylor and Arida 1989, Corden 1990).

First, when expenditures are reduced, there is a decline in spending on both tradeables and non-tradeables. Second, devaluation raises the domestic price level which in turn decreases the real value of assets.

Such a negative real balance or wealth effect has the potential of lowering expenditures, mainly consumption expenditures. Third, devaluation also increases the price of imports which consequently increases the costs of production, resulting in a contraction of real output (or aggregate supply). In addition, if credit in nominal terms to the private and public sectors is kept constant (as a result of credit ceilings), investment in real terms would decline. These essentially summarize the main expenditure-reducing effects.

In addition, there are expenditure-switching arguments. That is, there is a shift in the pattern of domestic demand from tradeables towards nontradeables and in the pattern of output produced from nontradeables towards tradeables. The switch in demand from foreign goods towards domestic goods occurs because devaluation increases the price of tradeables relative to nontradeables. However, there is a need to ensure that the decline in the demand for nontradeables resulting from the expenditure reduction does not lead to an excess supply of output of nontradeables. The switching policy ensures that external balance occurs with internal balance being maintained.

By increasing the price of imports, a devaluation raises the general price level in the domestic economy, and thus there is a pressure to increase nominal wages, especially in countries where wages are indexed. A real devaluation will not occur if wages rise proportionately with import prices and consumer prices. However, to the extent that devaluation lowers the 'rents' accruing to import quota holders as import prices are driven up, there is a profit squeeze on rent-seekers.

As far as its impact on the fiscal deficit is concerned, devaluation decreases (increases) imports (exports) and if the loss in revenues from falling imports is more than offset by taxing export income, then such an exchange rate adjustment can be instrumental in reducing the fiscal deficit. However, a devaluation increases the local currency value of external debt service payments which would *ceteris paribus* worsen the fiscal deficit unless government expenditures are reduced or taxes increased.

The above analysis assumes that the Marshall–Lerner condition, that is the sum of demand elasticities for exports and imports is greater than unity, is satisfied. If these elasticities are low (called elasticity pessimism), then devaluation is ineffective in improving the current account balance. However, empirical evidence suggests that while short-run elasticities could be low, the long-run elasticities are much higher. Therefore, devaluation is more likely to improve the current account in the long run than in the immediate future.

Apart from the price effects on imports and exports, the response of quantities to these price changes is also important because such responses usually involve considerable delays. If exports are invoiced in local currency while imports are invoiced in foreign currency, the initial effect of the devaluation is to worsen the trade balance as the value of exports in foreign currency falls, while the dollar value of imports increases. Thus, as a result of a devaluation, the trade balance may get worse initially before it gets any better. This particular phenomenon gives rise to the so-called 'J-curve effect'. One way of mitigating this effect is for the devaluing country to invoice its exports in foreign currency.

The above analysis indicates the necessity for a real devaluation to take place as a result of a nominal devaluation. The initial impact of a nominal devaluation is a real devaluation but, over time, the persistence effects of a nominal devaluation gradually die down. In the absence of supporting demand-management policies that limit the increase in domestic prices, a nominal devaluation will only have a transitory effect on the real exchange rate. In the medium-term, domestic prices will rise by the full amount of the devaluation and the real exchange rate will return back to its original level. Therefore, any sustainable real exchange rate requires policies to restrain aggregate demand, and the extent to which a devaluation will affect the real exchange rate is a direct function of these supporting policies.

In principle, the alternative to exchange rate policies is to have an incomes policy of government control of wages and prices. In general, however, the latter is likely to be a much more expensive way of achieving the desired objectives because these deflationary policies are designed to reduce domestic prices and wages which, in most countries, tend to be 'sticky downwards' unless accompanied by substantial falls in output and employment.

3.4.3 *The Extent of Exchange Rate Adjustment*

The task of determining the degree of exchange rate adjustment required, in conjunction with other policies, so as to achieve a targeted BOP is an extremely complicated one. This is because it is often very difficult to predict the impact of an exchange rate adjustment on all types of external transactions especially if the previous misalignment was so large so as to have encouraged a sizeable parallel market. Moreover, the results may be all the more uncertain if the policy package includes liberalization of the foreign trade and payments system. In view of these problems, it is not surprising that the move to an appropriate exchange rate is often accomplished gradually and by utilizing market forces to some extent.

In many instances, however, there is a reluctance to depend upon the market to determine an appropriate rate because often the market attaches an excessive degree of importance to relatively small and transient changes. For example, in the case of a decline in export prices due to a recession, a country has the option of waiting out the cyclical downturn with the expectation that export prices would increase eventually with the recovery, rather than instantly devaluing the exchange rate appropriately in order to restore profitability to the export sector. In any event, one may wish to arrive at an independent judgment of what such an 'appropriate' rate ought to be rather than depending entirely on market sentiments in such matters.

One possible approach to exchange rate analysis is to estimate export supply and import demand functions, and to use the resulting elasticities to arrive at that exchange rate which would produce the desired changes in trade flows. This technique is however open to the criticism that it takes only a partial equilibrium view of the economy and that ultimately the correct level of the 'equilibrium' exchange rate cannot be determined without taking a general equilibrium view; in effect, by examining the interactions between the exchange rate and the other principal macroeconomic variables, all of which are simultaneously determined not only by the exchange rate itself, but also by all the other policy actions that are part of the stabilization programme.

In attempting to do this, it would be necessary to take account of the time element. One approach to incorporating lags in a general equilibrium model of trade flows is to employ the error-learning model that was discussed in the context of the demand for money. However, such models may not be realistic in this case for a variety of reasons. First, the appropriate lag pattern for modelling trade flows could have a '∩' shape rather than the steadily decaying pattern emerging from the error-learning framework. This becomes particularly important in the case of export supply functions. Second, the error-learning model assumes that the lag in response of the dependent variable is identical irrespective of whether the change is prompted due to variations in prices or the scale variable. While there seems to be some agreement that the effect of real income (capacity) on imports (exports) is largest in the initial period and declines rapidly thereafter, there is much less consensus on the proper distributed-lag pattern for price changes. These two problems have led researchers to experiment with alternative lag structures; and, consequently, the timing issue in modelling trade relationships in general-equilibrium models of the economy is still far from settled. The only consensus that seems to emerge is that the lags will be, to a large extent, country-specific.

3.4.4   The Impact of Exchange Rate Changes

One of the standard criticisms against devaluation as an adjustment policy is that it induces stagflation and increases unemployment. As mentioned earlier, whether a devaluation exerts a net contractionary or expansionary effect on domestic output and employment depends on the relative strengths of the effects it has on aggregate demand and supply, and the time frame in question. As long as devaluation succeeds in altering the real exchange rate by raising product prices in domestic currency relative to factor incomes, it should exert a stimulative effect to the extent that the short-run marginal cost curves of the relevant (tradeable goods) industry are upward sloping. Naturally, the longer a real devaluation persists, the larger are the gains to be achieved. Also, if the wealth and distributional effects of devaluation stimulate savings, a long-run increase in potential output can be realized.

Despite the controversy surrounding the output and employment effects of the exchange rate policy, there is surprisingly little empirical evidence available on the subject. Furthermore, the relatively few studies examining this issue yield rather mixed results. Thus, given the state of empirical knowledge currently, it would be futile to draw conclusions one way or the other.

The experience of developing countries with exchange rate actions during the 1980s suggests that exports are responsive to exchange rate changes. However, export diversification is only possible in the medium- to long-term when exchange rate changes are accompanied by trade liberalization measures and a favourable external environment, including financial support. The effectiveness of exchange rate actions on import-substitution has been limited in certain cases because a large share of imports are often tied to aid.

Of equal relevance are the effects of devaluation on inflation. The evidence in this regard indicates that countries which followed expansionary domestic credit policies and large fiscal deficits after a nominal devaluation experienced a high erosion of the initial effects. Based on 28 episodes of nominal devaluation, Edwards (1988) noticed that, on an average, a 10 per cent nominal devaluation resulted in a real devaluation of about 7 per cent in the first year, and about 5 per cent by the end of three years.

Associated with all these questions is the related one of whether the overall impact of an exchange rate adjustment varies if it is made in one single step, or if it is made gradually over time in a series of small steps, after an initial large step. It is sometimes felt that a more gradual adjustment softens the inflationary consequences; against this, there is the consideration that a 'front-loaded' adjustment brings about a quicker change in the foreign trade balance. The choice of the relative speeds of adjustment is essentially a variant of the 'gradualism versus shock' issue; graphically the problem is illustrated in Figure 3.2, where Route (1) denotes the shock approach (the so-called 'cold turkey' strategy), while Route (2) indicates the gradualist approach. Against this, however, it is sometimes argued that if a country is unwilling to make frequent exchange rate adjustments, it might wish to devalue by more than what is initially necessary in order to avoid possible capital flight which might arise as a result of an expectation of a further imminent devaluation. This type of an 'overshooting' approach is denoted by Route (3) in Figure 3.2.

3.5 CONCLUSIONS

The design of adjustment programmes is often a difficult task, involving analysis of a complex set of macroeconomic relationships as well as hard political decisions. Stabilization programmes must be aimed at meeting the country's principal economic objectives, including both a satisfactory rate of growth of output and general macroeconomic balance. The goal of sustaining a viable BOP position is closely related to the specification of domestic macroeconomic objectives: the targeted excess of domestic expenditure (or absorption) over income must not exceed the amount of external debt that can be accumulated without undue increase in the relative burden of debt service. The formulation of a feasible set of objectives is therefore the first step in designing a programme; for this, a general framework of analysis is needed. The next step is to choose the instruments with which to achieve the objectives of the programme; this, in turn, requires knowledge about the transmission process whereby policy variables affect the BOP, prices, and output.

The relationship between external and internal balance, as shown in the accounting framework for financial programming, provides the basis for defining the fundamental macroeconomic adjustments necessary. Macroeconomic balance, while a necessary condition for sustained growth, is certainly not a sufficient condition, and where resources are poorly utilized and growth rates are inadequate, it is necessary to undertake measures of various sorts to raise savings and investment, as well as the return on investment.

Another major argument is that the financial programming framework is consistent with a wide range of hypothesis about the transmission mechanism between stabilization policies and the macroeconomic variables targeted, and therefore with different overall policy strategies. In particular, the time lags between policy changes and changes in the target variables will have an important bearing on the choice of policy measures and the timing of their implementation. This last point is especially noteworthy because of the difficult decision that must always be made with regard to the pace at which various measures, such as the reduction of the *CAD,* should be implemented. In such a context, the role of exchange rate policies often raises questions as it influences the choices with respect to the conduct of monetary policy. This is because with limited exchange rate flexibility, not much scope exists for the authorities to influence the stock of money in an open economy. With flexible rates, there may be circumstances under which a monetary aggregate other than domestic credit would be a more appropriate, or at least a desirable supplementary, policy variable, especially when inflation is a major concern.

In the ultimate analysis, the most important factors in the design and implementation of adjustment programmes are the institutional and political settings. Aside from the question of exchange rate regime, which in the extreme case of membership in a currency union limits the scope for the use of both exchange rate and monetary policies in carrying out the needed adjustments, there are other institutional features of crucial importance. For example, the degree and the modalities of planning in an economy often affect the scope for the use of prices to affect economic decision making in the non-government sector. Even in economies that are not 'planned', the adherence to government controls and the resistance to structural reforms could severely limit the pace with which adjustment programmes can be implemented.

NOTES

[1] If commercial banks are assumed to hold no foreign exchange assets, then the net foreign assets of the central bank will be equal to the overall foreign exchange reserves of the banking system, that is $NFA = R$.

[2]All the assumptions regarding the application of financial programming techniques will be discussed in Chapter 4.

[3]After the Mexican debacle in December 1994, it has become fashionable to argue in favour of a currency board. The suggestion is that the Mexican crisis could have been averted had it introduced a currency board such as the one existing in Argentina since 1991. Under a currency board, the central bank commits itself to a fixed exchange rate and to zero domestic credit expansion. In such a system, the central bank cannot act as a lender of the last resort, because it is unable to provide liquidity (because the change in net domestic assets must be zero) even when domestic banks are faced with a depositor panic. Equally true, an exchange rate depreciation is no longer an option even when there is a run on reserves. This lack of flexibility has made currency boards unattractive to many countries, although for small and very open economies, such as the Eastern Caribbean states, Hong Kong, and Lithuania, this is a good option as it enforces fiscal and monetary discipline.

[4]The general government includes, in addition to the central government, the budgetary and extra-budgetary activities of state and local governments as well.

ANALYTICAL FRAMEWORK FOR STABILIZATION AND ADJUSTMENT

4

Financial Programming and Stabilization

4.1 INTRODUCTION

The International Monetary Fund (IMF) was founded together with the World Bank, formally known as the International Bank for Reconstruction and Development (IBRD), at the Bretton Woods Conference in July 1944. It was no coincidence that, rather than one international economic and financial institution, two institutions were established as the founding fathers of the Bretton Woods (of whom Lord Keynes was the leading figure) were consciously trying to establish a division of labour among the two.

The IMF was initially set up to promote international monetary cooperation by providing a machinery for consultation and collaboration and, until 1973, the IMF monitored members' compliance with their obligations within the then-prevailing fixed exchange rate system. However, in 1976, the original expression 'a system of stable exchange rates' was changed in the Second Amendment of the IMF Articles of Amendment to 'a stable system of exchange rates' and new procedures for IMF surveillance of exchange rate policies as well as balance of payments (BOP) problems of member countries were introduced in line with the changed international and financial environment. As such, the current mandate of the IMF is, in general, limited to financing temporary BOP disequilibria in attempts to stabilize the economy. When BOP deficits are not inherently temporary, they must be rendered so by stabilization programmes.

Broadly defined, a stabilization (or financial) programme is a package of policies designed to eliminate disequilibrium between aggregate demand and supply in the economy, which typically manifests itself in the form of rising prices and BOP deficits. Thus, the fundamental objective of a stabilization package is to find 'a suitable relationship between resource availabilities and needs that causes minimum strain on the internal price level and produces a desired balance of payments result' (Robichek 1967, pp. 1–2).

The formulation of such stabilization measures requires the possession of an implicit or explicit model that links policy instruments controlled by the authorities to the BOP. While there is no single theoretical model underlying all financial programmes, a broad framework within which most of them are formulated has evolved in the Fund over the years. This approach of the IMF to macroeconomic stabilization is generally referred to as 'financial programming', the basis for which was articulated and formalized principally by Polak (1957) and Robichek (1967). The more recent work in this area has also tended to stay broadly within the Polak–Robichek tradition (see IMF 1977, 1987; Robichek 1985). The Polak model, which postulates a well-defined relationship between domestic credit, nominal income, imports, and the BOP, with the supply of and the demand for money playing a central linking role, is considered by many (see Taylor 1987) to be the most influential piece of work in macroeconomics after the *General Theory* of Keynes (1936), especially as it currently forms the cornerstone of most IMF-supported programmes and policy prescriptions.

However, partly because of the inaccessible nature of most Fund-related work on financial programming and partly due to the tendency of the Fund to set the rules for internal discussions in terms of its own model(s), there have been several acrimonious debates on the IMF approach which, unfortunately, have been translated into an ideological level by IMF critics, thereby pre-empting a proper understanding of some of the more important issues at stake or how they may be resolved.

The purpose of this chapter is to describe the analytical framework behind the design of Fund-supported adjustment programmes. Given the eclectic nature of the IMF approach, it is not possible to offer a unified or unique theory underlying such programmes. However, it is hoped that, by providing a description of the 'state of the art' with respect to the theoretical nexus, we would be able to dispel the notion that these programmes are based on a particular view of the economy or on the convictions of any single school of economic thought. That money and monetary policy play an important role in determining inflation and BOP outcomes, and therefore clearly also in the design of adjustment programmes, does not necessarily make Fund-supported adjustment programmes 'monetarist' in character. The concentration on monetary flows in such programmes can be justified on several grounds, ranging from the view that the BOP is essentially a monetary phenomenon to the more pragmatic reason that data on monetary variables contain important macroeconomic information and are more accurate and timely than data on real variables.

We initially discuss the original Polak model and set it against the backdrop of the theory which it was partly responsible for subsequently creating. We then specify a representative model of BOP and inflation which captures the essence of the Fund approach to macroeconomic stabilization. An empirical attempt is then made to assess the adequacy of this approach and a few stabilization options within the postulated framework are considered. Finally, we formulate, construct, and test a financial programming model on the lines suggested by the IMF approach.

4.2   THE SIMPLE MONETARY STABILIZATION MODEL

4.2.1   The 'Empty' Framework
Any financial programming exercise revolves around the macroeconomic accounts reviewed in Chapter 2. The national balance given by (eqn 2.2), the external balance given by (eqn 2.19), the monetary balance given by (eqn 2.20) and the savings–investment balance given by (eqn 2.25) are usually singled out as being the most important. The order in which these balances are listed are not accidental. Early IMF work on BOP issues was framed within the absorption approach associated with Alexander (1951, 1952). This approach, which combines (eqn 2.2) and (eqn 2.19), played a key role in the design of early Fund-supported programmes prior to the formulation of the Polak model.

Towards the end of the 1950s, however, with the advent of the Polak model, the absorption approach became integrated with the view that the BOP is principally a monetary phenomenon, and attention was focused on the relationship between money supply and the external sector, that is the monetary balance given by (eqn 2.20), which was 'added' to the first two balance equations.

With the introduction of the 'two-gap' models into the literature by Chenery and his associates (see Chenery and Bruno 1962, Chenery and Strout 1966), attention was subsequently drawn to the savings–investment balance and the role of foreign savings in supplementing domestic savings. Thus, (eqn 2.25) was 'added' to the basic framework and, in summary form, the set of four identities can be presented as follows:

- National Balance: $Y = (C + I) + (X - Z)$
- External Balance: $(X - Z) + \Delta F = \Delta R$
- Monetary Balance: $\Delta M = \Delta DC + \Delta R$
- Savings–Investment Balance: $I = S + (Z - X)$.

The above set of equations which are singled out for further study in the IMF framework is just a subset of the overall balances that make up the national accounts. Furthermore, the subset of balances do not amount to a model as no behavioural equations have been specified. While *ex ante* gaps must close during the period so that they are in balance *ex post,* the above identities do not provide any clue as to how this adjustment process takes place. For this, it is essential to provide the necessary causal links in the economy, without which the above set of equations would be just an 'empty' framework devoid of any macroeconomic implications.

4.2.2   *The Polak Model*
The first transformation of the above 'empty' framework into an analytic model took place in the seminal article by Polak (1957) who, being dissatisfied with the Keynesian overemphasis on fiscal policy and the inappropriate treatment meted out to monetary policy in the *General Theory,* attempted to streamline the monetary side of the analysis. He, however, clearly stressed that his model was not an alternative to Keynesian economics and, on the contrary, '. . . by focusing on the monetary side of the same circular process, we can approach the problem from another angle, which makes it tractable in many situations' (Polak 1957, p. 11).

In line with the IMF mandate, an improvement in the BOP was established as the key objective. The Polak model was specified in nominal terms and, consequently, no explicit distinction was made between price and real income changes. The two key behavioural assumptions made were: (i) the demand for money (Md) depends on nominal income (Y) only, with the income velocity of money (v) being assumed to be a constant; and (ii) imports (Z) are a constant fraction (m) of nominal income. Furthermore, it was assumed that money supply (M) was determined through the identity for monetary balance, that is (eqn 2.20), while reserves (R) were determined through the identity for external balance, that is (eqn 2.19). Assuming that the money market is in flow equilibrium, that is $\Delta Md = \Delta M$, the structure of the Polak model can be given as follows:

$$\Delta M = \Delta DC + \Delta R, \tag{4.1}$$
$$\Delta R = X - Z + \Delta F, \tag{4.2}$$
$$\Delta Md = \Delta M, \tag{4.3}$$
$$(\Delta Md)v = \Delta Y, \tag{4.4}$$
$$Z = mY. \tag{4.5}$$

Polak used the above system to reach a series of conclusions regarding the effects of changes in the policy variable, domestic credit (DC), on the target variable, foreign exchange reserves (R), assuming that exports (X) and capital inflows (ΔF) were given exogenously. The transmission mechanism through which an increase in domestic credit (ΔDC) works is initially to increase money supply by the same amount, that is ΔDC, through (eqn 4.1). This brings about an identical increase in money demand, given (eqn 4.3), and consequently nominal income increases by $v\Delta DC$ through (eqn 4.4). This increase in nominal income increases imports by $mv\Delta DC$, given (eqn 4.5), and consequently there would be a reserve change by an identical amount, that is $-mv\Delta DC$, given (eqn 4.2). As the initial increase in domestic credit remains fixed at ΔDC, this would, in turn, imply that money supply, in the next round, would increase only by $(1 - mv)\Delta DC$.

The above process will go on in the standard multiplier fashion and it can easily be shown that the initial expansion in money supply through the increase in domestic credit is eventually exactly offset by the depletion in foreign exchange reserves, implying that money supply would return back to its original level.[1] This implies that nominal income as well as imports will also return back to their original levels after an initial increase and, consequently, the only lasting impact of the credit expansion would be a fall in reserves (to the exact extent of the credit expansion) brought about by the temporary increase in imports.

Thus, the Polak model focused attention on the links between changes in money supply and changes in the external account. If a BOP target (ΔR) is set, a corresponding maximum 'permissible' expansion of domestic credit extended by the monetary system can be estimated. If credit expansion exceeds this amount, which is the amount the economy can 'afford', the resulting consequence will be declining international reserves implying that the ΔR target will not be met. Thus, the policy conclusion is that improving the external balance implies domestic credit restraint. In this way, it becomes obvious as to why the IMF places such great emphasis on controlling domestic credit expansion by the monetary system.

It is thus easy to see why Polak's 1957 article is widely regarded as the first model formally designed to analyse BOP problems in a monetary setting. The values of nominal income, imports, and money (including international reserves) are the direct result of the behaviour of domestic credit policies, given the exogenous elements in the BOP (exports and capital flows). While its results are similar in nature to those obtained later on in the subsequent academic literature, the Polak model emphasized in great detail the dynamics of the adjustment path and concentrated *inter alia* on the short- and long-run consequences of monetary policies for the external sector.

While the approach outlined in his paper still forms the basis of most structural adjustment programmes recommended by the IMF, several events in the 1970s, notably the switch to a system of floating exchange rates amongst major currencies and the sharp increases in real interest rates in international credit markets, implied that the design structure of financial programming models used by the IMF has evolved over time in an attempt to absorb many of the developments that have taken place in the study of open-economy macroeconomics, notably the monetary approach to the balance of payments.

4.3   THE MONETARY APPROACH TO THE BALANCE OF PAYMENTS

4.3.1   *The Background*

In the early 1970s, there was a strong revival of interest in the re-examination of monetary relationships for an open economy as well as in the analysis of the interactions between the behaviour of monetary aggregates and the determination of the BOP. This interest led to the formalization of what has come to be known in the literature as 'the monetary approach to the balance of payments' (MABP) which, from the mid-1970s until the mid-1980s, held centre stage in the theoretical and empirical debates that characterized the literature on open-economy macroeconomics.

By 1975, the MABP was well established as a more realistic alternative to the 'Keynesian' as well as the 'elasticities' approach. As the MABP gained popularity, there arose a debate regarding its origins and 'ownership'. While all those involved in the development of the approach routinely acknowledged that its origins could be traced back to the eighteenth century contributions of David Hume, credit for the modern revival of the MABP was simultaneously claimed in two professional circles. While there is no doubt that the academic version of the MABP originated with the writings of James Meade in the early 1950s (Meade 1951) and continued with the contributions of Harry Johnson and Robert Mundell in the 1960s (Johnson 1958, Mundell 1968), years before the standard expositions of the MABP arising from these and other contributions became prominent, a number of important analytical and empirical studies in this area had already been carried out at the IMF largely under the leadership of Jacques Polak.

Although many of these studies were intended only to yield analytical foundations to the Fund's practices and, therefore, in many ways, were geared only to the IMF's operational procedures, they greatly promoted the subsequent development of a rigourous monetary framework for the examination of BOP performance that essentially became the forerunner to the MABP which emerged later on in the academic literature in a more robust formulation. Despite this, the IMF work was largely disregarded because of the dominance of Keynesian views in the 1950s and '. . . the relative impotence and disrepute of the Fund as an international monetary institution at that time' (Johnson 1977, p. 261).

However, since the 1970s, the precursory role played by the Polak model in the development of the MABP has been universally acknowledged to the extent that this approach has come to be identified, rather controversially, as the 'theory' underlying IMF supported programmes. While it is generally accepted by the Fund that the MABP is a central part of the theoretical underpinning of IMF-supported programmes, it believes that identifying 'IMF theory' with the MABP is outright erroneous (see IMF 1987, p. 12) not only because the significance accorded to monetary phenomena is very much different in the 'Chicago' version of the MABP which followed the Polak model in chronological time, but also because the actual design of a programme is far more pragmatic as there are '. . . various possible interpretations of the theoretical mechanisms forming the adjustment process, and consequently a variety of theoretical models can be used as the framework for constructing adjustment programmes' (IMF 1987, p. 2).

4.3.2 *The Chicago Version*

A simple model along the 'Chicago' line of thinking was developed by Johnson (see Frenkel and Johnson 1976) and, to illustrate its essential similarities and differences *vis-à-vis* the Polak model, it is summarized below. In Johnson's model, nominal and real variables are separated explicitly through the introduction of the domestic price level (P). Thus, nominal income (Y) can be written as Py where y is real income which is assumed to be given exogenously. It is further assumed that the law of one price holds,[2] implying that the domestic price level is equal to the foreign price level (P_f) times the nominal exchange rate (E) which is defined as the domestic currency price per unit of foreign currency.

The real demand for money (Md/P) is assumed to be a stable function (f) of real output and the rate of interest, although to keep the model as simple as possible, the interest rate can be ignored without loss of generality. The nominal money supply (M) is determined endogenously as the sum of domestic credit (DC) and foreign exchange reserves (R). Finally, the money market is assumed to be in continuous equilibrium, implying that $Md = M$. Consequently the Chicago version of the MABP can be specified as follows:

$$Y = Py, \tag{4.6}$$
$$P = EPf, \tag{4.7}$$
$$Md/P = f(y), \tag{4.8}$$
$$M = DC + R, \tag{4.9}$$
$$Md = M. \tag{4.10}$$

It therefore follows that:

$$R = Pf(y) - DC. \tag{4.11}$$

Partially differentiating (eqn 4.11) with respect to time (t) yields the following expression where the dot (.) on top of a variable indicates its time derivative, that is $\delta/\delta t$:

$$\dot{R} = f(y)\dot{P} + P[\delta f(y)/\delta y]\dot{y} - \dot{DC}, \tag{4.12}$$

that is the change in reserves is equal to the difference between the change in money demand and the change in domestic credit, which are independent of each other. If it is further assumed that the nominal exchange rate, the foreign price level, and real output remain constant, then (eqn 4.12) reduces to:

$$\dot{R} = -\dot{DC}. \tag{4.13}$$

This is the fundamental result of the 'Chicago' version of the MABP which states that, under fixed exchange rates, the money supply is endogenous, and any increase in domestic credit will automatically lead to a decrease in foreign exchange reserves on a 'one-for-one basis'. If the economy is growing, the demand for money will also be growing, and so domestic credit can expand without causing any BOP problems. But if the rate of credit expansion exceeds the flow demand for money, reserves will fall. Therefore, a good BOP performance depends on controlling domestic credit expansion.

This central conclusion was also reached by Polak, but there is one fundamental difference between the two models. In the 'Chicago' version, any increase in domestic credit expansion *ceteris paribus* will instantly 'crowd out' foreign exchange reserves by an equivalent amount. In the Polak model, this complete 'crowding out' is also true but only in the long run, where the end result is reached through a transmission mechanism involving changes in money supply, nominal income, and imports. As the instantaneous depletion in reserves as a result of credit expansion is substantially lower in the Polak model,[3] this implies the possibility of short- and medium-term disequilibria. This result appears far more realistic than that of the 'Chicago' version.

4.3.3 *Summing-Up*

While there are some evident differences between the earlier Fund work and the academic versions of the MABP, there is no doubt that both these versions deal with similar questions using comparable methodologies. The essence of the MABP is an analytical formulation that emphasizes the interaction between the supply of and demand for money in determining a country's overall BOP. It could be seen, in fact, as a logical extension of the conventional closed-economy monetary models to an open economy which, by assuming a stable money demand function, assess the consequences of changes in money supply under different conditions. When the expansion of money supply is not consistent with the equivalent change in the demand for money, a stock disequilibrium in the money market arises, which affects the spending patterns of economic agents. When money supply grows faster than real money demand, the excess flow supply of money so generated gives rise to a corresponding excess demand for goods and non-monetary financial assets. In a closed economy, the resulting disequilibrium in the money market is eliminated by an increase in prices, interest rates, and possibly output. These changes affect the nominal demand for money and bring it to a level commensurate with the increased money supply, thereby restoring monetary equilibrium.

Unlike in a closed economy, in an economy open to trade and financial flows, the central bank can influence the increase in money supply by domestic credit creation as well as by foreign exchange accretion. Under these circumstances, the MABP emphasizes that money market disequilibria are reflected not only in changes in nominal income (prices and output), but also in changes in the country's foreign exchange reserves. Therefore, the approach concentrates on the relationships between the supply of and demand for money, on the one side, and prices, output, interest rates, and the BOP, on the other.

An important implication of this analysis is that, under a regime of fixed exchange rates, the aggregate money supply is beyond the direct control of the monetary authority and is consequently rendered endogenous. The central bank, however, retains control over the volume of credit which is one of the sources of monetary expansion. Thus, within the framework of the MABP, the distinction between the monetary base and its domestic-credit component becomes central: the monetary authority can control the latter but not the former. For any given expansion in the demand for real money balances, an equivalent growth in the money supply can be realized through a suitable increase in domestic credit. However, if the actual rate of domestic credit creation diverges from this suitable level, the difference is automatically adjusted by equivalent changes in foreign exchange reserves resulting from either a BOP surplus or deficit.

The MABP was extended in several ways to analyse the consequences of once-and-for-all devaluations as well as the abandonment of the fixed exchange rate assumption. Monetary research on exchange rate determination in a flexible exchange rate system was seen as the logical, and inevitable, extension to the original monetary approach formulation. Despite the appeal of these and other extended formulations, both the MABP under fixed exchange rates and the monetary approach to the exchange rate began to lose ground in the mid-1980s. The impact of the debt crisis after 1982 (with the consequent intensification of the phenomenon of currency substitution) and the seemingly exogenous upsurge of capital inflows into emerging markets in the 1990s weakened the credibility of some of the central tenets of the MABP, particularly with regard to the endogeneity or exogeneity of the various monetary aggregates (see Blejer, Khan, and Masson 1995).

Despite these failings, the MABP has had a lasting influence on macroeconomic thought because some of the major propositions it brought to the forefront (that is the importance of money demand in BOP analysis) have been widely accepted and have been largely incorporated into the macroeconomic framework of the financial programming models currently used by the Fund.

4.4 THE FUND APPROACH: THE BASIC FRAMEWORK

With the Polak–MABP apparatus in hand, we can now describe the Fund model, referred to as the Representative Model—Version 1 (RM1). The fundamental ingredient of this basic framework is the specification of nominal income (Y) which, following the MABP approach, is given by:

$$Y = Py, \tag{4.14}$$

where, as before, P denotes the domestic price level and y is real output which is assumed to be given exogenously. The change in nominal income can therefore be approximated by:

$$\Delta Y = \Delta Py(-1) + P(-1)\Delta y, \tag{4.15}$$

where we assume that both ΔP and Δy are small, so that the second-order interaction term $\Delta P\Delta y$ can be ignored, that is $\Delta P\Delta y = 0$. As real output growth rate (g) and the inflation rate (π) are defined as $g = \Delta y/y(-1)$ and $\pi = \Delta P/P(-1)$, we rewrite (eqn 4.15) as follows:

$$\Delta Y = (g + \pi) \, Y(-1). \tag{4.16}$$

In the above equation, $Y(-1)$ is pre-determined, the real growth rate is exogenous, and the inflation rate is endogenous.[4]

The remaining two essential ingredients of the model are the financing constraints for the monetary and external sectors.

The monetary sector financing constraint is given by (eqn 2.20), that is,

$$\Delta M = \Delta DC + \Delta R, \tag{4.17}$$

while the external sector financing constraint is given by (eqn 2.19), that is,

$$(Z - X) = \Delta F - \Delta R. \tag{4.18}$$

In both these equations, foreign exchange reserves appear explicitly and, consequently, the external and monetary sectors can be linked together to identify proximate sources of inflation and BOP disequilibria. In order to solve these two simultaneous equations involving six unknowns, we make a series of simplifying assumptions which are set out below.

4.4.1 *Monetary Sector Equilibrium*
(Eqn 4.17) expressing monetary sector equilibrium can be rewritten as:

$$\Delta R = \Delta M - \Delta DC, \tag{4.19}$$

where ΔR is the target variable, ΔM is an endogenous variable, and ΔDC is an instrument. Following Polak, the demand for nominal money balances (Md) depends only on nominal income, with the income velocity of money (v) assumed to remain constant. Thus, we have:

$$\Delta Md = (1/v)\Delta Y. \tag{4.20}$$

The money market is assumed to be in flow equilibrium, implying therefore:

$$\Delta Md = \Delta M. \tag{4.21}$$

(Eqn 4.19)–(eqn 4.21), together with (eqn 4.16), permit the BOP outcome (ΔR) to be expressed as follows:

$$\Delta R = (1/v) \ (g + \pi) \ Y(-1) - \Delta DC, \tag{4.22}$$

where ΔR and π are the targets, ΔDC is an instrument, g is an exogenous variable, $Y(-1)$ is a predetermined variable, and v is a parameter. (Eqn 4.22) is instantly recognizable as the fundamental equation of the MABP where the BOP is expressed as the difference between the flow demand for money and the expansion of domestic credit and where increases in domestic credit will be offset by decreases in reserves on a one-for-one basis.

(Eqn 4.22) contains two endogenous variables—ΔR and π—and it is not possible to find a unique solution for both conditional on a chosen expansion of domestic credit. This situation can be depicted better by regrouping the variables in (eqn 4.22) and rewriting it as:

$$\Delta R = [(g/v) \ Y(-1) - \Delta DC] + (1/v) \ Y(-1) \ \pi, \tag{4.23}$$

which is a straight line in $\Delta R - \pi$ space with intercept $[(g/v) \ Y(-1) - \Delta DC]$ and a positive slope $(1/v) \ Y(-1)$. This is shown by the MM line in Figure 4.1 which represents monetary sector equilibrium. It is obvious from the negative coefficient of ΔDC that any reduction in domestic credit will shift the MM line upwards, implying either an increase in reserves (for a given rate of inflation) or a fall in the inflation rate (for a given level of reserves).

It is also obvious that given a targeted reserve position and a desired inflation rate, along with an exogenously specified real growth rate, it is possible to solve (eqn 4.22) for the requisite expansion in domestic credit compatible with these targets. (Eqn 4.22) thus provides a rationale for the use of credit ceilings as a performance criteria or a conditionality clause in Fund programmes. By monitoring the expansion in domestic credit, it is possible to determine whether the programme would achieve the targeted BOP.[5]

4.4.2 *External Sector Equilibrium*

(Eqn 4.18) expressing external sector equilibrium can be rewritten as:

$$\Delta R = (X - Z) + \Delta F, \tag{4.24}$$

where ΔR is the target variable, Z is an endogenous variable, and X and ΔF are exogenous variables. As the above equation forms part of the overall system, it is obvious that the desired level of reserves and the rate of inflation cannot be arbitrarily selected because these targets may also affect some of the variables (specifically imports) defining external sector equilibrium. Thus, the values of ΔR, π, and ΔDC which satisfy (eqn 4.23) may not necessarily satisfy (eqn 4.24). In order to eliminate this indeterminacy, we need to assume an import demand function and incorporate it into the above equation.

However, it needs to be noted that the assumed import demand function cannot be of the Polak type, that is $Z = mY$, because the model, as it currently stands, has two targets (ΔR, π) and only one instrument (ΔDC) implying that we are essentially one instrument short in the Tinbergen sense. The use of the exchange rate (E) as an instrument provides a way out of this dilemma because it can easily be introduced into the model.[6]

We do so by assuming that imports depend linearly on nominal income (Y), *à la* Polak, and the nominal exchange rate (E). We therefore have:

$$Z = mY - bE, \tag{4.25}$$

where m is the marginal propensity to import out of income, and b measures the responsiveness of imports to the exchange rate.[7]

We therefore have:

$$Z = Z(-1) + m(g + \pi) \, Y(-1) - b\Delta E, \tag{4.26}$$

which is derived by substituting $[Z(-1) + m\Delta Y - b\Delta E]$ for Z and using (eqn 4.16).

Substituting (eqn 4.26) into (eqn 4.24) yields:

$$\Delta R = X - [Z(-1) + m(g + \pi) \, Y(-1) - b\Delta E] + \Delta F, \tag{4.27}$$

where ΔR and π are the targets; ΔE is an instrument; X, ΔF, and g are the exogenous variables; $Y(-1)$ and $Z(-1)$ are the predetermined variables; and m and b are parameters.

Regrouping variables as before yields:

$$\Delta R = [X + \Delta F - Z(-1) - mgY(-1) + b\Delta E] - mY(-1)\pi \tag{4.28}$$

which is a straight line in $\Delta R - \pi$ space with intercept $[X + \Delta F - Z(-1) - mgY(-1) + b\Delta E]$ and slope $-mY(-1)$. This is shown by the EE line in Figure 4.1 which represents external sector equilibrium. It is obvious from the positive coefficient of ΔE that any devaluation ($\Delta E > 0$) will shift the EE line outwards implying either an increase in reserves (for a given rate of inflation) or a rise in the inflation rate (for a given level of reserves).

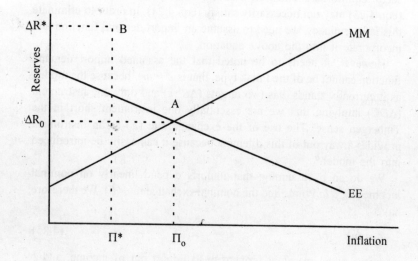

FIGURE 4.1   THE IMF MODEL

In Figure 4.1, at the intersection of the MM and EE lines, denoted by A, we have values of $\Delta R(0)$ and $\pi(0)$ that simultaneously satisfy the constraints of the monetary and external sectors. If the objective now is to attain B, given by $(\Delta R^*,\ \pi^*)$, which represents an improvement in the reserve position and the inflation rate *vis-à-vis* A, then the structure of the model would suggest a reduction in domestic credit to shift the MM line upwards towards B and a devaluation to shift the EE line outwards towards B.

Both policies are necessary to attain B because, for example, a decrease in domestic credit will only shift the MM line, and there is no guarantee that it will intersect the EE line at B. The impossibility of reaching two targets with only one instrument illustrates a general principle in the modelling of such deterministic systems: it is not possible to attain n targets with less than n instruments.

The above analysis is a simplified representation of the actual dynamics of inflation and reserves which, for the present, can be considered as a first approximation of how these variables interact. Important modifications in its dynamic structure will be carried out in the subsequent chapters.

The structure of the Fund approach is set out in Table 4.1.

TABLE 4.1   STRUCTURE OF THE FUND APPROACH

Targets	ΔR	:	change in foreign exchange reserves
	π	:	rate of inflation
Instruments	ΔDC	:	change in domestic credit
	ΔE	:	change in the nominal exchange rate
Endogenous	ΔM	:	change in the money supply
	Z	:	imports
Exogenous	X	:	exports
	ΔF	:	change in foreign borrowings (i.e., capital inflows)
	g	:	real growth rate
Predetermined	$Y(-1)$	:	nominal income in the previous period
	$Z(-1)$	:	imports in the previous period
Parameters	v	:	income velocity of money
	m	:	marginal propensity to import out of income
	b	:	import response to exchange rate changes

4.5 STABILIZATION THEORY

4.5.1 *The Analytical Framework*

The theory of macroeconomic stabilization is an extremely broad one and is discussed in several contexts in the literature (see Turnovsky 1977). In this section, we consider only that part dealing with the stabilization of a static, linear, non-stochastic system such as the one described above.

In order to examine how stabilization theory can be applied within the framework of the specified Fund approach, we rewrite (eqn 4.23) and (eqn 4.28) in matrix notation as follows:

$$\begin{bmatrix} 1 & -(1/v)Y(-1) \\ 1 & mY(-1) \end{bmatrix} \begin{bmatrix} \Delta R \\ \pi \end{bmatrix} = \begin{bmatrix} -1 & 0 \\ 0 & b \end{bmatrix} \begin{bmatrix} \Delta DC \\ \Delta E \end{bmatrix}$$

$$+ \begin{bmatrix} (g/v)Y(-1) \\ X + \Delta F - Z(-1) - mgY(-1) \end{bmatrix} \qquad (4.29)$$

which can be written as:

$$Ax = Bu + z, \qquad (4.30)$$

where: $x = [\Delta R \ \pi]'$ is a (2×1) vector of targets;
   $u = [\Delta DC \ \Delta E]'$ is a (2×1) vector of instruments;
   $z = (2 \times 1)$ vector of exogenous and predetermined variables;
   $A = (2 \times 2)$ matrix of time-varying coefficients;
   $B = (2 \times 2)$ matrix of constant coefficients.

Solving (eqn 4.30) for u yields:

$$u = B^{-1}[Ax - z], \qquad (4.31)$$

where x is now the desired target vector and u is the corresponding instrument vector which achieves all these targets. In the Fund approach, as B is non-singular, u will exist and will be unique.

In order to apply the above theory, we need numerical estimates of the matrices listed out in (eqn 4.29). We use data on the Indian economy for this purpose, the objective being to determine heuristic guidelines regarding alternative stabilization policy options which were available for 1995–6.[8]

From Table 4.1, we realize that, in order to use the model in its so-called 'positive' mode and generate *ex-post* forecasts of the two targets (ΔR, π) for 1995–6, we need data on: (i) the two instruments, ΔDC and ΔE, for 1995–6; (ii) the three exogenous variables, X, ΔF, and g, for

1995–6; (iii) the two predetermined variables, $Y(-1)$ and $Z(-1)$, for 1994–5; and (iv) the three parameters, v, m, and b. These are as follows:[9] (i) $\Delta DC = 585.33$, $\Delta E = 1.63$; (ii) $X = 940.32$, $\Delta F = 80.20$, $g = 0.0620$; (iii) $Y(-1) = 8541.03$, $Z(-1) = 904.36$; and (iv) $v = 2.22$, $m = 0.1524$, $b = 5.1160$.

Substituting the above values into (eqn 4.29) yields:

$$\begin{bmatrix} 1 & -3847.31 \\ 1 & 1301.65 \end{bmatrix} \begin{bmatrix} \Delta R \\ \pi \end{bmatrix} = \begin{bmatrix} -1 & 0 \\ 0 & 5.116 \end{bmatrix} \begin{bmatrix} \Delta DC \\ \Delta E \end{bmatrix} + \begin{bmatrix} 238.53 \\ 35.46 \end{bmatrix} \qquad (4.32)$$

which simplifies to:

$$\begin{bmatrix} \Delta R \\ \pi \end{bmatrix} = \begin{bmatrix} -0.2528 & 3.8227 \\ 0.000194 & 0.000994 \end{bmatrix} \begin{bmatrix} \Delta DC \\ \Delta E \end{bmatrix} + \begin{bmatrix} 86.796 \\ -0.0394 \end{bmatrix}. \qquad (4.33)$$

The *ex-post* forecasts of the two targets (ΔR and π) for 1995–6, can now be obtained by merely setting the two instruments (ΔDC and ΔE) at their actual levels given above, that is $\Delta DC = 585.33$ and $\Delta E = 1.63$. This yields $\Delta R = -54.94$ and $\pi = 0.0759$, implying a reserve drawdown to the extent of approximately Rs 55 billion and an inflation rate of about 7.6 per cent. Given that the actual depletion of foreign exchange reserves in 1995–6 was Rs 62.35 billion while the actual inflation rate was 7.7 per cent, it is seen that the Fund approach provides robust BOP and inflation forecasts despite its apparent simplicity.

In order to use the above model in its so-called 'programming' mode, we rewrite (eqn 4.33) in the form suggested by (eqn 4.31). This yields:

$$\begin{bmatrix} \Delta DC \\ \Delta E \end{bmatrix} = \begin{bmatrix} -1 & 0 \\ 0 & 0.1955 \end{bmatrix} \begin{bmatrix} \Delta R - 3847.31\pi - 238.53 \\ \Delta R + 1301.65\pi - 35.46 \end{bmatrix}. \qquad (4.34)$$

Thus, it is seen that domestic credit is inversely related to reserves and positively related to inflation, while the exchange rate is positively related to both reserves and inflation. The programming mode implies that target values for reserve accumulation (ΔR) and the inflation rate (π) must initially be assigned in order to obtain the corresponding instrument values which attain these targets. Setting, idealistically, $\Delta R = 0$ (that is no reserve depletion) and $\pi = 0.05$ (that is a five per cent inflation rate), we solve (eqn 4.34) above, obtaining: $\Delta DC = 430.90$ and $\Delta E = 5.79$. This implies that domestic credit expansion should have been restrained at only Rs 431 billion and the nominal exchange rate should have been allowed to depreciate from Rs 31.37 per US dollar to Rs 37.16 per US dollar. The tight credit ceiling would not only have prevented a reserve depletion, but it would have contained the inflation rate from rising as a result of the exchange rate depreciation. It is interesting to note, in this context, that by allowing domestic credit to expand upto Rs 585 billion, not only was there a reserve depletion to the extent of nearly Rs 62 billion and a 7.7 per cent inflation in 1995–6, but the nominal exchange rate did ultimately depreciate to Rs 36.50 per US dollar as a result of the high inflation rate. Thus, the usefulness of a credit ceiling while formulating policy can hardly be overemphasized.

4.5.2 Policy Options

In order to obtain greater insights into the trade-offs implicit in designing stabilization policy, we expand (eqn 4.34) obtaining:

$$\Delta DC = -\Delta R + 3847.31\pi + 238.53, \qquad (4.35a)$$
$$\Delta E = 0.1955\ \Delta R + 254.47\pi - 6.93. \qquad (4.35b)$$

The above system comprises a set of two equations in four unknowns, and the logic of solving it implies that *any* two of them (not necessarily belonging exclusively to the target or instrument set) can be assigned values exogenously in order to solve for the remaining two. This implies that we have six possible pairs of alternative 'instruments' and 'targets' from which we can choose. The Fund approach deals with only two of them: (i) the 'positive' mode where the instrument pair (ΔDC and ΔE) is projected exogenously, thereby forecasting the target pair (ΔR and π); and (ii) the 'programming' mode where the desired target pair (ΔR and π) is specified exogenously, thereby solving for the optimal instrument pair (ΔDC and ΔE). Thus, we are still left with four other possible policy options which we shall refer to as the 'option' mode.

Option 1: On the assumption that the strategy proposed by the programming mode implies a very tight credit ceiling which could be difficult to implement in practice, in the first option, we relax this constraint and set $\Delta DC = 585.33$ (its actual historical level) and pair it along with an idealistic BOP target of $\Delta R = 0$. Substituting these values into (eqn 4.35a) yields $\pi = 0.0901$ which, when substituted into (eqn 4.35b) along with $\Delta R = 0$, yields $\Delta E = 16.01$. Thus, this policy option implies a 9 per cent inflation rate and calls for a devaluation of the exchange rate from Rs 31.37 per US dollar to Rs 47.38 per US dollar. While the latter strategy does prevent a reserve drawdown, it is an unfeasible policy option because of the almost 50 per cent devaluation that it entails. Moreover, it is also an unsustainable option as the rising inflation rate would soon put pressure on the nominal exchange rate to depreciate still further in the future.

Option 2: As the first strategy is unfeasible because of the high devaluation that it implies, in this second option, we attempt to prevent any erosion in the exchange rate by setting $\Delta E = 0$, while still retaining the idealistic BOP target of $\Delta R = 0$. Substituting these values into (eqn 4.35b) yields $\pi = 0.0272$ which, when substituted into (eqn 4.35a) along with $\Delta R = 0$, yields $\Delta DC = 343.2$. Thus, this policy option, in view of the extremely tight targets that are being tracked, implies a domestic credit crunch of a very high magnitude which, despite the ensuing low inflation rate of 2.7 per cent, would be impossible to implement. Thus, the most important lesson learned from this stabilization option is the impossiblity of tracking idealistic targets and the definite need to consider possible trade-offs while devising a strategy.

Option 3: As the second strategy is unfeasible because of the deep credit cut that it envisages, in this third option, we set the desired inflation rate at a more reasonable level of five per cent ($\pi = 0.05$). Although abandoning our earlier quest for an ideal BOP position, we still target a fixed nominal exchange rate, that is $\Delta E = 0$. Substituting these two values into (eqn 4.35b) yields $\Delta R = -29.63$ which, when substituted into (eqn 4.35a) along with $\pi = 0.05$, yields $\Delta DC = 460.5$. In view of the substantial reduction in foreign exchange outflow, this policy option does seem quite reasonable although the credit crunch that it imposes is still considerable. However, it does suggest a strategy for reducing reserve depletion considerably and indicates the feasibility of targeting a (near) fixed nominal exchange rate.

Option 4: Based upon the possibilities raised by the earlier strategy, in this final option, we further relax the credit ceiling to $\Delta DC = 500$ and track a more reasonable inflation rate of 6.25 per cent (that is $\pi = 0.0625$). Substituting these values into (eqn 4.35a) yields $\Delta R = -21.01$ which, when substituted into (eqn 4.35b) along with $\pi = 0.0625$, yields $\Delta E = 4.86$. Thus, this strategy indicates that the exchange rate needs to depreciate from Rs 31.37 per US dollar to Rs 36.23 per US dollar and the ensuing reserve depletion would be of the order of approximately Rs 21 billion (which is substantially lower than its projected level of Rs 55 billion). Thus, a bare 15 per cent reduction in domestic credit expansion would have resulted not only in a 1.35 percentage point reduction in the inflation rate but in a saving of almost Rs 34 billion in foreign exchange reserves.

In this manner, the 'option' mode of the Fund approach can be used to analyse alternative stabilization policies in an attempt to identify the most feasible and robust strategy.

4.6 FINANCIAL PROGRAMMING

4.6.1 *Theory*

Providing advice to developing countries on macroeconomic policy is an important responsibility of the Fund. In addition, the IMF extends financial support to stabilization programmes which are consistent with the principles set out in the institution's articles of agreement and offer a convincing prospect of repayment. However, this assistance is conditional on the borrowing country's compliance with a set of quantitative policy performance criteria drawn up in consultation with the Fund and embodied in a financial (or standby) programme. The design of such a programme and specification of such criteria rely on a conceptual framework referred to as 'financial programming'.

There is, surprisingly enough, very little written material readily accessible on financial programming, in general, and the financial programming model of the IMF, in particular. Even until the late 1970s, not much was available even on its theoretical underpinnings, apart from Kragh (1970), Robichek (1971), and a compendium of earlier papers on the Fund's approach to financial programming (IMF 1977). Although the analytical basis for financial programming was introduced by Polak (1957) and later on formalized by Polak and Argy (1971) on the lines suggested by Christ (1969), their model was incomplete in the sense that it only considered the financial constraints for the monetary and external sectors, and not those for the private and government sectors.

Crockett (1981) and Guitian (1981) then provided general descriptions of the policy content of adjustment programmes in terms of all these four sectors for developing economies, while Goldstein (1986) covered the global effects of such adjustment programmes. However, none of these discussed the theoretical details regarding the implicit inter-sectoral relationships. The theoretical aspects of the design of stabilization issues and Fund-supported adjustment programmes were explained in IMF (1987) which, along with Robichek (1985), Chand (1987) and Mills and Nallari (1992), put together a fairly consistent picture of the theory underlying financial programming. The Polak–Robichek tradition was continued by Khan, Montiel, and Haque (1990) whose specification of the financial programming framework, comprehensively discussed in Tarp (1993), remains probably the best description of the IMF practice to date.

The presentation, in this section, of the theory underlying financial programming is based on the modified form of the IMF model outlined earlier in Section 4.4, and attempts to distill the essence of the Fund approach without loss of accuracy. The minimum version of the financial programming model comprises ten equations, of which six form the core of the model. As this core has already been discussed, we state these main elements very briefly.

Nominal income (Y) is equal to Py where P is the domestic price level and y is real output which is exogenously determined. Nominal money demand (Md) is positively related to nominal income, with the velocity of money (v) assumed to be a constant. Nominal money supply (M) is determined endogenously as the sum of domestic credit (DC) and foreign exchange reserves (R). The money market is assumed to be in equilibrium, implying that money supply equals money demand. Imports are assumed to be a linear function of nominal income and the exchange rate. From the BOP identity, it follows that the change in reserves (ΔR) equals the sum of the surplus/deficit on the trade account (that is $X - Z$) and other capital flows on the capital account (that is ΔF). Thus, the core of the approach is given by the following six equations:

$$Y = Py, \tag{4.36}$$
$$(Md)v = Y, \tag{4.37}$$
$$M = DC + R, \tag{4.38}$$
$$M = Md, \tag{4.39}$$
$$Z = mY - bE, \tag{4.40}$$
$$\Delta R = (X - Z) + \Delta F. \tag{4.41}$$

The remaining four equations, explaining the 'credit' block of the minimum version, form the periphery of the model. Domestic credit comprises credit to the government (DCg) and credit to the private sector (DCp), that is

$$DC = DCg + DCp. \tag{4.42}$$

The expansion of credit to the private sector is postulated to keep pace with the increase in nominal income. This so-called 'demand for private credit' relationship is therefore given by:

$$\Delta DCp = k\Delta Y, \tag{4.43}$$

where k [$= DCp(-1)/Y(-1)$] denotes the private sector 'entitlement' ratio which is predetermined. Therefore, the expansion of credit to the public sector is determined residually as follows:

$$\Delta DCg = \Delta DC - \Delta D\mathcal{C}p. \tag{4.44}$$

The final equation of the model states that given the exogenously projected increases in domestic borrowings by the government (ΔB) and foreign borrowings by the government (ΔFg), the constraint on public sector credit expansion effectively fixes the government fiscal deficit, defined as the excess of public sector investment (Ig) over public sector savings (Sg), that is

$$Ig - Sg = \Delta DCg + \Delta B + \Delta Fg. \tag{4.45}$$

(Eqn 4.36)–(eqn 4.45) thus constitute the minimum version of the financial programming approach of the Fund. As noticed earlier, the above framework can be reduced to two linear equations in ΔR and π that reflect the changes in foreign exchange reserves and inflation. These are the two main targets in IMF-supported stabilization programmes. The amount of domestic credit outstanding and the nominal exchange rate are assumed to be under the direct control of the authorities. Thus, the policy instruments in the model are ΔDC and ΔE.

The reduction is carried out on the same lines as spelt out in Section 4.4. Therefore, the equation for defining monetary sector equilibrium, that is (eqn 4.23), is given by:

$$\Delta R = \gamma(0) - \Delta DC + \gamma(1)\ \pi, \tag{4.46}$$

where:
$$\gamma(0) = (g/v)\ Y(-1), \tag{4.47a}$$
$$\gamma(1) = (1/v)\ Y(-1). \tag{4.47b}$$

Similarly, the equation for defining external sector equilibrium, that is (eqn 4.28), is given by:

$$\Delta R = \rho(0) + \rho(1)\ \Delta E - \rho(2)\ \pi, \tag{4.48}$$

where:
$$\rho(0) = X + \Delta F - Z(-1) - mgY(-1), \tag{4.49a}$$
$$\rho(1) = b, \tag{4.49b}$$
$$\rho(2) = mY(-1). \tag{4.49c}$$

As both (eqn 4.46) and (eqn 4.48) define ΔR, they can be linked together to solve for π in terms of ΔDC and ΔE. This yields:

$$\pi = \frac{\rho(0) - \gamma(0)}{\gamma(1) + \rho(2)} + \frac{\rho(1)}{\gamma(1) + \rho(2)}\Delta E + \frac{1}{\gamma(1) + \rho(2)}\Delta DC \tag{4.50}$$

which when substituted either into (eqn 4.46) or (eqn 4.48) yields:

$$\Delta R = \frac{\gamma(0)\rho(2) + \gamma(1)\rho(0)}{\gamma(1) + \rho(2)} + \frac{\gamma(1)\rho(1)}{\gamma(1) + \rho(2)}\Delta E - \frac{\rho(2)}{\gamma(1) + \rho(2)}\Delta DC \tag{4.51}$$

(Eqn 4.50) and (eqn 4.51) are based upon the 'positive' mode of the financial programming approach wherein instrument values (ΔDC and ΔE) are initially projected in order to make baseline forecasts of the targets (ΔR and π).

If these baseline forecasts are not up to the expectations of the policy makers in as much as they do not correspond broadly to the target values assigned to the inflation rate and the BOP, then the 'programming' mode of the financial programming approach comes into play. Here, the instrument values are derived by solving (eqn 4.46) and (eqn 4.48) for ΔDC and ΔE in terms of ΔR and π. By mere inspection of these two equations, we note that:

$$\Delta DC = \gamma(0) - \Delta R + \gamma(1)\ \pi, \tag{4.52}$$

and

$$\Delta E = - [\rho(0)/\rho(1)] + [1/\rho(1)]\ \Delta R + [\rho(2)/\rho(1)]\ \pi . \tag{4.53}$$

Therefore, given desired target values (ΔR, π), we can obtain the optimal instrument settings (ΔDC, ΔE). Given the desired inflation rate (π) and the exogenously assumed real growth rate (g), we can project the expansion in nominal income (ΔY), given (eqn 4.16), which, in conjunction with the private sector demand-for-credit relationship, given by (eqn 4.43), will determine the entitlement of the private sector (ΔDCp). Given the overall credit ceiling (ΔDC) and the share of the private sector in this expansion, we can determine, using (eqn 4.44), the amount available for the public sector (ΔDCg). This residual share, along with the projected levels of domestic borrowings by the government (ΔB) and external borrowings by the government (ΔFg) will, given (eqn 4.45) effectively fix the overall fiscal deficit ($Ig - Sg$).

4.6.2 *Practice*

Following the review of the theoretical underpinnings of IMF-supported adjustment programmes, this section briefly describes the actual process of formulating an IMF financial stabilization programme. Strictly speaking, the term 'financial programming' describes the process of determining the values of the policy instruments that are required to achieve desired values of the target variables. The process normally follows the same routine, but there are always local variations in the computational or negotiating procedures.

For the purpose of empirically demonstrating the steps behind this exercise, we use data on the Indian economy, the objective being to formulate a financial stabilization programme for any given programme period, say, 1996–7, which, by way of illustration, *is assumed to be in the future from the viewpoint of the policy planner.* The essential idea is to show numerically how such a programme, based upon the existing IMF practice, can be devised. The formulation of a financial programme involves the following steps:

Step 0: (i) Generate projections for the values of the three exogenous variables, X, ΔF, and g, for the programme period, that is 1996–7 (ii) Specify values for the three parameters, v, m, and b; and (iii) Use historical values for the two predetermined variables, $Y(-1)$ and $Z(-1)$, for 1995–6. All these estimates are provided below:

$$X = 1050; \quad g = 0.0600; \quad m = 0.1524; \quad Y(-1) = 9637.48;$$
$$\Delta F = 150; \quad v = 2.2167; \quad b = 5.1160; \quad Z(-1) = 1075.26.$$

(iv) Based upon the above data set, derive the set of parameters given by (eqn 4.47) and (eqn 4.49). These parameters are estimated as:

$$\gamma(0) = 260.86; \quad \gamma(1) = 4347.67;$$
$$\rho(0) = 36.61; \quad \rho(1) = 5.116; \quad \rho(2) = 1468.75.$$

(v) Based upon these estimated parameters, derive the numerical versions of (eqn 4.50)–(eqn 4.53). The equations specifying the 'positive' mode are:

$$\Delta R = 93.24 + 3.8241\ \Delta E - 0.2525\ \Delta DC, \qquad (4.54)$$
$$\pi = -0.0386 + 0.000880\ \Delta E + 0.000172\ \Delta DC, \qquad (4.55)$$

while those specifying the 'programming' mode are:

$$\Delta DC = 260.86 - \Delta R + 4347.67\ \pi, \qquad (4.56)$$
$$\Delta E = -7.15 + 0.1955\ \Delta R + 287.09\ \pi. \qquad (4.57)$$

Step 1:[10] Generate baseline forecasts of the target variables, ΔR and π, given plausible forecasts of the instrument variables, ΔDC and ΔE. Based upon their past trends, we set $\Delta DC = 650$ and $\Delta E = 3.50$ for 1996–7. These forecasts, when substituted into the 'positive' mode, that is (eqn 4.54) and (eqn 4.55), yield $\Delta R = -57.5$ and $\pi = 7.63$, implying a reserve depletion of about Rs 58 billion and an inflation rate of about 7.6 per cent in 1996–7 (as against an actual reserve drawdown of Rs 62 billion and an actual inflation rate of 7.7 per cent in 1995–6).

Step 2: Specify the desired values of the target variables, ΔR and π. Going by the forecasts of Step 1 and the policy implications of the 'option' mode in Section 4.5.2, we set reasonable targets of $\Delta R = -20.0$

and $\pi = 0.0625$, that is a reserve drawdown of Rs 20 billion and an inflation rate of 6.25 per cent.

Step 3: Substitute these desired target values into the 'programming' mode, that is (eqn 4.56) and (eqn 4.57), in order to determine the necessary extent of credit expansion and devaluation in order to meet these targets. Doing so yields $\Delta DC = 552.6$ and $\Delta E = 6.88$, implying that credit expansion should be about Rs 553 billion and that the nominal exchange rate should be devalued to Rs 40.33 per US dollar.

Step 4: Formulate a judgment on the feasibility of implementing these policies. Given that the targeted credit expansion in 1996–7 would be Rs 30 billion *less* than what it was in 1995–6, it is obvious that imposing such a 'liquidity crunch' would be unfeasible in practice. The same holds true for the projected devaluation, what with its order of magnitude being almost 21 per cent. This implies that both the BOP and the inflation targets need to be revised. Accordingly, we reset $\Delta R = -45.0$ and $\pi = 0.0675$ and resolve (eqn 4.56) and (eqn 4.57). This yields: $\Delta DC = 599.3$, implying that the increase in ΔDC in 1996–7 would be of the same order of magnitude as it was in 1995–6; and $\Delta E = 3.43$, implying that a 10 per cent depreciation would be necessary. As both these policy responses seem feasible, we now have a consistent policy package.

Step 5: Given the assumed real growth rate $(g = 0.06)$ and the projected inflation rate $(\pi = 0.0675)$, along with the historical level of nominal income in the previous period, that is $Y(-1) = 9637.48$, we can project the change in nominal income (ΔY) given (eqn 4.16). This yields: $\Delta Y = 1228.78$, and consequently nominal income in 1996–7 is projected around Rs 10,866 billion.

Step 6: Using this projected value of nominal income, the expansion of credit to the private sector (ΔDCp) is derived from (eqn 4.43), where the private sector 'entitlement' ratio $[k = DCp(-1)/Y(-1)]$ is predetermined. For 1995–6, $k = 0.3356$ and consequently we obtain: $\Delta DCp = 412.42$, and therefore the expansion in domestic credit for the private sector in 1996–7 would be about Rs 412 billion which is nearly 70 per cent of the total credit expansion.

Step 7: With overall credit expansion (ΔDC) limited to Rs 599 billion and with the private sector share (ΔDCp) fixed at Rs 412 billion, the projected expansion of credit to the public sector (ΔDCg), using (eqn 4.44), works out residually to be Rs 187 billion which is about 20 per cent less than its level in 1995–6. Thus, it is seen that the public sector must, by and large, bear the brunt of the credit squeeze.

Step 8: Finally, given the public sector budget constraint, (eqn 4.45), it is seen that this programmed expansion of credit to the public sector (ΔDCg), along with the exogenously projected levels of domestic borrowings by the government (ΔB) and foreign borrowings by the government (ΔFg), effectively fixes the overall public sector fiscal deficit, ($Ig - Sg$), from 'below the line', that is from the financing side. With ΔB projected at Rs 650 billion and ΔFg at Rs 85 billion, this would imply that the fiscal deficit cannot exceed Rs 922 billion which works out to be 8.5 per cent of projected nominal income for 1996–7 (as against 9.2 per cent in 1995–6). Herein lies the final impact of the stabilization programme because the expenditure and revenue items in the budget have now to be reconciled with this programmed deficit by either increasing revenue and/or reducing current or capital expenditures.

4.7   Critique of the Fund Approach

The stated objectives of the IMF are geared towards the achievement of a viable BOP position together with an acceptable level of inflation during the programme period. Adjustments are designed and policy measures prescribed with these overall targets in mind. In this context, the IMF does enjoy a distinct advantage over the World Bank because its framework uses monetary data which, apart from being more timely and accurate than data on real variables, has policy implications that concern variables over which the government does exert a reasonable amount of control.

While it is true that the structure of Fund-supported programmes has gradually evolved over time in order to incorporate many of the developments that have taken place in the study of open-economy macroeconomics, the basic core of the IMF theoretical framework has largely remained unchanged since the late 1950s. If prices and nominal exchange rates are assumed to be fixed, and if imports are assumed to be a function of nominal income alone (and not the nominal exchange rate as well, as we have assumed) then the existing financial programming model is undistinguishable from the original Polak model.

While the IMF is not monetarist in the strict sense of the word and does not view the BOP and inflation as a purely monetary phenomenon, the Fund model is monetary in nature as it is based, to a considerable extent, on some of the principal tenets of the MABP, especially the ones pertaining to the stability of the money demand function and the exogeneity of real output. Such an approach has implied that the IMF identifies policy failure in the form of an excessive expansion of money supply (that is, domestic credit plus foreign exchange reserves) over money demand as the prime cause of external and internal economic imbalances.

More importantly, although the IMF model is internally consistent, it fails to explain real variables and assumes that changes in domestic credit affect only foreign exchange reserves, ignoring, in the process, the possible impact of credit controls on output variations, that is how monetary variables interact with real variables. While IMF (1987) makes it clear that changes in domestic credit may have an affect on interest rates, consumption–savings decisions, prices, and the exchange rate, besides the level of foreign exchange reserves, very little has been said (or done) about the possible implications of Fund-supported policies on the productive capacity of the economy.

Yet, it is well known that working capital provided by the monetary system is an essential component of the production process and, therefore, a credit squeeze may affect output as well as demand and absorption. This implies that the use of credit ceilings could, under certain circumstances, become counter-productive if their adverse impacts on the real growth rate outweigh their favourable impacts on reserves and inflation.

If the burden of credit adjustment falls solely on the public sector, it could be possibly argued that there may be little impact on output, but the underlying 'crowding out' hypothesis that this argument is based on would have to be subjected to empirical verification. In the Indian context, for example, there is no evidence of public sector investment crowding out private sector investment, and therefore any credit squeeze on the public sector without a compensating expansion of credit to the private sector is bound to adversely affect growth.

Limiting demand may also, by itself, bring about lower domestic production rather than reduced absorption in the absence of effective policies to counteract the contractionary effects of stabilization measures. While a devaluation may eventually help through expenditure-switching, this policy is bound to take, at best, some time to have a favourable impact on the BOP (the so-called 'J-curve' hypothesis) and will, in the short-run, contribute to stagflation. The consistency of macroeconomic policies with specified overall long-term objectives has therefore to be carefully analysed rather than assumed and, in this context, the possibility of 'overkill' needs to be skilfully avoided through the explicit inclusion of dynamics and lags.

The above reservations, including the possibility of feedbacks between the monetary sector, the external sector, and the output block, implies the need for a theoretical redesign of the basic framework considered above. Many of these problems will be tackled in the subsequent chapters.

NOTES

[1]With the second-round increase in money supply being given by $(1 - mv)\Delta DC$, the second-round increase in imports would be $mv(1 - mv)\Delta DC$. This implies that the accumulated reserve changes by the end of the second-round would be $-[mv\Delta DC + mv(1 - mv)\Delta DC]$. Thus, the third-round increase in money supply would be given by:

$$\Delta M = \Delta DC - [mv + mv(1 - mv)]\Delta DC = (1 - mv)^2 \Delta DC, \qquad (4.a)$$

implying that the third-round increase in imports is $mv(1 - mv)^2 \Delta DC$. Thus, the total increase in imports over time is given by:

$$mv\Delta DC + mv(1 - mv)\Delta DC + mv(1 - mv)^2 \Delta DC + \ldots \qquad (4.b)$$

The limit of the above convergent expression (if $mv < 1$) as $t \to \infty$ is ΔDC. Using (eqn 4.2), it follows that the total change in reserves is $-\Delta DC$, and, therefore, from (eqn 4.1), it follows that there is no change in money supply.

[2]The law of one price states that the price of tradeables in the domestic and foreign economies must, at most, differ by tariffs and marketing costs. If the differences are any larger, profit-seeking entrepreneurs will enter the market and the ensuing competition will push prices towards equilibrium. Therefore, under the assumption that all goods are tradeables, the domestic price level (P) will equal the foreign price level (P_f) times the nominal exchange rate (E).

[3]The Polak model indicates that as a result of a given expansion in domestic credit by ΔDC, the instantaneous change in reserves (ΔR) would be only $-mv\Delta DC$. This is substantially less than $-\Delta DC$ which is the instantaneous change in reserves predicted by the MABP.

[4]The existing Fund approach (see Khan, Montiel, and Haque 1990) uses (eqn 4.15) and, therefore, the endogenous (target) variable is ΔP which is the change in the domestic price level. One of the basic drawbacks of such an approach is that the measurement of ΔP often raises problems as it depends on the choice of deflator as well as base year. By converting (eqn 4.15) into its equivalent version given by (eqn 4.16), we target the inflation rate (π) which, apart from being the more relevant outcome variable, largely bypasses these measurement problems. Thus, the specification of (eqn 4.16), which also converts the change in the output level (Δy) into its corresponding growth rate (g), represents a substantial improvement over the existing Fund design.

[5]In practice, however, the ceiling on the expansion of total domestic credit (ΔDC) is frequently accompanied by a sub-ceiling on the expansion of credit to the public sector (ΔDCg). This sub-ceiling plays a dual role. On the one hand, it assists in monitoring the overall credit ceiling since, in the Fund's experience, violations of overall credit ceilings frequently tend to originate from excessive expansion of credit to the public sector. More importantly, the public sector sub-ceiling ensures that the availability of credit to the private sector is not excessively curtailed by the overall credit ceiling. Formally, this implies that the expansion of credit to the private sector (ΔDCp) functions as a secondary target in Fund stabilization programmes (see Kelly 1982). The target value of private sector credit expansion (ΔDCp) is typically related to the projection of nominal GDP. For example, it is often postulated that the expansion of credit to the private sector should keep pace with the increase in nominal GDP. Thus, the targeted expansion of private credit would be derived from a 'demand for credit' relationship such as:

$$\Delta DCp = [DCp(-1)/Y(-1)] \; \Delta Y. \tag{4.c}$$

Now, given the ceiling on total credit expansion (ΔDC), this implies that public sector credit expansion is determined residually as:

$$\Delta DCg = \Delta DC - \Delta DCp, \tag{4.d}$$

and, therefore, the public sector deficit is effectively fixed from 'below the line' (that is from the financing side) by this programmed increase in public sector credit, given that both the domestic and foreign borrowings of the government are assumed to be exogenous.

[6]An alternative way to introduce the exchange rate into the analysis (see Khan, Montiel, and Haque 1990) has been to specify the following equation:

$$P = (1 - \Theta) \; Pd + \Theta \; EPf, \tag{4.e}$$

where P is the aggregate price level, Pd is an index of domestic prices, Pf is an index of foreign prices, E is the nominal exchange rate and Θ is the share of importables in the overall price index. While theoretically elegant, (eqn 4.e) poses several problems because, with two definitions of the domestic price level included in the model, it becomes difficult to distinguish between P and Pd. With nominal income (Y) being defined as the aggregate price level (P) times real output (y), the implication would be that P should be measured by the GDP deflator, and Pd by, say, the consumer price index. Once these two variables are specified, (eqn 4.e) can be estimated using restricted least squares. However, in most applied work, the resulting estimates of Θ, obtained in this manner, do not accurately reflect the share of importables in the aggregate price level.

In order to overcome this problem, Reinhart (1991) has suggested approximating this parameter by the average share of imports in total (private plus public) consumption, that is $\Theta = Z/(C + G)$. However, this implies that we would have to construct a time series of P (given Pd, E, Pf, and Θ) using (eqn 4.e) and replace the actual GDP deflator by this so-called 'virtual' price level. This would, in turn, imply that that we would have to redefine nominal income, given by (eqn 4.14), as well as velocity, given by (eqn 4.20). More importantly, we would have to endogenize Θ itself because it would depend upon imports (Z) which is endogenous. Moreover, by using this definition of P, we would be unable to solve the model in terms of the inflation rate (π) as we intend to do. In concluding, it needs to be noted that the only reason for introducing (eqn 4.e) into the model is to ensure that prices rise with devaluation. This result can just as well be obtained by assuming an import function of the type given by (eqn 4.25).

[7]Although this is the simplest possible specification of an import demand function, as is the case with the earlier behavioural equation (that is, the money demand function), it is not so much the particular specification that is important, but rather the stability of the function. Most works in this area (see Khan, Montiel, and Haque 1991) specify an import volume equation given by:

$$(Z/EPf) = my - b(EPf/P), \tag{4.f}$$

where the term in parentheses on the left-hand-side of (eqn 4.f) indicates the volume of imports while the term in parentheses on the right-hand-side denotes the real exchange rate. However, by incorporating the assumptions that $P(-1) = Pf(-1) = E(-1)Pf(-1) = 1$ and $\Delta Pf = 0$, the above equation may be simplified to:

$$Z = (1 + \Delta E) Z(-1) + m\Delta y + b\Delta P - b\Delta E, \tag{4.g}$$

which is broadly similar in structure to (eqn 4.26) as regards the effects of real output and prices on imports, except that a devaluation in the above case would reduce imports only if $b > Z(-1)$. Now, this is a very restrictive assumption which is unlikely to be satisfied in any empirical application. Therefore, in the merged Bank–Fund model discussed in Chapter 6, we specify a more robust (non-linear) import demand function which, without incorporating any restrictive assumptions of the kind specified above, overcomes such a shortcoming.

[8]The Indian financial year extends from 1 April to 31 March. Thus, 1995–6 would correspond to 1 April, 1995 to 31 March, 1996.

[9]Income (Y), exports (X), imports (Z), domestic credit (DC), foreign borrowings or capital inflows (F), and foreign exchange reserves (R) are all measured in billions of Indian rupees (Rs) where, under the then (in October 1996) existing exchange rate of approximately Rs 36.50 per US dollar, one billion Indian rupees would be roughly equal to $ 27.4 million. The nominal exchange rate (E) is defined in terms of Indian rupees per US dollar. The real growth rate (g) and the inflation rate (π) are measured directly in terms of rates of change and therefore have to be multiplied by 100 to obtain equivalent percentage growth rates and inflation rates, respectively.

[10]In practice, however, this step is overlooked in applications of financial programming by the Fund which directly proceed to Step 2. However, as clearly shown in the 'option' mode, targets (especially idealistic ones) cannot be set *à priori* because this could elicit unrealistic or unfeasible instrument responses. Therefore, a baseline forecast has to be initially carried out to obtain guideposts regarding the future state of the economy. It is only then that desired targets which, as far as possible, should be in the neighbourhood of these baseline forecasts can be set.

5

Growth Programming and Adjustment

5.1 INTRODUCTION

The World Bank, whose official title is the International Bank for Reconstruction and Development (IBRD), was established in 1944 and is also a creation of Bretton Woods along with the International Monetary Fund (IMF). As the name suggests, the World Bank was founded to initially finance the reconstruction and development of the Western European countries ravaged by World War II. As soon as this region achieved a degree of economic self-sufficiency, attention turned to the long-term task of financing economic growth in the developing countries, especially those which had gained independence in the 1950s and 1960s. In contrast to the IMF mandate which was, by and large, confined to helping countries to overcome their short-run BOP difficulties, the Bank was assigned the task of allocating resources to finance investment projects with the objective of increasing economic growth and thereby improving the standard of living in the long run. Thus, by emphasizing growth and supply-side aspects, the World Bank approach has involved grappling more directly with microeconomic and macroeconomic structural issues in an attempt to establish economic balances in an orderly manner. It is for this reason that some of the conditionalities imposed by the Bank have tended to be far more detailed than their Fund counterparts.

In the World Bank model, which is a variant of the two-gap growth model (or the Harrod–Domar model for the open economy), the financing needs for development purposes are in focus along with real variables and relationships. This framework, which currently forms the analytical basis of the growth and resource gap models used by the Bank, is discussed in Section 5.2. The core of the Revised Minimum Standard Model (RMSM), which is the most widely used economy-wide numerical programming model within the Bank, is presented in Section 5.3. Despite its usefulness, several criticisms have been levelled against the RMSM and a few of these are summarized in Section 5.4.

5.2 GROWTH AND RESOURCE GAP MODELS

5.2.1 *The Accounting Framework*

It may be recalled from Chapter 4 that the so-called 'empty framework' of the IMF financial programming model concentrates on monetary variables, and two key national accounts identities—the external balance and the monetary balance. The focus in the Bank model, apart from the external balance, is on the overall national balance as well as on the resource gaps in the economy. Thus, the three additional identities included by the World Bank are the national balance, the income–savings balance, and the savings–investment balance. Therefore, following Addison (1989), the basic identities of the 'empty' Bank framework are the following:

- National Balance: $Y = C + I + X - Z$
- Income–Savings Balance: $Y = C + S$
- Savings–Investment Balance: $I - S = Z - X$
- External Balance: $Z - X = \Delta F - \Delta R.$

Income (Y) is used for consumption (C) or savings (S), and it is clear that investment (I) must come out of either domestic savings or a negative resource (trade) balance. In other words, if domestic savings are inadequate to realize a targeted level of investment, imports (Z) must be larger than exports (X). This implies that foreign resources must be made available for use in the domestic economy—in effect, if international reserves (ΔR) are inadequate, then external borrowings (ΔF) are needed.

5.2.2 *The Basic Growth Model*

The focus on rapid growth and capital accumulation, characteristic of the early work in development economics, implied that the aggregate growth theory developed by Harrod (1939) and Domar (1946) became a natural first building block in the World Bank approach to economic development.

In a closed economy, given that real savings (S) should equal real investment (I), we have the following relationship:

$$I = S = sy, \tag{5.1}$$

where it is assumed that savings form a stable share (s) of real income (y).

As I is definitionally equal to the change in capital stock (K), we have:

$$I = \Delta K = \Delta y/k, \tag{5.2}$$

where k ($= \Delta y/\Delta K = y/K$) is the (incremental) output–capital ratio.

From (eqn 5.1) and (eqn 5.2), we get:

$$g = \Delta y/y = sk, \tag{5.3}$$

where g is the growth rate of real output.

(Eqn 5.3), which is the famed Harrod–Domar growth equation, states that the real rate of growth (g) is equal to the savings rate (s) times the (incremental) output–capital ratio; therefore focusing on capital accumulation as the key constraint to economic development. Thus, for economies to grow faster, they have to save and invest more, although the actual growth rate will depend eventually on the productivity of capital, given by the inverse of the ICOR (incremental capital–output ratio).

It automatically follows that the Harrod–Domar growth equation can be used in a 'predictive' sense to determine the output growth rate, based on the available level of savings and a constant k (determined historically or technologically). But, for an open economy, it can also be used as a planning tool to establish just how much investment is required to raise the growth rate to a given level. A 'savings gap' is said to exist when the actual domestic savings rate (s) is lower than the projected investment rate (s^*) required to achieve the desired target growth rate (g^*). In such a framework, (eqn 5.3) can be rewritten in its 'prescriptive' mode as follows to yield:

$$s^* = g^*/k, \tag{5.4}$$

and, consequently, the savings gap is given by:

$$s^* - s = (g^*/k) - s, \tag{5.5}$$

where, as mentioned earlier, s is the actual savings propensity.

Multiplying (eqn 5.5) throughout by real output (y) yields:

$$I - S = (g^*/k)y - sy,\tag{5.6}$$

where $I\ (= s^*y)$ is the projected investment requirements.

The heart of the Bank approach lies in establishing the amount of foreign borrowings (ΔF) needed to close this investment–savings gap $(I - S)$. To do so, we relate the savings–investment gap and external balances given above to obtain:

$$I - S = \Delta F - \Delta R.\tag{5.7}$$

Linking (eqn 5.6) and (eqn 5.7) yields the following expression for the desired level of foreign capital required to finance the targeted growth rate:

$$\Delta F = [(g^*/k) - s]y + \Delta R,\tag{5.8}$$

where ΔR is given exogenously and captures restrictions, if any, placed on changes in international reserves.

Such an approach was fundamental in the early World Bank work on the post-War reconstruction of Western Europe and provided, in fact, the main theoretical rationale for the massive American capital injected into Europe under the Marshall Plan. The early approach to development was built on much the same lines of thought with foreign capital as a supplement to domestic savings, the implication being that there was no difference whether growth was financed by domestic sources (savings) or foreign sources (external borrowings).

5.2.3 The Two-gap Growth Model

A second theoretical building block was added in the 1960s with the development of the two-gap model by Chenery and Bruno (1962), McKinnon (1964), and Chenery and Strout (1966). These fix-price models included the savings constraint but, in addition, considered the possibility of foreign exchange acting as a separate and independent constraint on economic growth. The rationale behind this extension was that developing countries not only needed foreign exchange to supplement domestic savings, but also to finance imports.

In such a context, rapid growth presupposes the availability of capital (and intermediate) goods which, under the assumption that no domestic substitutes exist, will have to be imported. Thus, the basic hypothesis of the two-gap approach is the specification of a stable relationship that links imports (Z) to output (y) and investment (I), commonly given by (see Blitzer, Clark, and Taylor 1975; Tarp 1993):

$$Z = \Theta I + my, \tag{5.9}$$

where $0 \leq \Theta \leq 1$ is the import content of investment, and m is the propensity to import out of income.

At the heart of such a specification is the hypothesis that the economy is characterized by structural rigidities as well as bottlenecks that may make it impossible for the economy to attain, at least in the short-run, the desired increase in investment required to attain the targeted growth rate. Moreover, the higher the target growth rate, the more likely (or quicker) it is that bottlenecks will appear. For example, if the feasible growth of exports is limited, then there is no guarantee that the *ex ante* capital flows implied by the savings gap, (eqn 5.8), will automatically correspond to the difference between the necessary level of imports, given by (eqn 5.9), and the feasible export level. Under the circumstances, a 'foreign exchange gap', also known as the 'trade gap', could exist.

As long as one assumes that savings and foreign exchange (or exports) are not perfect substitutes for each other, one of the two gaps will be binding. When the 'savings gap' is binding a shortage of domestic savings makes it impossible for the economy to transform foreign exchange into investment. Under the circumstances, increased exports (implying additional foreign exchange) cannot enhance growth. When the 'trade gap' is binding a shortage of foreign exchange (implying a shortage of imported goods) makes it impossible for the economy to transform all potential savings into investment. In such a case, additional savings cannot increase growth. These two gaps will, of course, be equal *ex post* as the necessary adjustments in the macroeconomic variables will take place in order to ensure the satisfaction of the overall savings–investment balance, given by (eqn 2.25).

The foreign borrowings (ΔF) needed to close the trade gap can be obtained by substituting (eqn 5.9) into the external balance equation to yield:[1]

$$\Delta F = [\Theta(g^*/k) + m]y - X + \Delta R, \tag{5.10}$$

where g^* is the targeted growth rate, and X and ΔR are given exogenously.

(Eqn 5.8) and (eqn 5.10) reflect two different relationships between the targeted growth rate and the external borrowings required to close the 'savings' and 'trade' gaps. The two gaps will only exceptionally be of the same size and in $y - \Delta F$ space, they can be represented by two straight lines with positive slopes equal to $[(g^*/k) - s]$ and $[\Theta(g^*/k) + m]$, respectively.

It is obvious that the issue of which constraint is most likely to be binding has significant implications since the two-gap model implies that the productivity of foreign borrowings can be different, depending on the binding constraint. Thus, the basic notion underlying the two-gap growth model is that two independent resource constraints inhibit the growth potential of a developing economy. First, the required level of investment to realize the desired growth potential is not available because of the inability of the economy to internally generate the needed savings. Second, domestic growth is restrained by the limited availability of foreign exchange, or the inability of a developing economy to run current account surpluses. Since foreign borrowings can both add to domestic savings as well as provide the foreign exchange for importing inputs for which there are no domestic substitutes, the latter constraint is usually hypothesized to be the dominant constraint, implying that 'external strangulation' is the major structural constraint. The main assumption in the above analysis is that some proportion of investment is imported. If foreign exchange is withdrawn, then either exports must rise or imports must fall. Beyond a point, however, it is investment and thus output, that will reduce in the face of such external strangulation (Taylor 1983).

5.3 THE BANK APPROACH: THE REVISED MINIMUM STANDARD MODEL (RMSM)

5.3.1 *The Model*

In contrast with the Fund's concern with temporary BOP disequilibria, the Bank has been charged with the financing of growth and development over the medium term. The basic approach that the Bank uses for its macroeconomic projections and policy work, as discussed above, emphasizes the relationship between savings, foreign capital inflows, investment, and growth. This approach is reflected in the Revised Minimum Standard Model (RMSM) that was originally constructed in the early 1970s after Hollis Chenery joined the World Bank as Chief Economist. This model was developed to ensure a consistent approach to World Bank projections as well as to facilitate comparisons across countries. The number of variables in the model was kept to a basic minimum, partly in view of the paucity of data available in the developing countries, and partly to enable the model to be easily adapted to country-specific circumstances. However, economists within the Bank were free to use the model as a 'thinking' tool and modify it to meet current operational requirements. As a result, the RMSM currently has over 425 variables, although a basic core can be identified.

A study of country-wide modelling activity in the Bank concluded that the RMSM remains the most widely used tool for making macroeconomic projections and analyzing macroeconomic policies (see Whalley 1984). While other modelling approaches have been used to study particular problems in particular countries (for example Egypt, Dominican Republic, Nepal), these models have remained country-specific and no clear and widely acceptable alternative to the RMSM (apart from its second generation version, the RMSM-X) has emerged as yet.

The basic concern of the RMSM is with medium-term growth and its financing and, as such, interest is focused on real variables only. Therefore, inflation is not determined within the model.[2] Like the earlier Fund model, it can be compressed into a small number of key relationships for a better scrutiny of its internal structure. In keeping with the spirit of the RMSM framework, prices are assumed to be constant ($\Delta P = 0$) in the remainder of this chapter. The RMSM basically posits the following five relationships.

The first is the national income accounting identity given by:[3]

$$y(-1) + \Delta y = Cp + Cg + I + X - Z, \qquad (5.11)$$

where Δy, which is the change in real output, that is $\Delta y = y - y(-1)$, is a target variable; private consumption (Cp), total investment (I), and imports (Z) are endogenous variables; government consumption (Cg) is a policy variable; exports (X) are exogenous; and lagged output, $y(-1)$, is a predetermined variable.

The second relationship, which highlights the so-called 'needs' or 'requirements' approach, specifies the desired level of investment (I) which is consistent with a target level of output expansion (Δy). In line with the Harrod–Domar growth equation (see (eqn 5.2)), this is given by:

$$I = \Delta y/k, \qquad (5.12)$$

where k, which is the inverse of the ICOR, is an exogenous variable, and is assumed to be either historically or technologically given. The above relationship also allows one to obtain the expansion in real output based on the available level of investment which is the so-called 'constraints' or 'availabilities' approach.

The third one specifies a stable relationship between imports (Z) and real output (y). Thus, the import demand function is given by:

$$Z = my, \tag{5.13}$$

where m is the propensity to import out of income.

The next specification relates to the behaviour of private sector savings which is essentially reduced to a stable historically given savings rate. Given such a savings rate, the implicit function for specifying private consumption (Cp) is given by:

$$Cp = (1 - s)[y - T], \tag{5.14}$$

where s is the private sector's propensity to save out of disposable income, which is defined as income (y) less taxes (T).

Rewriting the external balance as follows results in model closure:

$$\Delta R = (X - Z) + \Delta F, \tag{5.15}$$

where the change in reserves (ΔR) is a target variable, and net foreign borrowings (ΔF) is an instrument.

The main difference between the Fund and Bank approaches is that while the Fund uses the external sector to study short-run BOP disequilibria, the Bank uses it to model medium-term growth. However, the Bank approach does not provide an explicit relationship between the targets (Δy and ΔR) and the instruments (Cg, ΔF and T). For this purpose, the RMSM relies on the assumed behavioural relationships for investment, consumption (or savings), and imports.

To solve the model, therefore, we substitute (eqn 5.12), (eqn 5.13), and (eqn 5.14) into (eqn 5.11) and rewrite the resulting expression in terms of the projected change in real output (Δy). This yields:

$$\Delta y = [(1/k) - s - m]^{-1} [(s + m)y(-1) + (1 - s)T - (Cg + X)]. \tag{5.16}$$

Substituting (eqn 5.13) into (eqn 5.15) yields:

$$\Delta R = X - my(-1) - m\Delta y + \Delta F, \tag{5.17}$$

and, subsequently, substituting the solution for Δy, given by (eqn 5.16), into (eqn 5.17) above would yield the required reduced form expression for ΔR.

Thus, the logic of the RMSM essentially implies that policy prescription involves the following two recursive stages: in the first stage, using (eqn 5.16), taxes (T) and government expenditures (Cg) are manipulated in such a way that the output target (Δy) is realized; in the second stage, using (eqn 5.17), foreign borrowings are set at that level which, along with this output solution, ensures that the BOP target (ΔR) is achieved.

The structure of the Bank approach is set out in Table 5.1.

TABLE 5.1   STRUCTURE OF THE BANK APPROACH

Targets	Δy	:	change in output
	ΔR	:	change in foreign exchange reserves
Instruments	C_g	:	government consumption
	T	:	total tax revenues
	ΔF	:	change in foreign borrowings
Endogenous	I	:	investment
	C_p	:	private consumption
	Z	:	imports
Exogenous	X	:	exports
Predetermined	$y(-1)$	:	output in the previous year
Parameters	k	:	(incremental) output–capital ratio
	s	:	savings rate
	m	:	marginal propensity to import

5.3.2   Constraints on Capital Inflows: The Two-gap Extension

In theory, the RMSM can be closed in either of two ways: first, by suppressing the savings gap which amounts to running the model as a one-gap (trade) model. Under the circumstances, total consumption ($C = Cg + Cp$) would be determined residually from the national balance, (eqn 5.11), as follows:

$$C = Cg + Cp = y - I - X + Z, \tag{5.18}$$

which, on the assumption that public consumption (Cg) is controlled by the government, yields:

$$Cp = y(-1) + \Delta y^* - (\Delta y^*/k) - X + my(-1) + m\Delta y^* - Cg, \tag{5.19}$$

where Δy^* is the targeted level of output expansion; X is given exogenously; and Cg is a policy variable.

However, for obvious reasons, it is unrealistic to assume that private consumption can be derived residually in this manner as such a formulation is totally devoid of all insight into the consumption and savings processes governing private sector behaviour. Thus, the residual value of *Cp* obtained in this manner may make little economic sense.

The second way to close the RMSM is by suppressing the trade gap which is the procedure adopted above in the earlier section. This is tantamount to running the model as a one-gap (savings) model where, by assuming that the authorities exert sufficient control over capital inflows (Δ*F*), this policy variable can be chosen according to the closure mechanism:

$$\Delta F = Z - X + \Delta R, \tag{5.20}$$

which is equivalent to:

$$\Delta F = my(-1) + m\Delta y^* - X + \Delta R^*, \tag{5.21}$$

where Δ*y** and Δ*R** are the targeted levels of output expansion and reserve changes, respectively; and *X* is given exogenously.

Suppressing the trade gap in the above manner, and assuming that Δ*F* is perfectly controllable is also questionable because if there are limits to foreign borrowings, then (eqn 5.21) will operate as a constraint on output expansion or reserve changes, implying that either one or both of these targets would need to be scaled down to accommodate the foreign exchange restrictions. Such a model with foreign exchange constraints is immediately recognizable as one version of the familiar two-gap growth model discussed earlier. Therefore, the RMSM can be redesigned as a two-gap structural model in which neither constraint is suppressed *à priori* so that either of the two gaps might be binding in reality. In such a two-gap situation, depending upon which constraint is binding, observed domestic savings (imports) may be different from desired or required savings (imports). Following such a two-gap approach, the principal use of the RMSM is to determine the financing requirements for alternative rates of growth and, hence, to determine the feasibility of a particular rate of growth given reasonable foreign financing scenarios.

In order to integrate the two-gap approach into the RMSM, we rewrite the national income accounting identity, (eqn 5.11), as follows:

$$I = (y - T - Cp) + (T - Cg) + (Z - X) \tag{5.22}$$

which yields the condition that domestic investment (*I*) is the sum of private sector savings (*y* − *T* − *Cp*), public savings (*T* − *Cg*), and external savings (*Z* − *X*). Substituting the implicit savings function as well as the external balance equation into (eqn 5.22) above, and recalling that $y = y(-1) + \Delta y$, yields the following expression for investment in terms of constraint notation:

$$I \leq \alpha(0) + \Delta F, \tag{5.23}$$

where, $\alpha(0) = sy(-1) + [(1 - s)T - Cg] + [s\Delta y^* - \Delta R^*], \tag{5.24}$

which is a straight line in $\Delta F - I$ space with a slope of unity and an intercept term $\alpha(0)$ which will usually be positive. This is the 'savings constraint' which is depicted by the SS line in Figure 5.1. From (eqn 5.24), it is seen that the position of the savings constraint can be shifted by changing the values of the instruments (T, Cg) or the targets $(\Delta y^*, \Delta R^*)$.

We then invoke the external sector budget constraint which is given by:

$$Z - X = \Delta F - \Delta R. \tag{5.25}$$

Substituting the import demand function, (eqn 5.13), into (eqn 5.25) above, and recalling that $y = y(-1) + \Delta y$, yields the following expression for Δy:

$$\Delta y = (1/m)X - y(-1) - (1/m)\Delta R + (1/m)\Delta F. \tag{5.26}$$

From the growth equation, (eqn 5.12), we have the following expression for the 'constraints' approach to planning in the RMSM:

$$\Delta y = Ik. \tag{5.27}$$

(Eqn 5.26) and (eqn 5.27) together yield the following expression for investment (I) in terms of constraint notation:

$$I \leq \beta(0) + (1/mk)\Delta F, \tag{5.28}$$

where, $\beta(0) = [(1/mk)X - (1/k)y(-1)] - (1/mk)\Delta R^* \tag{5.29}$

which is a straight line in $\Delta F - I$ space with a slope $1/mk > 1$ and an intercept term $\beta(0)$ which, in all likelihood, will be negative. This is the 'trade constraint' which is depicted by the TT line in Figure 5.1. From (eqn 5.29), it is seen that the position of the trade constraint can be influenced by changing the value of the target (ΔR^*) or the exogenous variable (X).

Each of these constraints, (eqn 5.23) and (eqn 5.28), provide an estimate of investment, and the one yielding the lower level is called the binding constraint. As the slope of the trade constraint is larger than that of the savings constraint ($1/mk > 1$), the impact of foreign borrowings on investment, and thus output and growth, will be larger if the trade constraint is binding.

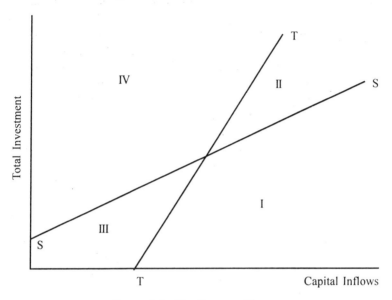

FIGURE 5.1 THE TWO-GAP MODEL

5.3.3 The Growth Programming Procedure

Under the assumption that foreign financing is constrained, then the process of iteratively determining the values of investment, output expansion, imports, and reserve expansion which are mutually consistent with each other as well as with the policy instruments and the exogenous variables, within a two-gap framework, would involve the following sequential steps:

Step 1: Specify the following values:

(a)   The parameters: k, s, and m;
(b)   The predetermined variable: $y(-1)$;
(c)   The exogenous constraints: X and ΔF;
(d)   The policy settings: T and Cg;
(e)   The target levels: Δy^* and ΔR^*.

Step 2: Determine the required level of investment (I^*) as follows:

$$I^* = \Delta y^*/k. \tag{5.30}$$

Step 3: Use the savings constraint, (eqn 5.23), and determine the level of investment it yields. Denote it by $I(S)$. Similarly, determine the corresponding level of investment from the trade constraint, (eqn 5.28). Denote it by $I(T)$. Obtain the binding level of investment (I_{min}) as follows:

$$I_{min} = min [I(S), I(T)], \qquad\qquad (5.31)$$

where *min* refers to 'minimum'. In the process, derive the binding constraint. If $I_{min} \geq I^*$, that is if the minimum level of investment so derived is equal to or exceeds the required level (implying that the intersection of ΔF and I^* takes place in Zone I in Figure 5.1), then proceed directly to Step 6. If not, proceed to either Step 4A or 4B or 4C, depending upon the binding constraint(s).

Step 4A: If $I_{min} < I^*$, and if the savings constraint is binding (implying that the intersection of ΔF and I^* takes place in Zone II in Figure 5.1), either increase taxes (T) and/or reduce government consumption (Cg) and/or reduce desired reserve accumulation (ΔR^*) until the constraint is relaxed or until further changes in the policy/ target variables are ruled out as infeasible. If the constraint is relaxed so that the required investment level can be achieved, proceed to Step 6. If not proceed to Step 5.

Step 4B: If $I_{min} < I^*$, and if the trade constraint is binding (implying that the intersection of ΔF and I^* takes place in Zone III in Figure 5.1), reduce the reserve accumulation target (ΔR^*) until the constraint is relaxed or until further reductions in the target variable become infeasible. If the constraint is relaxed so that the required investment level can be achieved, proceed to Step 6. If not, proceed to Step 5.

Step 4C: If $I_{min} < I^*$, and if both constraints are binding (implying that the intersection of ΔF and I^* takes place in Zone IV in Figure 5.1), make suitable changes in, both, the instruments (T, Cg) as well as the target (ΔR^*) until both the constraints are relaxed or until further changes become infeasible. If both constraints are relaxed so that the required investment level can be achieved, proceed to Step 6. If not, proceed to Step 5.

Step 5: If Step 4 fails to yield the required level of investment needed to achieve the desired level of output expansion, then a new (lower) target level has to be recomputed as follows:

$$\Delta y^* = k(I_{min}), \qquad\qquad (5.32)$$

and the old target level specified in Step 1 is replaced by this new estimate.

Step 6: Estimate import requirements as follows:

$$Z = my = my(-1) + m\Delta y^*. \tag{5.33}$$

Step 7: Given this level of required imports, as well as the exogenous levels of exports (X) and additional foreign borrowings (ΔF), re-estimate the targeted level of reserve expansion as follows:

$$\Delta R^* = (X - Z) + \Delta F. \tag{5.34}$$

To ensure consistency, this derived level of reserve expansion has to be compared to the (modified) one used in the savings and trade constraints. If both estimates are identical (most unlikely at the first iteration), go to Step 8. If not, go back to Step 3 and rework the exercise again with this new level of reserve expansion. Continue iterations until the estimate of ΔR^* used in Step 3 is identical to the one provided by Step 7.

Step 8: After convergence has been achieved, estimate the final levels of investment (I), output expansion (Δy^*), imports (Z), and reserve expansion (ΔR^*) which are mutually consistent with each other.

Step 9: Use (eqn 5.14), along with the new value of output, that is $y = y(-1) + \Delta y^*$ and the (modified) value of taxes (T), to estimate private consumption (Cp).

Step 10: Use (eqn 5.11) in order to determine public consumption (Cg) residually. Based upon the level of taxes, determine government savings $(T - Cg)$.

The above steps could also be followed to arrive at a set of projections that are consistent with the necessary amount of foreign financing which can be determined through a set of iterations.

The above model, by assuming that prices are constant, does not take account of changes in the terms of trade. As this is obviously unrealistic, in actual operational simulations, a separate module in the RMSM treats changes in the terms of trade as an income effect and distinguishes between gross domestic income (GDI) and gross domestic product (GDP) by using the identity:

$$GDI \equiv GDP \pm \textit{income due to changes in the terms of trade.} \tag{5.35}$$

Although the RMSM was originally designed as a two-gap structural model, by and large, it is often run as a one-gap model by suppressing either one of the two constraints *à priori*. Despite this unsatisfactory method of closing the model, the RMSM has served a useful purpose because it can be effectively used to find the time paths of various variables by easy manipulation of the model's parameters, predetermined variables, and initial conditions.

5.4   CRITIQUE OF THE BANK APPROACH

Despite the apparent usefulness of the two-gap model and, thus, the RMSM, many criticisms have been levelled against it. Some of them include:

- *Relative prices and policies are neglected*: The framework does not specifically determine policies that are needed to arrive at the targeted growth rate or BOP position. Moreover, exports are exogenous; and capacity utilization and labour are missing, as are the price, government, and monetary sectors, leading many economists to label it as an incomplete model.

- *Savings do not automatically flow from the developed to the developing countries*: It has been pointed out that the two-gap model is based on a 'sink' theory of international capital flows because it assumes that the developed countries save more than they can invest at home and so they need to transfer the surplus savings as foreign investment to developing countries which are in need of such funds. This premise is empirically questionable as Kuznets (1966) was unable to unearth historical evidence substantiating the claim that capital flows from high saving societies to low savings countries. Moreover, the recent experience of the United States is a testimony to the fact that rich nations do not always have surplus savings.

- *Difficult to decide the binding constraint à priori*: The framework assumes that imports are essential for investment and that the availability of foreign exchange, by allowing such imports, raises the growth rate of output. However, critics have argued that the savings gap can be closed by reducing imports or increasing exports or both, thereby freeing the foreign exchange necessary for investment. While the World Bank assumes that investment is constrained by the trade gap, different economies may be constrained differently. If import capacity is strictly limited by the availability of foreign exchange (as in Russia in 1990–1), then inflation and supply-induced recession are likely to result. On the other hand, high external debt (Poland and Hungary) can force cutbacks in public expenditures while a surge in capital inflows relative to the size of the economy may be hard to absorb (the Baltic countries). To counter this criticism, Gunning (1983), Waelbroeck (1984), and Standaert (1985) interpret the two-gap model as a 'disequilibrium' model in the tradition of Chenery; and van Wijnbergen (1986) demonstrates that in a two-sector model with traded and non-traded goods, an *exante* wedge between the savings and trade gaps implies an *exante* home goods market disequilibrium. In his view, a binding trade gap corresponds to an excess supply of home goods and thus leads to Keynesian unemployment, while a binding savings gap results in an excess demand for home goods and thus leads to classical unemployment.

In response to these shortcomings, the World Bank, since the 1980s, has moved away from the traditional version of the two-gap model in which exports are exogenous, the ICOR is predetermined, and the import propensity and the savings rate are given *exante*. For under the structural adjustment programmes (SAPs), among other things, the objective is to increase exports, raise efficiency levels by reducing the ICOR, change policies to affect expenditures and imports, and increase real interest rates to stimulate savings. In such a changing environment, we require a framework that is more complete than the existing RMSM–Bank or MABP–Fund versions and, to this end, a merged Bank–Fund model will be developed and extended in the subsequent chapters.

NOTES

[1]The external balance is given by:

$$Z - X = \Delta F - \Delta R. \tag{5.a}$$

Substituting (eqn 5.9) into (eqn 5.a) above and rewriting it in terms of ΔF yields the following:

$$\Delta F = \Theta I + mY - X + \Delta R. \tag{5.b}$$

From (eqn 5.6) we have:

$$I = (g^*/k)y. \tag{5.c}$$

Substituting (eqn 5.c) into (eqn 5.b) yields (eqn 5.10).

[2]On the other hand, the basic concern of the financial programming model of the Fund is with medium-term inflation and its determinants and, as such, interest is focused on monetary variables only. Therefore, the real growth rate is not determined within the Fund model.

[3]It needs to be noted that all variables are at constant prices.

6

Financial Programming and Growth-oriented Adjustment

6.1 INTRODUCTION

The 1980s witnessed a significant increase in the importance and influence of the World Bank and the International Monetary Fund (IMF) on macroeconomic policy formulation and implementation in the developing countries. Initially, however, the policy stance of these institutions was very restricted with the IMF mandate being, by and large, limited to the financing of temporary BOP disequilibria in attempts to stabilize the economy. When BOP problems were more of a permanent nature and needed to be corrected by appropriate policy measures (including supply-side structural policies), it was regularly argued by the IMF that such measures were beyond their purview as they would involve a gestation period far beyond the permissible time frame for IMF support. They were, it was held, within the competence of the IMF's sister institution, the World Bank.

Such a dividing line between the IMF and the World Bank implied that the IMF received guidance from the World Bank on development issues and, in turn, the World Bank followed the IMF advice on domestic macroeconomic and exchange rate policies, adjustment of temporary BOP disequilibria, and stabilization programmes. This distinction, however, became blurred during the turbulent years after the breakdown of the Bretton Woods par value system from 1968 to 1973 and the origin of the debt crisis in 1982 which brought in their wake substantial changes in the international, financial, and economic environment.

Spurred by the widespread criticisms which emanated during the 1980s—characterized as 'a lost decade of development'—that Fund programmes are in some sense inimical to growth, the growth aspects of adjustment programmes have now started receiving increasing attention (see Camdessus 1989). Growth is accepted as an indispensable component of any adjustment strategy aimed at macroeconomic stabilization; and 'growth-oriented adjustment' has become a concept which represents a measure of consensus on a possible solution to the problems of many developing economies (see Corbo, Goldstein, and Khan 1987).

In this context, the Fund, in collaboration with the Bank, now supports, for certain low-income countries, financial programmes which are formulated within the context of a long-term growth-oriented adjustment programme. These programmes have been further reinforced by the introduction of the more recent 'special' IMF facilities (as well as the introduction of structural adjustment loans by the World Bank for BOP support) to help low-income developing countries. The same accounts for debt rescheduling undertaken in a number of countries under the auspices of the IMF as this has forced the IMF into assessing the medium- and long-term growth prospects of the concerned countries. While the future of these facilities is still under debate, and is by no means certain, their mere existence and use implies that the IMF has started squaring up to supply side issues as it has *de facto* become involved in development finance.

Thus, while the IMF used to formerly insist that stabilization must precede any attempts at structural reform (see Mosley 1989), more recent statements seem to indicate a growing recognition by the Fund that, to the extent that efforts to channel resources away from inefficient uses are impeded by institutional rigidities, structural reform should, under certain circumstances, precede stabilization attempts as it can play a critical role in achieving BOP viability and growth. This switch in strategy, which entails a far greater level of coordination between the Bank and the Fund than that which currently exists, is bound to create difficulties at the operational level because of the differences that currently exist between the financial programming model of the Fund and the financial requirements model of the Bank. This lack of a common integrated framework has come into focus within the two institutions as well as within the development community at large.

In this context, several studies by Mohsin Khan and his associates at the Fund have suggested ways in which the financial programming framework can possibly be extended (see Khan and Knight 1985; Khan and Montiel 1989; Khan, Montiel, and Haque 1990). The essence of these approaches to linking growth-related elements with the basic financial programming model has been to incorporate into the latter a number of additional variables and relationships that characterize the model underlying the Bank's long-term projections of economic growth in developing countries.

While the resulting merged models have had the formal characteristics that represent the basic analytical features of both the Fund and Bank frameworks, most of them have been very large and elaborate and therefore the simplicity that accounted for part of the attraction of the two models has been lost in the merger which, needless to say, has provided substantive rewards in terms of new insights with respect to growth-oriented adjustment. Moreover, while these attempts to cross the Fund and Bank models have, to a large extent, facilitated each in doing its own job, the increasing size of every newer version of such merged models has implied greater uncertainty regarding many of their parameter values thereby limiting the usefulness of such 'hybrid' merged models in addressing themselves to practical issues related to the overall effects of Fund-assisted adjustment programmes on growth.

Consequently, there is a well-identified need for the development of a 'growth-oriented financial programme' that is applicable at the operational level. The purpose of this chapter is to describe the analytical framework behind the design of such a representative model which is seen to be internally consistent, and capable of serving the needs of both the Fund as well as the Bank. Moreover, its very simplicity and robustness allows it to be tailored to the circumstances and structural characteristics of individual countries.

We initially highlight the basic postulates of the merged Bank–Fund model of Khan, Montiel, and Haque (1990) and briefly review it against the backdrop of some of the criticisms it invoked from Polak (1990). Keeping in view some of the shortcomings of the merger, we extend our representative model of the Fund, developed in Chapter 4, by incorporating the basic economic variables and key relationships of the Bank model, developed in Chapter 5. After exploring the properties of this model, an empirical attempt is made to assess the adequacy of its framework as well as to determine the extent to which such a model can explain the nature and relevance of the policy advice rendered by these two institutions.

6.2 ADJUSTMENT WITH GROWTH: THE MERGED BANK–FUND MODEL

The paper by Khan, Montiel, and Haque (1990), which extended their earlier work (see Khan and Montiel 1989), is probably the most authoritative source which describes how it is possible to merge the Fund and Bank approaches within a consistent framework. Given the Fund's emphasis on financial variables (with real variables given exogenously) and the Bank's focus on real variables (with financial variables being given exogenously), it turns out to be relatively straightforward to merge the macroeconomic approaches of the two institutions because each of the models provides the 'missing' equation to its counterpart. Their general framework revolves around three key balance equations, that is the monetary balance, the external balance, and the savings–investment balance, which are reproduced below for convenience:

$$\Delta M = \Delta DC + \Delta R, \tag{6.1}$$
$$(Z - X) = \Delta F - \Delta R, \tag{6.2}$$
$$I = S + (Z - X). \tag{6.3}$$

These balance sheet constraints are then utilized to relate the approaches of the Fund and the Bank as well as to subsequently merge them.

6.2.1 *Relating the Analytical Approaches of the Fund and the Bank*

The essence of the Khan–Montiel–Haque approach can be synthesized in the following four simple steps:

The Fund Approach: The equations for monetary and external balances, that is (eqn 6.1) and (eqn 6.2), which together constitute the Fund approach, are initially used to solve for ΔR and ΔP, for given values of ΔDC, ΔE, and Δy.[1] This yields:

$$\Delta R = f(\Delta DC, \Delta E, \Delta y), \tag{6.4}$$

$$\Delta P = g(\Delta DC, \Delta E, \Delta y), \tag{6.5}$$

where from (eqn 4.51), it is seen that:

$$\frac{\delta \Delta R}{\delta \Delta DC} < 0, \text{ and } \frac{\delta \Delta R}{\delta \Delta E} > 0. \tag{6.6}$$

The 'Missing' Link: Substituting (eqn 6.2) into (eqn 6.3) yields:

$$I = S + \Delta F - \Delta R; \tag{6.7}$$

and substituting (eqn 6.4) into (eqn 6.7) above yields:

$$I = S + \Delta F - f(\Delta DC, \Delta E, \Delta y). \tag{6.8}$$

Therefore, given exogenously projected levels of domestic savings (S) and foreign borrowings (ΔF), and the solved value of ΔR by the Fund approach, it is possible to arrive at a given level of nominal investment (I).

The Bank Approach: It is assumed by the Bank that the change in real output (Δy) is equal to the incremental output–capital ratio (k) times the level of real investment, that is nominal investment (I) deflated by the aggregate price level ($1 + \Delta P$).[2] Therefore, we have:

$$\Delta y = k \ I/(1 + \Delta P), \tag{6.9}$$

which allows one to obtain the expansion of real GDP based on the available level of investment. This relationship can also be rewritten to provide the required level of investment consistent with a target level of output expansion as follows:

$$I = (1/k) \ \Delta y(1 + \Delta P). \tag{6.10}$$

The Merger: Substituting (eqn 6.8) into (eqn 6.10) and ignoring the second-order interaction term ($\Delta P \Delta y$) yields the merger:

$$S + \Delta F - f(\Delta DC, \Delta E, \Delta y) = (1/k)\Delta y, \tag{6.11}$$

which, given projected levels of S and ΔF and desired values of ΔDC and ΔE, can be solved to yield the equilibrium level of output expansion (Δy^*), and this solution, when substituted back into (eqn 6.4) and (eqn 6.5), yields the corresponding equilibrium levels of reserve accretion (ΔR^*) and price increase (ΔP^*), respectively. Therefore the resulting integration of the Fund and Bank approaches into a unified model goes a long way towards addressing what are perceived to be the principal weaknesses of the two models because by linking them up, it allows for the simultaneous determination of growth, inflation, and the BOP which is consistent with the projected set of exogenous and policy variables.

6.2.2   A 'Marriage' between the Fund and Bank Models: Some Comments

Despite its underlying appeal, Polak (1990) has criticized this so-called 'marriage' between the Fund and Bank models[3] by drawing attention to what he feels are the three principal weaknesses of the merged model: (1) The effort to cross these two models incapacitates each from doing its own job; (2) The simplicity that accounted for part of the attraction of the two models is lost in the merger; and (3) The merger provides scant rewards in terms of new insights with respect to growth-oriented adjustment.

Considering the fact that we shall be using the essence of this approach to provide an alternative design structure for integrating growth into the basic monetary model, it would be pertinent to examine the validity of these criticisms. As shown in the earlier section, the effort to cross these two models has implied that both of them have gained from the merger. The Fund model treats real output as exogenous and the Bank model supplies the missing output equation, that is (eqn 6.9), thus providing a way to close the Fund model with endogenous output. In a similar manner, the Bank model treats the flow of foreign savings as exogenous and the merger renders it partly endogenous because it supplies the missing reserve accretion equation, that is (eqn 6.7), thus providing a way to close the Bank model with endogenous foreign savings.

The basic drawback of the Bank approach is that if a country has spare reserves to finance a current account deficit, then this element of foreign savings enters the Bank model directly. However, this is a theoretically incorrect approach because spare reserves *per se* do not automatically translate into increased foreign savings, unless these reserves are used for import liberalization, as Polak himself has noted. However, with imports being given endogenously, and with the marginal propensity to import being treated as a fixed (technical) parameter, imports cannot be increased merely by the presence of spare reserves, unless these reserves are run down by domestic credit expansion which would, by increasing the demand for investment and output, lead to an increase in imports, thereby worsening the current account deficit. As increasing credit expansion is compatible with falling reserves which, in turn, is compatible with rising investment, the type of model closure used to merge the two approaches is not merely the only one of interest, but the only one feasible. Therefore, the first comment regarding the incapacitation of both models as a result of the merger is seen to be invalid.

As far as the third comment is concerned, it is obvious from (eqn 6.11) and (eqn 6.6) that:

$$\frac{\delta \Delta y}{\delta \Delta DC} > 0, \text{ and } \frac{\delta \Delta y}{\delta \Delta E} < 0, \tag{6.12}$$

which corroborates the empirical evidence (see IMF 1985) regarding the expansionary (contractionary) effects of credit expansion (devaluation) on output. Therefore, by endogenizing output and showing how policy variables associated with Fund programmes can affect its growth rate, the merger does provide substantive insights with regard to designing growth-oriented adjustment programmes.

The only substantive criticism by far is the second comment that the simplicity which accounted for part of the underlying appeal of the two models is lost in the merger. Ironically, however, it is not the complexity of the merged Bank–Fund model that is its principal weakness— although this criticism is certainly valid—but rather some of the simplifying assumptions it invokes in order to effect the merger.

The most damaging of these simplifications occurs in the final merger, (eqn 6.11), which, under the assumption that $\Delta P \Delta y$ can be ignored, technically yields the following 'simplified' version of the Bank equation:

$$\Delta y = k\ I, \tag{6.13}$$

implying that increases in the price level have no impact on real investment and, consequently, it is nominal investment which determines real output. This represents the most serious flaw in the overall design of the merged model.

As will be shown in the next section, the problem lies not so much with the omission of the interaction term but rather in the specification of the Bank equation itself which, under the present circumstances, needs to be modified in order to accommodate the adverse impact of inflation on the growth rate even after the inevitable simplification has been carried out.

6.3   INTEGRATING GROWTH INTO THE BASIC MONETARY MODEL

6.3.1   *The Analytical Framework*
The underlying principle for designing such a merged Bank–Fund model, referred to as the Representative Model—Version 2 (RM2), essentially follows the above approach, albeit with some major modifications, and was first spelt out in Rao and Singh (1995, 1996).

The various components of the RM2 are set out below. All the derivations spelt out in Chapter 4, as well as in Section 6.2.1 above, remain relevant for the ensuing analysis.

The equation defining monetary sector equilibrium continues to be given by (eqn 4.23) which is now rewritten as follows:

$$\Delta R - (1/v)Y(-1)\ \pi - (1/v)Y(-1)\ g = -\Delta DC, \qquad (6.14)$$

where the only difference *vis-à-vis* the earlier Fund version is that the growth rate (g) is now treated as an endogenous variable.

The equation defining external sector equilibrium continues to be given by (eqn 4.28) which is now rewritten as follows:

$$\Delta R + mY(-1)\ \pi + mY(-1)\ g = b\Delta E + [X + \Delta F - Z(-1)], \qquad (6.15)$$

where, as in (eqn 6.14), g is an endogenous variable.

It is assumed that nominal savings (S) are a linear function of nominal income (Y). Therefore, we have:

$$S = sY, \qquad (6.16)$$

where s is the marginal (assumed equal to the average) propensity to save.

Taking first-differences of (eqn 6.16) and writing in terms of S yields:

$$S = S(-1) + s(g + \pi)\ Y(-1), \qquad (6.17)$$

which is obtained by replacing ΔY by its definition given by (eqn 4.16).

Substituting (eqn 6.17) into (eqn 6.7) yields the following relationship between investment, growth, inflation, and reserves:

$$I = S(-1) + s(g + \pi)\ Y(-1) + \Delta F - \Delta R. \qquad (6.18)$$

We now assume that real output (y) is determined by a Harrod–Domar type growth equation given by:

$$y = (1 - d)\ y(-1) + k(I/P), \qquad (6.19)$$

where k is the incremental output–capital ratio, d is the fraction of capital stock depreciated each period, and (I/P) is real investment, that is nominal investment (I) divided by the price level (P).

As g is the growth rate, that is $g = [y - y(-1)]/y(-1)$, (eqn 6.19) yields:

$$g = k\frac{(I/P)}{y(-1)} - d. \qquad (6.20)$$

We now replace $y(-1)$ by $Y(-1)/P(-1)$ which is its definitional equivalent, and then replace $P(-1)/P$ by $1/(1 + \pi)$ which follows from the definition of the inflation rate, that is $\pi = [P/P(-1)] - 1$. (eqn 6.20) can then be written as:[4]

$$g = \frac{k[I/Y(-1)]}{(1+\pi)} - d. \tag{6.21}$$

Substituting (eqn 6.18) into (eqn 6.21), and setting $\pi g = 0$, yields:

$$[k/Y(-1)]\ \Delta R + (d - sk)\ \pi + (1 - sk)\ g = [k/Y(-1)]\ \Delta F + ks(-1) - d, \tag{6.22}$$

where ΔR, π, and g are the targets; ΔF is an exogenous variable; $Y(-1)$ and $s(-1)$ $[= S(-1)/Y(-1)]$ are the predetermined variables; and s, k, and d are parameters.

The structure of the merged model, comprising (eqn 6.14), (eqn 6.15) and (eqn 6.22), is set out in Table 6.1.

TABLE 6.1   STRUCTURE OF THE MERGED BANK–FUND APPROACH

Targets	ΔR	:	change in foreign exchange reserves
	π	:	rate of inflation
	g	:	real growth rate
Instruments	ΔDC	:	change in domestic credit
	ΔE	:	change in the nominal exchange rate
Endogenous	ΔM	:	change in money supply
	Z	:	imports
	I	:	investment
	S	:	savings
Exogenous	X	:	exports
	ΔF	:	change in foreign borrowings
Predetermined	$Y(-1)$	:	income in the previous period
	$Z(-1)$	:	imports in the previous period
	$s(-1)$	:	savings rate in the previous period
Parameters	v	:	velocity of money
	m	:	marginal propensity to import
	b	:	import response to exchange rate changes
	s	:	marginal propensity to save
	k	:	incremental output-capital ratio
	d	:	depreciation rate of capital stock

6.3.2 Structural Analysis of the Merged Model

In order to obtain insights into the structure of the merged model, we rewrite (eqn 6.14), (eqn 6.15), and (eqn 6.22) in matrix notation as follows:

$$\begin{bmatrix} 1 & -(1/v)Y(-1) & -(1/v)Y(-1) \\ 1 & mY(-1) & mY(-1) \\ k/Y(-1) & (d-sk) & (1-sk) \end{bmatrix} \begin{bmatrix} \Delta R \\ \pi \\ g \end{bmatrix} =$$

$$\begin{bmatrix} -1 & 0 \\ 0 & b \\ 0 & 0 \end{bmatrix} \begin{bmatrix} \Delta DC \\ \Delta E \end{bmatrix} + \begin{bmatrix} 0 \\ X + \Delta F - Z(-1) \\ [k/Y(-1)]\Delta F + ks(-1) - d \end{bmatrix} \qquad ...(6.23)$$

which can be written as:

$$Ax = Bu + z, \qquad (6.24)$$

where: $x = [\Delta R \ \pi \ g]'$ is a (3×1) vector of targets;

            $u = [\Delta DC \ \Delta E]'$ is a (2×1) vector of instruments;

            $z = (3 \times 1)$ vector of exogenous and predetermined variables;

            $A = (3 \times 3)$ matrix of time-varying coefficients; and

            $B = (3 \times 2)$ matrix of constant coefficients.

Solving (eqn 6.24) for x yields:

$$x = A^{-1}[Bu + z] \qquad (6.25)$$

which represents the 'positive' mode of the model. It needs to be noted that the model, as it currently stands, has no 'programming' mode as such because, as the number of targets exceeds the number of instruments, we cannot rewrite (eqn 6.24) in the form suggested by (eqn 4.31). This statement will be examined in detail shortly, and subsequently qualified, because we will show how a heuristic version of a programming mode can still be obtained for the system.

In order to apply the above theory of the merged Bank–Fund model, we need numerical estimates of the matrices listed out in (eqn 6.23). We once again use data on the Indian economy for this purpose, the objective being to determine the robustness of the approach as well as to carry out a structural analysis of the estimated model for 1995–6. We provide below the necessary data on:[5] (i) the two instruments: $\Delta DC = 585.33$ and $\Delta E = 1.63$; (ii) the two exogenous variables: $X = 940.32$ and $\Delta F = 80.20$; (iii) the three predetermined variables: $Y(-1) = 8541.03$,

$Z(-1) = 904.36$, and $s(-1) = 0.2700$; and (iv) the six parameters: $v = 2.22$, $m = 0.1524$, $b = 5.1160$, $s = 0.2440$, $k = 0.2442$, $d = 0.0183$.
Substituting these values into (eqn 6.23) and solving for x yields:

$$\begin{bmatrix} \Delta R \\ \pi \\ g \end{bmatrix} = \begin{bmatrix} -0.2528 & 3.8227 \\ 0.000179 & 0.001063 \\ 0.000016 & -0.000069 \end{bmatrix} \begin{bmatrix} \Delta DC \\ \Delta E \end{bmatrix} + \begin{bmatrix} 86.7948 \\ -0.0267 \\ 0.0493 \end{bmatrix}. \qquad ...(6.26)$$

The *ex-post* forecasts of the three targets (ΔR, π, and g) for 1995–6, can be obtained by setting the two instruments (ΔDC and ΔE) at their actual levels given above, that is $\Delta DC = 585.33$ and $\Delta E = 1.63$. This yields $\Delta R = -54.94$, $\pi = 0.0796$, and $g = 0.0583$, implying a reserve drawdown to the extent of about Rs 55 billion, an average inflation rate of about 8.0 per cent, and an average real growth rate of about 5.8 per cent. Comparing these forecasts with the actual depletion of foreign exchange reserves of Rs 62.35 billion, an actual inflation rate of 7.7 per cent, and an actual growth rate of 6.2 per cent, it is seen that the merged Bank–Fund model does provide rather realistic BOP, inflation, and growth forecasts despite its simplicity, testifying to the inherent robustness of the postulated framework.

6.3.3   *Inflation and Growth Determination*

It is also possible to solve the merged model in the positive mode by condensing it into two relationships between π and g. These relationships can be regarded as the 'Fund' component and the 'Bank' component.

The heart of the Fund component lies in the relationship that determines joint equilibrium between the monetary and external sectors. The equation determining monetary sector equilibrium which is given by (eqn 6.14) can be written in terms of ΔR as follows:

$$\Delta R = (1/v)Y(-1)\ \pi + (1/v)Y(-1)\ g - \Delta DC, \qquad (6.27)$$

while the equation defining external sector equilibrium which is given by (eqn 6.15) can be written in terms of ΔR as follows:

$$\Delta R = -mY(-1)\ \pi - mY(-1)\ g + b\Delta E + X + \Delta F - Z(-1). \qquad (6.28)$$

Equating the right-hand-sides of (eqn 6.27) and (eqn 6.28) above and solving uniquely in terms of g yields:

$$g = \phi - \pi, \qquad (6.29)$$

where: $$\phi = \frac{\Delta F + X - Z(-1) + \Delta DC + b\Delta E}{[(1/v) + m]Y(-1)}. \qquad (6.30)$$

(Eqn 6.29) which traces out a negatively-sloped locus in $\pi - g$ space, denoted by FF in Figure 6.1, thus specifies all combinations of inflation rates and growth rates at which, both, the monetary and external sectors are in simultaneous equilibrium.

The heart of the Bank component lies in the equations specifying investment and growth, that is (eqn 6.3) and (eqn 6.21). Substituting (eqn 6.17) and (eqn 4.26) into (eqn 6.3) yields:

$$I = S(-1) + s(g + \pi)\,Y(-1) + Z(-1) + m(g + \pi)\,Y(-1) - b\Delta E - X, \tag{6.31}$$

which when substituted back into (eqn 6.21) yields the following:

$$g = k\left[s(-1) + s(g+\pi) + \frac{Z(-1)}{Y(-1)} + m(g+\pi) - \frac{b\Delta E}{Y(-1)} - \frac{X}{Y(-1)}\right] - d - d\pi. \tag{6.32}$$

Solving the above expression uniquely in terms of g yields:

$$g = \psi(1) + \psi(2)\,\pi, \tag{6.33}$$

where:

$$\psi(1) = \left[ks(-1) + \frac{kZ(-1)}{Y(-1)} - \frac{kb\Delta E}{Y(-1)} - \frac{kX}{Y(-1)} - d\right]\bigg/(1 - sk - mk), \tag{6.34}$$

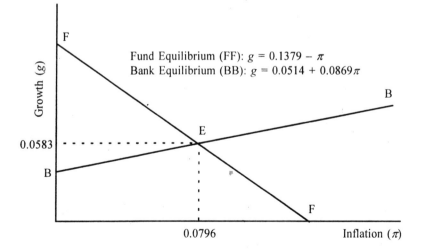

Fund Equilibrium (FF): $g = 0.1379 - \pi$
Bank Equilibrium (BB): $g = 0.0514 + 0.0869\pi$

FIGURE 6.1   JOINT FUND–BANK EQUILIBRIUM: INDIAN ECONOMY (1995–6)

$$\psi(2) = (sk + mk - d)/(1 - sk - mk). \qquad ...(6.35)$$

(Eqn 6.33) which traces out a positively-sloped locus in $\pi - g$ space, denoted by BB in Figure 6.1, thus specifies all combinations of inflation rates and growth rates at which the supply and demand for investment are equal.

These two equations, (eqn 6.29) and (eqn 6.33), can be solved simultaneously for π and g as functions of the instruments, exogenous and predetermined variables, as well as parameters.

Using the data (on the Indian economy) specified above yields the following estimated versions of these Fund and Bank equilibrium conditions:

Fund equilibrium:	$g = 0.1379 - \pi$	(6.36)
Bank equilibrium:	$g = 0.0514 + 0.0869\,\pi$	(6.37)

and it is these lines which are plotted in Figure 6.1, denoting, respectively Fund equilibrium (FF) and Bank equilibrium (BB).

Their intersection, which occurs at E where $\pi = 0.0796$ and $g = 0.0583$, is the solution we obtained using (eqn 6.26) and denotes simultaneous equilibrium of the monetary, external, and investment–output sectors.

Figure 6.1 lends itself easily to standard comparative-static analysis. An increase in the flow of domestic credit, for instance, would shift the FF locus outwards while leaving the BB locus unaffected. The result is an increase in g and π. Therefore, in contrast to the Fund model, a reduction in domestic credit expansion would have contractionary effects. Similarly, a devaluation would shift the FF and BB loci upwards and downwards, respectively. As shown in (eqn 6.26), the result is an increase in π and a decrease in g. Therefore, any unique point in this $\pi - g$ space (two targets only) can be attained considering that the two instruments, that is ΔDC and ΔE, are capable of shifting the FF and BB loci which implies that they can be made to intersect at any desired position.

6.3.4 *Robust Policy*

The excess of targets (ΔR, π, g) over instruments (ΔDC, ΔE) makes it impossible to solve the model in its programming mode because as B is a (3×2) matrix, its inverse is not defined and therefore the model cannot be directly put into the form suggested by (eqn 4.31). However, heuristic guidepost solutions for deriving a 'robust' policy can still be obtained.

To do so, we pre-multiply (eqn 6.24) by B', that is the transpose of B, and solve the resultant expression uniquely in terms of u obtaining:

$$u = (B'B)^{-1}B'Ax - (B'B)^{-1}B'z, \tag{6.38}$$

which will exist considering that the inverse of B'B exists.

Using the data (on the Indian economy) specified above, this yields the following heuristic version of the programming mode of the model:

$$\Delta DC = -\Delta R + 3847.31 \ \pi + 3847.31 \ g, \tag{6.39}$$
$$\Delta E = 0.1955 \ \Delta R + 254.4 \ \pi + 254.4 \ g - 22.7. \tag{6.40}$$

'In order to check the validity of these policy response functions, we substitute the forecast values of ΔR, π, and g into (eqn 6.39) and (eqn 6.40), that is $\Delta R = -54.94$, $\pi = 0.0796$ and $g = 0.0583$. Doing so yields: $\Delta DC = 585.5$ and $\Delta E = 1.64$ which are, indeed, the actual policy settings.

The reason as to why the above set of equations constitutes only a 'heuristic' version of the programming mode is that although it does prescribe policy on the basis of the three desired targets, this policy setting will be unable to attain all the three targets simultaneously and there will be a certain amount of deviation between the desired and realized targets.

In order to examine this concept more closely, consider tracking the following three targets: $\Delta R = -100$, $\pi = 0.1$, and $g = 0.07$, that is a reserve drawdown of Rs 100 billion, an inflation rate of 10 per cent, and a real growth rate of 7 per cent. Substituting these values into (eqn 6.39) and (eqn 6.40) yields the following policy setting: $\Delta DC = 754$ and $\Delta E = 0.9980$, that is a domestic credit expansion of Rs 754 billion and a nominal devaluation of one rupee.

Now substitute these values into (eqn 6.26) in order to forecast the targets given this policy setting. The forecasts are: $\Delta R = -100$, $\pi = 0.1093$, and $g = 0.0613$, implying that while the BOP target has been perfectly realized, the actual inflation rate is 10.93 per cent (higher than targeted), while the actual growth rate is 6.13 per cent (lower than targeted). However, for the given set of desired targets, this policy setting will be the best one in as much as the sum of squared deviations between the desired values of the three targets and their respective realizations will be minimal[6]. It is in this sense, that we refer to this policy setting as a 'robust' or 'best fit' policy as against the notion of an 'optimal' policy that tracks all targets simultaneously. In most actual situations involving stabilization, as there is bound to be an excess of targets over instruments, the above methodology does provide a useful technique to determine a 'robust' policy from an estimated model.

6.4   GROWTH-ORIENTED FINANCIAL PROGRAMMING: A CONCEPTUAL FRAMEWORK

6.4.1   *The Core*

The presentation, in this section, of the theory underlying growth-oriented financial programming is essentially an extension of RM2 outlined in the previous section. This revised model,[7] referred to as the Representative Model—Version 3 (RM3), has a core comprising the following eight equations.

Nominal income (Y) is equal to Py where P is the domestic price level and y is real output. Nominal money demand (Md) is related to nominal income, with the velocity of money (v) assumed to be a constant. Nominal money supply (M) is determined endogenously as the sum of domestic credit (DC) and foreign exchange reserves (R). The money market is assumed to be in equilibrium, implying that money supply equals money demand. The change in reserves (ΔR) equals the sum of the trade balance ($X - Z$) and other capital flows (ΔF). Investment (I) is the sum of domestic savings (S) and foreign savings, the latter being synonymous with the current account deficit ($Z - X$). Savings are positively related to income, with the savings propensity (s) assumed to be a constant. Real output is a function of real investment (I/P), with the incremental output–capital ratio (k) and the fraction of capital stock depreciated each period (d) assumed to be constants. Therefore, the theoretical core of the growth-oriented financial programming model is given by the following eight equations:

$$Y = Py, \tag{6.41}$$
$$(Md)v = Y, \tag{6.42}$$
$$M = DC + R, \tag{6.43}$$
$$M = Md, \tag{6.44}$$
$$\Delta R = (X - Z) + \Delta F, \tag{6.45}$$
$$I = S + (Z - X), \tag{6.46}$$
$$S = sY, \tag{6.47}$$
$$y = (1 - d)\, y(-1) + k[I/P]. \tag{6.48}$$

The above core will now be extended by incorporating certain important modifications in the design of the model.

6.4.2 *Monetary Sector Equilibrium*

Substituting (eqn 6.44) and (eqn 6.42) into (eqn 6.43), taking first-differences, and using (eqn 4.16) yields the, by now familiar, equation for monetary sector equilibrium:

$$\Delta R = (1/v) \ (g + \pi) \ Y(-1) - \Delta DC. \tag{6.49}$$

The most important modification in RM3 is that, unlike the earlier two versions, foreign exchange reserves will be measured in terms of foreign currency units. Therefore (eqn 6.49) above has to be changed to reflect the valuation effects of exchange rate changes on the balance sheet of the banking system. The stock of foreign exchange reserves in domestic currency units (R) is equal to the nominal exchange rate (E) times the stock of foreign exchange reserves in foreign currency units (R^*), that is

$$R = ER^*. \tag{6.50}$$

Therefore, changes in the domestic value of foreign exchange reserves may arise either due to changes in the exchange rate, changes in the stock of foreign exchange reserves in foreign currency units, or both. Therefore:

$$\Delta R = E(-1)\Delta R^* + R^*(-1)\Delta E, \tag{6.51}$$

which is obtained by ignoring the second-order interaction term, $\Delta E\Delta R^*$. Substituting (eqn 6.51) into (eqn 6.49) and solving the resulting expression for ΔR^* yields after simplification:

$$\Delta R^* = (1/v) \ Y^*(-1) \ \pi + (1/v)Y^*(-1) \ g - [1/E(-1)] \ \Delta DC - R^*(-1) \ e, \tag{6.52}$$

where $Y^*(-1) = Y(-1)/E(-1)$, that is nominal income in the previous period expressed in terms of foreign currency units, and $e = \Delta E/E(-1)$, that is the rate of change of the exchange rate.

Incorporating this valuation effect has two important implications: (1) The target variable is no longer the change in foreign exchange reserves measured in domestic currency units (ΔR) but rather the change in foreign exchange reserves measured in foreign currency units (ΔR^*) which is, by far, the more relevant target; and (2) The instrument variable is no longer the change in the exchange rate (ΔE) but rather the depreciation rate of the currency (e) which, once again, is the more relevant instrument.

(Eqn 6.52) can be rewritten as follows:

$$\Delta R^* - \alpha(1)\,\pi - \alpha(2)\,g = -\,\alpha(3)\,\Delta DC - \alpha(4)\,e, \qquad (6.53)$$

where: $\alpha(1) = \alpha(2) = (1/v)Y^*(-1),$ (6.54a)
                $\alpha(3) = 1/E(-1),$ (6.54b)
                $\alpha(4) = R^*(-1).$ (6.54c)

6.4.3   *External Sector Equilibrium*

There are three important modifications in (eqn 6.45), that is the equation defining external sector equilibrium. These are: (1) The estimates of exports and foreign borrowings will be denominated in terms of foreign currency units. This implies that the local currency value of exports (X) and capital inflows (ΔF) would depend upon exchange rate variations; (2) Rather than specifying imports in nominal terms (Z) to be a linear function of nominal income (Y) and the nominal exchange rate (E), we now assume, more realistically, that the volume of imports (QZ) is a non-linear function of real output (y) and the real exchange rate (RER); and (3) The increase in foreign borrowings denominated in foreign currency units (ΔF^*) will be treated as an instrument, rather than as an exogenous variable, to ensure an equality between targets and instruments, thereby allowing RM3 to be solved in its programming mode.

Exports in domestic currency units (X) is equal to the nominal exchange rate (E) times the value of exports in foreign currency units (X^*), that is

$$X = EX^* = [E(-1) + \Delta E]X^*. \qquad (6.55)$$

With the stock of foreign borrowings in domestic currency units (F) being equal to the nominal exchange rate (E) times the stock of foreign borrowings in foreign currency units (F^*), that is $F = EF^*$, the change in the domestic value of foreign borrowings, ignoring the interaction term, $\Delta E \Delta F^*$, is given by:

$$\Delta F = E(-1)\Delta F^* + F^*(-1)\Delta E. \qquad (6.56)$$

Imports in domestic currency units (Z) is equal to the nominal exchange rate (E) times the value of imports in foreign currency units (Z^*), that is

$$Z = EZ^*. \qquad (6.57)$$

Imports in foreign currency units (Z^*) is equal to the foreign price level (P_f) times the volume of imports (QZ), that is,

$$Z^* = P_f(QZ). \tag{6.58}$$

The import volume equation is given by:

$$QZ = Ay^m(RER)^{-b}, \tag{6.59}$$

where QZ is the volume of imports, y is real output, RER is the real exchange rate, that is $RER = E(P_f/P)$, and where m and b are positive parameters that measure the elasticity of the volume of imports to real output and to the relative price of importables, respectively.

Substituting (eqn 6.59) and (eqn 6.58) into (eqn 6.57), and replacing RER by its definition, yields:

$$Z = Ay^m E^{(1-b)} P^b P_f^{(1-b)}. \tag{6.60}$$

Logarithmic differentiation of (eqn 6.60) with respect to time yields:

$$\frac{\dot{Z}}{Z} = mg + (1-b)e + b\pi + (1-b)\pi_f, \tag{6.61}$$

where g is the growth rate of real output (y), e is the rate of change of the nominal exchange rate (E), π is the domestic inflation rate, and π_f is the foreign inflation rate.

In discrete-time representation, (eqn 6.61) implies that:

$$\Delta Z = [mg + (1-b)e + b\pi + (1-b)\pi_f] Z(-1), \tag{6.62}$$

and therefore:

$$Z = [1 + mg + (1-b)e + b\pi + (1-b)\pi_f] Z(-1). \tag{6.63}$$

Substituting (eqn 6.51), (eqn 6.55), (eqn 6.56), and (eqn 6.63) into (eqn 6.45) and solving the resulting expression for ΔR^* yields after simplification:

$$\Delta R^* = -bZ^*(-1)\pi - mZ^*(-1)g + [F^*(-1) + X^* - (1-b)Z^*(-1) \\ - R^*(-1)]e + \Delta F^* + [X^* - Z^*(-1) - (1-b)Z^*(-1)\pi_f]...(6.64)$$

Thus, the modifications made while defining external sector equilibrium are compatible with those made while defining monetary sector equilibrium.

(Eqn 6.64) can be rewritten as follows:

$$\Delta R^* + \beta(1)\pi + \beta(2)g = \beta(3)e + \Delta F^* + \beta(4), \tag{6.65}$$

where:
$$\beta(1) = bZ^*(-1), \tag{6.66a}$$
$$\beta(2) = mZ^*(-1), \tag{6.66b}$$
$$\beta(3) = F^*(-1) + X^* - (1 - b)Z^*(-1) - R^*(-1), \tag{6.66c}$$
$$\beta(4) = X^* - Z^*(-1) - (1 - b)Z^*(-1)\pi_f \tag{6.66d}$$

6.4.4 The Price-Output Block

The relationship between investment, growth, inflation and reserves continues to be given by (eqn 6.18) repeated below for convenience:

$$I = S(-1) + s(g + \pi) Y(-1) + \Delta F - \Delta R. \tag{6.67}$$

Replacing ΔF and ΔR by their current representations which are given by (eqn 6.56) and (eqn 6.51) yields:

$$I = S(-1) + s(g + \pi) Y(-1) + E(-1)\Delta F^* + F^*(-1)\Delta E - E(-1)\Delta R^* - R^*(-1)\Delta E. \tag{6.68}$$

The growth equation, (eqn 6.21), when simplified by setting $\pi g = 0$, yields:

$$g = k[I/Y(-1)] - d(1 + \pi). \tag{6.69}$$

Substituting (eqn 6.68) into (eqn 6.69) above yields:[8]

$$g = ks(-1) + ks(g + \pi) + k[1/Y^*(-1)]\Delta F^* + k[F^*(-1)/Y^*(-1)]e - k[1/Y^*(-1)]\Delta R^* - k[R^*(-1)/Y^*(-1)]e - d - d\pi \tag{6.70}$$

which can be written as:

$$\gamma(1)\Delta R^* + \gamma(2)\pi + \gamma(3)g = \gamma(4)e + \gamma(5)\Delta F^* + \gamma(6), \tag{6.71}$$

where:
$$\gamma(1) = \gamma(5) = k/Y^*(-1), \tag{6.72a}$$
$$\gamma(2) = d - sk, \tag{6.72b}$$
$$\gamma(3) = 1 - ks, \tag{6.72c}$$
$$\gamma(4) = k[F^*(-1) - R^*(-1)]/Y^*(-1), \tag{6.72d}$$
$$\gamma(6) = ks(-1) - d. \tag{6.72e}$$

6.5 STABILIZATION WITH GROWTH

6.5.1 The Model

The structure of the growth-oriented financial programming model, comprising (eqn 6.53), (eqn 6.65), and (eqn 6.71), can be set out in matrix notation as follows:

$$\begin{bmatrix} 1 & -\alpha(1) & -\alpha(2) \\ 1 & \beta(1) & \beta(2) \\ \gamma(1) & \gamma(2) & \gamma(3) \end{bmatrix} \begin{bmatrix} \Delta R^* \\ \pi \\ g \end{bmatrix} = \begin{bmatrix} -\alpha(3) & -\alpha(4) & 0 \\ 0 & \beta(3) & 1 \\ 0 & \gamma(4) & \gamma(5) \end{bmatrix} \begin{bmatrix} \Delta DC \\ e \\ \Delta F^* \end{bmatrix}$$

$$+ \begin{bmatrix} 0 \\ \beta(4) \\ \gamma(6) \end{bmatrix} \qquad ...(6.73)$$

which can be written as:

$$Ax = Bu + z \qquad (6.74)$$

where: $x = [\Delta R^*\ \pi\ g]'$ is a (3×1) vector of targets;
$u = [\Delta DC\ e\ \Delta F^*]'$ is a (3×1) vector of instruments;
$z = (3 \times 1)$ vector of exogenous and predetermined variables;
$A = (3 \times 3)$ matrix of time-varying coefficients; and
$B = (3 \times 3)$ matrix of time-varying coefficients.

In order to apply the above theory of growth-oriented financial programming, we need numerical estimates of the matrices listed out in (eqn 6.73). We use data on the Indian economy for this purpose, the objective being to determine heuristic guidelines regarding alternative stabilization-with-growth options that can be considered for 1996–7.

To do so, we require data on: (1) the three instruments, ΔDC, e, and ΔF^*, for 1996–7; (2) the two exogenous variables, X^* and π_f, for 1996–7; (3) The six predetermined variables, $Y^*(-1)$, $Z^*(-1)$, $R^*(-1)$, $F^*(-1)$, $E(-1)$, and $s(-1)$, for 1995–6; and (4) the six parameters, v, m, b, s, k, and d. All these are given below:[9]

$\Delta DC = 650$	$Y^*(-1) = 288.55$	$v = 2.22$
$e = 0.1061$	$Z^*(-1) = 32.19$	$m = 4.2997$
$\Delta F^* = 4.11$	$R^*(-1) = 17.046$	$b = 1.4838$
$X^* = 28.77$	$F^*(-1) = 64.04$	$s = 0.25$
$\pi_f = 0.03$	$E(-1) = 33.4$	$k = 0.2442$
	$s(-1) = 0.2440$	$d = 0.0183$

The above data set, along with (eqn 6.54), (eqn 6.66), and (eqn 6.72), yields the estimated parameters of (eqn 6.73) which can then be used to solve the model in its positive, programming and option modes.

6.5.2 *The Positive Mode*

The estimated parameters of the model are given below:

$$\alpha(1) = 129.98 \qquad \beta(1) = 47.76 \qquad \gamma(1) = 0.000846$$
$$\alpha(2) = 129.98 \qquad \beta(2) = 138.41 \qquad \gamma(2) = -0.0428$$
$$\alpha(3) = 0.0299 \qquad \beta(3) = 91.34 \qquad \gamma(3) = 0.9390$$
$$\alpha(4) = 17.046 \qquad \beta(4) = -2.95 \qquad \gamma(4) = 0.0398$$
$$\gamma(5) = 0.000846$$
$$\gamma(6) = 0.0413$$

Substituting these values into (eqn 6.73) yields the estimated forms of the matrices A and B, as well as the vector z. Solving (eqn 6.74) for x yields the positive mode of the model which is given by:

$$x = A^{-1}Bu + A^{-1}z, \tag{6.75}$$

whose estimated form is given by:

$$\begin{bmatrix} \Delta R^* \\ \pi \\ g \end{bmatrix} = \begin{bmatrix} -0.009014 & 61.2879 & 0.698542 \\ 0.000146 & 0.588662 & 0.004880 \\ 0.000015 & 0.013999 & 0.000494 \end{bmatrix} \begin{bmatrix} \Delta DC \\ e \\ \Delta F^* \end{bmatrix} + \begin{bmatrix} -5.1247 \\ -0.0842 \\ 0.0448 \end{bmatrix}.$$

$$...(6.76)$$

The *exante* forecasts of the three targets (ΔR^*, π, and g) for 1996–7 can be obtained by setting the three instruments (ΔDC, e, and ΔF^*) at their predicted levels given above, that is $\Delta DC = 650$, $e = 0.1061$, and $\Delta F^* = 4.11$. This yields: $\Delta R^* = -1.61$, $\pi = 0.0933$, and $g = 0.0581$, implying a reserve drawdown of about \$ 1.6 billion, an inflation rate of about 9.3 per cent, and a growth rate of about 5.8 per cent. All these three forecasts, which are inherently plausible, testify to the robustness and stability of the merged framework.

In Table 6.2 which is based upon the estimated form of the matrix $A^{-1}B$ in (eqn 6.76), the elements of each column represent the total impact of the concerned instrument, as a result of setting it at its predicted level given above, upon the corresponding target. The sum of the differential impacts of these three policy settings (inclusive of the intercept term) provides the overall forecast of the concerned target variable.

The preliminary results suggest that within the Indian context: (1) Domestic credit is a powerful instrument as it has a considerable impact on reserves, inflation, and growth; (2) Devaluation, although inflationary, has considerable potential in increasing reserves without causing a contraction in output; and (3) Capital inflows are inflationary and their impact on output expansion is insignificant. The results also indicate that a 10 per cent nominal devaluation, by increasing the rate of inflation by 5.9 percentage points, would result in a real devaluation of about 4.1 per cent.

TABLE 6.2 DIFFERENTIAL IMPACTS OF THE POLICY SETTINGS

	Impact on:		
Contribution of	*Reserves*	*Inflation*	*Growth*
Domestic credit ($\Delta DC = 650$)	−5.86	0.0949	0.0098
Exchange rate ($e = 0.1061$)	6.50	0.0625	0.0015
Capital inflows ($\Delta F^* = 4.11$)	2.87	0.0201	0.0020
Exogenous Factors:	−5.12	−0.0842	0.0448
Total	−1.61	0.0933	0.0581

6.5.3 The Programming Mode

Solving (eqn 6.74) in terms of u yields the programming mode of the model:

$$u = B^{-1}Ax - B^{-1}z, \qquad (6.77)$$

whose estimated form is:

$$\begin{bmatrix} \Delta DC \\ e \\ \Delta F^* \end{bmatrix} = \begin{bmatrix} -33.44 & 3081.33 & 16851.10 \\ 0.0 & 2.22 & -21.93 \\ 1.0 & -155.05 & 2141.76 \end{bmatrix} \begin{bmatrix} \Delta R^* \\ \pi \\ g \end{bmatrix} - \begin{bmatrix} 666.28 \\ -1.17 \\ 103.80 \end{bmatrix} \dots (6.78)$$

Thus, it is seen that domestic credit is inversely related to reserves and positively related to both inflation and growth, while the exchange rate is positively related to inflation and negatively related to growth.[10] The programming mode implies that target values for reserve accumulation (ΔR^*), the inflation rate (π), and the growth rate (g) must initially be assigned in order to obtain the corresponding instrument values. Setting, realistically, $\Delta R^* = -1.00$ (that is a reserve depletion of $ 1 billion), $\pi = 0.07$ (that is a seven per cent inflation rate), and $g = 0.06$ (that is a six per cent growth rate), we solve (eqn 6.78) above obtaining: $\Delta DC = 593.9$, $e = 0.0082$, and $\Delta F = 12.85$. This implies that domestic credit expansion would have to be restrained at only Rs 594 billion, the nominal exchange rate should be allowed to depreciate by just about one per cent from its level of Rs 33.4 per US dollar in 1995–6 and foreign borrowings should be around $ 12.85 billion. The stability in the exchange rate would contribute to controlling inflation, the tight credit ceiling would not only prevent reserve depletion but also contain inflation, while the increased capital inflows would spur output expansion.

6.5.4 *The Option Mode*

In order to obtain greater insights into the trade-offs implicit in designing growth-oriented stabilization policy, we expand (eqn 6.78) obtaining:

$$\Delta DC = -33.4\Delta R^* + 3081.33\pi + 16851.10g - 666.28, \qquad (6.79a)$$
$$e = 2.22\pi - 21.93g + 1.17, \qquad (6.79b)$$
$$\Delta F^* = 1.0\Delta R^* - 155.05\pi + 2141.76g - 103.80. \qquad (6.79c)$$

The above system comprises a set of three equations in six unknowns which implies that *any* three of them (except the combination e, π, and g) can be assigned values exogenously to solve for the remaining three. As the objective is to probe alternative options for improving upon the forecasts and designing a growth-oriented stabilization policy with limited inflation, we target a 6 per cent growth rate and a 9 per cent inflation rate. Therefore, we set $g = 0.06$ and $\pi = 0.09$. Substituting these two values into (eqn 6.79) above yields:

$$\Delta DC = -33.4\Delta R^* + 622.11, \qquad (6.80a)$$
$$e = 0.0540, \qquad (6.80b)$$
$$\Delta F^* = 1.0\Delta R^* + 10.75, \qquad (6.80c)$$

implying that the exchange rate must depreciate by about 5.4 per cent. Thus, it is seen that, once the growth rate and inflation rate are fixed, the desired change in the exchange rate is uniquely determined. We still have one degree of freedom left, and with three variables to choose from, this implies that we have three alternative stabilization options.

Option 1: On the assumption that the strategy proposed by the programming mode implies a very tight credit ceiling, in this first option, we relax this constraint and set $\Delta DC = 650$ (its projected level). Substituting this value into (eqn 6.80a) yields $\Delta R^* = -0.84$ which, when substituted into (eqn 6.80c), yields $\Delta F^* = 9.91$. Thus, this policy option implies a reserve drawdown of $ 0.84 billion and total foreign borrowings of about $ 10 billion. While the reserve depletion is sustainable, this option is rendered infeasible because of the prohibitively high level of foreign borrowings (capital inflows) required to finance it.

Option 2: As the first strategy is unfeasible because of the high foreign borrowings involved, in this second option, we place an upper limit of $ 6 billion(which has been achieved in the past) on the amount of capital inflows. Setting $\Delta F^* = 6$ in (eqn 6.80c) yields $\Delta R^* = -4.75$ which, when substituted into (eqn 6.80a), yields $\Delta DC = 780.76$. Thus, this policy option envisages a domestic credit expansion of Rs 781 billion and a reserve drawdown of $ 4.75 billion. While the domestic credit expansion is feasible enough, this option is ruled out because the reserve depletion is definitely unsustainable.

Option 3: As the second strategy is unfeasible because of the unsustainable reserve depletion that it envisages, in this third and final option, we set a maximal level of $ 3 billion on reserve depletion. Setting $\Delta R^* = -3$ in (eqn 6.80a) and (eqn 6.80c) yields $\Delta DC = 722.31$ and $\Delta F^* = 7.75$. Thus, this policy option invokes a credit expansion of about Rs 722 billion and total foreign borrowings of about $ 7.75 billion.In view of the fact that both estimates seem feasible enough, this strategy seems to be the only reasonable one, given the existing framework of the merged mode, to achieve our objectives.

6.6 CONCLUSIONS

The merged model therefore suggests that an appropriate policy response to promote 'adjustment with growth' in the face of a negative external shock, typified by reduced foreign borrowings or capital inflows (ΔF^*), is to increase credit expansion (ΔDC) and/or run down reserves (ΔR^*) against the backdrop of a better aligned exchange rate (e).

It is thus seen that, despite the misgivings of Reinhart (1991) regarding the usefulness of such an approach due to the inherent instability of some of its key parameters, our merged model not only provides fairly accurate forecasts of the BOP, inflation, and reserves, but also captures the essence of growth-oriented adjustment as it ensures a robust framework for designing a stabilization package in the face of external shocks.

The attractiveness that characterizes the financial programming framework of the Fund and the financial requirements framework of the Bank is that they require little data to work with and are relatively easy to utilize. However, these two models *per se* do not contribute much to an understanding of the complex policy responses that are required to design a stabilization package that will simultaneously eliminate macroeconomic imbalances (in the form of BOP disequilibria and rising inflation) as well as raise the growth rate.

The composite model which represents a synthesis in technical terms of these two sub-models not only carries forward their appealing simplicity and their potential flexibility, but is also better equipped to investigate issues involving growth-oriented adjustment. More importantly, the merged model endogenously eliminates unattainable growth paths, and therefore the planner does have the option of modifying the instruments in order to achieve the BOP and inflation targets consistent with the remaining set of feasible growth trajectories. So, if used flexibly and with the necessary care, the merged model is capable of drawing attention to the possible trade-offs which policy makers have to face while designing growth-oriented stabilization programmes.

The only limitation of the merged model, as it currently stands, is that because the multipliers associated with the growth rate are relatively small, it takes large modifications in ΔDC and ΔF^* to affect the growth target in any significant manner. While this is not a design flaw *per se*, it essentially implies that more instruments, especially fiscal policy variables (including the interest rate), need to be incorporated into the model to make it better suited for addressing a number of critical issues in structural adjustment. Moreover, the merged model can very easily be expanded to include domestic and external debt, as well as the interactions between the banking system, the fiscal sector, and the private sector. All these steps will be taken up, one at a time, in the subsequent chapters where it will be shown that introducing such changes alter the policy conclusions in certain fundamental ways.

Thus, in line with Khan, Montiel, and Haque (1990), we conclude that while the merged model does yield very useful insights into the relationships between the BOP, inflation, and growth that would need to be taken into account while designing programmes in which growth is an explicit objective, the present version represents only a natural first step in the search for an integrated framework within which growth-oriented adjustment issues can be analysed.

NOTES

[1]As discussed in Chapter 4 (Note 4), the Khan–Montiel–Haque approach involves solving the Fund model in terms of ΔP, for exogenously given values of Δy. Needless to say, there are other exogenous and predetermined variables which have been omitted for the sake of convenience.

[2]As mentioned in Chapter 4 (Note 7), the Khan–Montiel–Haque approach assumes that $P(-1) = 1$. Therefore, the current price level (P), which is given by $P = P(-1) + \Delta P$, is merely $1 + \Delta P$.

[3]These criticisms, which were replied to later on by Khan and Montiel (1990), were primarily directed against the earlier version of the merged Bank–Fund model by Khan and Montiel (1989).

[4]Multiplying (eqn 6.21) by $(1 + \pi)$ and setting $\pi g = 0$ yields:

$$g = k \, [I/Y(-1)] - d(1 + \pi), \tag{6.a}$$

which implies that, despite the simplification involved by ignoring the interaction term, inflation does have an adverse impact on growth. Thus, the re-specification of the Bank equation by the specific introduction of the rate of capital stock depreciation serves to overcome the flaw in the Khan–Montiel–Haque approach where it was seen that, by omitting the interaction term, $\Delta P \Delta Y$, an increase in the price level has no impact on the output level.

[5]The units of measurement for all these variables have been provided in Chapter 4 (Note 9). As before, as we are forecasting for 1995–6, the estimates of the two instruments and two exogenous variables correspond to 1995–6, while the estimates of the three predetermined variables correspond to 1994–5.

[6](Eqn 6.38) is analogous to the OLS (ordinary least squares) technique as it applies the same principle to determine the so-called 'line of best fit'. Just as in the case of estimating 'n' parameters with 'n' data points available, the OLS approach yields an equation whose predictions of the dependent variable are exactly equal to its actual values, similarly with 'n' targets and 'n' instruments, (eqn 4.31) yields response functions which would track the desired targets exactly. However, when there are 'n' data points and less than 'n' parameters to be estimated, the OLS principle estimates the 'best fit' equation which minimizes the sum of squared residuals between the actual and predicted values of the dependent variable. Correspondingly, when there are 'n' targets and less than 'n' instruments, the underlying principle employed in (eqn 6.38), selects 'best fit' policy response functions which minimize the sum of squared deviations between the desired values of the targets and their respective realizations.

[7]We present here only the minimum version of the financial programming model with the peripheral block, regarding the allocation of domestic credit between the private sector (ΔDCp) and the public sector (ΔDCg), being omitted for the sake of simplicity. An empirical analysis of a growth-oriented financial programming model, which includes all these features, will be carried out in Chapter 8.

[8]It should be noted that:

$$F^*\,(-1)\frac{\Delta E}{Y(-1)} = F^*\,(-1)\frac{\Delta E}{E(-1)}\frac{E(-1)}{Y(-1)} = \frac{F^*\,(-1)}{Y^*\,(-1)}e. \qquad (6.b)$$

[9]As before, domestic credit (DC) is measured in billions of Indian rupees, while income (Y^*), exports (X^*), imports (Z^*), foreign borrowings (F^*), and foreign exchange reserves (R^*) are all measured in billions of US dollars. The predetermined variable, $E(-1)$, is the lagged value of the nominal exchange rate which is defined in terms of Indian rupees per US dollar, while the instrument (e) is the rate of change of the exchange rate, given by $e = \Delta E/E(-1)$.

[10]That there is no relationship between ΔR^* and e is a very important corollary of such a merger and needs to be explained carefully. To do so, we

shall invoke the assumptions of the simpler RM2 although the final result can easily be generalized to the more complicated RM3 as well.

Substitute the imports function given by: $Z = Z(-1) + m\Delta Y - b\Delta E$, into the external sector financial constraint given by: $\Delta R = (X - Z) + \Delta F$, and rewrite the equation in terms of ΔE to yield:

$$\Delta E = (1/b)\Delta R - (1/b)X + (1/b)Z(-1) + (m/b)\Delta Y - (1/b)\Delta F. \qquad (6.c)$$

(Eqn 6.c) implies that to increase ΔR by one unit, the increase in ΔE should be $(1/b)$. (Eqn 6.c) is valid for the programming mode provided all its explanatory variables are either target or exogenous variables, and the latter set of variables are not affected by exchange rate changes. In the merged model, as ΔF is an instrument, it can no longer remain on the right-hand-side of (eqn 6.c) and must be replaced appropriately.

To do so, substitute the investment constraint given by: $I = S + \Delta F - \Delta R$, into an output equation given simplistically by: $\Delta Y = kI$, and rewrite the resulting equation in terms of ΔF to yield:

$$\Delta F = (1/k)\Delta Y - S + \Delta R. \qquad (6.d)$$

(Eqn 6.d) implies that to increase ΔR by one unit, ΔF should be increased by one unit. However, from (eqn 6.c), this implies that the decrease in ΔE should be $(1/b)$. Therefore, the requisite change in the exchange rate is seen to be zero, as the devaluation in the exchange rate required to increase ΔR by one unit is exactly offset by the revaluation that will be required as a result of the consequent increase in ΔF. This result can be obtained by directly substituting (eqn 6.d) into (eqn 6.c) yielding:

$$\Delta E = (1/b)S - (1/b)X + (1/b)Z(-1) - [(1 - mk)/bk]\Delta Y, \qquad (6.e)$$

and it is seen that the coefficient of ΔR is zero, implying that desired reserves have no bearing on exchange rate changes. The basic stabilization implication of the result is that, once the target inflation and growth rates are specified, the desired change in the exchange rate is uniquely determined, and any subsequent changes in desired reserves will have to be met either by changes in domestic credit or foreign borrowings.

MONETARY, FISCAL, AND EXTERNAL SECTOR ADJUSTMENTS

7

Growth-oriented Adjustment and Monetary Reform

7.1 INTRODUCTION

A key economic feature that differentiates developed and developing countries is the structure of their financial system which is very often characterized by the presence of, what has come to be called, financial repression. The term 'financial repression' is due to McKinnon (1973) and Shaw (1973) who were the first to present a systematic account of some of the specific characteristics of financial markets in developing countries. According to McKinnon (1973), the financial system in most developing countries is 'repressed' by a series of government interventions that have the effect of keeping very low (often negative) real interest rates that domestic banks offer to savers. To a large extent, the motivation for this set of measures is a fiscal one; the government wants to actively promote development and, lacking the direct fiscal means to do so, it uses the financial system to fund its spending. It does this in two ways: first, by imposing large reserve and liquidity requirements on banks, it creates a captive demand for its own (low or non) interest-bearing instruments. Thus, it can finance its own high-priority spending by issuing debt. Second, by keeping interest rates at artificially low levels through the imposition of ceilings on lending rates, it creates an excess demand for credit. It then orders the banking system to set aside a fixed fraction of the available credit to priority sectors.

Apart from these reasons, financial repression has been motivated by a variety of other factors including the concern that market-determined interest rates would produce serious imperfections. For example, it has been argued that such imperfections would arise because domestic financial markets are 'thin' in the sense that they have an oligopolistic structure. In such situations, freeing interest rates from controls would lead to sharply higher lending rates that would increase the cost of capital and thereby discourage investment. Moreover, high nominal interest rates would also increase the cost of servicing government debt. There would also be adverse effects on income distribution, especially if holdings of financial instruments are narrowly distributed.

Be that as it may, such a system of financial repression has had serious implications for economic efficiency because the combination of low rates of return on assets and high reserve requirements has implied that even competitive banking systems have been forced to offer low interest rates on their liabilities. This, along with moderate to high inflation, has often resulted in negative real rates of return on financial assets for extended periods, at least in regulated financial markets, which has had adverse effects on savings and the financial intermediation process. Moreover, in such instances, the real holdings of domestic financial assets have grown less rapidly than the real economy and capital flight has been a serious problem. All these developments have severely restricted the availability of real credit thereby inhibiting investment. Since available credit is often initially allocated to large enterprises, credit for small- and medium-sized firms has been severely rationed, even though their investments could have yielded a higher rate of return.

In such a context, Park (1991) has drawn a useful distinction between monetary reform and financial liberalization. The former is defined as an increase in administered interest rates to near-equilibrium levels, with the remaining set of restrictions on the banking system being left untouched. By contrast, financial liberalization comprises a much more ambitious set of reforms which, apart from freeing official interest rates, is directed at removing at least some of the restrictions on the behaviour of banks. Full financial liberalization involves privatization of public financial institutions, the removal of restrictions on entry into banking (including those preventing access by foreign banks), measures aimed at spurring competition in financial markets, the reduction of reserve requirements, the elimination of directed lending, and the freeing of official interest rates.

Both monetary reform and the various forms of financial liberalization are becoming increasingly common in the developing world, and this chapter focuses attention on the effects of monetary reform as a structural policy designed to complement growth-oriented adjustment programmes and enhance economic growth by promoting the accumulation and efficient use of productive assets.

7.2 MONETARY REFORM AND INTEREST RATE POLICY

Growth-oriented adjustment programmes place considerable emphasis on achieving external adjustment through policies that will ensure a satisfactory rate of economic growth over the longer term. Although a substantial increase in output can be achieved in the short run through more efficient and fuller utilization of existing resources, long-run economic growth essentially requires an increase in productive capacity. This can come about either through a higher rate of investment, or the choice of investments that yield a higher rate of return (implying a lower ICOR), or both.

In general, the goal of stimulating higher levels of investment, and thus higher output growth, has been implemented via measures to increase domestic savings. Investment in developing countries has frequently been constrained by the availability of savings, thereby giving policies that favour public and private savings a special importance in growth-oriented adjustment programmes. For the public sector, this involves steps to improve the overall fiscal position, while the focus as far as fostering private savings is concerned has been on interest rate policy.

In growth-oriented adjustment programmes, interest rate policy is regarded as having a major influence not only on short-run adjustments of spending, inflation, and external payments, but also on the long-term accumulation of financial wealth and the level and composition of investment. This argument for monetary reform as a structural policy conducive to a higher growth path is a direct corollary of the McKinnon–Shaw financial repression hypothesis; their basic theory underlying interest rate policy as a means of increasing savings and investment can be summarized briefly as follows (see Agenor and Montiel 1996): In a context in which the saving instruments available in the formal financial system are limited to cash, demand deposits, and time deposits, raising controlled interest rates to near-equilibrium levels may induce an increase in the savings rate as well as a portfolio shift out of non-financial assets into the formal financial system. The high real interest rates resulting from the monetary reform would actually increase rather than reduce aggregate investment, either because the need to accumulate funds to undertake lumpy investments makes money and capital complementary, rather than substitute, assets (the McKinnon hypothesis), or because of a credit availability effect (the Shaw hypothesis). The latter works as follows: When real interest rates are low, total investment is limited by the availability of savings. By increasing total savings and attracting it into the banking system, higher real interest rates would increase investment through enhanced credit availability. Moreover, many high-return projects, not previously funded, would be undertaken after monetary reform because banks, having scale economies relative to the informal sector, would be more efficient in channeling funds towards them. It is equally true that many low-return projects, previously funded, would not be undertaken because the increase in the real rates of return would now make them economically unviable. This analysis therefore suggests that elimination of distortions in the market for financial savings can be expected to yield a higher growth rate not only because the quantity of investment increases (as a result of gains in the savings rate), but also because the quality of investment improves (as a result of gains in productivity).

7.2.1   *Empirical Evidence*

According to the above arguments, raising controlled interest rates should raise the supply of domestic time and savings deposits, which should increase the quantity and improve the quality of domestic investment, in turn increasing the rate of growth. Econometric studies, in this context, have looked at each of these propositions separately, and have examined the links between the primary instrument (interest rate), intermediate targets (savings and investment rates), and the final target (growth rate).

One of the most systematic studies in this context has been the work by Fry (1988) who examined each step in the set of propositions linking monetary reform to economic growth. Using pooled cross-section and time-series data for several samples of Asian countries, it was found that the weight of evidence did support a positive correlation between real deposit rates and national savings as well as between real deposit rates and the supply of credit. Credit supply, in turn, was found to have a strong positive effect on investment, thereby supporting the 'credit availability' effect. However, there was no evidence of the 'complementarity' effect which was tested by including the investment rate in the money demand function. More recently, in a study focusing on a larger sample of countries, Fry (1993) found further evidence of two types in support of improved quality of investment. First, real deposit rates were found to be positively correlated with the incremental output-capital ratio which was used as a proxy for the efficiency of investment. Second, the real deposit rate had a positive effect on the growth rate in a simple regression of one variable on the other.[1]

Based upon these and other studies, including Gelb (1989), it can be concluded that real deposit rates have a weak positive association with the savings and investment rates, a strong positive association with the growth rate, and a strong negative association with the ICOR, implying, overall, that the efficiency effect on investment, and not the volume effect, accounts for the positive relationship between real interest rates and growth. Moreover, it has also been found that an increase in the real deposit rate increases the share of domestic savings intermediated through the formal financial system, and this share has a stronger effect on growth than the level of savings *per se* which can be interpreted as establishing the causal chain between real deposit rates and growth through more effective intermediation into higher-productivity investment.

7.2.2   Policy Implications
The above evidence indicates why raising real interest rates on domestic financial instruments is a key element in growth-oriented adjustment programmes. However, in actually setting the level of nominal interest rates, considerable judgment and caution needs to be exercised especially regarding the future course of inflation. Establishing the perception that holders of domestic financial instruments will earn positive real returns that are to some extent comparable with the real yields that can be obtained on foreign instruments appears to be a vital element in promoting BOP adjustment, preventing capital flight, and increasing domestic savings.

In such a context, interest rate policy needs to be coordinated with exchange rate policy to avoid problems with capital flows. Although many developing countries have restrictions on external capital movements, holdings of foreign assets and liabilities have nevertheless become important components of resident portfolios in a number of countries since the 1970s. Moreover, while the linkages between domestic and financial markets are often imperfect, significant differences in the perceived yields on domestic and foreign instruments have at times stimulated periods of capital inflows or capital flight. As the relevant yield on foreign instruments would equal the foreign interest rate adjusted for anticipated changes in the exchange rate, there is a need to coordinate interest rate and exchange rate policies because they have the potential to sharply alter the relative yields on domestic and foreign financial instruments. For example, the initial phase of a stabilization programme could involve an increase in domestic interest rates (to stimulate savings) and a significant devaluation of the exchange rate (to improve the BOP). If this devaluation is viewed as a once-and-for-all measure aimed at eliminating the need for further exchange rate adjustments, then the resulting combination of interest rate and exchange rate changes may make domestic assets quite attractive relative to foreign assets and make foreign credit appear relatively less expensive. The resulting capital inflows could result in a significant expansion of reserve money as the central bank intervenes to maintain the exchange rate. Such monetary growth could create strong inflationary pressures, which could seriously destabilize any monetary reform, thereby placing the entire financial liberalization process in jeopardy.

All these potential problems make specifying the equilibrium interest rate a particularly hazardous issue because while an excessive increase in interest rates could adversely affect investment and create problems with capital inflows, an insufficient increase in interest rates might be unable to garner domestic savings to the extent necessary to carry through the reform process. In such a situation, it is imperative to specify a proper model of interest rate determination which can be integrated into the merged Bank–Fund framework in order to ensure the success of the growth-oriented adjustment programme.

7.3 THEORETICAL MODELS OF INTEREST RATE DETERMINATION

Once the process of financial liberalization gets under way, policy makers are faced with quite a different set of issues because the focus of attention shifts away from investigating the effects of freeing interest rates to examining how interest rates ought in fact to be determined. The interest in this particular issue has been heightened by two factors. The first is the experience of some of the countries in Latin America where domestic interest rates rose to extraordinarily high levels following the implementation of financial reform policies. The second is the evidence that has accumulated over the recent past that high and volatile world interest rates can be partially transmitted into developing countries. Both these factors have been a cause of concern to policy makers and have generated some fundamental questions regarding the behaviour of interest rates in developing countries—in particular, about what should be expected when controls on interest rates are eliminated.

It is obvious that the process of determination of interest rates will be significantly different under alternative degrees of openness of the capital account of the BOP. For example, in the case of countries with a fully open capital account, some form of interest arbitrage will hold, with domestic interest rates depending on world interest rates, expected devaluation, and perhaps some risk factors. In contrast, in countries with a completely closed economy, open-economy factors will obviously play no role whatsoever, and the nominal interest rate will depend only upon expected inflation and the prevailing conditions in the domestic money market. Most developing countries, however, do not fall in either of these two categories, so that interest rates will in general depend both on domestic as well as on foreign money market conditions. From a policy perspective, it is important to determine the way in which these different factors actually affect domestic interest rates, because the success of any growth-oriented adjustment programme depends critically upon an appropriate interest rate policy.

In this context, Edwards and Khan (1985) were probably the first to propose a framework for empirically analysing the determination of nominal interest rates in developing countries. Their model combines features of both closed- and open-economy characteristics and specifically examines the respective influences of domestic monetary conditions and foreign factors on interest rates. Even though the model is quite general, the discussion is carried out with special reference to those developing countries that have liberalized their domestic financial sectors in the sense of removing controls on interest rates.

In this section, which is based on Edwards and Khan (1985), three basic models for analysing interest rate behaviour in developing economies are briefly presented. The first one assumes that the economy is a completely closed one and, consequently, the nominal interest rate depends only on the real interest rate and expected inflation. The second model considers a completely open economy in which case domestic interest rates are closely linked to world interest rates through interest arbitrage. Finally, a more general model that allows both domestic and foreign factors to affect the nominal interest rate, thereby treating the other two models as special cases, is developed and empirically estimated.

7.3.1 *Interest Rates in a Closed Economy*

Following the standard Fisher approach and ignoring, for the time being, the effects of taxation on the relation between expected inflation and the nominal interest rate, we can specify the nominal interest rate as equal to:

$$i = r + \pi^e, \tag{7.1}$$

where i is the nominal rate of interest; r is the real (*exante*) rate of interest; and π^e is the expected rate of inflation.

The real rate of interest can be specified as:

$$r = \rho - \lambda EMS + \omega, \tag{7.2}$$

where ρ is a constant representing the long-run equilibrium real rate of interest; EMS represents the excess supply of money; λ is a parameter ($\lambda > 0$); and ω is a random error term. According to (eqn 7.2), the real rate of interest deviates from its long-run equilibrium level ρ only if there is a monetary disequilibrium in the form of an excess demand for or supply of real money balances. This relation has been termed as the 'liquidity effect' in the literature (Mundell 1963). Introducing this liquidity effect into the model allows the real rate of interest to be variable in the short run. As such, even though the Fisher equation, (eqn 7.1), is assumed to hold continuously, the possibility of a slow adjustment of the real interest rate (given by λ) implicitly allows for the possibility of a delayed response of the nominal interest rate to monetary reform.

Substituting (eqn 7.2) into (eqn 7.1) provides the solution for the nominal interest rate in a closed economy which is given by:

$$i = \rho - \lambda EMS + \pi^e + \omega. \tag{7.3}$$

While the expected rate of inflation could have been modelled in a variety of ways, in this study, we assume, for the sake of simplicity, that the actual and expected rates of inflation are identical, implying a strict form of rational expectations (that is, perfect foresight).

The excess supply of money is defined in this study as:

$$EMS = \ln m - \ln m^d, \tag{7.4}$$

where m ($= M/P$) is the actual stock, and m^d is the desired equilibrium stock, of real money balances.

In an economy that is undergoing a financial reform process, we would expect substitution to take place between both money and goods, as well as between money and financial assets, so that the demand for money would be a function of two opportunity cost variables, that is the expected rate of inflation (π^e) and the rate of interest, along with the scale variable, that is real income (y). The equilibrium demand for money is therefore given by:

$$\ln m^d = \alpha(0) + \alpha(1) \ln y - \alpha(2) [\rho + \pi^e] - \alpha(3) \pi^e. \tag{7.5}$$

It needs to be noted that the long-run equilibrium demand for money is assumed to be a function of the equilibrium nominal interest rate, defined as the sum of the equilibrium real interest rate (ρ) and the expected rate of inflation (π^e), rather than the current nominal interest rate (i).

The model is then closed by assuming that the stock of real money balances adjusts according to:

$$\Delta\ln m = \beta[\ln m^d - \ln m(-1)], \tag{7.6}$$

where $\Delta\ln m = \ln m - \ln m(-1)$; and β ($0 \le \beta \le 1$) is the coefficient of adjustment. If the nominal money supply was completely exogenous, then (eqn 7.6) would have described an adjustment mechanism for domestic prices. In our case, it essentially describes the process by means of which the nominal interest rate returns eventually to its equilibrium level.

Rewriting (eqn 7.6) as:

$$\ln m = \beta \ln m^d + (1 - \beta) \ln m(-1), \tag{7.6a}$$

and combining it with (eqn 7.4) yields:

$$EMS = (1 - \beta) [\ln m(-1) - \ln m^d]. \tag{7.7}$$

Using (eqn 7.3), (eqn 7.5), and (eqn 7.7), we can derive the following reduced-form equation for the nominal interest rate:

$$i = \gamma(0) + \gamma(1) \ln y - \gamma(2) \ln m(-1) + \gamma(3) \pi^e + \omega, \tag{7.8}$$

where the composite parameters are:

$$\gamma(0) = \rho + \lambda(1 - \beta)[\alpha(0) - \alpha(2)\rho],$$
$$\gamma(1) = \lambda(1 - \beta)\alpha(1),$$
$$\gamma(2) = \lambda(1 - \beta),$$
$$\gamma(3) = [1 - \lambda(1 - \beta)\{\alpha(2) + \alpha(3)\}].$$

During estimation of (eqn 7.8), the sign of $\gamma(3)$ would depend on whether $[\lambda(1 - \beta)\{\alpha(2) + \alpha(3)\}]$ is greater or less than unity.

7.3.2   *Interest Rates in an Open Economy*

If the economy is completely open to the rest of the world and there are no impediments to capital flows, domestic and foreign interest rates will be closely linked. In particular, if there are no transaction costs and all agents are assumed to be risk-neutral, then the following uncovered interest arbitrage relationship will hold:

$$i = i_f + e^e, \tag{7.9}$$

where i_f is the world interest rate (for a financial asset of similar characteristics), and e^e is the expected rate of change of the exchange rate, that is $e^e = \Delta E^e / E(-1)$.

If we assume that, because of frictions arising from transactions costs and information lags, domestic interest rates respond with delay to any changes in the foreign rate of interest or in exchange rate expectations, then (eqn 7.9) can be rewritten in a partial adjustment framework as follows:

$$\Delta i = \Theta[\{i_f + e^e\} - i(-1)], \tag{7.10}$$

where Θ is the adjustment parameter, $0 \leq \Theta \leq 1$. If the domestic financial market adjusts rapidly, the parameter Θ will tend towards unity. Conversely, a small value of Θ would imply slow adjustment of the domestic interest rate. The solution of (eqn 7.10) in terms of the domestic interest rate is therefore given by:

$$i = \Theta [i_f + e^e] + (1 - \Theta) i(-1). \tag{7.11}$$

7.3.3   *The General Case*

Having examined interest rate determination under the two polar cases related to the degree of openness of the economy, it is possible to visualize that both open as well as closed economy factors will affect the behaviour of domestic interest rates, at least in the short run. Under the circumstances, we assume that the equation for the nominal interest rate can be specified as a weighted average of the open and closed economy expressions. Denoting these weights by ψ and $(1 - \psi)$, and combining (eqn 7.1) and (eqn 7.11), we obtain:

$$i = \psi[\Theta\{i_f + e^e\} + (1 - \Theta) i(-1)] + (1 - \psi) [r + \pi^e], \tag{7.12}$$

where the parameter ψ can be interpreted as an index measuring the degree of financial openness of the country with ψ ranging from 0 (completely closed economy) to 1 (completely open economy). Thus, given the data, it is possible to determine the degree of openness of the financial sector for a given economy, and this estimated degree of openness will provide some information on the actual degree of integration of the domestic capital market with the world financial markets. Substituting (eqn 7.2), (eqn 7.7), and (eqn 7.5) into (eqn 7.12) above, we obtain the following expression for the nominal interest rate for a semi-open economy:

$$i = \delta(0) + \delta(1) [i_f + e^e] + \delta(2) \ln y - \delta(3) \ln m(-1) + \delta(4) \pi^e$$
$$+ \delta(5) i(-1) + \varepsilon, \qquad \qquad \qquad ...(7.13)$$

where:
$$\delta(0) = (1 - \psi)[\rho + \lambda(1 - \beta)\{\alpha(0) - \alpha(2)\rho\}], (7.14a)$$
$$\delta(1) = \psi\Theta, \qquad \qquad (7.14b)$$
$$\delta(2) = (1 - \psi)\lambda(1 - \beta)\alpha(1), \qquad (7.14c)$$
$$\delta(3) = (1 - \psi)\lambda(1 - \beta), \qquad (7.14d)$$
$$\delta(4) = (1 - \psi) [1 - \lambda(1 - \beta)\{\alpha(2) + \alpha(3)\}], (7.14e)$$
$$\delta(5) = \psi(1 - \Theta), \qquad (7.14f)$$

and ε is a random error term. (Eqn 7.13) is quite general because it not only incorporates closed- and open-economy features, it also permits the possibility of slow adjustment on both the domestic and foreign sides.

7.3.4 Empirical Evidence
To apply the above methodology for the Indian economy, we initially need estimates of i, i_f, π^e, and e^e. The domestic rate of interest (i) was proxied by the 3-year term deposit rate.[2] The foreign rate of interest (i_f) was proxied by the 1-year London Inter-Bank Offer Rate (LIBOR) although, strictly speaking, we should have chosen a financial asset of the same characteristics (maturity and so on) as the 3-year term deposit rate. Both, the expected rate of inflation (π^e) as well as the expected rate of depreciation (e^e) were replaced by the actual rate of inflation (π) and the actual rate of depreciation (e), respectively.[3]

The estimated reduced-form parameters of (eqn 7.13), using annual time-series data on the Indian economy over the period 1970–95, are given below:

$$-0.3815 = \delta(0) = (1 - \psi)[\rho + \lambda(1 - \beta)\{\alpha(0) - \alpha(2)\rho\}], \quad (7.15a)$$
$$0.0540 = \delta(1) = \psi\Theta, \qquad (7.15b)$$
$$0.0549 = \delta(2) = (1 - \psi)\lambda(1 - \beta)\alpha(1), \qquad (7.15c)$$
$$0.0209 = \delta(3) = (1 - \psi)\lambda(1 - \beta), \qquad (7.15d)$$
$$0.0686 = \delta(4) = (1 - \psi)[1 - \lambda(1 - \beta)\{\alpha(2) + \alpha(3)\}], \quad (7.15e)$$
$$0.4594 = \delta(5) = \psi(1 - \Theta). \qquad (7.15f)$$

Based upon the above composite reduced-form parameters, the following information on the Indian economy can be extracted: (1) Adding together (eqn 7.15b) and (eqn 7.15f) yields $\psi = 0.5134$ implying that the current index of financial openness is about 0.5 on a scale ranging from 0 (completely closed economy) to 1 (completely open economy). This estimated index of openness thus provides some information on the actual degree of integration of the Indian capital market with the world financial markets. (2) Substituting this result into either of these two equations yields $\Theta = 0.1052$, implying slow adjustment of the domestic interest rate to a change in either the foreign interest rate or the exchange rate. (3) The coefficient of $i(-1)$, given by $\delta(5)$, is equal to 0.4594, implying that the time-constant of the lag in adjustment of the nominal interest rate is about 1.28 years.[4]

In order to predict the equilibrium interest rate for the Indian economy for 1996–7, we have to project the independent variables in (eqn 7.13). These projections are as follows:[5] (i) the set of exogenous variables: $e = 0.1061$, $\pi = 0.0933$, $\ln y = 12.5154$, and $i_f = 0.0590$; and (ii) the set of predetermined variables: $i(-1) = 0.12$ and $\ln m(-1) = 12.0539$. Substituting these values into (eqn 7.13) above and using the estimated parameters provided in (eqn 7.15a)–(eqn 7.15f) yields: $i = 0.1241$ implying that the 3-year term deposit rate, which was set at 12 per cent, should have been increased to about 12.4 per cent which was its actual equilibrium level.

However, this recursive forecast ignores the possibility of an interactive feedback between interest rates and growth. As discussed in Section 7.2, higher interest rates would increase savings which would translate itself into increased investment and growth. And this, in turn, via (eqn 7.13) would imply a still higher interest rate. As the ensuing positive feedback would result in, both, higher growth as well as interest rates, the estimation of an equilibrium level of the interest rate needs to be carried out within such a simultaneous framework. This is why it is necessary to integrate the interest rate into the merged Bank–Fund model (RM3) developed in Chapter 6 to ensure the joint determination of the interest rate, along with the BOP, inflation, and growth.

7.4   INTEGRATING THE INTEREST RATE INTO THE MERGED MODEL

From a policy perspective, it is essential to determine the way in which such a feedback can actually affect equilibrium growth and interest rates. For example, the manner in which changes in domestic monetary conditions and expected devaluation affect interest rates in developing countries is crucial for assessing the significance of one of the possible mechanisms by means of which stabilization policies can affect aggregate demand. Most stabilization programmes typically involve both tighter credit policies as well as devaluation to restrain demand and if these policies generate an increase in the domestic interest rate, there will be an additional channel (usually overlooked in formal studies on growth-oriented adjustment programmes in developing countries) through which aggregate demand will be affected. By overlooking the role of the interest rate in the transmission process while analysing the effects of stabilization policies on output, prices, and the BOP, the danger of implementing an 'overkill' strategy, which is a criticism most often directed against stabilization programmes in developing countries, can never be ruled out.

In order to pre-empt this possibility, it will now be shown how the above interest-rate determination equation can be ideally integrated into the merged Bank–Fund model developed in Chapter 6 so as to ensure an additional channel through which growth impulses can be transmitted into the economy.

7.4.1 The Core

The basic components for designing such an integrated model, referred to as the Representative Model—Version 4 (RM4), are set out below. All the derivations spelt out for RM3, which is the direct precursor of the current version, remain relevant for the ensuing analysis.

The equation defining monetary sector equilibrium continues to be given by (eqn 6.53) which is provided below for convenience:

$$\Delta R^* - \alpha(1)\pi - \alpha(2)g = -\alpha(3)\,\Delta DC - \alpha(4)e, \qquad (7.16)$$

where $\alpha(1)$, $\alpha(2)$, $\alpha(3)$, and $\alpha(4)$ are given by (eqn 6.54a)–(eqn 6.54c).

The equation defining external sector equilibrium continues to be given by (eqn 6.65) which is provided below for convenience:

$$\Delta R^* + \beta(1)\pi + \beta(2)g = \beta(3)e + \Delta F^* + \beta(4), \qquad (7.17)$$

where $\beta(1)$, $\beta(2)$, $\beta(3)$, and $\beta(4)$ are given by (eqn 6.66a)–(eqn 6.66d).

It is now assumed, following the discussion in Section 7.2, that nominal savings (S) are a linear function of nominal income (Y) and the nominal interest rate (i). Therefore, we have:

$$S = sY + \iota i, \qquad (7.18)$$

where s is the marginal propensity to save, and ι measures the responsiveness of savings to the interest rate.

Taking first-differences of (eqn 7.18) and writing in terms of S yields:

$$S = S(-1) + s(g + \pi) \, Y(-1) + \iota\Delta i, \qquad\qquad (7.19)$$

which is obtained by replacing ΔY by its definition given by (eqn 4.16).

Substituting (eqn 7.19) into (eqn 6.7) yields the following relationship between investment, growth, inflation, reserves, and the interest rate:

$$I = S(-1) + s(g + \pi) \, Y(-1) + \iota\Delta i + \Delta F - \Delta R. \qquad (7.20)$$

Replacing ΔF and ΔR by their definitions given by (eqn 6.56) and (eqn 6.51), respectively, and substituting the result into (eqn 6.69) yields:

$$
\begin{aligned}
g = {} & ks(-1) + ks(g + \pi) + k[\iota^*/Y^*(-1)]\Delta i + k[1/Y^*(-1)]\Delta F^* \\
& + k[F^*(-1)/Y^*(-1)]e - k[1/Y^*(-1)]\Delta R^* \\
& - k[R^*(-1)/Y^*(-1)]e - d - d\pi, \qquad\qquad ...(7.21)
\end{aligned}
$$

where $\iota^* = \iota/E(-1)$.[6] This can be written as:

$$
\gamma(1)\Delta R^* + \gamma(2)\pi + \gamma(3)g - \gamma(7)i = -\gamma(8)\, i(-1) + \gamma(4)e + \gamma(5)\Delta F^* \\
+ \gamma(6), \qquad\qquad ...(7.22)
$$

where, as before, $\gamma(1)$, $\gamma(2)$, $\gamma(3)$, $\gamma(4)$, $\gamma(5)$ and $\gamma(6)$ continue to be given by (eqn 6.72a)–(eqn 6.72e); and where:

$$\gamma(7) = \gamma(8) = k[\iota^*/Y^*(-1)]. \qquad\qquad (7.23)$$

It needs to be noted that in the above formulation, apart from ΔR^*, π, and g, the rate of interest (i) becomes an additional target.

7.4.2   *The Integration*

We now have to formally integrate the nominal interest rate determination equation, given by (eqn 7.13), into the merged model given above. In order to do so, we initially simplify (eqn 7.13) and assume that the income elasticity of the demand for money is unity, that is $\alpha(1) = 1$. In such a case, from (eqn 7.14c) and (eqn 7.14d), it is seen that $\delta(2) = \delta(3)$, and real income and lagged money balances can be combined into one composite term, that is $[\ln y - \ln m(-1)]$, while estimating (eqn 7.13).

Therefore, (eqn 7.13) can now be rewritten as:

$$i = \delta(0) + \delta(1) \, [i_f + e] + \delta(2) \, [\ln y - \ln m(-1)] + \delta(4)\pi + \delta(5)i(-1), \\
(7.24)$$

where, in line with the empirical testing of the model in Section 7.3.4, we have set $\pi^e = \pi$ and $e^e = e$, and the error term ε has been dropped.

Considering that: $y = (1 + g) y(-1)$ and $v = y/m$, that is velocity is the ratio of real income to real money stock, (eqn 7.24) can be further simplified to yield the following expression:[7]

$$i = \delta(0) + \delta(1) [i_f + e] + \delta(2)g + \delta(2)\ln v(-1) + \delta(4)\pi + \delta(5)i(-1).$$

$$(7.25)$$

It is thus obvious that the above equation is easily capable of being integrated into the merged framework as the interest rate is seen to be influenced by two of the three targets of the merged model, that is inflation (π) and growth (g), as well as by an instrument, that is exchange rate changes (e).

(Eqn 7.25) can be rewritten as:

$$-\delta(4)\pi - \delta(2)g + i = \delta(5) i(-1) + \delta(1)e + \delta(6), \qquad (7.26)$$

where: $\quad \delta(6) = \delta(0) + \delta(1)i_f + \delta(2) \ln v(-1) \qquad (7.27)$

The structure of the integrated model, comprising (eqn 7.16), (eqn 7.17), (eqn 7.22), and (eqn 7.25), is set out in Table 7.1.[8]

TABLE 7.1   STRUCTURE OF THE INTEGRATED APPROACH

Targets	ΔR^*	: change in foreign exchange reserves
	π	: rate of inflation
	g	: real growth rate
	i	: nominal interest rate
Lagged Target	$i(-1)$	: nominal interest rate in the previous period
Instruments	ΔDC	: change in domestic credit
	e	: rate of change in the nominal exchange rate
	ΔF^*	: change in foreign borrowings
Exogenous	X^*	: exports
	π_f	: foreign inflation rate
	i_f	: foreign interest rate
Predetermined	$Y^*(-1)$	: nominal income in the previous period
	$Z^*(-1)$	: nominal imports in the previous period
	$R^*(-1)$	: stock of foreign exchange reserves in the previous period
	$F^*(-1)$	: stock of foreign debt in the previous period

Table 7.1 contd.

Table 7.1 contd.

	$E(-1)$	: nominal exchange rate in the previous period
	$s(-1)$	: savings propensity in the previous period
	$v(-1)$	: velocity in the previous period
Parameters	v	: velocity of money
	m	: marginal propensity to import
	b	: import response to exchange rate changes
	s	: marginal propensity to save
	k	: incremental output–capital ratio
	d	: depreciation rate
	ι^*	: savings response to interest rate changes

7.5 POLICY ANALYSIS WITH THE INTEGRATED MODEL

In order to obtain insights into the dynamic structure of the integrated model, we rewrite (eqn 7.16), (eqn 7.17), (eqn 7.22), and (eqn 7.25) in matrix notation:

$$\begin{bmatrix} 1 & -\alpha(1) & -\alpha(2) & 0 \\ 1 & \beta(1) & \beta(2) & 0 \\ \gamma(1) & \gamma(2) & \gamma(3) & -\gamma(7) \\ 0 & -\delta(4) & -\delta(2) & 1 \end{bmatrix} \begin{bmatrix} \Delta R^* \\ \pi \\ g \\ i \end{bmatrix} = \begin{bmatrix} 0 & 0 & 0 & 0 \\ 0 & 0 & 0 & 0 \\ 0 & 0 & 0 & -\gamma(8) \\ 0 & 0 & 0 & \delta(5) \end{bmatrix} \begin{bmatrix} \Delta R^*(-1) \\ \pi(-1) \\ g(-1) \\ i(-1) \end{bmatrix}$$

$$+ \begin{bmatrix} -\alpha(3) & -\alpha(4) & 0 \\ 0 & \beta(3) & 1 \\ 0 & \gamma(4) & \gamma(5) \\ 0 & \delta(1) & 0 \end{bmatrix} \begin{bmatrix} \Delta DC \\ e \\ \Delta F^* \end{bmatrix} + \begin{bmatrix} 0 \\ \beta(4) \\ \gamma(6) \\ \delta(6) \end{bmatrix} \qquad \dots(7.28)$$

which can be written as:

$$A(0)\ x = A(1)\ x(-1) + B(0)\ u + z(0), \qquad (7.29)$$

where: $x = [\Delta R^*\ \pi\ g\ i]'$ is a (4×1) target vector, and
            $x(-1) = [\Delta R^*(-1)\ \pi(-1)\ g(-1)\ i(-1)]'$ is a (4×1)
            lagged target vector.

It is the presence of the lagged state (target) vector, that is $x(-1)$, which converts the hitherto static model into a dynamic one. Solving (eqn 7.29) for x yields the following positive mode of the integrated system:

$$x = Ax(-1) + Bu + z, \qquad (7.30)$$

where: $A = A(0)^{-1}A(1),$ \qquad (7.31a)

$$B = A(0)^{-1}B(0), \tag{7.31b}$$
$$z = A(0)^{-1}z(0). \tag{7.31c}$$

In order to apply the above integrated theory to the Indian economy for determining growth-oriented adjustment guidelines for 1996–7, we require the following additional data (apart from those listed for RM3 in Section 6.5.1) which are given below: (i) the lagged target variable: $i(-1) = 0.12$; (ii) the exogenous variable: $i_f = 0.0590$; (iii) the predetermined variable: $\ln v(-1) = 0.4052$; and (iv) the parameter $\iota^* = 357.92$. The complete data set, along with (eqn 7.15), (eqn 7.23), and (eqn 7.27), yields the following additional parameters which are necessary for solving the model.[9]

$$\delta(1) = 0.0540 \qquad \delta(4) = 0.0686 \qquad \gamma(7) = 0.3029$$
$$\delta(2) = 0.9430 \qquad \delta(5) = 0.4594 \qquad \gamma(8) = 0.3029$$
$$\delta(6) = 0.0038$$

Substituting these above parameters, along with those given in Section 6.5.2, into (eqn 7.28) yields the estimated form of (eqn 7.30) given by:

$$\begin{bmatrix} \Delta R^* \\ \pi \\ g \\ i \end{bmatrix} = \begin{bmatrix} 0 & 0 & 0 & 15.6575 \\ 0 & 0 & 0 & 0.3567 \\ 0 & 0 & 0 & -0.2362 \\ 0 & 0 & 0 & 0.2611 \end{bmatrix} \begin{bmatrix} \Delta R^*(-1) \\ \pi(-1) \\ g(-1) \\ i(-1) \end{bmatrix}$$

$$+ \begin{bmatrix} -0.009710 & 58.171940 & 0.675352 \\ 0.000130 & 0.517686 & 0.004352 \\ 0.000025 & 0.061003 & 0.000844 \\ 0.000033 & 0.147039 & 0.001094 \end{bmatrix} \begin{bmatrix} \Delta DC \\ e \\ \Delta F^* \end{bmatrix} + \begin{bmatrix} -6.29006 \\ -0.11073 \\ 0.06234 \\ 0.05499 \end{bmatrix}.$$

$$\dots(7.32)$$

The *exante* forecasts of the four targets (ΔR^*, π, g, and i) for 1996–7 can be obtained by setting: (i) the lagged target variable at its historical level for 1995–6 given above, that is $i(-1) = 0.12$; and (ii) the three instruments at their predicted levels for 1996–7 (given in Section 6.5.1), that is $\Delta DC = 650$, $e = 0.1061$ and $\Delta F^* = 4.11$. This yields: $\Delta R^* = -1.77$, $\pi = 0.0895$, $g = 0.0603$, and $i = 0.1277$, implying a reserve drawdown of about $ 1.8 billion, an inflation rate of about 9.0 per cent, a growth rate of about 6.0 per cent, and an (equilibrium) interest rate of about 12.8 per cent. Thus, it is seen that by integrating the rate of interest into the merged Bank–Fund framework, the ensuing positive feedback between growth and interest rates results in higher growth and lower inflation (*vis-à-vis* the forecasts obtained using RM3 in Section 6.5.2) with the same policy setting. This clearly highlights the role of monetary reform with an appropriate interest rate policy in determining the eventual success of any growth-oriented adjustment programme.

7.5.1 *Designing a Consistent Interest Rate Policy*

Once again, the excess of targets (ΔR^*, π, g, i) over instruments (ΔDC, e, ΔF^*) makes it impossible to solve the model in its pure programming mode. However, as before, heuristic guidepost solutions for deriving a 'robust' policy can still be obtained.

To do so, we pre-multiply (eqn 7.30) by B and solve the resultant expression uniquely in terms of u obtaining:

$$u = B^*x - z^*, \tag{7.33}$$

where: $B^* = (B'B)^{-1}B'$, (7.34a)

$z^* = (B'B)^{-1}B'[Ax(-1) + z]$, (7.34b)

which will exist considering that the inverse of $B'B$ exists.

Using the estimated matrices A, B and z specified in (eqn 7.32) above, and setting $i(-1) = 0.12$, we obtain the estimated form of (eqn 7.33) which, when expanded, yields the following set of equations:

$$\Delta DC = -33.4\ \Delta R^* + 3489.1\pi + 16328.9g - 5827.2i + 37.391,$$
$$\tag{7.35a}$$
$$e = 1.6898\pi - 21.2536g + 9.6690i + 0.0027 \tag{7.35b}$$
$$\Delta F^* = 1.0\ \Delta R^* - 95.407\pi + 2065.39g - 916.60i + 6.8471 \tag{7.35c}$$

However, as noted in Section 6.3.4, the above set of policy response functions constitutes only a 'heuristic' version of the programming mode because although it does prescribe the levels at which the three instruments should be set on the basis of the four desired targets, this policy setting will be unable to attain all the targets simultaneously and there will be a certain amount of deviation between the desired and realized targets. However, the ensuing policy prescription will be the most 'robust' one in as much as the sum of squared deviations between the desired values of the three targets and their respective realizations will be minimal.

Based upon the results of the previous section, which clearly indicated how a well-integrated interest rate policy can complement an adjustment programme, the objective in this section is to design an even more ambitious growth-oriented stabilization package (than the one attempted in Section 6.5.4) and obtain guidelines regarding the spectrum of alternative 'robust' policy options which can attain the desired objectives.

As such, we target a 6.25 per cent growth rate and a 8.25 per cent inflation rate. Therefore, setting $g = 0.0625$ and $\pi = 0.0825$ in (eqn 7.35) above yields:

$$\Delta DC = -33.4\Delta R^* - 5827.2i + 1345.8, \qquad (7.36a)$$
$$e = 9.6690i - 1.1862, \qquad (7.36b)$$
$$\Delta F^* = 1.0\Delta R^* - 916.60i + 128.06. \qquad (7.36c)$$

The above system which is now used to determine 'robust' policy options comprises a set of three equations in five unknowns which implies that *any* two of them (except the combination e and i) can be targeted exogenously and this would yield solutions for the remaining three. However, a monetary-reform perspective would suggest that the interest rate ought to be determined endogenously and, as such, we shall not target it *à priori*. Therefore, with two degrees of freedom and with only four variables to choose from, this implies that we have six alternative stabilization options. The results of these alternative simulation exercises are provided in Table 7.2.[10]

The results clearly highlight that there exist a wide spectrum of alternative and, more important, feasible policy options which are capable of attaining the desired objectives (of a 6.25 per cent growth rate with a 8.25 per cent inflation rate). Options 1 and 2 are essentially base-run scenarios obtained by setting the concerned variables at either their projected levels or forecasts or both.[11] By and large, they indicate that if credit expansion and the exchange rate remain in the neighbourhood of their current projections, then the nominal interest rate needs to be increased to about 13.3 per cent. In such a case, the desired level of foreign borrowings (ΔF^*) can be substantially reduced by almost 25 per cent with the offsetting amount of reserve drawdown (ΔR^*) remaining within tolerable levels.

Options 3 and 4 are diametrically opposed to each other and provide an interesting study in contrasts. The former is essentially a 'cold turkey' strategy as it calls for a strong dose of credit restraint and devaluation (the classic Fund prescriptions) coupled with a substantial increase in the interest rate. Contrariwise, the latter invokes a highly expansionary credit policy coupled to a milder devaluation and a lesser increase in the interest rate. However, and this is important, both of them track the desired growth and inflation objectives, and thus the criticism that Fund policies necessarily involve a slow-down in growth is not warranted. Moreover, the second strategy requires a higher level of foreign borrowings and entails a much greater drawdown of foreign exchange reserves and, to that extent, it is unsustainable in the long-run, which is the reason as to why macroeconomic management, comprising credit, exchange rate, and interest rate policy, is so important, not only for short-run stabilization, but for long-term growth as well.

TABLE 7.2   INTEREST RATE POLICY AND STABILIZATION OPTIONS

Option	ΔDC	e	ΔF^*	ΔR^*	i
1	(650)	(0.1061)	3.02	−2.49	0.1337
2	628.2	0.1027	(4.11)	(−1.77)	0.1333
3	581.3	(0.1250)	(3.00)	−0.77	0.1356
4	(675)	0.0959	(3.50)	−3.02	0.1326
5	(600)	0.1210	2.89	(−1.25)	0.1352
6	638.4	(0.1125)	2.71	(−2.25)	0.1343

Options 5 and 6 are basically 'gradualist' strategies with a lesser 'compressionary' bias towards credit expansion. The latter option, which seems to be the most feasible one in terms of implementation, broadly suggests that a moderate restraint in credit expansion coupled to a higher-than-projected depreciation in the rupee needs to be accompanied by a substantially higher interest rate of about 13.4 per cent. This would allow the desired objectives to be realized with a much lesser requirement of foreign borrowings, although it will involve a slightly higher-than-projected level of reserve drawdown.

The most important lesson learnt from these exercises is that, unlike in the earlier chapter involving RM3, most of these policy options are feasible and sustainable as they do not involve excessive reliance on foreign borrowings or reserve depletion. Thus, by integrating the interest rate in the merged Bank–Fund framework, the RM4 is better suited for analysing alternative stabilization options as it invokes the underlying complementarity between monetary reform and growth-oriented adjustment programmes.

7.6 CONCLUSIONS

All this highlights the need for sound financial policies to back growth-oriented adjustment programmes in order to create an atmosphere of confidence in the future of an economy and its management. Without such confidence, savings will tend to be transferred abroad and private investors will either postpone or cancel domestic capital investments. One of the unfortunate consequences of weak confidence in macroeconomic management is that domestic interest rates would have to be raised to very high levels to avoid capital flight, but at such levels, borrowings for productive purposes could well be discouraged leading to a dampening of economic activity.

Therefore, changes in interest rates and other financial reforms must be coordinated with the policy actions that are part of the stabilization programme. The experiences of a number of developing countries with financial reform seem to suggest that this coordination is especially vital during the early phases of the adjustment programme. In particular, certain combinations of policies can be potentially destabilizing for a financial system undergoing major structural change. For example, if a large fiscal deficit is being financed through excessive issuance of central bank credit to the government, then there could be limited scope for the successful implementation of a sound interest rate policy or a financial reform programme. The rapid monetary growth and inflation that would be associated with such a fiscal deficit could potentially lead to destabilizing changes in the flow of funds in and out of the financial system as well as between different types of financial institutions or instruments. The inability to control fiscal deficits is often considered to be one of the most important factors that contribute to the failure of growth-oriented adjustment programmes and, as such, until the fiscal accounts can be brought under control, major financial reforms may have to be deferred.

While all these potential pitfalls make the process of monetary reform and financial liberalization a rather hazardous one, they should not be viewed as a rationale for maintaining high negative yields on domestic financial instruments and an inefficient financial system. While growth-oriented adjustment programmes often warrant a sharp increase in interest rates, very often such an excessive increase could affect investment and create problems with capital flows. In such a situation, it may be more appropriate to adjust interest rates gradually as the new stabilization and financial reform policies take hold. For this to be successful, however, the public would have to believe that the authorities were committed to carrying out the reforms based on realistic objectives. If such a perception is established, then the maintenance of positive yields on domestic financial instruments would strengthen domestic savings and the financial system.

With many developing countries irrevocably committed to liberalizing their domestic financial systems, the twin issues of interest rate determination, in general, and the manner in which interest rates can be expected to behave in the changed environment and respond to domestic and foreign influences, in particular, are becoming increasingly important. Only when the behaviour of interest rates is well understood will it be possible to predict its effects on key macroeconomic variables such as BOP, inflation, savings, investment, and, above all, economic growth. After all, to affect these variables is the real purpose for which liberalization policies have to be designed.

NOTES

[1]It needs to be noted that such a finding is equally consistent with causation from growth to interest rates, or from a common third factor (such as inflation) to both growth and interest rates.

[2]Both, the domestic interest rate (i) and the world interest rate (i_f) were measured, not in terms of percentage points, but as rates in order to make them compatible with the inflation rate (π) and the rate of change in the exchange rate (e). Thus, $i = 0.10$ would imply a 10 per cent interest rate.

[3]The expected rate of inflation could have been specified in a variety of other ways. One of them would have been to use the traditional adaptive expectations model, in which the expected rate of inflation is assumed to be a (geometrically) distributed lag function of the past rates of inflation. An empirical generalization of this approach is to assume an autoregressive process for the rate of inflation and to use the predicted values as representing the expected rate of inflation. In such a formulation, the weights of the lag distribution are not assumed to follow any specific pattern. It was seen that using such a methodology did not produce any significant difference in the results. As there is no compelling theoretical reason for preferring one method over any other, the choice was ultimately governed by the fact that by assuming $\pi^e = \pi$ and $e^e = e$, it would be possible to directly integrate (eqn 7.13) into the merged Bank–Fund framework which is, indeed, our primary objective.

[4]Given an autoregressive model: $Y(t) = \alpha + \beta X(t) + \lambda Y(t-1)$, the time constant of the lag, which is given by $-(1/\ln \lambda)$, indicates the time required for the first half, or 50 per cent, of the total change in Y following a unit sustained change in X. Thus, in our case, with $\delta(5) = 0.4594$, the time constant

of the lag is: $-(1/\ln 0.4594) = 1.2856$, implying that 50 per cent of the total change in the domestic interest rate, as a result of a unit sustained change in any of the independent variables, would be completed in about 1.29 years.

[5]In RM3 (see Section 6.5.1), it is seen that by setting $e = 0.1061$ *inter alia* implies that $\pi = 0.0933$ and $g = 0.0581$. The latter estimate, along with $y(-1) = 257579$, implies that $\ln y = 12.5154$. Thus, these three variables, that is e, π, and $\ln y$, form a consistent set of exogenous variables which, along with the given values of i_f, $i(-1)$, and $\ln m(-1)$, are used to forecast the nominal interest rate.

[6]It should be noted that:

$$\frac{\iota}{Y(-1)} = \frac{\iota}{E(-1)} \frac{E(-1)}{Y(-1)} = \frac{\iota^*}{Y^*(-1)}. \tag{7.a}$$

[7]The term $[\ln y - \ln m(-1)]$ can be written as $[\ln (1 + g) + \ln y(-1) - \ln m(-1)]$ considering that: $y = (1 + g) y(-1)$ and $\ln ab = \ln a + \ln b$. Now, we know that for small values of g, $\ln (1 + g) \approx g$, and therefore the expression reduces to: $[g + \ln y(-1) - \ln m(-1)]$. Given that $v = y/m$, we have $\ln v = \ln y - \ln m$. Lagging this equality by one period and substituting it in the above expression yields: $[g + \ln v(-1)]$. This helps to converts (eqn 7.24) into (eqn 7.25).

[8]All starred (*) variables indicate that they are measured in terms of foreign currency units which, in our case, happens to be US dollars ($).

[9]The parameters $\gamma(7)$ and $\gamma(8)$ were derived from (eqn 7.23). We obtained $\delta(0)$, $\delta(1)$, $\delta(4)$, and $\delta(5)$ from (eqn 7.15a), (eqn 7.15b), (eqn 7.15e), and (eqn 7.15f). The parameters $\delta(2)$ and $\delta(3)$, given by (eqn 7.15c) and (eqn 7.15d), were not applicable in this case as, by assuming $\alpha(1) = 1$, we were implying that $\delta(2) = \delta(3)$. Therefore, the parameter $\delta(2)$ was obtained by re-estimating (eqn 7.13) using restricted least squares as follows:

$$i^* = \delta(2) [\ln y - \ln m(-1)], \tag{7.b}$$

where: $i^* = i - \delta(0) - \delta(1)[i_f + e] - \delta(4)\pi - \delta(5)i(-1)$. This procedure yielded: $\delta(2) = 0.9430$ which, along with $\delta(0)$, $\delta(1)$, and the estimates of $v(-1)$ and i_f, yielded $\delta(6) = 0.0038$ by using (eqn 7.27).

[10]In each of the options, the two figures in parentheses are the values fixed exogenously for the corresponding target variables. The 3-equation system was then solved for the remaining 3 unknowns.

[11]Based upon Section 7.5, in Option 1, we set the two target variables at: $\Delta DC = 650$ and $e = 0.1061$ which were their corresponding projections; and in Option 2, we set the two target variables at: $\Delta F^* = 4.11$ and $\Delta R^* = -1.77$ which were their corresponding projection and forecast, respectively.

8

Fiscal Adjustments, Deficits, and Growth

8.1 ANALYTICAL ASPECTS OF FISCAL POLICY

In the broadest possible sense, fiscal policy encompasses the government's spending, taxing, and financing decisions. Most of these issues fall in the area related to public finance. Two of these issues are particularly important. The first issue concerns the size of the budget deficit with its resulting implications for absorption and the external balance. The second issue concerns the financing of imbalances in the budget with its ensuing consequences on inflation and debt.

8.1.1 *The Size of the Deficit*

A change in fiscal policy, whether through changes in government spending or taxes, will be reflected in changes in the size of the budget deficit which will directly affect aggregate demand and hence, via absorption, the allocation of resources and the external balance. Public sector spending on currently-produced goods and services is itself a component of total domestic spending and this, of course, represents a direct contribution to absorption. If government spending is limited only to non-tradeable goods, they also represent an addition to aggregate demand for domestic goods. On the other hand, government spending on traded goods will only contribute to a worsening of the trade balance while having no effects on real aggregate demand or output.

However, it is the indirect effects of government expenditures that have generated some controversy. The crux of the issue is whether an increase in public sector expenditures reduces or increases private sector spending. There are a variety of mechanisms through which private spending would fall as a result of increased public spending. For example, increased public spending could raise domestic economic activity and thereby the private sector's demand for money. If interest rates adjust to maintain portfolio balance, then the higher interest rates associated with the increased demand for money would, other things remaining equal, tend to reduce aggregate demand. This is, of course, the familiar 'financial crowding out' hypothesis associated with the IS–LM approach. Even if interest rates do not adjust immediately, and portfolio imbalances persist, the excess demand for money may cause households to curtail spending in order to accumulate cash balances.

Private spending can also be reduced if the increased public spending gives rise to an equal tax liability for the private sector, either in the present through tax-financing or in the future through the need to retire the additional public debt associated with the increased public spending. This is the well-known 'Ricardian equivalence' proposition developed by Barro (1974). Finally, if nominal wages are flexible, or if the increase in public spending was foreseen at the time when wage contracts were entered into, then the domestic price level could rise sufficiently enough to reduce private spending by an amount equal to the increase in public spending, thereby leaving total aggregate demand unchanged. This 'policy neutrality' result has come to be known as the Lucas–Sargent–Wallace (LSW) proposition (Lucas 1972, Sargent and Wallace 1975) although the validity of such rational-expectations models relating public and private sector expenditures has yet to be proved for developing countries.

Tax receipts from the private sector have no direct effect on total absorption. They do, however, affect private disposable income and will therefore have an indirect effect on private spending. The effects of a given tax on private spending will depend *inter alia* on whether the tax is viewed as permanent or temporary (temporary taxes are expected to reduce savings), and on the nature of the financial system (which will affect the extent to which taxpayers are liquidity-constrained). Transfers are essentially the negative of taxes and, consequently, an increase in transfer payments should increase private absorption. Their effects on total domestic absorption will, however, depend on how the government finances these transfer payments.

In summary, therefore, the effects of fiscal policy on overall aggregate demand would appear to be more complex than standard Keynesian macroeconomics would seem to suggest. Ultimately, whether a restrictionary fiscal policy would, on balance, reduce aggregate demand (and therefore growth) or not is an empirical issue which will require to be tested.

8.1.2   *Financing the Deficit*

Rapid increases in fiscal deficits are often the source of macroeconomic imbalances, primarily because of the manner in which they are financed, and it is often argued that the key to successful stabilization is a lower fiscal deficit. However, even if fiscal deficits are not the original source of imbalance, an improvement in the current account can take place only if public savings rise relative to public investment, with the savings–investment gap of the private sector remaining unchanged (see Dornbusch and Helmers 1988).

The overall government budget constraint, (eqn 2.11) shows that a fiscal deficit can be financed through three ways: (i) increased domestic credit from the banking system (ΔDCg); (ii) an increase in borrowings from the private sector (ΔB); and (iii) an increase in foreign borrowings (ΔFg). However, financing from these three different sources will have dissimilar impacts on BOP, inflation, and growth.

The most visible dangers of borrowing from either the banking system or from abroad is that both of them imply an expansion in money supply[1] which is inflationary. On the other hand, the direct effects of domestic or external borrowings is the increased future costs of debt servicing. As these costs are not very apparent, governments may overborrow and sink into a debt crisis. Even if they do not, the arithmetical fact remains that by the very act of borrowing, there is an increase in, both, the interest burden of the debt and *ceteris paribus* future fiscal deficits which, in turn, would require additional financing. Moreover, by borrowing from the private sector, interest rates will increase and may either crowd out private investment, leading to a fall in output, or force the private sector to borrow from the banking system (ΔDCp) or from abroad (ΔFp), both of them leading to a further expansion in the money supply.

However, not all money-financed deficits need to be inflationary. Some increase in money demand might occur due to real growth or because of an expansion in the monetized sector of the economy. Thus, if output is below capacity limits, money-financed deficits can be used to stimulate economic development.[2] Under such circumstances, the expansion in money supply can be absorbed without causing inflation. However, if output is close to capacity limits, closing the fiscal deficit through monetization implies that a part of the fiscal deficit is transferred to the private sector through the inflation tax mechanism.[3] However, because inflation tax reduces private spending, it does not leave behind the burden of debt for the future.

While this might seem to justify resorting to inflationary finance, the consequences of such a strategy become most imminent when the inflation tax revenue starts falling with rising inflation because this usually signals the onset of hyperinflation (see Rao and Bhogle 1990) which is invariably accompanied by massive portfolio shifts out of money. Vast reserves of foreign exchange would be lost if the central bank then decides to defend the existing exchange rate; if it did not, the exchange rate would collapse. In this sense, borrowing from abroad seems a less visible way of running deficits because the exchange rate crisis can be postponed, until such time that credit rationing in the world markets suddenly opens a foreign exchange gap (Dornbusch 1988).

8.2   SOME UNPLEASANT FISCAL ARITHMETIC

'Milton Friedman's famous statement that inflation is always and everywhere a monetary phenomenon is correct. However, while rapid money growth is conceivable without an underlying fiscal balance, it is unlikely. Thus rapid inflation is almost always a fiscal phenomenon' (Fischer and Easterly 1990, p. 138–9). This interaction between monetary and fiscal policy exemplified by the relationship between fiscal deficits and inflation is often considered the heart of macroeconomics and has been the focus of extensive empirical research. For instance, Haan and Zelhorst (1990) investigated the relationship between government deficits and money growth in seventeen developing countries over the period 1961–85 and found strong support for a positive long-run relationship between budget deficits and inflation in high-inflation countries. Various arguments have been proposed to explain the presence of close correlations between budget deficits and inflation. One common explanation for the inflationary consequences of fiscal deficits in developing countries is the lack of sufficiently developed domestic capital markets that can absorb newly issued government debt. Moreover, in many developing countries, the central bank, being under the direct control of the government, often passively finances deficits through money creation.

On a purely theoretical plane, however, there is an appealing argument which relies on the existence of strong expectational effects linked to perceptions about future government policy. Private agents in an economy with high fiscal deficits may at different times form different expectations about how the deficit will eventually be closed. For instance, if the public believes at a given moment that the government will attempt to reduce its fiscal deficit through inflation (thus eroding the real value of the public debt), current inflation—which reflects expectations of future price increases—will rise. If, later on, the public starts believing that the government will eventually introduce an effective fiscal adjustment programme to lower the deficit, inflationary expectations will adjust downwards and current inflation—reflecting, once again, expectations about the future behaviour of prices—will fall (see Drazen and Helpman 1990).

In this context, a particularly well-known example of the role of expectations about future policy is provided by the 'monetarist arithmetic' or the so-called tight-money paradox. In a seminal contribution, Sargent and Wallace (1981) showed that when a financing constraint forces the government to finance its deficit through the inflation tax, any attempts to lower the rate today, even if successful, will require a higher inflation rate tomorrow. For a given level of government spending and 'conventional' taxes, the reduction in revenue from money creation raises the level of government borrowing. If a solvency constraint imposes an upper limit on public debt, the government will be forced to eventually return to money financing. At that stage, however, the rate of money growth will be much higher as it will have to finance not only the original primary deficit that prevailed before the initial policy change, but also the higher interest payments due to the additional debt accumulated as a result of the policy change. Solvency and macroeconomic consistency thus impose constraints on policy options in attempts to reduce the long-run inflation rate.

In their theoretical analysis of the interaction between monetary and fiscal policy, Sargent and Wallace focus primarily on the case where the time paths of both government spending and tax revenues are fixed—a situation in which it is the central bank that must, by design, eventually give in to the fiscal authority. However, the same framework is equally applicable to the case where the central bank moves first and sets policy independently. Here, lower rates of money growth sooner or later require lower fiscal deficits, and, in this modified framework, it is therefore the fiscal authority that must capitulate to the central bank.

Thus, given such a long-run constraint on deficit growth, it can be argued that if the fiscal authority faces an independent central bank committed to an anti-inflationary policy, then the expectation that deficits will not be accommodated tomorrow may deter the government from running a high deficit today (see Burdekin and Langdana 1992). The possible importance of such a reverse direction of influence was originally suggested by Sargent (1985), who characterized the combination of tight money and large deficits suggested at the inception of the Reagan administration as coordination via resort to a 'game of chicken'. Here, 'if the monetary authority could successfully stick to its guns and forever refuse to monetize any government debt, then eventually the arithmetic of the government's budget constraint would compel the fiscal authority to back down and to swing its budget back into balance' (Sargent 1985, p. 248). Under such circumstances, if the central bank does not yield by monetizing (a large proportion of) the deficit, then fiscal policy is necessarily constrained.

It follows therefore that if no further borrowings from domestic or foreign sources are available, then a ceiling on domestic credit to the public sector will fix the overall fiscal deficit from the financing side. In such a case, the government will have no other option but to adjust either by increasing revenues or decreasing expenditures or both. It is towards such efforts that financial programming techniques are often directed.

8.3 MONETARY AND FISCAL LINKS

Thus, an extension that can be made to the basic financial programming approach is to link the monetary and fiscal accounts through expanding the underlying balance sheet relationships. This is done by discriminating between the expansion of credit to the private sector and that to the public sector, and taking into account the connections between the government budgetary position and official foreign borrowings on one hand and the growth of domestic credit on the other. In practice, because of the central role of fiscal expenditures and revenues in a government's economic policy, and because of the dependence of private sector economic activity on an adequate supply of credit, this stage of the financial programming exercise is often regarded as the one involving the most crucial decisions.

The inclusion of fiscal deficits which is presented here as an extension of the basic financial programming approach should not obscure the underlying importance of these deficits in creating initial imbalances and the inescapable fact that these imbalances have to be tackled through fiscal adjustments. In summary, the fact remains that fiscal policies are amongst those most directly amenable to strong and rapid government action and, often, a more satisfactory growth performance may require a reallocation of resources away from the public sector to more directly productive non-public sectors.

Fiscal policy can be grafted into the financial programming framework in a fairly straightforward manner. To do so, requires three additional *ex post* identities: first, that the total change in net foreign indebtedness of the country (ΔF) is the sum of changes in the private sector's (ΔFp) and public sectors's (ΔFg) net foreign debt position, that is

$$\Delta F = \Delta Fp + \Delta Fg. \tag{8.1}$$

Second, a similar decomposition between the private and public sectors can be made with respect to changes in domestic credit:

$$\Delta DC = \Delta DCp + \Delta DCg, \tag{8.2}$$

where, as indicated in Section 4.6.1, ΔDCp is the change in credit channeled to the private sector and ΔDCg is the change in credit going to the government.

Finally, the government budget constraint (GBC) is introduced, which states that the overall fiscal deficit ($Ig - Sg$) can be financed either by borrowing from the banking system (ΔDCg), or by selling debt to the private (non-bank) sector (ΔB), or by borrowing from abroad (ΔFg), that is

$$Ig - Sg = \Delta DCg + \Delta B + \Delta Fg, \tag{8.3}$$

where Ig is public sector investment, Sg is public sector savings which is defined as the excess of total government revenue (T) over total government expenditures (G), which includes interest payments, that is $Sg = T - G$.

These three equations not only directly establish the relationship between monetary expansion and the fiscal position of the government, but indirectly provide the rationale for determining the impact of fiscal policy on growth.

8.3.1 *Empirical Evidence*

In order to draw attention to the links between fiscal policy and growth, the overall savings–investment balance, (eqn 2.25), can be written as follows:

$$I = Ip + Ig = Sp + (T - G) + (Z - X), \qquad (8.4)$$

which indicates that total investment, that is the sum of private investment (Ip) and public investment (Ig), is financed by domestic savings, that is the sum of private savings (Sp) and public savings ($Sg = T - G$), and external savings ($Z - X$).

While (eqn 8.4) suggests a relationship between growth (via investment) and changes in government spending (G) or taxes (T), direct evidence of such a link in developing countries is quite scarce (see Khan and Villanueva 1991). In standard Keynesian models, a reduction in government expenditure or an increase in taxation is expected to have a multiplier effect on the level of real income, at least in the short run. While this proposition is well known, remarkably few studies have introduced fiscal variables directly into a growth model, and those that have done so (see Orsmund 1990) have generally found the effect to be statistically insignificant. The lack of positive results is a reflection of the fact that the relationship between fiscal variables and the level of output in developing countries is more complicated than basic Keynesian theory would imply. The effects of fiscal deficits ($G - T$) on growth also turn out to be difficult to establish empirically because of the tight linkage between fiscal policy and monetary policy. As such, in models that include domestic credit expansion or the growth of money, empirical tests tend to suggest that fiscal variables have only a relatively modest role to play.

Other than through the demand side, fiscal policy can influence output through the effects of public sector investment on private sector investment. Despite the many difficulties, both conceptual and data-related, involved in modelling private investment behaviour in developing countries, recent studies (see Rama 1993) have identified a positive effect of public investment on private capital formation. In addition, when a distinction is made between infrastructural and other types of public investment, more significant results emerge. Blejer and Khan (1984), for instance, show that a $ 1.00 increase in real infrastructural public sector investment would increase real private investment by about $ 0.25. On the other hand, an equivalent increase in all other forms of public investment would reduce real private investment by $ 0.30. These results are consistent with the hypothesis that infrastructural investment is complementary to private investment, while increases in other types of public investment tend to crowd out the private sector.

However, the issue of whether a contractionary fiscal policy, taking the form of a cut in real public sector investment, will tend to 'crowd in' private capital formation is far from settled. Although the direction of the effect is uncertain, it is apparent that, by varying the level and composition of public investment, the government can alter private investment, and thereby influence the long-run growth rate of the economy. As such, in the course of reducing the fiscal deficit, it would be necessary for the government to weigh carefully the short-run consequences of cuts in current spending *vis-à-vis* the long-term effects if these reductions fell more heavily on investment expenditures.[4]

8.4   FISCAL DEFICIT, MONEY CREATION, AND DEBT

The relationship between fiscal deficit, money growth, and inflation, in particular, has long been a central element in the 'orthodox' view of the inflationary process in many developing countries (see Rao 1992a). In view of this, the focus of recent attention has been on assessing the macroeconomic effects of fiscal deficits within the context of their sustainability. In order to analyse this aspect, we have to initially assess whether fiscal deficits are consistent with the other macroeconomic targets, in particular, output growth and the inflation rate. In such a framework, consistency implies that fiscal deficits, which have alternative sources of financing, have to be compatible with targets which imply restrictions on these sources of financing. These restrictions set the permissible deficit at a certain level; and consistency requires that the actual deficit be brought in line with it. If the actual deficit exceeds this limit, then one or more of the macroeconomic targets will have to be revised, or else the fiscal stance would have to be adjusted.

This section and the next discuss the measurement, sustainability, and macroeconomic effects of fiscal deficits. Here, we begin by providing a brief overview of the government budget constraint and relate it to some commonly used budget concepts. We then examine the role of seignorage and the inflation tax as sources of deficit finance. In this context, the concept of an optimal inflation rate, which maximizes seignorage revenue, and the impact of collection lags on this optimal rate are also discussed.

8.4.1   *The Analytical Framework*
In an attempt to analyse some of these questions, we now set out the basic analytical framework that will be used in this chapter and extended

in the next. In order to keep the ensuing analysis as simple as possible, we shall rewrite (eqn 8.3) as follows which states that when fiscal revenues fall short of current and capital expenditures (including interest payments on the public debt), the government incurs a fiscal deficit (*FD*) that can be financed either by money financing (ΔM) or debt financing (ΔB),[5] that is

$$FD = D + iB = \Delta M + \Delta B, \tag{8.5}$$

where D is the primary (non-interest) deficit (surplus, if negative); and iB refers to interest payments on public debt.

(Eqn 8.5), commonly referred to as the government budget constraint (GBC), provides the necessary links between deficits, money, and debt, and is essential for understanding the relationship between monetary and fiscal policies, and more generally the macroeconomic effects of fiscal deficits.

On the basis of (eqn 8.5), several commonly used budget concepts can be derived. The first one refers to the primary deficit. Measured as a fraction of nominal income (*Py*), it is given by:

$$d = D/Py, \tag{8.6}$$

which is important for evaluating the sustainability of government deficits and the consistency of macroeconomic policy targets, as will be discussed below.

The second concept is the conventional deficit, which is equal to the primary deficit augmented by interest payments on the public debt. Measured as a fraction of nominal income, the conventional deficit is defined as:

$$f = FD/Py = (D/Py) + i(B/Py) = d + ib, \tag{8.7}$$

where b ($= B/Py$) is the debt–GNP ratio.

Finally, the operational (inflation-adjusted) deficit is defined as:

$$f(\pi) = d + (i - \pi)b = d + rb, \tag{8.8}$$

where π and r denote the inflation rate and real interest rate, respectively.

The operational deficit deducts from the conventional deficit the inflation component of interest payments on public debt. The rationale for this adjustment is the presumption that inflation-induced interest payments are tantamount to amortization payments in their economic impacts; that is, they do not represent 'new' income to asset holders, and therefore do not affect real aggregate expenditure. The conventional deficit therefore is nothing but the operational deficit the government would face at a zero inflation rate.

8.4.2 *Seignorage and Inflationary Finance*

Seignorage is an important implicit tax levied by the government. Broadly defined, it consists of the amount of real resources appropriated by the government by means of money creation. With the increase in money supply being denoted by ΔM and the price level by P, real seignorage revenue (as a fraction of real output), denoted by S^*, can be defined as:

$$S^* = \frac{\Delta M/P}{y} = \frac{\Delta M}{Py} = \mu m = \Delta m + gm + \pi m, \tag{8.9}$$

where: $\mu = \Delta M/M$, that is the rate of growth of money supply,[6]

$m = M/Py$, that is real money balances as a fraction of real output,

g = growth rate, and

π = inflation rate.

The first two terms in (eqn 8.9), that is $(\Delta M/P)/y$ and $\Delta M/Py$, are identical and define real seignorage revenue as a fraction of real output. The third term (μm) equates this fraction with the product of the rate of nominal money growth and real balances (as a fraction of real output) held by the public.[7] By analogy with the public finance literature, μ is often referred to as the tax rate and m, which is equal to the demand for money balances under the assumption of money market equilibrium, as the tax base. The last expression specifies the value of resources (as a fraction of income) extracted by the government as the sum of three components: (i) the increase in the money–income ratio (Δm); (ii) the increase in nominal money supply needed to maintain a constant money–income ratio in the face of real growth (gm); and (iii) the change in nominal money supply needed to offset inflation effects and maintain a constant money–income ratio (πm). The last term in this expression represents the inflation tax as a fraction of real output, I^t. Therefore:

$$I^t = \pi m, \tag{8.10}$$

so that:

$$S^* = \Delta m + gm + I^t, \tag{8.11}$$

which implies that in a stationary state, with $\Delta m = g = 0$, seignorage will be equal to the inflation tax revenue.[8] To the extent that money

creation causes inflation, thereby affecting the real value of nominal
assets, seignorage can be viewed as a tax on the nominal money
holdings of the private sector.

TABLE 8.1 SEIGNORAGE AND THE INFLATION TAX

(percentage averages over 1980–91)

Country	Annual Inflation Rate	Seignorage Revenue (a)	(b)	Inflation Tax Revenue
		Industrial (G7) Countries		
Canada	6.3	1.1	0.2	0.8
France	7.4	0.9	0.4	1.8
Germany	2.9	1.6	0.5	0.5
Italy	10.5	5.9	1.6	4.0
Japan	2.6	5.4	0.6	0.8
United Kingdom	7.5	0.6	0.2	1.7
United States	5.4	1.8	0.4	0.9
		Developing Countries		
Asia				
India	9.5	14.7	2.0	1.5
Pakistan	7.8	13.4	2.3	2.2
Philippines	15.3	10.0	1.4	1.2
Singapore	2.9	5.2	1.6	0.7
Sri Lanka	13.5	8.1	1.6	1.7
Latin America				
Bolivia	1155.8	111.6	5.0	91.5
Chile	21.8	40.9	10.7	1.5
Brazil	547.9	11.0	3.8	14.2
Mexico	61.7	25.0	3.8	4.7
Peru	1058.7	65.3	6.9	110.4

Notes: (i) Inflation tax revenue is measured as a percentage of GDP.
(ii) Seignorage revenue is measured as a percentage of GDP in column (b) and
as a percentage of total government revenue in column (a).
Source: Agenor and Montiel (1996)

Table 8.1 presents data on seignorage, the inflation tax, and the rate
of inflation for a group of developed and developing countries during
the 1980s. The table shows considerable differences across nations in

the reliance on seignorage. In recent years, seignorage has been a negligible source of revenue in almost all industrial countries except Italy. In developing countries, by contrast, seignorage accounts for a substantially higher share of government revenue, especially in India, Pakistan, and almost all Latin American countries. Seignorage and the inflation tax also amount to a large fraction of output.

Certain useful information can be extracted from this table based on the analytical framework presented above. In order to do so, we combine (eqn 8.9) and (eqn 8.10) in order to provide the basic definition of seignorage revenue:

$$S^* = \mu m = \Delta m + gm + I^t. \tag{8.12}$$

Using the data on India provided in Table 8.1, we note that: (i) the annual rate of inflation was 9.5 per cent, that is $\pi = 0.095$; (ii) seignorage revenue was 2 per cent of GDP, that is $S^* = \mu m = 0.02$; and (iii) inflation tax revenue was 1.5 per cent of GDP, that is $I^t = \pi m = 0.015$.

Substituting $\pi = 0.095$ in the equation for inflation tax revenue: $I^t = \pi m = 0.015$ yields $m = 0.1579$, implying that real money balances (M/P) were about 15.8 per cent of real output (y) over the period 1980–91. Substituting this value in the equation for seignorage revenue: $S^* = \mu m = 0.02$ yields $\mu = 0.1267$, implying that money supply (M) grew at an annual rate of about 12.7 per cent over this decade. As the annual average real growth rate in the Indian economy was about 5.53 per cent over the period 1980–91, that is $g = 0.0553$, we have $gm = 0.0087$. Therefore the change in the money–income ratio (Δm) can be computed as a residual from (eqn 8.12). This works out to: $\Delta m = -0.0037$, implying that the current money–income ratio, defined as $m + \Delta m$, would be about 0.1542.

8.4.3   The Optimal Inflation Tax

While the inflation tax has long been recognized as an important source of government revenue, Phelps (1973) was the first to emphasize that the inflation rate can be determined *optimally* in such a context. To prove this, assume that expectations are fulfilled, that is $\pi = \pi^e$, and that the demand for real money balances (M/P) follows a generalized Cagan specification given by:

$$M/P = Ay^\alpha e^{-\beta \pi}, \qquad \alpha, \beta > 0, \tag{8.13}$$

where A is a constant, α is the income elasticity of real money demand and β is the (semi) elasticity of the demand for money with respect to

the expected—and, in our case, actual—inflation rate (see Blanchard and Fischer 1989):
By assuming $\alpha = 1$, (eqn 8.13) can be rewritten as:

$$M/Py = m = Ae^{-\beta\pi}. \tag{8.14}$$

Combining (eqn 8.10) and (eqn 8.14) yields:

$$I^t = A\pi e^{-\beta\pi}. \tag{8.15}$$

(Eqn 8.15) can be depicted as a curve in $\pi - I^t$ space and it is seen that when $\pi = 0$, the revenue from inflation tax is also zero. Thereafter, with an increase in the inflation rate, inflation tax revenue rises initially (at a decreasing rate) and then, beyond a certain point, starts falling (at an increasing rate). Maximum revenue is therefore reached when $\delta I^t / \delta\pi = 0$ and at that unique point, the (*inflation tax*) revenue-maximizing rate of inflation is:

$$\pi(1) = 1/\beta, \tag{8.16}$$

which is the inverse of the inflation rate semi-elasticity of the demand for money.[9]
The above analysis can easily be extended to determine the seignorage-maximizing rate of inflation. Suppose that the economy is in steady-state equilibrium, that is $\Delta m = 0$, with a constant growth rate (g), then from (eqn 8.11), (eqn 8.14), and (8.15), we have:

$$S^* = A(g + \pi)e^{-\beta\pi}. \tag{8.17}$$

In such a framework, the revenue-maximizing rate of inflation works out to be:[10] $\pi(2) = (1/\beta) - g$. However, as $\Delta m = 0$, this implies that the rate of money growth must equal the sum of the inflation rate and the real growth rate,[11] that is $\mu = \pi + g$. Substituting the value of $\pi(2)$ into this relationship yields: $\mu^* = 1/\beta$ which is the unique (*seignorage*) revenue-maximizing rate of money growth. Thus, given specific assumptions regarding the formation of inflationary expectations, the parameter β can be estimated for individual countries which could provide guidelines for determining an 'optimal' revenue-maximizing monetary policy.

8.4.4 Collection Lags, Fiscal Erosion, and the Olivera–Tanzi Effect

An important element that ought to be considered in the debate over the optimal use of inflationary finance relates to the effects of inflation on the tax system, and in particular, the links between inflation and the collection lag in conventional tax revenue. This factor, which was first emphasized by Olivera (1967) and, more emphatically, by Tanzi (1978), has come to be known as the Olivera–Tanzi effect which plays an important role in the analysis of fiscal, monetary, and inflationary dynamics in developing countries.

Taxes are collected with lags in almost all countries. In developing countries, the average collection lag, defined as the time between the moment taxes are due and the moment that they are actually paid to the fiscal authority, appears to be about 6.5 months for total revenue, but varies widely from 4 months for taxes on international trade and transactions to about 13.7 months on profits and capital gains (see Choudhry 1991). Under such conditions, an increase in the inflation rate will bring a fall in real conventional tax revenue, the extent of which will depend on the average collection lag and the prevalent tax burden, that is, the initial ratio of taxes to aggregate output.

Formally, let v denote the average lag in the collection of conventional taxes (measured in years), and let π denote the annual inflation rate. The real value of conventional tax revenue (as a fraction of income) is therefore given by (see Tanzi 1978, p. 426):

$$t(\pi, v) = t(0)e^{-v\pi}, \tag{8.18}$$

where $t(0)$ denotes the conventional tax rate at zero inflation. In effect, therefore, $t(0)$ corresponds to the *exante* tax rate set by the government, while $t(\pi, v)$ corresponds to the *expost* tax rate actually observed as a result of fiscal erosion arising out of inflation and collection lags.

Total government revenue (inclusive of seignorage revenue) measured as a fraction of nominal income, der.oted by t, is obtained by combining (eqn 8.17) and (eqn 8.18) together yielding:

$$t = S^* + t(\pi, v) = A(\pi + g)e^{-\beta\pi} + t(0)e^{-v\pi}. \tag{8.19}$$

Setting the derivative of (eqn 8.19) with respect to π equal to zero yields the following expression:

$$\delta t/\delta\pi = A(1 - \beta\pi)e^{-\beta\pi} - Ag\beta e^{-\beta\pi} - vt(0)e^{-v\pi} = 0, \tag{8.20}$$

which being a transcendental function of π does not yield an analytical solution to estimate the unique (*total*) revenue-maximizing rate of inflation, $\pi(3)$. However, because $\delta t/\delta\pi < 0$ at, both, $\pi(1) = 1/\beta$ as well as at $\pi(2) = (1/\beta) - g$, it is obvious, that this (total) revenue-maximizing rate of inflation, $\pi(3)$, has to be even lower than the (seignorage) revenue-maximizing rate of inflation, $\pi(2)$, which, in turn, is lower than the (inflation tax) revenue-maximizing rate of inflation, $\pi(1)$. This implies that the fall in the conventional tax rate as a result of inflating the economy beyond $\pi(3) < \pi(2) < \pi(1)$ will be large enough to outweigh the increase in the seignorage or inflation tax revenue rate, yielding an overall decline in the total tax rate (see Tanzi 1988). In this context, it should be noted that, based on the evidence provided by Phylaktis and Taylor (1992, 1993) as well as Easterly and Schmidt-Hebbel (1994) on some recent episodes of high inflation in Latin America, the assumption that the average inflation rate which prevailed in some of these countries during the 1970s and the 1980s was equal to—or even higher than—the rate which maximized steady-state revenue from the inflation tax, that is $\pi(1)$, cannot be rejected.

Certain additional useful information can be extracted from Table 8.1 based on the analytical framework presented above. In order to do so, we rewrite (eqn 8.19) as follows so as to provide the link between total government revenue, seignorage revenue, and conventional tax revenue:

$$t = S^* + t(0)e^{-v\pi}. \tag{8.21}$$

Once again, using the data on India, we note that while seignorage (S^*) was 2 per cent of GDP, it was 14.7 per cent of total government revenue. This implies that total *expost* government revenue was 13.61 per cent of GDP [= $(2/14.7) \times 100$], that is $t = 0.1361$. Based upon Choudhry (1991), we assume that the average collection lag for total revenue is 6.5 months, which implies that $v = 0.5417$ (= $6.5/12$). Given that $S^* = 0.02$ and $\pi = 0.095$, this implies that, both, the *ex ante* tax rate, $t(0)$, as well as the *ex post* tax rate, $t(\pi, v)$, can be computed from (eqn 8.21) and (eqn 8.18), respectively. This works out to be: $t(0) = 0.1222$ and $t(\pi, v) = 0.1161$, indicating that, as a result of the Olivera–Tanzi effect, there was an average annual fiscal erosion to the extent of 0.61 (= 12.22–11.61) per cent of GDP over the decade 1980–91.

8.5 TOWARDS A CONSISTENT FISCAL POLICY DESIGN

The GBC derived earlier, (eqn 8.5), while useful *per se* for assessing the static nature of the fiscal stance adopted by the government at any given moment in time, does not highlight the dynamic nature of the financing constraint that the public sector typically faces. Governments cannot indefinitely accumulate public (domestic and foreign) debt.

They, therefore, also face a dynamic budget constraint which imposes restrictions on the paths followed by different components of the GBC. In addition, this dynamic budget constraint imposes consistency requirements on the overall formulation (specification) of macroeconomic policy (targets) that must be taken into account while designing stabilization programmes. The first part of this section examines how the GBC can be used to derive the dynamic budget constraint which helps to evaluate the sustainability of fiscal policy. The second part analyses the requirements imposed by the dynamic nature of this budget constraint on the formulation of macroeconomic policy objectives within a consistent framework.

8.5.1 *The Sustainability of Fiscal Policy*

(Eqn 8.5) can be rewritten in terms of the behaviour over time of stocks and flows per unit of nominal output as follows:

$$(D/Py) + i(B/Py) = (\Delta M/Py) + (\Delta B/Py), \tag{8.22}$$

which, using (eqn 8.6), (eqn 8.7), and (eqn 8.9), yields:[12]

$$d + ib = S^* + [\Delta b + (\pi + g)b], \tag{8.23}$$

where Δb is the change in the debt–output ratio.

Therefore, we have:

$$\Delta b = (r - g)b + d - S^*, \tag{8.24}$$

which indicates that, in a stationary state, that is $g = 0$, the difference between the operational deficit, (eqn 8.8), and seignorage revenue (S^*) is equal to the changes in the debt–output ratio.

(Eqn 8.24) yields:

$$\frac{\Delta b}{b} = (r - g) + \frac{(d - S^*)}{b}, \tag{8.25}$$

which implies that ultimately the debt–output ratio must grow at a rate equal to the real rate of interest minus the rate of growth of output.

If the real interest rate remains below the growth rate of output forever, that is $r(t) < g(t)$, for all t, the government will, in each period, be able to service the existing debt by borrowing further and, regardless of the excess of the primary deficit (d) over seignorage revenue (S^*), in the long run, the steady-state debt–output ratio will converge to a finite value given by:[13]

$$b^* = (d - S^*)/(g - r).$$ (8.26)

If we, however, assume that this condition will not hold for an indefinite period of time and eventually, after some point $t = T$, the real rate of interest will exceed the growth rate, that is $r(t) > g(t)$, for all $t > T$, then the government cannot forever pay the interest on its outstanding debt simply by borrowing more. After this point, the debt must be serviced by reducing the primary deficit or by increasing seignorage revenue.

More specifically, the solvency restriction eventually requires positive values for $(S^* - d)$, that is the difference between seignorage revenue and the primary deficit.[14] Although running a conventional primary surplus is not strictly necessary to ensure solvency, positive operational surpluses are eventually required in the absence of growth or seignorage revenue.

For different paths of $(r - g)$ and for a given value of seignorage revenue, the size of the primary surplus required to stabilize the debt–output ratio can, in principle, be computed. Let s^* denote the 'permanent' primary surplus, which is a constant value of the primary surplus equal in present value to a given stream of future primary surpluses. Then, from (eqn 8.24), solvency requires that this permanent primary surplus be equal to:[15]

$$s^* = (r - g) - (1/v)(\pi + g),$$ (8.27)

where r and g are, respectively, the long-term real interest rate and the economy's long-run growth rate; π the 'equilibrium' rate of inflation chosen by policy makers; and v the velocity corresponding to this inflation rate.

In practice, however, the use of such a solvency constraint to determine a sustainable path of fiscal policy is fraught with difficulties, which result from the uncertainty involved in projecting future revenue and expenditure flows. As such, not many attempts have been made to evaluate the sustainability of fiscal deficits using such a solvency constraint. Among the few developing-country studies available are those by Buiter and Patel (1992) for India, and Haque and Montiel (1994) for Pakistan. More importantly, in theory, solvency is a weak criterion with which to evaluate the sustainability of fiscal policy because while several alternative fiscal policy rules can be consistent with the solvency constraint, not all of them may be necessarily sustainable in the long run. Thus, the sustainability of alternative fiscal strategies must be evaluated in the context of the overall macroeconomic policy mix, taking into account all the necessary targets.

8.5.2   *Financing Constraints and Policy Consistency*

Macroeconomic programmes typically consist of specifying targets for the BOP, inflation, and growth as well as for domestic and foreign borrowings. The existence of such targets imposes restrictions on the use of alternative sources of financing the public sector deficit. The GBC thus determines a 'financeable' or sustainable level of the fiscal deficit, given these policy targets. If the actual fiscal deficit exceeds its sustainable level, then either some of the macroeconomic targets must be compromised or else fiscal policy adjustment must take place.

A convenient accounting framework for the analysis of consistency requirements between fiscal deficits, inflation and growth is provided by substituting (eqn 8.7) and (eqn 8.17) into (eqn 8.23) to yield:

$$\Delta b = f - (\pi + g)b - A(\pi + g)e^{-\beta\pi}. \tag{8.28}$$

(Eqn 8.28), which links up the conventional fiscal deficit (f) with the other macroeconomic indicators, is the essential analytical tool for determining whether a given fiscal policy path is sustainable or not. For instance, given the fiscal stance (f), it can be used to project the future course of the debt–output ratio (b) for given predictions about the desired inflation rate (π) and the growth rate (g), under the assumption of a stable money demand function, that is under the assumed constancy of the parameters A and β. If the analysis shows the debt–output ratio to be rising continually, that is $\Delta b > 0$, eventually violating the solvency constraint, fiscal adjustment or adjustments in other targets is required.

Thus, if the policy target is to maintain a fixed debt–output ratio (for both internal and external debt), then setting $\Delta b = 0$ in (eqn 8.28), yields:

$$f = (\pi + g)b + A(\pi + g)e^{-\beta\pi}, \tag{8.29}$$

which determines the 'financeable' or sustainable level of the fiscal deficit. In (eqn 8.29) above, the given inflation and growth targets, (π^*, g^*), together with the parameters A and β help to determine the level of revenue from money creation; and this together with the initial level of the debt–output ratio, $b(0)$, helps to determine the level of revenue from debt creation.

Equally true, for a given size of the fiscal deficit (f^*), (eqn 8.29) can be used to derive an 'equilibrium' inflation rate for which no fiscal adjustment is required by rewriting it as follows:

$$A(\pi + g)e^{-\beta\pi} = f^* - (\pi + g)b, \tag{8.30}$$

implying essentially that the inflation rate should ensure that the revenue from seignorage covers the difference between the government's financing needs and its issuance of debt. A similar strategy would lead to the determination of the appropriate path of domestic and foreign borrowings, given the fiscal deficit, as well as the inflation and growth targets. Whatever the 'closure rule' applied, the resulting path of the policy variables will depend critically upon assumptions regarding the behaviour of the predetermined variables (especially output growth), as well as the estimated form and assumed constancy of the demand for real money balances.

Thus, consistency checks amongst the different objectives of macroeconomic policy and their financing implications for fiscal policy are an integral aspect of the design of macroeconomic stabilization programmes. However, the mere fact that a given fiscal stance is sustainable *vis-à-vis* other macroeconomic targets does not imply that it is necessarily the optimal choice (see Fischer and Easterly 1990). For instance, if a financeable fiscal deficit is large enough to crowd out private investment, then reducing the debt–output ratio would be a more appropriate policy choice since it could 'crowd in' private capital expenditures and allow for a higher growth rate of output.

8.6 EXTENDING THE INTEGRATED FRAMEWORK

In order to answer such questions which are related to the overall design of consistent macroeconomic policy, it is essential to determine the extent of feedback between fiscal deficits, growth rates, and inflation. In such a context, the manner in which changes in interest rates affect fiscal deficits is crucial for assessing one of the most significant mechanisms by means of which stabilization programmes can be either rendered ineffective or completely neutralized. Most stabilization policies typically involve lower primary deficits as well as higher interest rates to increase private investment and savings. However, if the increase in interest payments (as a result of a rise in the interest rate) more than offsets the reduction in the primary deficit, then these policies would generate rising fiscal deficits which could crowd out private investment, thereby affecting growth. Thus, by overlooking this transmission mechanism, the possibility of implementing a 'self-defeating' strategy, which is yet another criticism directed against growth-oriented adjustment programmes, is always very high.

In order to guard against this eventuality, it will now be shown how the fiscal deficit can be neatly incorporated into the integrated Bank–Fund model developed in Chapter 7 so as to ensure an additional channel through which growth impulses can be transmitted into the economy.

8.6.1 *The Core*

The basic components for designing such an extended model, referred to as the Representative Model—Version 5 (RM5), are set out below. All the derivations spelt out for RM4, which is the direct precursor of the current version, remain relevant for the ensuing analysis.

The equation defining monetary sector equilibrium continues to be given by (eqn 6.53) which is provided below for convenience:

$$\Delta R^* - \alpha(1)\pi - \alpha(2)g = -\alpha(3)\ \Delta DC - \alpha(4)e, \tag{8.31}$$

where $\alpha(1)$, $\alpha(2)$, $\alpha(3)$, and $\alpha(4)$ are given by (eqn 6.54a)–(eqn 6.54c).

The equation defining external sector equilibrium continues to be given by (eqn 6.65) which is provided below for convenience:

$$\Delta R^* + \beta(1)\pi + \beta(2)g = \beta(3)e + \Delta F^* + \beta(4), \tag{8.32}$$

where $\beta(1)$, $\beta(2)$, $\beta(3)$, and $\beta(4)$ are given by (eqn 6.66a)–(eqn 6.66d).

The equation for defining interest rate equilibrium continues to be given by (eqn 7.26) which is provided below for convenience:

$$-\delta(4)\pi - \delta(2)g + i = \delta(5)\ i(-1) + \delta(1)e + \delta(6), \tag{8.33}$$

where $\delta(1)$, $\delta(2)$, $\delta(4)$, $\delta(5)$, and $\delta(6)$ are given by (eqn 7.14b), (eqn 7.14c), (eqn 7.14e), (eqn 7.14f), and (eqn 7.27) respectively.

8.6.2 *Incorporating the Fiscal Deficit into the Integrated Model*

To integrate the fiscal deficit into the model, we split up total savings (S) into private sector savings (Sp) and public sector savings (Sg), that is

$$S = Sp + Sg. \tag{8.34}$$

Public sector savings is given by the identity:

$$Sg = T - G, \tag{8.35}$$

where T stands for total taxes collected from the private sector (net of transfer payments) and G stands for total government expenditures (inclusive of interest payments on, both, the domestic and external debt).

As far as private savings are concerned, let 's' represent the average (as well as marginal) propensity to save out of disposable income, that is $Y - T$. Then the implicit savings function of the private sector is given by:

$$Sp = s(Y - T). \tag{8.36}$$

Substituting (eqn 8.35) and (eqn 8.36) into (eqn 8.34) and taking first-differences yields:

$$\Delta S = s\Delta Y + (1 - s)\Delta T - \Delta G, \tag{8.37}$$

which indicates that an increase in taxes (ΔT), other things being equal, leads to an increase in total savings (ΔS).[16] Thus, tax revenues can be used as an additional instrument in this extended framework.

However as private savings also depend upon the nominal rate of interest (i), the explicit savings function of the private sector is given by:

$$Sp = s(Y - T) + \iota i, \tag{8.38}$$

where i is the responsiveness of private sector savings to the interest rate.

As before, taking first-differences of (eqn 8.38), replacing ΔY by its definition given by (eqn 4.16), and writing the result in terms of Sp yields:

$$Sp = Sp(-1) + s(g + \pi) Y(-1) - s\Delta T + \iota \Delta i. \tag{8.39}$$

Following the logic of Sections 8.4 and 8.5, public sector savings, given by (eqn 8.35), can now be written as follows:[17]

$$Sg = (T - Cg) - \Theta iB(-1) - i_f Fg(-1), \tag{8.40}$$

where Cg is the non-interest consumption expenditure of the government; i and i_f are the domestic and foreign rates of interest; $B(-1)$ and $Fg(-1)$ are the stocks of internal and external debt, denominated in domestic currency units, in the previous period; and $0 \leq \Theta \leq 1$ is an index which measures the captive nature of the domestic financial system.[18] Thus, effectively, $0 \leq \Theta i \leq i$ is the interest rate paid by the government on its domestic debt.

As Fg is the stock of foreign debt denominated in domestic-currency units, we have, as before: $Fg = EFg^*$, where E is the nominal exchange rate and Fg^* is the stock of external debt denominated in foreign-currency units. Lagging this relationship by one period and substituting it into (eqn 8.40) yields:

$$Sg = (T - Cg) - \Theta iB(-1) - i_f E(-1)Fg^*(-1). \tag{8.41}$$

Substituting (eqn 8.39) and (eqn 8.41) into (eqn 8.34) yields:

$$S = Sp(-1) + s(g + \pi)Y(-1) + [\iota - \Theta B(-1)]i - \iota i(-1) + (1 - s)\Delta T$$
$$+ T(-1) - Cg - i_f E(-1)Fg^*(-1), \tag{8.42}$$

which is obtained by using the definitions: $T = T(-1) + \Delta T$ and $\Delta i = i - i(-1)$.

Substituting (eqn 8.42) into (eqn 6.7) yields the following relationship between investment and all its proximate determinants including taxes and debt:

$$I = Sp(-1) + s(g + \pi)Y(-1) + [\iota - \Theta B(-1)]i - \iota i(-1) + (1 - s)\Delta T$$
$$+ T(-1) - Cg - i_f E(-1)Fg^*(-1) + \Delta F - \Delta R. \tag{8.43}$$

As before, replacing ΔF and ΔR by their definitions given by (eqn 6.56) and (eqn 6.51), respectively, and substituting the result into (eqn 6.69) yields:

$$g = ks(-1) + ks(g + \pi) + k[\{\iota^*/Y^*(-1)\} - \Theta b(-1)]i$$
$$- k[\iota^*/Y^*(-1)]i(-1) + k(1 - s)t(-1)\tau + kt(-1) - kc(1 + g + \pi)$$
$$- ki_f fg^*(-1) + k[1/Y^*(-1)]\Delta F^* + k[\{F^*(-1) - R^*(-1)\}/Y^*(-1)]e$$
$$- k[1/Y^*(-1)]\Delta R^* - d - d\pi, \tag{8.44}$$

where: $b = B/Y$ is the internal debt–output ratio; $t = T/Y$ is the tax rate with $\tau = \Delta T/T(-1)$ being the rate of growth of nominal tax revenues;[19] $c = Cg/Y$ is the ratio of government consumption to income;[20] and $fg^* = Fg^*/Y^*$ is the external debt–output ratio (denominated in foreign currency units).[21]

This can be written as follows:

$$\gamma(1)\Delta R^* + \gamma(2)\pi + \gamma(3)g - \gamma(7)i = -\gamma(8)i(-1) + \gamma(4)e + \gamma(5)\Delta F^*$$
$$+ \gamma(9)\tau + \gamma(6), \tag{8.45}$$

where the expressions for $\gamma(1)$, $\gamma(4)$, $\gamma(5)$ and $\gamma(8)$ continue to be given by (eqn 6.72a), (eqn 6.72d), (eqn 6.72a), and (eqn 7.23), respectively; and where:

$$\gamma(2) = d - sk + ck, \tag{8.46a}$$
$$\gamma(3) = 1 - sk + ck, \tag{8.46b}$$

$$\gamma(6) = ks(-1) - d + kt(-1) - ck - kfg^*(-1)i_f, \qquad (8.46c)$$
$$\gamma(7) = k[\{i^*/Y^*(-1)\} - \Theta b(-1)], \qquad (8.46d)$$
$$\gamma(9) = k(1 - s)t(-1). \qquad (8.46e)$$

It needs to be noted that in the above formulation, apart from e and ΔF^*, the growth rate of tax revenues (τ) becomes an additional instrument.

8.7 FISCAL POLICY, INTEREST RATES, AND GROWTH

The dynamic structure of the extended model, comprising (eqn 8.31)–(eqn 8.33) and (eqn 8.45), is set out below in matrix notation as follows:

$$
\begin{bmatrix}
1 & -\alpha(1) & -\alpha(2) & 0 \\
1 & \beta(1) & \beta(2) & 0 \\
\gamma(1) & \gamma(2) & \gamma(3) & -\gamma(7) \\
0 & -\delta(4) & -\delta(2) & 1
\end{bmatrix}
\begin{bmatrix}
\Delta R^* \\ \pi \\ g \\ i
\end{bmatrix}
=
\begin{bmatrix}
0 & 0 & 0 & 0 \\
0 & 0 & 0 & 0 \\
0 & 0 & 0 & -\gamma(8) \\
0 & 0 & 0 & \delta(5)
\end{bmatrix}
\begin{bmatrix}
\Delta R^*(-1) \\ \pi(-1) \\ g(-1) \\ i(-1)
\end{bmatrix}
$$

$$
+
\begin{bmatrix}
-\alpha(3) & -\alpha(4) & 0 & 0 \\
0 & \beta(3) & 1 & 0 \\
0 & \gamma(4) & \gamma(5) & \gamma(9) \\
0 & \delta(1) & 0 & 0
\end{bmatrix}
\begin{bmatrix}
\Delta DC \\ e \\ \Delta F^* \\ \tau
\end{bmatrix}
+
\begin{bmatrix}
0 \\ \beta(4) \\ \gamma(6) \\ \delta(6)
\end{bmatrix}
\quad ...(8.47)
$$

which can be written as:

$$A(0)\ x = A(1)\ x(-1) + B(0)\ u + z(0), \qquad (8.48)$$

where: $\qquad$ $x = [\Delta R^*\ \pi\ g\ i]'$ is a (4×1) target vector, and
$\qquad\qquad\qquad$ $u = [\Delta DC\ e\ \Delta F^*\ \tau]'$ is a (4×1) instrument vector.
Solving (eqn 8.48) for x yields the following positive mode of the system:

$$x = Ax(-1) + Bu + z, \qquad (8.49)$$

where A, B and z can be computed once all the composite parameters are known.

In order to apply the above extended theory to the Indian economy for determining growth-oriented adjustment guidelines for 1996–7, we require the following additional data (apart from those listed for RM3 in Section 6.5.1 and RM4 in Section 7.5) which are given below: (i) the current and lagged estimates of the private sector's propensity to save out of disposable income: $s = 0.3250$ and $s(-1) = 0.2916$; (ii) the responsiveness of private sector savings (in foreign currency units) to the interest rate: $i^* = 232.24$; (iii) the projected ratio of government consumption to income: $c = 0.1750$; (iv) the lagged values of the tax rate, as well as the internal and external debt–output ratios: $t(-1) = 0.1849$, $b(-1) = 0.6971$, and $fg^*(-1) = 0.2219$; and (v) the parameter $\Theta = 0.525$. The complete data set, along with (eqn 8.46a)–(eqn 8.46e) and (eqn 7.23), yields the following additional composite parameters which are necessary for solving the model:

$$\gamma(2) = -0.0183 \qquad \gamma(6) = 0.0521 \qquad \gamma(8) = 0.1965$$
$$\gamma(3) = 0.9634 \qquad \gamma(7) = 0.1072 \qquad \gamma(9) = 0.0305$$

Substituting these parameters, along with those given in Sections 6.5.2 and 7.5, into (eqn 8.47) yields the estimated form of (eqn 8.49) given by:

$$
\begin{bmatrix} \Delta R^* \\ \pi \\ g \\ i \end{bmatrix} =
\begin{bmatrix} 0 & 0 & 0 & 11.5527 \\ 0 & 0 & 0 & 0.2632 \\ 0 & 0 & 0 & -0.1743 \\ 0 & 0 & 0 & 0.3131 \end{bmatrix}
\begin{bmatrix} \Delta R^*(-1) \\ \pi(-1) \\ g(-1) \\ i(-1) \end{bmatrix}
$$

$$
+ \begin{bmatrix} -0.008910 & 61.541360 & 0.702134 & -2.392880 \\ 0.000148 & 0.594436 & 0.004962 & -0.054510 \\ 0.000013 & 0.010175 & 0.000440 & 0.036096 \\ 0.000023 & 0.104374 & 0.000755 & 0.030300 \end{bmatrix}
\begin{bmatrix} \Delta DC \\ e \\ \Delta F^* \\ \tau \end{bmatrix}
$$

$$
+ \begin{bmatrix} -6.38656 \\ -0.11293 \\ 0.06380 \\ 0.05621 \end{bmatrix} . \qquad\qquad\qquad ...(8.50)
$$

The forecasts of the targets for 1996–7 were obtained by setting: (i) the lagged interest rate at its actual level for 1995–6: $i(-1) = 0.12$; and (ii) the instruments at their predicted levels for 1996–7: $\Delta DC = 650$, $e = 0.1061$, $\Delta F^* = 4.11$, and $\tau = 0.1350$. This yielded: $\Delta R^* = -1.70$, $\pi = 0.0912$, $g = 0.0592$, and $i = 0.1267$, implying a reserve drawdown of \$ 1.7 billion, an inflation rate of 9.1 per cent, a growth rate of 5.9 per cent, and an (equilibrium) interest rate of 12.7 per cent. Thus, it is seen that the negative feedback between interest rates and growth (via fiscal deficits) results in lower growth and higher inflation (*vis-à-vis* the forecasts obtained using RM4 in Section 7.5). This clearly highlights the possibility that monetary reform (with its emphasis on increasing interest rates) could, by increasing fiscal deficits, have an adverse impact on growth-oriented adjustment programmes unless such reform is backed up by designing a sustainable and consistent fiscal policy.

8.7.1 Designing a Consistent Fiscal Policy

This time the equality between the number of targets (ΔR^*, π, g, i) and the number of instruments (ΔDC, e, ΔF^*, τ) makes it possible to solve the model in its programming mode. Solving (eqn 8.49) uniquely in terms of u yields:

$$u = B^{-1}x - B^{-1}[Ax(-1) + z], \tag{8.51}$$

which will exist considering that B is a non-singular matrix.

Using the estimated matrices A, B, and z specified in (eqn 8.50) above, and setting $i(-1) = 0.12$, we obtain the estimated form of (eqn 8.51) which, when expanded, yields the following set of four equations:

$$\Delta DC = -33.4\ \Delta R^* + 5071.4\pi + 14302.8g - 10557.4i + 622.13, \tag{8.52a}$$
$$e = -1.2704\pi - 17.4630g + 18.5185i - 1.0913, \tag{8.52b}$$
$$\Delta F^* = 1.0\ \Delta R^* + 163.80\pi + 1733.48g - 1691.48i + 102.63, \tag{8.52c}$$
$$\tau = -3.4856\pi + 6.29195g + 19.2379i - 2.3577. \tag{8.52d}$$

The essence of the argument regarding the complementarity between monetary reform and fiscal sustainability is contained in (eqn 8.52d) which indicates that higher interest rates have to be offset by rising tax revenues in order to ensure the eventual success of any growth-oriented adjustment programme. Based upon these policy response functions, the objective now is to obtain guidelines regarding the spectrum of alternative policy options which can be considered to be consistent with the desired objectives.

To obtain options which are comparable with those obtained in Section 7.5.1, we once again target a 6.25 per cent growth rate and a 8.25 per cent inflation rate. Therefore, setting $g = 0.0625$ and $\pi = 0.0825$ in (eqn 8.52) yields:

$$\Delta DC = -33.4\Delta R^* - 10557.4i + 1934.4, \tag{8.53a}$$
$$e = 18.5185i - 2.2875, \tag{8.53b}$$
$$\Delta F^* = 1.0\Delta R^* - 1691.48i + 224.48, \tag{8.53c}$$
$$\tau = 19.2379i - 2.2520. \tag{8.53d}$$

The above system which is now used to determine policy options comprises a set of four equations in six unknowns which implies that *any* two of them, except the pairs (e, i), (τ, i) and (e, τ), can be targeted exogenously and this would yield solutions for the remaining four variables. However, as before, allowing the interest rate to be determined endogenously implies that we have nine alternative stabilization options. The results of these alternative simulation exercises are provided in Table 8.2 below.[22]

TABLE 8.2 ALTERNATIVE FISCALLY CONSISTENT POLICY OPTIONS

Option	ΔDC	e	ΔF^*	τ	ΔR^*	i
1	974.8	0.0102	(4.11)	(0.1350)	−10.49	0.1241
2	716.4	0.0247	10.29	(0.1500)	(−3.00)	0.1249
3	(675.0)	0.0487	8.92	(0.1750)	−2.17	0.1262
4	678.2	(0.0625)	7.33	0.1893	(−2.50)	0.1269
5	727.5	(0.0750)	(4.50)	0.2023	−4.19	0.1276
6	(700.0)	0.0780	(5.00)	0.2054	−3.42	0.1277
7	(675.0)	0.0973	3.65	0.2255	(−3.00)	0.1288
8	(650.0)	(0.1061)	3.45	0.2346	−2.40	0.1293
9.	627.6	0.1072	(4.00)	0.2357(−1.75)		0.1293

The underlying macroeconomic logic of these simulation results, which are arranged in increasing order of the rate of growth of tax revenues (τ), can be summarized briefly as follows: With the growth rate of tax revenues constrained to low levels, it becomes infeasible to increase the rate of interest because of the additional burden it would involve in terms of interest payments on the domestic debt. As a result of the relatively lower interest rate, private sector savings are insufficient to fuel the required growth rate. Consequently, aggregate investment needs to be increased either by increasing foreign borrowings ($\Delta F^* > 0$) or by drawing down foreign exchange reserves ($\Delta R^* < 0$). The latter policy would require an increase in domestic credit expansion which would need to be reinforced by a lower rate of depreciation.

The results clearly highlight that with increasing tax revenues, the permissible increase in the interest rate, by increasing private savings, not only reduces the dependence on foreign borrowings, but also simultaneously pre-empts the drawdown of foreign exchange reserves, thereby guaranteeing the long-run sustainability of such a projected fiscal path. The inescapable conclusion is that increasing tax revenues are absolutely *de rigueur* for the success of any growth-oriented adjustment programme. Thus the arrangement of all the nine options also corresponds, more-or-less, to an increasing order of their perceived short-run feasibility in terms of foreign borrowings as well as their long-term sustainability in terms of foreign exchange depletion.

Options 1–4, with the increase in tax revenues being of the order of less than 20 per cent, that is $\tau \le 0.20$, are totally infeasible, even in the short-run, considering the excessive reserve depletion or foreign borrowings that they entail. While Options 5–7, with $0.2 < \tau < 0.23$, seem feasible enough in the short-run at least, the extent of drawdown in reserves that they invoke (partly because of the high level of credit expansion and partly because of the less-than-optimal rate of depreciation) make them unsustainable in the long run. In this respect, Options 8 and 9 are not only totally feasible in the short run with respect to foreign borrowings but entirely sustainable in the long run with regard to reserve depletion.

By and large, it is seen that the last two options invoke the same policy settings for credit expansion, the exchange rate, and capital inflows that were used while carrying out *ex ante* forecasts of the target variables for 1996–7 in the preceding section. The only difference is that in this exercise they envision a rate of growth of tax revenues in the range of about 23.5 per cent (as against the projected level of 13.5 per cent in the previous one)[23] along with an accompanying interest rate which is about a percentage point higher than the existing level.

In this context, it is important to note that all the policy options presented above, by and large, suggest lower equilibrium interest rates as well as exchange rates *vis-à-vis* those projected in Section 7.5.1.[24] Therefore, it is evident that changes in interest rates and exchange rates need to be coordinated with other policy actions, including tax reforms, that are part of the ongoing stabilization programme. At a narrower level, the results suggest that in the presence of large fiscal deficits, there is lesser scope for implementing a sound interest rate policy or a trade reform programme. At a broader level, they imply that certain combinations of policies could be potentially destabilizing and, therefore, policy coordination is vital during the entire phase of an adjustment programme.

8.8 CONCLUSIONS

An important component of any programme of internal (fiscal) adjustment is the extent to which the public sector contributes directly to improving the savings surplus. In this context, it has long been recognized that reducing the fiscal deficit is an appropriate indicator of the magnitude of the adjustment effort undertaken by a country in the course of a stabilization programme. The key to understanding the macroeconomic effects of government fiscal deficits is provided by linking together the economy's savings–investment or resource constraint, given by (eqn 8.4), and the government budget constraint, given by (eqn 8.3). Doing so yields:

$$FD \equiv (Ig - Sg) \equiv (Sp - Ip) + (Z - X) = \Delta DCg + \Delta B + \Delta Fg, \text{(8.54)}$$

which indicates that the fiscal deficit ($FD = Ig - Sg$) is financed either by surpluses from the private sector ($Sp - Ip$) or from the rest of the world ($Z - X$) or, alternatively, by issuing domestic debt (ΔB) or foreign debt (ΔFg) or by borrowing from the banking system (ΔDCg).

However, regardless of the sources of financing the fiscal deficit, the attainment of certain specified macroeconomic targets, in addition to the constraints implicit in remaining solvent or creditworthy, would restrict each of these financing methods. All these raise the question of fiscal consistency, the lack of which forebodes future changes in policy and thus undermines the credibility of the growth-oriented adjustment programme envisaged.

The nature of the effects of public deficits on the economy thus depends, to a very large extent, on the components of (eqn 8.54) that actually adjust to this deficit. Adjustment depends on the scope for domestic and foreign financing, the degree of diversification of financial markets (which determines to some extent the choice between money or bond financing), and the composition of the deficit. While large fiscal deficits do have, in addition to an inflationary impact, a negative output effect because they crowd out private sector investment, the adverse effect of such deficits may, however, be largely mitigated if they reflect predominantly an increase in public investment. Thus, in general, whether fiscal deficits have a negative impact on private investment, output, and growth depends to a large extent on the sources of the deficit and the composition of government expenditure.

The broad message of this chapter is that adequate fiscal policy is crucial for the achievement of macroeconomic stability. The empirical exercises carried out suggest that there is a considerable amount of interaction between fiscal deficits and other macroeconomic variables, including the BOP, output growth, inflation, and interest rates, that influence fiscal consistency. They also highlight the trade-offs that exist between fiscal policy adjustment and sustainable growth, besides indicating how this trade-off is affected by monetary reform and exchange rate policies as well as by interest rates on domestic and foreign debt. The essence of the argument, however, is that although fiscal policy must eventually confront a number of alternative objectives, such as economic efficiency and equity, in addition to macroeconomic stabilization, tax reform has to be viewed as a short-run rather than a long-term objective because increasing *real* tax revenues is imperative for the successful implementation of any growth-oriented adjustment programme.

NOTES

[1]The former through its direct effect on ΔDC and the latter through its indirect effect on ΔR.

[2]See Table 6.2 where it is shown that increasing domestic credit (and, consequently, money supply) can increase the real growth rate.

[3]When the monetary system provides domestic credit in excess of the flow demand for money, the resulting inflation diminishes the real value of money balances held by individual agents who are then 'forced' to increase their savings (in terms of their holdings of nominal balances) in an attempt to maintain intact the purchasing power of their money balances. This increase in nominal money holdings is termed as the inflation tax (The exact concept and measurement of inflation tax revenue and its relationship with seignorage will be discussed in Section 8.4.2).

[4]The complementarity between public and private investment has important implications for growth and employment when adjustment measures aimed at reducing the fiscal deficit take the form of severe cuts in public sector expenditure on infrastructure. Buffie (1992) has argued that this link may explain the protracted recession associated with adjustment programmes in certain Latin American countries, in the aftermath of the debt crisis.

[5]Setting $Sg = T - G$, and letting ΔB refer to total (domestic and foreign) borrowings, (eqn 8.3) can be written as:

$$(Ig + G) - T = \Delta DCg + \Delta B. \tag{8.a}$$

Splitting up G into its non-interest expenditure component (Cg) and interest payments on total (internal and external) public debt (iB), that is the interest rate on public debt (i)—it is assumed for simplicity that the interest rate on internal debt is identical to that on external debt—times the stock of total public debt (B), yields:

$$(Ig + Cg + iB) - T = \Delta DCg + \Delta B, \tag{8.b}$$

which can be written as:

$$D + iB = \Delta M + \Delta B, \tag{8.c}$$

where D $(= Ig + Cg - T)$ is the primary (non-interest) deficit; and where ΔM is the increase in money supply (The exact nature of the balance sheet linkages between the government sector and the banking system which allows us to substitute ΔM in place of ΔDCg will be clarified in Chapter 9).

[6]In order to simplify the ensuing analytical presentation in Sections 8.4 and 8.5, we shall adopt this definition of the growth rate which is true if Δ is defined as the forward-difference operator. Needless to say, when we incorporate the GBC into the integrated model of Chapter 7, we shall revert back to our earlier notation.

[7]Note that: $(\Delta M/Py) = (\Delta M/M)(M/Py) = \mu m$.

[8]Many macroeconomists use the terms 'seignorage' and 'inflation tax' interchangeably. As shown by (eqn 8.11), this is not true, except in a stationary state.

[9]Differentiating (eqn 8.15) with respect to the inflation rate (π) and setting the resulting partial derivative equal to zero yields:

$$\delta I^t/\delta\pi = A(1 - \beta\pi)e^{-\beta\pi} = 0, \tag{8.d}$$

which leads to (eqn 8.16).

[10]Differentiating (eqn 8.17) with respect to the inflation rate (π) and setting the resulting partial derivative equal to zero yields:

$$\delta S^*/\delta\pi = A(1 - \beta\pi - \beta g)e^{-\beta\pi} = 0 \tag{8.e}$$

which implies that: $\pi = (1/\beta) - g$.

[11]As $m = M/Py$, it implies that:

$$(\Delta m/m) = (\Delta M/M) - (\Delta P/P) - (\Delta y/y) = \mu - \pi - g. \tag{8.f}$$

However, if $\Delta m = 0$, then (eqn 8.f) reduces to: $\mu = \pi + g$.

[12]As $b = B/Py$, it implies that:

$$(\Delta b/b) = (\Delta B/B) - \pi - g. \tag{8.g}$$

Multiplying (eqn 8.g) throughout by $b(= B/Py)$ yields:

$$(\Delta B/Py) = \Delta b + (\pi + g)b, . \tag{8.h}$$

which is used to replace $(\Delta B/Py)$ in (eqn 8.22).

[13]As $\Delta b(t) = b(t + 1) - b(t)$, (eqn 8.24) yields:

$$b(t + 1) = [1 + r - g]b(t) + [d - S^*]. \tag{8.i}$$

Now, given that $r < g$, it implies that:

$$|\, 1 + r - g \,| < 1, \tag{8.j}$$

which is a necessary and sufficient condition for the stability of (eqn 8.i). Thus, the debt-output ratio will converge to a steady-state solution given by, say, b^* which implies that in the long run, we have:

$$b(t) = b(t + 1) = b^*. \tag{8.k}$$

Substituting (eqn 8.k) into (eqn 8.i) and solving for b^* yields:

$$b^* = (d - S^*)/(g - r). \tag{8.l}$$

[14]The solvency restriction ensures only that the existing debt is ultimately serviced by current and future primary surpluses or by current and future seignorage revenue; it does not imply that the debt is actually paid off (see Buiter 1985, 1989).

[15]Setting $\Delta b = 0$ in (eqn 8.24) yields:

$$-d = s^* = (r - g)b - S^*. \tag{8.m}$$

Setting $\Delta m = 0$ in (eqn 8.9) and substituting the result into (eqn 8.m) above yields:

$$s^* = (r - g)b - (\pi + g)m, \tag{8.n}$$

where the steady-state value of m ($= M/Py$) must equal the inverse of the velocity ($v = Py/M$) at this inflation rate.

[16]Because government savings increase by the full amount of the tax (ΔT) while private savings decrease only by a fraction of that amount ($s\Delta T$).

[17]While from an analytical viewpoint, it is acceptable to view interest payments on public debt as the interest rate (i) times the current stock of public debt (B), from an accounting viewpoint, it needs to be noted that the government pays interest on the stock of debt existing at the end of the previous period, that is $B(-1)$. Therefore, total interest payments on the stock of internal debt is given by $iB(-1)$, while total interest payments on the stock of external debt would be given by $i_f Fg(-1)$. In this context, given the definition of ΔFg, that is the change in foreign borrowings by the public sector which corresponds to the change in the public sector's net debt position, we have: $Fg = Fg(-1) + \Delta Fg$, which merely states that the existing level of government external debt (Fg) is the sum of all past borrowings of the public sector.

[18]While analytically it is convenient to assume that the rate of interest on the public debt is equal to the market rate of interest (i), in most developing countries, especially with a nationalized banking system, it is often the case that the government, by imposing large reserve and liquidity requirements on banks, creates a captive demand for its own non- or low-interest-bearing instruments, thereby financing its own spending by issuing debt. Under such circumstances, the actual interest rate paid by the government on its domestic debt will be some fixed (by assumption) fraction, $0 \leq \Theta \leq 1$, of the market interest rate, with Θ ranging from 0 (completely repressed financial system) to 1 (completely free financial system). However, regardless of the actual value of Θ, as it is assumed to be fixed, it would imply that the rate of interest on domestic debt, $0 \leq \Theta i \leq i$, would have to rise *pari passu* with the market interest

rate. Thus the theoretical results, discussed in Sections 8.4 and 8.5, regarding the impact of rising nominal interest rates on deficits continue to hold.

[19]Note that: $[\Delta T/Y(-1)] = [\Delta T/T(-1)][T(-1)/Y(-1)] = t(-1)\tau.$

[20]Note that: $[Cg/Y(-1)] = [Cg/Y][Y/Y(-1)] = c(1 + g + \pi).$ This implies that once the parameter 'c' is fixed exogenously (as is done in this study), nominal government expenditures (Cg) would rise inexorably with inflation (π) and growth (g) which is in keeping with the behaviour of this variable. To this extent, therefore, it is more precise to consider government expenditure as an endogenous rather than as a policy variable.

[21]Note that: $[E(-1)Fg^*(-1)]/Y(-1) = Fg^*(-1)/Y^*(-1) = fg^*(-1).$

[22]For the reasons specified in the previous chapter, we do not target the rate of interest. Therefore, with two degrees of freedom and five variables to choose from, we have 9 possible options, considering that the pair (e, τ) cannot be targeted *a priori*. As before, in each of the options, the two figures in parentheses are the values fixed exogenously for the corresponding target variables. The 4-equation system was then solved for the remaining 4 unknowns.

[23]It needs to be noted that a 23–4 per cent rate of growth in tax revenues is not infeasible considering that growth rates in this range were attained for two consecutive years in 1991–2 and 1992–3.

[24]For example, if we compare Option 9 (in Table 8.2) and Option 2 (in Table 7.2) which have almost identical policy settings for domestic credit expansion (ΔDC), exchange rate adjustments (e) and foreign borrowings (ΔF^*), we note that they both yield a similar depletion of foreign exchange reserves (ΔR^*). However, the equilibrium rate of interest in the present version (12.9 per cent) is 0.4 percentage points less than the corresponding equilibrium interest rate in the earlier version.

9

External Adjustments, Debt, and Growth

9.1 INTRODUCTION

The suspension of payments to its creditors abroad by Mexico in August 1982 triggered off an international debt crisis that has dominated macroeconomic policy making in heavily indebted countries (HICs) ever since. The crisis, which manifested itself in the form of an overwhelming reduction in the volume of voluntary lending to developing countries by foreign commercial banks, led to a prolonged period during which time several HICs in the developed world experienced drastically reduced economic growth accompanied by sharp contractions in domestic investment, substantial capital flight and, in some cases, greatly increased inflation rates. Despite the overriding emphasis on Latin America, other regions have not escaped the problems caused by these adverse shifts in the world economy. As such, the formulation of strategies that not only deal with external debt but also allow sustainable output growth within the limits of creditworthiness have begun to occupy the attention of policy makers in most developing countries.

The debt crisis gave rise to a voluminous professional literature on a wide range of issues, including the cause of the crisis, its macroeconomic consequences for the HICs, its likely evolution, and possible scope for its resolution. A great deal of policy oriented discussion on the debt problem originally centred on the question of whether the crisis was one of solvency or one of liquidity until Kletzer (1988) argued that HICs were clearly solvent in the sense that the present value of their prospective resources (as measured by the discounted value of real output flows, for instance) was several times greater than their debt obligations. However, if these countries were indeed solvent, then it becomes necessary to explain why they should have been considered illiquid, that is, why external creditors should have been unwilling to sustain the pace of lending.

One possible approach to this question lies in the distinction between the ability to pay and the willingness to pay. Thus, it is argued that while HICs may have been solvent (able to pay), the fact of sovereign immunity has the implication that, since legal sanctions to compel payment—of the type that can be applied to domestic debtors—are unavailable against sovereign debtors, debt contracts negotiated with such debtors have to be self-enforcing in the sense that debtors must find it in their own interest to comply with their payment obligations. From that perspective, the debt crisis can be viewed as one where the willingness to pay declined, setting off a recontracting process. Much of the theoretical debt literature has followed this line of thought, essentially modelling the process of lending to sovereign states.

However an alternative, and what seems more promising, resolution to the solvency–liquidity problem is based on examining the issue from a more disaggregated perspective. Thus, while debtor *countries* may have been solvent, debtor *governments* may not have been. The relevance of this perspective is supported by the empirical observation that an overwhelming proportion of the external debt outstanding in the HICs at the time of the outbreak of the debt crisis was owed by these countries' public sectors implying that they represented either a direct liability of the public sector or bore a public sector guarantee. This suggests that approaching the crisis from a fiscal perspective may yield additional insights that would otherwise tend to be blurred by treating the debtor country as a single agent—in particular, the crisis can be viewed as one of debtor solvency.

The sustainability of any external debt strategy depends to a very large extent on the internal policies that form the counterpart of any external adjustments undertaken. External adjustment requires that a transfer be made to foreigners (or an adjustment made to a lower transfer received from them); internal adjustment brings about a matching internal surplus of savings over investment. The role that the public sector can play in synchronizing these adjustments is central to the fundamental issue faced while formulating any growth-oriented adjustment programme, that of creating a surplus of savings over investment and *still* having sufficient investment to sustain output growth.

By integrating the external adjustment constraint into the model developed in the previous chapter, we show below that fiscal adjustment has a more fundamental role to play in resolving macroeconomic problems associated with external debt than would be inferred solely from its contribution to short-run macroeconomic stabilization. In effect, we highlight the formulation of an external debt strategy, with monetary and fiscal factors playing a key role in determining the overall sustainability of output growth.

9.2 TOWARDS FORMULATING AN EXTERNAL DEBT STRATEGY

The literature on the macroeconomics of developing-country debt suggests that three factors have to be considered while analysing external adjustment because an increase in the debt–output ratio can be traced to them: first, the non-interest current account (*NICA*) which is the measure of the net transfer of resources between a borrowing country and the rest of the world; second, real interest rates paid on external debt which interact with the growth rate of the economy and set the pace at which the dynamics of debt and output growth evolve over time; and third, exchange rate changes between the borrower and its trading partners which are an important determinant of creditworthiness.

The *NICA* is the fundamental measure of a country's external imbalance: it equals the difference between total expenditure (net of interest payments on foreign debt) and nationally generated income. Its counterpart is the net transfer of resources from foreigners:[1] the increase in debt less the interest payments made on debt. If the *NICA* is zero, the increase in debt will equal the interest payments on external debt, which implies that the rate of growth of external debt is equal to the rate of interest on external debt. As long as there is a surplus on the *NICA*, foreign borrowings will be less than the interest paid to foreigners or, alternatively, the growth of debt will be less than the rate of interest and a net transfer of resources to the rest of the world will occur. Exactly the opposite will happen when there is a deficit on the *NICA*: in that case, the debt will grow faster than the rate of interest, which will result in eventual insolvency.

The second factor captures what might be called an autonomous effect inherent in the dynamics of debt, real interest rates, and output growth. If the *NICA* is zero, then nominal debt will grow, as indicated above, at the rate of interest while nominal output will grow, as it always does, at a rate equal to the inflation rate plus the (real) growth rate of the economy. Therefore, the debt–output ratio will grow at a rate equal to the real rate of interest minus the real growth rate. This implies that if the real interest rate exceeds (falls short of) the real growth rate of the economy, the debt–output ratio will rise (fall), provided the *NICA* is zero. This term therefore measures the dynamics inherent in the interplay between real interest rates and real growth rates, referred to as the debt dynamics component. If the real interest rate exceeds the real growth rate by a significant margin, then the dynamics component will dominate the evolution of the debt–output ratio. Under the circumstances, the scope, even for a surplus on the *NICA,* to limit the increases in the debt–output ratio will be considerably attenuated.

The third factor measures the capital loss a country incurs on its external debt when the exchange rate depreciates. The debt–output ratio measures the debt in domestic currency units which, by definition, equals the debt denominated in foreign-currency units times the nominal exchange rate. Therefore, if there is a depreciation, the value of the debt (in domestic currency units) rises and, consequently, the debt–output ratio also rises. This adverse effect however could be offset by the favourable impact of a depreciation on exports, which is an important determinant of creditworthiness.

9.2.1 *A Sustainable Debt–Output Ratio*

Under current economic conditions, an external debt strategy involves making choices in two areas: how to achieve a sustainable ratio of external debt to output and the role of the real exchange rate. The first choice is essentially between two ways of restraining the debt–output ratio:

(i)   Transfer net resources to creditors through sufficiently large surpluses on the non-interest current account.

(ii) Pursue a policy of high output growth thereby slowing down the extent to which external debt feeds on itself through escalating debt service costs.

The first option has been pursued by most Latin American and Eastern European HICs since 1981–2. The problem with this approach however is vividly demonstrated by their experiences which suggest that the only practical and reliable way to create a surplus on the *NICA* is to reduce government spending drastically. However, as indicated in the earlier chapter, if these cutbacks come out of public sector investment, then the effects of such expenditure-reducing policies could be highly recessionary in the short run. Thus, any reductions made in the debt–output ratio through improvements in the *NICA per se* could be offset by the resulting increase in the gap between the real rate of interest and the growth rate. Arithmetically, it implies that whatever gains are made by slowing down the rate of increase in the numerator (of the debt–income ratio) are lost because the rate of increase in the denominator slows down as well. This is precisely what happened in most of the HICs which adopted the first strategy and were consequently trapped in a destabilizing spiral.

Under the circumstances, it must be asked as to whether all those HICs that opted for this strategy did so by design or because no other option was available to them. In this context, van Wijnbergen *et al* (1992) have noted that those countries (Turkey, for instance) which adopted internal policies that gave the private sector sufficient incentive to fund either private capital formation or public sector debt encouraged repatriation of past and current earnings; while those countries that did not adopt such policies (Brazil and Mexico, for instance) were faced with a substantial outflow of private capital (the capital flight problem). Consequently, HICs not experiencing capital flight required much less restraint on expenditures. Thus, although the eventual external constraints, in the form of a surplus on the *NICA,* imposed on the latter group of countries were clearly not of their own choosing, the internal policies that contributed ultimately to these external constraints were. In this sense, therefore, Latin American countries may have had much more choice than is often asserted and, in exercising this choice, they literally 'painted' themselves into a high-surplus, low-growth 'corner'.

The second option relies on a policy of encouraging high output growth, which is intended to slow down the dynamic process in which debt feeds on itself as debt service costs (as a share of output) escalate. The main problem with this strategy of low trade surplus and high growth is that the government has to ensure that the additional investible resources allowed by the reduced trade surplus is channelled into productive trade-oriented capital formation. However, even if this is done, through increased public sector investment and incentives for private investment, the fact remains that higher investment expenditures would increase aggregate demand which, by pushing up the price level and reducing the real exchange rate, would crowd out exports and jeopardize creditworthiness by diverting production away from traded goods. Under the circumstances, the only way to expand exports, which is essential for the eventual success of any external debt strategy, is to restrain both public and private consumption. This would alleviate further pressure on imports and the trade balance that would result if consumption is not restrained as investment (and output) expenditures are increased. All these aspects concern problems of internal adjustment which therefore are central to much of the discussion on external debt management.

Thus, the options are mutually exclusive. Running high surpluses on the *NICA* typically leads to slower growth as investment decays. As a consequence, the debt dynamics component increases as the growth rate starts falling far below the real interest rate on external debt. Conversely, higher growth and the resulting investment expenditures would require continued net transfer of resources from abroad which, if unchecked, would lead to a steady rise in the debt–output ratio and, thereby, defeat the very purpose of the strategy.

9.2.2   *The Role of the Exchange Rate*

The second choice determining an external debt strategy concerns the role of the exchange rate. A depreciation while raising the debt–output ratio could lower the ratio of debt to exports. Thus, whether a country should opt for a devaluation and accept the associated losses on its external debt depends on the scope for expanding exports as a result of the devaluation: in effect, on the elasticity of exports with respect to the exchange rate.

However, if the scope for sustaining an export drive is limited, does there exist an alternative set of policies involving less exchange rate depreciation or maybe even an appreciation? In such a context, it needs to be noted that a revaluation would instantly lower the debt–output ratio by reducing the value of the external debt denominated in domestic currency units. However, such a strategy, by increasing imports, would lead to a deteriorating *NICA* which would have to be financed by additional foreign borrowings implying, once more, a steady increase in the debt–output ratio. Consequently, the strategy would be unsustainable and would eventually have to be abandoned entirely, if not completely reversed. It is the anticipation of such events that have formed the genesis of the exchange rate crises that have characterized many Latin American countries over the past decade or so.

All this suggests that it is essential for HICs to be committed to an exchange rate strategy which is designed to maintain, if not steadily improve, their external competitiveness. Moreover, as most commercial credit ratings invariably place a great deal of emphasis on the degree of export orientation in the economy, this would require a real depreciation of the exchange rate which is essential to ensure creditworthiness.

The conclusion therefore seems to be that while, in theory, external debt management involves making one of two choices, in practice, both these choices are not mutually exclusive given that the exchange rate has a considerable role to play in achieving a sustainable debt–output ratio. In effect, therefore, an optimal external debt management strategy implies no choice whatsoever and involves encouraging high output growth with an export orientation based on exchange rate adjustments, notwithstanding the associated capital losses on the external debt that it will entail.

9.3 SOLVENCY, CREDITWORTHINESS, AND SUSTAINABLE EXTERNAL BORROWINGS

Based upon the above conclusions, it is seen that external debt management, which, in the broadest possible sense, implies stabilizing the debt–output ratio, needs to be essentially concerned with the three possible factors that bring about an increase in this ratio: increased resource transfers from the rest of the world to the borrowing country, interest payments on past debt at a rate higher than the real growth rate of the economy, and capital losses incurred on outstanding debt as a result of a depreciation of the nominal exchange rate. In such a framework, the central problem while formulating an external debt management strategy is to determine whether there exists a sustainable level of external borrowings (increased resource transfers) which, when coupled with the existing exchange rate policy (determining the rate of depreciation of the exchange rate), is consistent not only with the other macroeconomic targets, especially inflation and growth, but also with sustained creditworthiness (that is eventually determined by the evolution of the debt–output ratio).

In order to analyse such issues, in this section, we initially provide a brief overview of the decomposition method which is designed to highlight the extent to which each of these factors contribute to changes in the overall debt–output ratio. We then use the analytical framework to distinguish between the concepts of solvency and creditworthiness.

9.3.1 *The Dynamics of Debt, Output Growth, and the Current Account*

In order to keep the ensuing analysis as simple as possible, we shall rewrite the external balance, (eqn 2.19), as follows which states that the non-interest current account deficit, denominated in foreign-currency units (say, dollars), that is $Z^* - X^*$, has to be financed by a gross transfer of resources received from foreigners, in foreign-currency units, that is ΔF^*, *less* the interest payments on the external debt denominated, once again, in foreign-currency units, that is $i_f F^*$, where i_f is the interest rate on external debt and F^* is the external debt in foreign-currency units. Therefore, we have:[2]

$$NICA^* = \Delta F^* - i_f F^*, \tag{9.1}$$

where $NICA^*$ is the non-interest current account deficit (surplus, if negative) denominated in foreign-currency units. In essence, therefore, the non-interest current account measures the net transfer of resources received from abroad.

(Eqn 9.1) is the fundamental concept of external balance and is essential for understanding the relationship between exchange rate policies and external debt management, and more generally the macroeconomic effects of external debt.

Let f^* denote the ratio of external debt (F^*) to nominal output, denominated in foreign currency units (Y^*), i,e.,

$$f^* = F^*/Y^* = (EF^*)/(EY^*) = EF^*/Y, \tag{9.2}$$

where E is the nominal exchange rate and Y is nominal output (denominated in domestic currency units).

Taking first-differences of (eqn 9.2) and substituting the expression for ΔF^*—obtained from (eqn 9.1) above—into it yields:[3]

$$f^*\Delta Y + Y\Delta f^* = E\Delta F^* + F^*\Delta E = NICA + i_f EF^* + F^*\Delta E, \tag{9.3}$$

where $NICA$, which is the non-interest current account denominated in domestic-currency units, is merely $NICA^*$, that is the non-interest current account in foreign-currency units, times the nominal exchange rate (E).

Rewriting the above result in terms of the change in the debt–income ratio (Δf^*) yields the following after simplification:[4]

$$\Delta f^* = n + (r - g)f^* + ef^*, \tag{9.4}$$

where 'n' is the ratio of the $NICA$ to nominal income, that is $n = NICA/Y$; 'r' is the real interest rate on external debt, that is $r = i_f - \pi$; 'g' is the real growth rate; and 'e' is the rate of change in the nominal exchange rate, that is $e = \Delta E/E$.

(Eqn 9.4) isolates three components underlying an increase in the debt–output ratio: the deficit in the non-interest current account or the net transfer of resources received from abroad; the debt dynamics term measuring the extent to which real interest payments offset the tendency of real output growth to reduce the debt–income ratio; and the capital losses on foreign debt arising from a depreciation of the nominal exchange rate.

9.3.2 Solvency and Creditworthiness

The decomposition of (eqn 9.4) leads naturally to the concepts of solvency and creditworthiness which are now discussed. Consider the decomposition of the debt–output ratio corrected for exchange rate fluctuations. By setting $e = 0$, (eqn 9.4) becomes:

$$\Delta f^* = (r - g)f^* + n, \tag{9.5}$$

which implies that ultimately the debt–output ratio must grow at a rate equal to the real rate of interest on external debt less the growth rate of output.

If the real interest rate remains below the growth rate of output forever, that is $r(t) < g(t)$, for all t, the government will, in each period, be able to service its existing debt by borrowing further and, regardless of the magnitude of n, in the long run, the steady-state debt–output ratio will converge to a finite limit given by:[5]

$$\overline{f} = n/(g - r). \tag{9.6}$$

If we, however, assume that this condition will not hold for an indefinite period of time and eventually, after some point $t = T$, the real rate of interest will exceed the growth rate, that is $r(t) > g(t)$, for all $t > T$, then the government cannot forever pay the interest on its outstanding debt merely by borrowing more. After this point, the debt will have to be serviced by reducing the NICA. Denoting by n^* the minimum non-interest current account deficit that will hold the debt–output ratio constant, that is $\Delta f^* = 0$, yields:

$$n^* = -(r - g)f^*, \tag{9.7}$$

and, clearly, if $r > g$, then $n^* < 0$, that is the NICA must be in surplus. Thus, if the real interest rate exceeds the growth rate of the economy, only a surplus on the non-interest current account is compatible with a constant debt–output ratio. A non-interest current account deficit, and in fact any surplus less than $(r - g)f^*$ will lead to escalating debt growth and interest payments that rise faster than income. This will eventually lead to insolvency.

In this context, it is important to distinguish between solvency and creditworthiness. Solvency involves the ability to pay; while creditworthiness involves both the ability as well as the willingness to pay. From the above result, it is obvious that the solvency restriction eventually requires negative values for the non-interest current account.

Now, from (eqn 9.1), it is clear that if $n < 0$, then the rate of growth of debt ($\Delta F^*/F^*$) has to be less than the rate of interest on external debt (i_f). This implies that, effectively, even if $r > g$, a country does not need to reduce the balance of its debt to remain solvent. Strictly speaking, all solvency requires is that eventually the external debt be made to grow less rapidly than the rate of interest on external debt, which is a very weak condition indeed. An equivalent condition is that the discounted value of current and future surpluses on the non-interest current account be at least as large as the initial debt (see van Wijnbergen *et al* 1992).

The distinction between creditworthiness and solvency is unique to the subject of external debt. In the case of ordinary debt, for example, a debt owned by a corporation, a firm's assets can be seized through the legal system if it does not meet its debt–service obligations. Thus, where such domestic debt is concerned, creditworthiness and solvency are near identical concepts.

However, foreigners will be unable to seize domestic assets on a significant scale, especially if these assets belong to the debtor government. For this reason, the cost of defaulting on external debt is generally less than the value of the debtor's assets. This implies that a country can fail to be creditworthy (that is, it can seriously consider defaulting) even before it actually becomes insolvent.

To assess a country's creditworthiness therefore requires gauging whether the cost to the country of defaulting is less than the cost of its debt. A practical problem is that the cost of defaulting cannot be assessed reliably. However, a country that has not yet defaulted clearly perceives that the burden of debt falls short of the cost of defaulting. Otherwise it would have defaulted already. Creditworthiness, in such a context, can thus be maintained by preventing the burden of debt from increasing further (Cohen 1988). A prudent debt strategy would, therefore, be not to raise the debt burden above its current level. This may sound tautological, but it has important implications. For example, the trade surpluses that many Latin American countries were obliged to run after 1982 were, in fact, not prudent under this approach because it raised the burden of external debt, by slowing down the rate of growth of output, thereby triggering default in certain cases.

Such an approach to creditworthiness thus requires that the debt burden be prevented from increasing. This implies that $\Delta f^* = 0$ in (eqn 9.4). Solving the resultant expression in terms of the *NICA* ($= nY$) yields:

$$NICA = -(r + e - g)EF^*, \tag{9.8}$$

which implies that creditworthiness generally requires a non-interest current account surplus equal to the debt times the excess of the real interest rate and the change in the nominal exchange rate over the output growth rate. This is a far more stringent condition than that required for solvency. However, sustained creditworthiness, that is when $e = 0$, requires a *NICA* equal to the debt times the excess of (only) the real interest rate over the real growth rate.

Considering that the overall current account deficit (*CAD*) is equal to the sum of the *NICA* plus interest payments on external debt, we have:

$$CAD = NICA + i_f EF^* \tag{9.9}$$

Substituting (eqn 9.8) into (eqn 9.9) above yields:

$$CAD = -(e - \pi - g)EF^*, \tag{9.10}$$

implying that as long as the growth of nominal income ($\pi + g$) exceeds the change in the nominal exchange rate (e), a deficit on the current account, inclusive of interest payments on the external debt, is perfectly compatible with the constraints imposed by sustained creditworthiness.

9.4 EXTERNAL DEBT MANAGEMENT IN FINANCIAL PROGRAMMING

9.4.1 *The Fiscal Approach to Sustained Inflation*

This section presents an integrated framework to assess the overall consistency of monetary and fiscal policy, including exchange rate and external debt management policies. The expanded model, which centres on the GBC and the sources of financing it, determines the financeable deficit that is not only compatible with sustainable external and internal borrowings, implying sustainable creditworthiness, but also consistent with the existing targets for inflation and output growth.

The resulting fully expanded model can be used to assess the effects of fiscal and external adjustment policies as well as various other stabilization measures, including financial sector reform affecting interest rates, changes in interest rates paid on foreign and domestic public sector debt, and changes in exchange rate policy on sustainable inflation and growth rates. It can also be used to ascertain the consequences of either postponing fiscal adjustment or not coordinating monetary reform with the given fiscal stance.

The framework for integrating the sources of financing the GBC into the model is based on a view of inflation from the perspective of public finance. Phelps (1973) and Dornbusch (1977) were amongst the first to develop an analysis along these lines; although the actual specification of the linkages between fiscal deficits and other macroeconomic variables presented here is based upon the works of Anand, Rocha, and van Wijnbergen (1988); van Wijnbergen *et al* (1992); and Agenor and Montiel (1996) which are suitably modified to ensure that the resulting financing constraint is compatible with and can be integrated into the model developed in Chapter 8.

The most important aspect regarding such an integration is that the resulting view of inflation is one of 'sustained' inflation. Needless to say, the methodology does not deny that, in the short run, demand pressures or cost-push factors may be important determinants of inflation. However, such factors contribute little to understanding sustained inflation. Excess demand pressure, as pointed out by Friedman (1968) in his celebrated presidential address, should lead to accelerating rather than sustained inflation. Cost-push factors, such as changes in the wage or exchange rate, or, for that matter, in public sector prices, can explain once-and-for-all shifts in the price level, but not sustained inflation. Continued nominal devaluation could explain the excess of domestic over foreign inflation rates, but not the factors underlying the need for such a policy of devaluation. A similar objection can be raised against the strict monetarist interpretations of inflation. The claim that sustained inflation is impossible without a matching growth of nominal money supply is almost a truism since without that growth, the real money stock would approach zero rapidly even with moderate inflation. The claim does not, however, explain what drives the process of sustained monetization.

To explain sustained inflation rates requires analysing the fiscal implications of sustained inflation, which is what the current integrated approach does. Such an approach has received considerable attention after Sargent and Wallace (1981) used it to explain the paradoxical negative links between inflation and money growth sometimes observed in practice. The concept of sustainability plays an important role in their analysis because it requires that inflation targets be consistent with their implied consequences for revenue generated by seignorage, on the one hand, and with the public sector's excess of expenditure over other sources of revenue, on the other. In such a context, the fiscal view on inflation posits that while any short-term links between inflation and deficits could be tenuous, for any given fiscal deficit, coupled with constant and sustainable debt–output ratios, there would exist a particular and, more important, sustained inflation rate.

Exchange rate policy also plays an important role in this analysis[6] because the exchange rate policy of many moderate- and high-inflation countries increases the relevance of public finance in analysing inflation. This is because inflation often forces countries to offset the resulting inflation differentials through nominal devaluation in order to prevent the real exchange rate from appreciating. Such a policy, however, eliminates the role of the exchange rate as a nominal anchor, since an increase in the price level will be automatically offset by a corresponding adjustment in the nominal exchange rate. Thus, in such a policy environment, the exchange rate does not restrain domestic price increases: in effect, it accommodates them. If now, monetary policy is also accommodating because the central bank cannot resist monetization of fiscal deficits, then there are absolutely no monetary anchors left to tie down the price level. Under such circumstances, the public finance approach to inflation is probably the only relevant one for explaining short-run as well as medium-term inflation.

Even if a fixed exchange rate regime is adhered to, the approach suggested here is still relevant. A fixed (or a predetermined) exchange rate regime implies a medium-term inflation rate: foreign inflation plus the rate of nominal devaluation imbedded in the exchange rate regime (zero, if the regime is truly fixed). In such a framework, policy coordination in terms of consistency between fiscal policy and the inflation rate implied by the exchange rate policy is essential. Empirical evidence in this regard (see Cumby and van Wijnbergen 1989) shows conclusively that policy inconsistency is an important determinant of a lack of credibility and the eventual collapse of a fixed exchange rate regime. The integrated approach suggested here can thus be used to assess the sustainability of a fixed exchange rate regime.

In this section, we extend the formal framework developed in Chapter 8 by incorporating the external adjustment constraint into the model. By doing so, it would be possible to assess the extent of fiscal deficit correction required in order to ensure consistency between the macroeconomic targets and the stabilization measures implemented to achieve them. We initially establish the appropriate concept of the fiscal deficit which is used in the relationship between deficits and growth. We then discuss the links between these deficits and the changes in monetary aggregates as well as, both, internal and external debt. In this context, we highlight the importance of the financial structure in determining the feedback between inflation, debt, and fiscal deficits. In the next section, using data on the Indian economy, the theoretical base is used to assess, in particular, the effects of alternative policy measures, including financial sector reforms, on sustainable deficits and, in general, the concept of overall fiscal consistency given growth and inflation targets. In the process, we also show how to derive deficit levels that are consistent with internal and external debt strategies as well as with the exchange rate policy.

9.4.2 *Sectoral Equilibrium and Fiscal Policy*

The basic components for designing such a fully expanded model, referred to as the Representative Model—Version 6 (RM6), are set out below. All the derivations spelt out for RM5, which is the direct precursor of the current version, remain relevant for the ensuing analysis.

In order to graft fiscal policy into the financial programming framework, we initially need to use the two identities, given by (eqn 8.1) and (eqn 8.2), which are reproduced below for convenience:

$$\Delta DC = \Delta DCg + \Delta DCp, \tag{9.11a}$$
$$\Delta F^* = \Delta Fg^* + \Delta Fp^*. \tag{9.11b}$$

The first identity states that overall credit expansion can be decomposed into the change in credit channelled to the government (ΔDCg) and the change in credit going to the private sector (ΔDCp); while the second one states that the overall change in net foreign indebtedness of the country (ΔF^*) is the sum of changes in the government's net external debt position (ΔFg^*) and the private sector's net external liabilities position (ΔFp^*).

Incorporating (eqn 9.11a) into the equation defining monetary sector equilibrium, that is (eqn 6.53), yields the following:

$$\Delta R^* - \alpha(1)\pi - \alpha(2)g = -\alpha(3)\Delta DCg - \alpha(3)\Delta DCp - \alpha(4)e, \tag{9.12}$$

where $\alpha(1)$, $\alpha(2)$, $\alpha(3)$, and $\alpha(4)$ continue to be given by (eqn 6.54a)–(eqn 6.54c). In this expanded framework, both, ΔDCg and ΔDCp are treated as instruments.

Similarly, incorporating (eqn 9.11b) into the equation defining external sector equilibrium, that is (eqn 6.65), yields the following:

$$\Delta R^* + \beta(1)\pi + \beta(2)g = \beta(3)e + \Delta Fg^* + \Delta Fp^* + \beta(4), \qquad (9.13)$$

where $\beta(1)$, $\beta(2)$, $\beta(3)$, and $\beta(4)$ continue to be given by (eqn 6.66a)–(eqn 6.66d). However, as the stock of external debt, denominated in foreign currency units, that is Fg^*, is now treated as a target variable, we incorporate the identity: $\Delta Fg^* = Fg^* - Fg^*(-1)$; into (eqn 9.13) above and rewrite the result as follows:

$$\Delta R^* + \beta(1)\pi + \beta(2)g - Fg^* = -Fg^*(-1) + \beta(3)e + \beta^*(4), \qquad (9.14)$$

where: $\beta^*(4) = \beta(4) + \Delta Fp^*$. $\qquad (9.15)$

In this expanded framework, Fg^* and $Fg^*(-1)$ are considered as current and lagged target variables; while ΔFp^* is now treated as an exogenous variable.

The equation defining interest rate equilibrium remains unchanged and continues to be given by (eqn 7.26) which is provided below for convenience:

$$-\delta(4)\pi - \delta(2)g + i = \delta(5)i(-1) + \delta(1)e + \delta(6), \qquad (9.16)$$

where $\delta(1)$, $\delta(2)$, $\delta(4)$, $\delta(5)$, and $\delta(6)$ continue to be given by (eqn 7.14b), (eqn 7.14c), (eqn 7.14e), (eqn 7.14f), and (eqn 7.27), respectively.

9.4.3 *External Debt, Fiscal Deficits and Output Growth*

We continue grafting fiscal policy into the financial programming framework by invoking the following three definitional identities which, although having been defined earlier, are reproduced below for convenience:

$$I = Ig + Ip, \qquad (9.17a)$$
$$S = Sg + Sp, \qquad (9.17b)$$
$$FD = Ig - Sg, \qquad (9.17c)$$

where FD is the overall fiscal deficit which is defined as the excess of public sector investment (Ig) over public sector savings (Sg).

Incorporating (eqn 9.17a) into the growth equation, (eqn 6.69), yields:[7]

$$g = k[Ig/Y(-1)] + k[Ip/Y(-1)] - d(1 + \pi). \tag{9.18}$$

Substituting (eqn 9.17a) and (eqn 9.17b) into (eqn 6.7) and then using (eqn 9.17c) yields the following expression for private sector investment:

$$Ip = Sp - FD + [E(-1)\Delta F^* + F^*(-1)\Delta E]$$
$$- [E(-1)\Delta R^* + R^*(-1)\Delta E], \tag{9.19}$$

where, as before, we have replaced ΔF and ΔR by (eqn 6.56) and (eqn 6.51).

Substituting (eqn 8.39) into (eqn 9.19) and the resultant into (eqn 9.18) above yields the following modified growth equation:

$$g = ks(-1) + ks(g + \pi) + k[\iota^*/Y^*(-1)]i - k[\iota^*/Y^*(-1)]i(-1)$$
$$- kst(-1)\tau - k[1/Y(-1)]FD + k[1/Y(-1)]Ig + k[1/Y^*(-1)]Fg^*$$
$$- k[1/Y^*(-1)]Fg^*(-1) + k[1/Y^*(-1)]\Delta Fp^* + k[\{F^*(-1)$$
$$- R^*(-1)\}/Y^*(-1)]e - k[1/Y^*(-1)]\Delta R^* - d - d\pi, \quad ...(9.20)$$

where, as before, ΔF^* is decomposed into ΔFg^* and ΔFp^* and, subsequently, the former is split up into $[Fg^* - Fg^*(-1)]$.

This can be written as follows:

$$\gamma(1)\Delta R^* + \gamma(2)\pi + \gamma(3)g - \gamma(7)i + \gamma(10)FD - \gamma(5)Fg^* = -\gamma(8)i(-1)$$
$$- \gamma(5)Fg^*(-1) + \gamma(4)e - \gamma(9)\tau + \gamma(11)Ig + \gamma(6), \quad ...(9.21)$$

where $\gamma(1) = \gamma(5)$, $\gamma(2)$, $\gamma(3)$, $\gamma(4)$, and $\gamma(7) = \gamma(8)$ are given by (eqn 6.72a), (eqn 6.72b), (eqn 6.72c), (eqn 6.72d), and (eqn 7.23), respectively; and where:

$$\gamma(6) = ks(-1) - d + \gamma(5)\Delta Fp^*, \tag{9.22a}$$
$$\gamma(9) = kst(-1), \tag{9.22b}$$
$$\gamma(10) = \gamma(11) = k/Y(-1). \tag{9.22c}$$

In the expanded framework, *FD* becomes an additional target variable; while *Ig* becomes an additional instrument.

9.4.4 *The Dynamics of Fiscal Deficits*

Grafting of fiscal policy into the financial programming framework continues by invoking the identity for public sector savings, (eqn 8.35), which is reproduced below for convenience:

$$Sg = T - G, \tag{9.23}$$

which states that public sector savings is the excess of total taxes collected from the private sector (net of transfer payments) over total government expenditures (inclusive of interest payments on the domestic and foreign debt).

Substituting (eqn 9.23) into (eqn 9.17c) and using (eqn 8.41) yields:

$$FD = Ig - T + Cg + \Theta iB(-1) + i_fE(-1)Fg^*(-1). \tag{9.24}$$

In order to ensure compatibility with the growth equation above, we divide (eqn 9.24) throughout by $Y(-1)$ yielding:[8]

$$[1/Y(-1)]FD = [1/Y(-1)]Ig - t(-1) - t(-1)\tau + c(1 + g + \pi) \\ + \Theta b(-1)i + [i_f/Y^*(-1)]Fg^*(-1). \tag{9.25}$$

This can be written as:

$$-\varepsilon(1)\pi - \varepsilon(2)g - \varepsilon(3)i + \varepsilon(4)FD = \varepsilon(5)Fg^*(-1) - \varepsilon(6)\tau \\ + \varepsilon(7)Ig + \varepsilon(8). \quad ...(9.26)$$

where:

$$\varepsilon(1) = \varepsilon(2) = c, \tag{9.27a}$$
$$\varepsilon(3) = \Theta b(-1), \tag{9.27b}$$
$$\varepsilon(4) = \varepsilon(7) = 1/Y(-1), \tag{9.27c}$$
$$\varepsilon(5) = i_f/Y^*(-1), \tag{9.27d}$$
$$\varepsilon(6) = t(-1), \tag{9.27e}$$
$$\varepsilon(8) = c - t(-1), \tag{9.27f}$$

9.4.5 Model Closure: Deficits, Borrowings, and Debt

The final grafting of fiscal policy into the financial programming framework is carried out by invoking the financing constraint for the public sector deficit, (eqn 8.54), which is reproduced below for convenience:

$$FD = \Delta DCg + \Delta B + \Delta Fg, \tag{9.28}$$

which states that the overall fiscal deficit is financed either by borrowing from the banking system (ΔDCg), or by issuing domestic debt (ΔB), or by recourse to external borrowings (ΔFg).

From (eqn 9.24) and (eqn 9.28), we obtain the following relationship between borrowing, deficits and debt:

$$\Delta DCg + \Delta B + \Delta Fg = (Ig - T + Cg) + \Theta iB(-1) \\ + i_fE(-1)Fg^*(-1). \tag{9.29}$$

While (eqn 9.29) is correct in an accounting sense, it cannot ascertain the consistency of fiscal policy with other macroeconomic targets. First, if used to derive restrictions on fiscal deficits, it would leave a major loophole because it does not cover the entire public sector. At issue is the treatment of the central bank or, more generally, the entire banking system if it has been nationalized.[9] The government could easily shift a substantial part of its deficit into the accounts of the banking system merely by changing its bookkeeping practices. After all, if the entire banking system is part of the public sector, it could undertake many quasi-fiscal activities (QFAs) normally handled by the government. To close this loophole, the profit-and-loss account of the central bank, the so-called 'quasi-fiscal deficit', must be reconciled with the budget balance equation and the banking system must be consolidated with the public sector.

The importance of the latter cannot be overstressed. Many countries run a balanced budget, often because of a constitutional amendment, but in fact continue deficit spending by shifting government expenditure on to the banking system. In fact, in many developing countries, a substantial portion of the interest payments on the central government's external debt is handled by the central bank and thereby not recorded in the central government's budget.

The second issue is related to the first. Bank credit to the government (DCg) is in fact one public sector entity's claim on another. Debt consolidation would make that claim disappear because it does not correspond to any asset in the portfolio of the private sector. In order to effectively establish the link between bank credit to the government and money, the following table presents a simplified balance sheet of the entire banking system.

TABLE 9.1 BALANCE SHEET OF THE BANKING SYSTEM

Assets	Liabilities
DCg	M
DCp	NW
R	

The balance sheet shows that the liabilities of the banking system consist of money supply (M) which is used to hold foreign exchange reserves (R) and to extend credit to the government (DCg) as well as to the private sector (DCp). The balancing item is the net worth of the banking system (NW) and, thus, M can be interpreted as its net liability. The balance sheet also indicates the uses made of the funds raised by issuing zero-interest debt (money supply):

Balance Sheet Restriction: $M = DCg + DCp + R - NW,$

which implies that money supply is issued to cover credit creation and the banking system's accumulation of foreign exchange reserves that has not been covered by the banking system's accumulated profits or net worth.

The profits of the banking system are assumed to comprise only interest earnings on foreign exchange reserves, that is $i_f R(-1)$. Therefore, in this simplified set-up, the counterpart is an increase in its net worth, and the profit-and-loss account of the banking system would read as:

$$\Delta NW = i_f R(-1) = i_f E(-1)R^*(-1). \tag{9.30}$$

In order to incorporate the banking system into the public sector deficit identity, the profits of the banking system, that is $i_f E(-1)R^*(-1)$, must be subtracted from the fiscal deficit (FD) and, to ensure consistency, the corresponding increase in net worth (ΔNW) must be subtracted from the public sector's increase in liabilities, that is from the sources of financing. Thus, subtracting (eqn 9.30) from (eqn 9.29) yields:

$$\Delta DCg + \Delta B + \Delta Fg - \Delta NW = (Ig - T + Cg) + \Theta iB(-1)$$
$$+ i_f E(-1)[Fg^*(-1) - R^*(-1)]. \tag{9.31}$$

Although (eqn 9.31) includes the entire public sector and therefore closes one important loophole, it is difficult to interpret. On the right-hand-side, it lists interest payments on the *net* foreign debt of the public sector, that is gross foreign debt, $Fg^*(-1)$, less foreign exchange reserves of the banking system, $R^*(-1)$. On the left-hand-side, however, it lists increases in *gross* foreign debt as a financing source, thereby excluding the banking system. It also includes claims of one government entity on another: ΔDCg which being an intergovernmental agency debt technically ought to be netted out. Consolidating the debt of the banking system and the government is, therefore, necessary to arrive at an economically meaningful concept of net public sector debt.

This can be done in two steps. First, the gross public sector external debt must be made net debt throughout by subtracting the change in the banking system's foreign exchange reserves (ΔR) from the change in the government's external debt, ΔFg, on the left-hand-side of (eqn 9.31). To maintain equality, it must be added back in. The net result is:

$$\Delta DCg + \Delta B + (\Delta Fg - \Delta R) + \Delta R - \Delta NW = (Ig - T + Cg) + \Theta iB(-1)$$
$$+ i_f E(-1)[Fg^*(-1) - R^*(-1)]. \tag{9.32}$$

(Eqn 9.32) consolidates the foreign debt and assets of all the various government agencies, but it still includes what is essentially an inter-agency debt, that is expansion in bank credit to the government (ΔDCg). However, this can be rectified by recognizing (see Table 9.1) that the last two terms on the left-hand-side of (eqn 9.32), that is $\Delta R - \Delta NW$, equal the change in the supply of money less the change in total credit expansion, that is $\Delta M - (\Delta DCg + \Delta DCp)$. Substituting this money supply identity into (eqn 9.32) yields:

$$\Delta M - \Delta DCp + \Delta B + (\Delta Fg - \Delta R) = (Ig - T + Cg) + \Theta iB(-1)$$
$$+ i_f E(-1)[Fg^*(-1) - R^*(-1)], \qquad (9.33)$$

which indicates the precise nature of the relationship between money supply, borrowings, debt and fiscal deficits.

Replacing ΔM, ΔFg, and ΔR by their definitions given by (eqn 4.20), (eqn 6.56), and (eqn 6.51), respectively, yields:

$$(1/v)\Delta Y - \Delta DCp + \Delta B + [E(-1)\Delta Fg^* + Fg^*(-1)\Delta E] - [E(-1)\Delta R^*$$
$$+ R^*(-1)\Delta E] = (Ig - T + Cg) + \Theta iB(-1) + i_f E(-1)[Fg^*(-1) - R^*(-1)].$$
$$...(9.34)$$

In order to ensure compatibility with the growth and deficits equations developed above, we divide (eqn 9.34) throughout by $Y(-1)$ yielding:[10]

$$(1/v)(g + \pi) - [1/Y(-1)]\Delta DCp + b(-1)\Gamma + [1/Y^*(-1)]\Delta Fg^*$$
$$+ fg^*(-1)e - [1/Y^*(-1)]\Delta R^* - [R^*(-1)/Y^*(-1)]e = [1/Y(-1)]Ig$$
$$- t(-1) - t(-1)\tau + c(1 + g + \pi) + \Theta b(-1)i + i_f[1/Y^*(-1)]Fg^*(-1)$$
$$- i_f[R^*(-1)/Y^*(-1)] \qquad\qquad ...(9.35)$$

where: $\Gamma = \Delta B/B(-1)$ is the rate of growth of domestic borrowings.

Splitting up ΔFg^* into $[Fg^* - Fg^*(-1)]$, (eqn 9.35) can be written as:

$$-\phi(1)\Delta R^* + \phi(2)\pi + \phi(3)g - \phi(4)i + \phi(5)Fg^* = \phi(6)Fg^*(-1)$$
$$+ \phi(7)\Delta DCp + \phi(8)e - \phi(9)\tau + \phi(10)Ig - \phi(11)\Gamma + \phi(12), \quad ...(9.36)$$

where:

$$\phi(1) = \phi(5) = 1/Y^*(-1), \qquad\qquad (9.37a)$$
$$\phi(2) = \phi(3) = (1/v) - c, \qquad\qquad (9.37b)$$
$$\phi(4) = \Theta b(-1), \qquad\qquad (9.37c)$$
$$\phi(6) = [1 + i_f][1/Y^*(-1)], \qquad\qquad (9.37d)$$
$$\phi(7) = \phi(10) = 1/Y(-1), \qquad\qquad (9.37e)$$
$$\phi(8) = [R^*(-1)/Y^*(-1)] - fg^*(-1), \qquad\qquad (9.37f)$$
$$\phi(9) = t(-1), \qquad\qquad (9.37g)$$
$$\phi(11) = b(-1), \qquad\qquad (9.37h)$$
$$\phi(12) = c - t(-1) - i_f[R^*(-1)/Y^*(-1)]. \qquad\qquad (9.37i)$$

In the above formulation, the growth rate of domestic borrowings (Γ) is treated as an additional instrument.

The model comprises six equations describing the following phenomena:

(1) Monetary Sector equilibrium: ... (eqn 9.12)
(2) External Sector equilibrium: ... (eqn 9.14)
(3) Interest Rate equilibrium: ... (eqn 9.16)
(4) Growth–Inflation dynamics: ... (eqn 9.21)
(5) Fiscal Deficit dynamics: ... (eqn 9.26)
(6) External Debt dynamics: ... (eqn 9.36)

Each of these equations, by highlighting the relevant feedbacks between targets and instruments, therefore describe the nature of (dis)equilibrium dynamics that link up all these alternative phenomena.

9.4.6   *The Model: A Summing Up*

The structure of the model, in terms of all the targets, instruments, variables and parameters that it contains, is set out in Table 9.2.[11]

TABLE 9.2   STRUCTURE OF THE COMPLETELY INTEGRATED APPROACH

Targets	ΔR^*	: change in foreign exchange reserves
	π	: rate of inflation
	g	: real growth rate
	i	: nominal interest rate
	FD	: gross fiscal deficit
	Fg^*	: external debt
Lagged Targets	$i(-1)$	: nominal interest rate in the previous period
	$Fg^*(-1)$:	external debt in the previous period
Instruments	ΔDCg	: change in domestic credit to the public sector
	ΔDCp	: change in domestic credit to the private sector
	e	: rate of change in the nominal exchange rate
	τ	: rate of growth of nominal tax revenues
	Ig	: public sector investment
	Γ	: rate of growth of domestic borrowings
Exogenous	X^*	: exports
	π_f	: foreign inflation rate
	i_f	: foreign interest rate
	ΔFp^*	: private sector capital inflows

Table 9.2 contd.

Table 9.2 contd.

Predetermined		
$Y^*(-1)$	:	nominal income in the previous period
$Y(-1)$	:	nominal income in the previous period
$Z^*(-1)$	:	nominal imports in the previous period
$R^*(-1)$	:	stock of foreign reserves in the previous period
$F^*(-1)$	:	stock of foreign debt in the previous period
$E(-1)$	:	nominal exchange rate in the previous period
$s(-1)$	:	private savings propensity in the previous period
$v(-1)$	:	velocity in the previous period
$t(-1)$	:	tax rate in the previous period
$b(-1)$	:	internal debt–income ratio in the previous period
$fg^*(-1)$	:	external debt–income ratio in the previous period
Parameters v	:	velocity of money
m	:	marginal propensity to import
b	:	import response to exchange rate changes
s	:	marginal propensity to save of the private sector
k	:	incremental output–capital ratio
d	:	depreciation rate of capital stock
ι^*	:	private sector savings response to the interest rate
Θ	:	repression index of the domestic financial system
c	:	ratio of government consumption to income

9.5 TOWARDS A CONSISTENT GROWTH-ORIENTED ADJUSTMENT POLICY

9.5.1 *The Dynamic Structure of the Model*

The dynamic structure of the 6-equation completely integrated model is set out as follows in matrix notation:

$$
\begin{bmatrix}
1 & -\alpha(1) & -\alpha(2) & 0 & 0 & 0 \\
1 & \beta(1) & \beta(2) & 0 & 0 & -1 \\
\gamma(1) & \gamma(2) & \gamma(3) & -\gamma(7) & \gamma(10) & -\gamma(5) \\
0 & -\delta(4) & -\delta(2) & 1 & 0 & 0 \\
0 & -\varepsilon(1) & -\varepsilon(2) & -\varepsilon(3) & \varepsilon(4) & 0 \\
-\phi(1) & \phi(2) & \phi(3) & -\phi(4) & 0 & \phi(5)
\end{bmatrix}
\begin{bmatrix}
\Delta R^* \\
\pi \\
g \\
i \\
FD \\
Fg^*
\end{bmatrix}
=
$$

$$\begin{bmatrix} 0 & 0 & 0 & 0 & 0 & 0 \\ 0 & 0 & 0 & 0 & 0 & -1 \\ 0 & 0 & 0 & -\gamma(8) & 0 & -\gamma(5) \\ 0 & 0 & 0 & \delta(5) & 0 & 0 \\ 0 & 0 & 0 & 0 & 0 & \varepsilon(5) \\ 0 & 0 & 0 & 0 & 0 & \phi(6) \end{bmatrix} \begin{bmatrix} \Delta R*(-1) \\ \pi(-1) \\ g(-1) \\ i(-1) \\ FD(-1) \\ Fg*(-1) \end{bmatrix} +$$

$$\begin{bmatrix} -\alpha(3) & -\alpha(3) & -\alpha(4) & 0 & 0 & 0 \\ 0 & 0 & \beta(3) & 0 & 0 & 0 \\ 0 & 0 & \gamma(4) & \gamma(9) & \gamma(11) & 0 \\ 0 & 0 & \delta(1) & 0 & 0 & 0 \\ 0 & 0 & 0 & -\varepsilon(6) & \varepsilon(7) & 0 \\ 0 & \phi(7) & \phi(8) & -\phi(9) & \phi(10) & -\phi(11) \end{bmatrix} \begin{bmatrix} \Delta DCg \\ \Delta DCp \\ e \\ \tau \\ Ig \\ \Gamma \end{bmatrix} + \begin{bmatrix} 0 \\ \beta*(4) \\ \gamma(6) \\ \delta(6) \\ \varepsilon(8) \\ \phi(12) \end{bmatrix}$$

$$...(9.38)$$

which can be written as:

$$A(0) \; x = A(1) \; x(-1) + B(0) \; u + z(0), \tag{9.39}$$

where: $x = [\Delta R* \; \pi \; g \; i \; FD \; Fg*]'$ is a (6×1) target vector,

and

$u = [\Delta DCg \; \Delta DCp \; e \; \tau \; Ig \; \Gamma]'$ is a (6×1) instrument vector.

Solving (eqn 9.39) for x yields the following positive mode of the system:

$$x = Ax(-1) + Bu + z, \tag{9.40}$$

where A, B, and z can be computed once all the composite parameters are known.

9.5.2 Solving the Model: Unsustainable Deficit–Debt Dynamics

In order to apply the above fully integrated theory for the purpose of determining stabilization policy options, we initially require to estimate the following composite parameters of the model. The entire set of equations defining all these parameters are reproduced below *in toto* for convenience:[12]

$$\alpha(1) = \alpha(2) = (1/v)Y*(-1), \tag{6.54a}$$
$$\alpha(3) = 1/E(-1), \tag{6.54b}$$

$$\alpha(4) = R^*(-1), \tag{6.54c}$$

$$\beta(1) = bZ^*(-1), \tag{6.66a}$$

$$\beta(2) = mZ^*(-1), \tag{6.66b}$$

$$\beta(3) = F^*(-1) + X^* - (1 - b)Z^*(-1) - R^*(-1), \tag{6.66c}$$

$$\beta(4) = X^* - Z^*(-1) - (1 - b)Z^*(-1)\pi_f, \tag{6.66d}$$

$$\beta^*(4) = \beta(4) + \Delta Fp^*, \tag{9.15}$$

$$\gamma(1) = \gamma(5) = k/Y^*(-1), \tag{6.72a}$$

$$\gamma(2) = d - sk, \tag{6.72b}$$

$$\gamma(3) = 1 - sk, \tag{6.72c}$$

$$\gamma(4) = k[F^*(-1) - R^*(-1)]/Y^*(-1), \tag{6.72d}$$

$$\gamma(6) = s(-1)k - d + \gamma(5)\Delta Fp^*, \tag{9.22a}$$

$$\gamma(7) = \gamma(8) = k[\iota^*/Y^*(-1)], \tag{7.23}$$

$$\gamma(9) = skt(-1), \tag{9.22b}$$

$$\gamma(10) = \gamma(11) = k/Y(-1), \tag{9.22c}$$

$$\delta(0) = -0.3815, \tag{7.15a}$$

$$\delta(1) = 0.0540, \tag{7.15b}$$

$$\delta(2) = 0.9430, \tag{7.b}$$

$$\delta(4) = 0.0686, \tag{7.15e}$$

$$\delta(5) = 0.4594, \tag{7.15f}$$

$$\delta(6) = \delta(0) + \delta(1)i_f + \delta(2) \ln v(-1), \tag{7.27}$$

$$\varepsilon(1) = \varepsilon(2) = c, \tag{9.27a}$$

$$\varepsilon(3) = \Theta b(-1), \tag{9.27b}$$

$$\varepsilon(4) = \varepsilon(7) = 1/Y(-1), \tag{9.27c}$$

$$\varepsilon(5) = i_f Y^*(-1), \tag{9.27d}$$

$$\varepsilon(6) = t(-1), \tag{9.27e}$$

$$\varepsilon(8) = c - t(-1), \tag{9.27f}$$

$$\phi(1) = \phi(5) = 1/Y^*(-1), \tag{9.37a}$$

$$\phi(2) = \phi(3) = (1/v) - c, \tag{9.37b}$$

$$\phi(4) = \Theta b(-1), \tag{9.37c}$$

$$\phi(6) = [1 + i_f][1/Y^*(-1)], \tag{9.37d}$$

$$\phi(7) = \phi(10) = 1/Y(-1), \tag{9.37e}$$

$$\phi(8) = [R^*(-1)/Y^*(-1)] - fg^*(-1), \tag{9.37f}$$

$$\phi(9) = t(-1), \tag{9.37g}$$

$$\phi(11) = b(-1), \tag{9.37h}$$

$$\phi(12) = c - t(-1) - i_f[R^*(-1)/Y^*(-1)], \tag{9.37i}$$

The above set of equations indicate that in order to estimate all these composite parameters of the model, we require data on 9 basic parameters, 11 predetermined variables, and 4 exogenous variables (see Table 9.2). In Table 9.3, we provide this entire data set for the Indian economy:[13]

TABLE 9.3 PARAMETERS AND EXOGENOUS VARIABLES OF THE MODEL

Parameters	Predetermined Variables	Exogenous Variables
$v = 2.22$	$Y^*(-1) = 288.55$	$X^* = 28.77$
$b = 1.4838$	$E(-1) = 33.4$	$\pi_f = 0.03$
$m = 4.2997$	$R^*(-1) = 17.046$	$\Delta Fp^* = 1.74$
$k = 0.2442$	$Z^*(-1) = 32.19$	$i_f = 0.059$
$d = 0.0183$	$F^*(-1) = 64.04$	
$s = 0.3250$	$\ln v(-1) = 0.4052$	
$\iota^* = 232.24$	$s(-1) = 0.2916$	
$c = 0.1750$	$t(-1) = 0.1849$	
$\Theta = 0.5250$	$Y(-1) = 9637.6$	
	$b(-1) = 0.6971$	
	$fg^*(-1) = 0.2219$	

The above data set, along with the equation set, yields the following 44 composite parameters, given in Table 9.4, which are necessary for solving the full model:

TABLE 9.4 COMPOSITE PARAMETERS OF THE MODEL

$\alpha(1) = 129.9775$	$\gamma(8) = 0.1965$	$\varepsilon(5) = 0.0002045$
$\alpha(2) = 129.9775$	$\gamma(9) = 0.01467$	$\varepsilon(6) = 0.1849$
$\alpha(3) = 0.02994$	$\gamma(10) = 0.00002534$	$\varepsilon(7) = 0.0001038$
$\alpha(4) = 17.046$	$\gamma(11) = 0.00002534$	$\varepsilon(8) = -0.0099$
$\beta(1) = 47.7635$	$\delta(1) = 0.0540$	$\phi(1) = 0.003466$
$\beta(2) = 138.4073$	$\delta(2) = 0.9430$	$\phi(2) = 0.2755$
$\beta(3) = 91.3375$	$\delta(4) = 0.0686$	$\phi(3) = 0.2755$
$\beta^*(4) = -1.2128$	$\delta(5) = 0.4594$	$\phi(4) = 0.3660$
$\gamma(1) = 0.0008463$	$\delta(6) = 0.0038$	$\phi(5) = 0.003466$
$\gamma(2) = -0.06107$	$\varepsilon(1) = 0.1750$	$\phi(6) = 0.003670$
$\gamma(3) = 0.9206$	$\varepsilon(2) = 0.1750$	$\phi(7) = 0.0001038$
$\gamma(4) = 0.03977$	$\varepsilon(3) = 0.3660$	$\phi(8) = 0.1628$
$\gamma(5) = 0.0008463$	$\varepsilon(4) = 0.0001038$	$\phi(9) = 0.1849$
$\gamma(6) = 0.05438$		$\phi(10) = 0.0001038$
$\gamma(7) = 0.1965$		$\phi(11) = 0.6971$
		$\phi(12) = -0.01339$

Substituting these parameters into (eqn 9.38) yields the following estimated form of (eqn 9.40):

$$
\begin{bmatrix} \Delta R^* \\ \pi \\ g \\ i \\ FD \\ Fg^* \end{bmatrix} =
\begin{bmatrix}
0 & 0 & 0 & 52.2743 & 0 & 0.063844 \\
0 & 0 & 0 & 0.5510 & 0 & 0.000513 \\
0 & 0 & 0 & -0.1488 & 0 & -0.000022 \\
0 & 0 & 0 & 0.3569 & 0 & 0.000015 \\
0 & 0 & 0 & 1937.04 & 0 & 2.851490 \\
0 & 0 & 0 & 57.9950 & 0 & 1.085353
\end{bmatrix}
\begin{bmatrix} \Delta R^*(-1) \\ \pi(-1) \\ g(-1) \\ i(-1) \\ FD(-1) \\ Fg^*(-1) \end{bmatrix} +
$$

$$
\begin{bmatrix}
-0.03 & 0.00253 & 37.1633 & -57.7864 & 0.03247 & -218.12 \\
0 & 0.00023 & 0.4222 & -0.44594 & 0.00023 & -1.5414 \\
0 & 0.00002 & -0.0051 & 0.00135 & 0.00002 & -0.1367 \\
0 & 0.00004 & 0.0781 & -0.02932 & 0.00004 & -0.2347 \\
0 & 0.54449 & 978.933 & -2635.25 & 1.54449 & -3658.1 \\
-0.03 & 0.01630 & -34.720 & -78.8993 & 0.04624 & -310.67
\end{bmatrix}
\begin{bmatrix} \Delta DCg \\ \Delta DCp \\ e \\ \tau \\ Ig \\ \Gamma \end{bmatrix}
$$

$$
+ \begin{bmatrix} -4.9362 \\ -0.1067 \\ 0.0687 \\ 0.0613 \\ 56.577 \\ 0.6883 \end{bmatrix}. \qquad\qquad ...(9.41)
$$

The forecasts of the targets for 1996–7 were obtained by setting: (i) the lagged interest rate and the lagged value of the external debt at their actual levels for 1995–6:[14] $i(-1) = 0.12$; $Fg^*(-1) = 64.03$; and (ii) the instruments at their predicted levels for 1996–7: $\Delta DCg = 300$; $\Delta DCp = 350$; $e = 0.1061$; $\tau = 0.1350$; $Ig = 1150$; and $\Gamma = 0.15$. This yielded: $\Delta R^* = -1.91$, $\pi = 0.0898$, $g = 0.0591$, $i = 0.1266$, $FD = 1637.73$, and $Fg^* = 66.11$ implying a reserve drawdown of $ 1.9 billion, an inflation rate of 9.0 per cent, a growth rate of 5.9 per cent, an (equilibrium) interest rate of 12.7 per cent, a consolidated fiscal deficit of Rs 1638 billion, and an external debt of $ 66.1 billion.[15]

Thus, it is seen that by incorporating external debt dynamics into the analysis, the resulting positive feedback between the fiscal deficit and the external debt results in considerably enhanced reserve depletion (*vis-à-vis* the forecasts obtained using RM5 in Section 8.7). This implies that although a fiscal stance may seem consistent *per se* in terms of the given static financing constraints, the interactive deficit–debt dynamics could render it unsustainable. Despite the fact that the growth and inflation prospects remain *momentarily* the same, the results clearly indicate that fiscal reform is essential in order to pre-empt, what could eventually be, an unsustainable drawdown of foreign exchange reserves. If such a fiscal stance cannot be designed, then the only other alternative to halting reserve losses would be the inevitable exchange rate depreciation accompanied by a contraction in credit expansion which, as is clearly evident from the impact multipliers, would imply sacrificing short-term growth prospects.[16]

In view of this possibility, we have now to extend our earlier attempts and determine, not merely consistent, but sustainable growth-oriented adjustment guidelines for 1996–7 using the programming mode of the model.

9.6 TOWARDS A SUSTAINABLE GROWTH-ORIENTED ADJUSTMENT PROGRAMME

In such a context, it needs to be noted that although the current version of the model has an equal number of targets and instruments, the sparseness of B(0) in (eqn 9.39) renders this matrix singular. Thus, it is not possible to solve the model, as it stands, in its programming mode.[17] In order to circumvent this problem, we reduce the dimension of the system by carrying out the following three steps:

Step 1: We initially set the lagged target variables at their actual levels for 1995–6, that is we set $i(-1) = 0.12$ and $Fg^*(-1) = 64.03$ in (eqn 9.41).

Step 2: We then stabilize credit expansion to the private sector at its predicted level for 1996–7, that is we set $\Delta DCp = 350$ in (eqn 9.41).

Thus, the lagged impact of the target variables as well as the policy impact of this instrument setting is automatically absorbed by the intercept term, that is the vector 'z' in (eqn 9.41).

Step 3: We then extend our earlier resolve—of not targeting the interest rate and allowing it to be determined by market forces—to its logical conclusion, and delete the interest rate determination equation from (eqn 9.41).[18]

By doing so, the system of equations given by (eqn 9.41) now becomes:

$$
\begin{bmatrix} \Delta R^* \\ \pi \\ g \\ FD \\ Fg^* \end{bmatrix} = \begin{bmatrix} -0.03 & 37.1633 & -57.7864 & 0.03247 & -218.12 \\ 0 & 0.4222 & -0.44594 & 0.00023 & -1.5414 \\ 0 & -0.0051 & 0.00135 & 0.00002 & -0.1367 \\ 0 & 978.933 & -2635.25 & 1.54449 & -3658.1 \\ -0.03 & -34.720 & -78.8993 & 0.04624 & -310.67 \end{bmatrix} \begin{bmatrix} \Delta DCg \\ e \\ \tau \\ Ig \\ \Gamma \end{bmatrix}
$$

$$+ \begin{bmatrix} 6.309 \\ 0.073 \\ 0.057 \\ 662.18 \\ 82.849 \end{bmatrix} \qquad \qquad \text{...(9.42)}$$

which can be written as:

$$x^* = \overline{B}u^* + z^*, \qquad\qquad (9.43)$$

where: $x^* = [\Delta R^* \ \pi \ g \ FD \ Fg^*]'$ is a (5 × 1) target vector,
$u^* = [\Delta DCg \ e \ \tau \ Ig \ \Gamma]'$ is a (5 × 1) instrument
vector,
$\overline{B}$ = (5 × 5) reduced-form coefficient matrix of the
compressed system,

and where z^* is a (5 × 1) vector of intercept terms incorporating the effects of: (i) the original exogenous and predetermined variables, z; (ii) the lagged target variables, $Ax(-1)$; and (iii) the former instrument variable, ΔDCp.

Solving (eqn 9.43) uniquely in terms of u yields:

$$u^* = \overline{B}^{-1}x^* - \overline{B}^{-1}z^*, \qquad\qquad (9.44)$$

which will exist considering that $\overline{B}$ is now a non-singular matrix.

9.6.1   Fiscal Adjustments, Exchange Rate Policy, and External Debt

The estimated form of (eqn 9.44), when expanded, yields the following set of five policy response functions:

$$\Delta DCg = -39.634\Delta R^* + 4043.5\pi + 3478.5g + 6.23335Fg^*$$
$$- 756.68, \qquad\qquad (9.45a)$$
$$e = 0.01095\Delta R^* + 0.5229\pi + 1.5153g - 0.01095Fg^*$$
$$+ 0.7143, \qquad\qquad (9.45b)$$
$$\tau = 0.01140\Delta R^* - 1.6240\pi + 26.025g - 0.01140Fg^*$$
$$- 0.4817, \qquad\qquad (9.45c)$$
$$Ig = 18.2317\Delta R^* - 4922.1\pi + 41076g + 1.0FD - 18.2317Fg^*$$
$$- 1233.1, \qquad\qquad (9.45d)$$
$$\Gamma = 0.00241\Delta R^* - 0.7683\pi - 1.0001g + 0.000149FD$$
$$- 0.00241Fg^* + 0.1986. \qquad\qquad (9.45e)$$

The essence of the argument as to why controlling the deficit–debt dynamics is necessary to ensure sustainable reserve depletion is brought out by examining the coefficients of ΔR^* and Fg^* in each of the policy response functions above. It is seen that, as far as four instrument settings are concerned, these coefficients are equal in magnitude but opposite in sign, thereby indicating that efforts to reduce external debt or increase reserve accumulation (by equal amounts) would elicit identical responses from these four instruments. This implies that policies that attempt to control the external debt are perfectly compatible with those that attempt to increase reserve accumulation. Thus, a mix of such policies, which are needed to ensure the success of any growth-oriented adjustment programme, would be mutually self-reinforcing and there would be no off-setting trade-offs involved.

We now attempt to obtain policy options which are consistent with the objectives of growth-oriented adjustment. To do so, we initially solve the model in its programming mode and extract the 'optimal' set of stabilization policy responses. We then solve the model in its option mode with the target choices being made from within the neighbourhood of this 'optimal' set.

Solving the model in the programming mode implies imputing values for all the unknowns on the right-hand-side of (eqn 9.45a)–(eqn 9.45e). To do so, we specify, as before, a growth rate of 6.25 per cent and an inflation rate of 8.25 per cent; coupled to a reserve drawdown of \$ 1.75 billion, a fiscal deficit of Rs 1350 billion and an external debt of \$ 64 billion. In this context, it needs to be noted that this target set completely dominates the forecast set in as much as there are no trade-offs. Setting $\Delta R^* = -1.75$, $\pi = 0.0825$, $g = 0.0625$, $FD = 1350$, and $Fg^* = 64$, yields the following optimal policy package: $\Delta DCg = 262.6$; $e = 0.1323$; $\tau = 0.2613$; $Ig = 1079.3$, and $\Gamma = 0.1149$. Substituting these estimates into (eqn 9.41) yields the equilibrium value of the interest rate given by $i = 0.1307$.

The macroeconomic logic of this stabilization package suggests that the credit contraction would enable a sustainable level of reserve depletion. Increasing tax revenues, coupled to the reduction in public sector investment, would enable a reduction in the fiscal deficit. The fall in public investment would not reduce growth; in effect, the rise in the interest rate would increase private savings which, in association with the reduced fiscal deficit, would increase private investment more than adequately to compensate for the decrease in public investment. The fact that the external debt remains constant despite the associated capital losses on account of the exchange rate adjustment indicates a substantial reduction in the non-interest current account deficit as a result of the exchange rate depreciation.

9.6.2 *Policy Coordination Options: Financing the, Deficit*

In order to obtain guide-post solutions as to the possible growth-oriented adjustment options that are available, we once again target a 6.25 per cent growth rate and a 8.25 per cent inflation rate. Moreover, based upon the results of Section 8.7.1 (see Options # 8 and 9 in Table 8.2), as well as the forecasts just carried out, we accept the conclusion that: (i) a reserve depletion of $ 1.75 billion is a sustainable drawdown rate, and (ii) an exchange rate depreciation of 10.61 per cent will, more or less, enable the nominal exchange rate to lie in the approximate neighbourhood of its equilibrium level. Therefore, we set $\Delta R^* = -1.75$; $\pi = 0.0825$; $g = 0.0625$; and $e = 0.1061$ in (eqn 9.45). This yields the following set of equations:

$$\Delta DCg = 6.23335 Fg^* - 136.323, \tag{9.46a}$$
$$0.1061 = -0.01095 Fg^* + 0.83299, \tag{9.46b}$$
$$\tau = -0.01140 Fg^* + 0.99093, \tag{9.46c}$$
$$Ig = 1.0 FD - 18.2317 Fg^* + 896.169, \tag{9.46d}$$
$$\Gamma = 0.000149 FD - 0.00241 Fg^* + 0.06845. \tag{9.46e}$$

From (eqn 9.46b), we have, $Fg^* = 66.38$, which when substituted into (eqn 9.46a) and (eqn 9.46c) yields: $\Delta DCg = 277.5$ and $\tau = 0.2341$. Thus, it is seen that once the targets for reserve accumulation, inflation, growth, and exchange rate adjustments are fixed exogenously, the set of policy response functions yields a unique level of the external debt ($ 66.4 billion) which, in turn, yields unique values for the amount of credit expansion to the public sector (Rs 277.5 billion) and the rate of growth of tax revenues (23.4 per cent). Thus, no compromises are possible in the context of these two instruments (ΔDCg and τ) nor can there be any trade-off in the context of this target (Fg^*).

With values for Fg^*, ΔDCg, and τ uniquely established, the above system of equations reduces to the following:

$$Ig = 1.0 FD - 314.099, \tag{9.47a}$$
$$\Gamma = 0.000149 FD - 0.09153. \tag{9.47b}$$

This system which is now used to determine policy options comprises a set of two equations in three unknowns which implies that model closure can take place by specifying any one of them exogenously. Once the system has been solved, the optimal values of the six instruments (including $\Delta DCp = 350$), when substituted back into (eqn 9.41), would allow the (equilibrium) interest rate to be determined endogenously.

Option 1: In this first option, model closure is affected by assuming that the gross fiscal deficit will be held at the level set in the programming mode, that is $FD = 1350$. Substituting this value into (eqn 9.47a) and (eqn 9.47b) yields: $Ig = 1035.9$ and $\varGamma = 0.1096$, implying that public sector investment must be substantially curtailed to Rs 1036 billion while the rate of growth of domestic borrowings should not exceed 11 per cent. Substituting all the six instrument values, that is $\Delta DCg = 277.5$; $\Delta DCp = 350$; $e = 0.1061$; $\tau = 0.2341$; $Ig = 1035.9$; and $\varGamma = 0.1096$, into (eqn 9.41) yields $i = 0.1292$, implying that the equilibrium rate of interest would be around 12.9 per cent which is about a percentage point above its actual level. It is this increase in the interest rate that would ensure adequate private savings to offset the fall in public investment.

Option 2: However, the constraints on, both, public sector investment as well as public borrowings seem too tight to be feasible in practice. As such, in this second option, we relax the constraint on public sector investment and affect model closure by fixing $Ig = 1150$ (which is its predicted level). Substituting this value into (eqn 9.47a) yields $FD = 1464.1$ which, when substituted into (eqn 9.47b), yields $\varGamma = 0.1266$, implying that the fiscal deficit would now be Rs 1464 billion while the rate of growth of domestic borrowings can be slightly relaxed to 12.7 per cent. Although these changes would marginally increase the interest rate, it would be insufficient to increase private savings in a significant manner. Consequently, the increase in the fiscal deficit would tend to partially crowd out private investment.

Option 3: On the assumption that the second option still implies a rather tight domestic borrowing constraint which might be difficult for the government to adhere to, in this third and final option, we affect model closure by relaxing this constraint and setting $\varGamma = 0.15$ (its actual predicted level). Substituting this value into (eqn 9.47b) yields $FD = 1621.0$ which, when substituted into (eqn 9.47a), yields $Ig = 1306.9$, implying a lower fiscal deficit of Rs 1621 billion (*vis-à-vis* its predicted level of Rs 1638 billion) despite a higher public investment of Rs 1307 billion (*vis-à-vis* its predicted level of Rs 1150 billion). Thus, on the face of it, this last option seems to be the most feasible and sustainable of all.

The above options indicate that, by and large, the key to a successful implementation of growth-oriented adjustment programmes lies in the extent of policy coordination that exists between public investment (Ig) and public borrowings ($\varGamma$). To obtain a coordination rule between these two key instruments, we factor out *FD* from (eqn 9.47a) and (eqn 9.47b) thereby obtaining the following relationship between this instrument pair:

$$\Gamma = 0.000149Ig - 0.04473, \qquad (9.48)$$

which indicates that for every additional Rs 100 billion worth of public sector investment, the rate of growth of domestic borrowings must be stepped up by approximately 1.5 percentage points to ensure a balance between this subset of payments (classified 'above the line') and the corresponding subset of financing such payments (shown 'below the line').

To sum it up, a growth-oriented adjustment strategy for the Indian economy in 1996–7 which involves targeting: (1) a real growth rate of 6.25 per cent, (2) an inflation rate of 8.25 per cent, (3) a sustainable reserve depletion of $ 1.75 billion, and (4) an equilibrium exchange rate of about Rs 36.5 per US dollar; would require the following *approximate* stabilization measures: (1) public sector credit expansion of Rs 277.5 billion; (2) private sector credit expansion of Rs 350 billion; (3) a 23.5 per cent rate of growth of nominal tax revenues; (4) public sector investment of Rs 1307.5 billion; and (5) a rate of growth of domestic borrowings of 15 per cent. Under the circumstances, the equilibrium rate of interest would be around 12.9 per cent (which is almost a percentage point above its actual level), the consolidated fiscal deficit (that is the gross fiscal deficit of the central and state governments, plus the quasi-fiscal deficit of the entire banking system) would be around Rs 1621.5 billion, while the (interest-adjusted) external debt would be around $ 66.4 billion (about 21.9 per cent of GDP).

9.7 CONCLUSIONS

In conclusion, the debt crisis was triggered off by a widespread perception that the public sectors in many HICs were rendered effectively insolvent by their large stocks of both external and internal debt as well as by domestic constraints that impeded credible fiscal and monetary adjustments to the circumstances. In addition to the severe repercussions that the crisis had in terms of engendering uncertainty for private agents and thereby creating disincentives for private sector investment in the debtor countries, the drying up of external financing due to insolvency resulted in a liquidity crisis that required some form of fiscal adjustment as a matter of accounting arithmetic. The actual fiscal response—

involving increased reliance on domestic financing, the inflation tax, and the curtailment of public investment—was highly inefficient in many countries, leading to capital flight, reduced investment and stagnation, resulting in neither actual nor prospective full debt service, leaving the problem of insolvency well and truly in place.

In such a context, the central question therefore that needs to be asked and one that this chapter has attempted to address is whether there exists a sustainable level of external borrowings which, when coupled to a fiscal policy consistent with other macroeconomic targets (notably, reserve accumulation and inflation), permits enough investment for satisfactory output growth to be achieved. In effect, the integrated analytical framework presented here also examines the proposition as to whether the deficit–debt dynamics and reserve accumulation can be reconciled, or whether they are inherently opposed. The analysis of these issues raises three groups of related questions:

1. The first question is, how much borrowings are consistent with fiscal sustainability? The answer to this question sets the limits on fiscal deficits. Internal adjustments to these deficits require a matching surplus of private savings over private investment.
2. The second question is, how much of the matching internal adjustment can be actually brought about by the private sector? In other words, what should be the extent of monetary reform to increase private savings and is such a reform process consistent with these deficits?

The answers to the first two questions define the extent of private investment that is essential to reconcile the fiscal deficit target (obtained from the first question) with the private savings target (obtained from the second question).

3. The third question, then, is, what policies are required to induce the public sector to achieve this deficit without sacrificing investment?

Although each question is well defined in its own right, the separation is more apparent than real. The answer to each question has implications for the others; the sequential presentation does an injustice to the feedbacks that exist between them. The approach of this as well as the earlier chapters does, however, attempt to take account of these interactions as far as possible. However, the extent to which macro-economic dislocations are due to direct 'debt overhang' effects, rather than to the nature of the fiscal response to the liquidity aspects of the debt crisis, remain matters for future research.

NOTES

[1]The ensuing analysis, by assuming that $\Delta R = 0$, is based upon the following simplified version of the external balance:

$$Z - X = \Delta F - i_f F, \tag{9.a}$$

where ΔF is gross external borrowings and $i_f F$ are the interest payments on external debt. As such, the right-hand-side of (eqn 9.a), which is equal to the net transfer of resources from foreigners, must correspond to the *NICA* given by $(Z - X)$. All the analytical results spelt out in this section are based on the above equation.

[2]As before, the analysis continues to assume, from the viewpoint of analytical tractability, that $\Delta R^* = 0$. As a consequence, a non-interest current account deficit can only be financed by a net transfer of resources from abroad and not by a drawdown of foreign exchange reserves as is ordinarily possible. Needless to say, when the relationship between the fiscal deficit, current account, and external debt are finally integrated into our model, we shall revert back to the operational definition of the external balance.

[3]As in the earlier chapter, in order to simplify the ensuing analytical presentation, we shall adopt the following first-difference version of (eqn 9.2) which is true if Δ is defined as the forward difference operator. As before, however, when we incorporate the external adjustment equation into the model of Chapter 8, we shall revert back to our earlier notation.

[4](Eqn 9.3) can be written in terms of Δf^* as follows:

$$\Delta f^* = [NICA/Y] + i_f[EF^*/Y] + [F^*\Delta E/Y] - f^*[\Delta Y/Y]. \tag{9.b}$$

which yields (eqn 9.4) given the definitions: $n = NICA/Y, f^* = EF^*/Y, \Delta Y/Y = \pi + g,$ and $r = i_f - \pi;$ as well as the following simplification:

$$F^*[\Delta E/Y] = F^*[\Delta E/E][E/Y] = e[EF^*/Y^*] = ef^*. \tag{9.c}$$

[5]As $\Delta f^*(t) = f^*(t + 1) - f^*(t)$, (eqn 9.5) yields:

$$f^*(t + 1) = [1 + r - g]f^*(t) + n. \tag{9.d}$$

Now, if $r < g$, then, following the logic outlined in Chapter 8 (Note 13), in the long-run we shall have:

$$f^*(t) = f^*(t + 1) = \overline{f}, \tag{9.e}$$

where $\overline{f}$ is the long-run steady-state value of the external debt–income ratio. Substituting (eqn 9.e) into (eqn 9.d) yields (eqn 9.6):

[6]The analysis of Sargent and Wallace (1981) was extended to an open economy by Drazen and Helpman (1987), and van Wijnbergen (1991) thereby facilitating the incorporation of exchange rate policy into the framework.

[7]While we could have used differential ICORs for public and private sector investment, it would have needlessly complicated the resulting analytical framework. As such, we have assumed that both these categories of investment are equally productive.

[8]Note that: $T/Y(-1) = [T(-1) + \Delta T]/Y(-1) = [T(-1)/Y(-1)]$
$$+ [\Delta T/T(-1)][T(-1)/Y(-1)]$$
$$= t(-1) + t(-1)\tau. \tag{9.f}$$

[9]If the entire banking system has been nationalized, the terms 'central bank' and 'banking system' can be used interchangeably. The deficit of the central bank is often referred to as the 'quasi-fiscal' deficit.

[10]The following definitional equations were used in the derivation:

$$\Delta Y/Y(-1) = g + \pi, \tag{9.g}$$
$$\Delta B/Y(-1) = [\Delta B/B(-1)][B(-1)/Y(-1)] = b(-1)\Gamma, \tag{9.h}$$
$$[Fg^*(-1)\Delta E]/Y(-1) = [Fg^*(-1)/Y(-1)][\Delta E/E(-1)]E(-1)$$
$$= [Fg^*(-1)/Y^*(-1)]e = fg^*(-1)e, \quad ...(9.i)$$
$$[R^*(-1)\Delta E]/Y(-1) = [R^*(-1)/Y(-1)][\Delta E/E(-1)]E(-1)$$
$$= [R^*(-1)/Y^*(-1)]e. \quad ...(9.j)$$

[11]All starred (*) variables indicate that they are measured in terms of foreign currency units which, in our case, happens to be US dollars ($).

[12]It needs to be noted that the set of parameters corresponding to the interest rate determination equation, that is $\delta(0) - \delta(6)$, cannot be considered as composite parameters as they were estimated on the basis of a regression equation. As such, we have directly provided these estimated values unlike in the case of the other composite parameters wherein we have specified the equation determining each of them.

[13]The predetermined variables correspond to 1995–6 while the exogenous variables correspond to 1996–7.

[14]The actual value of the external debt at the end of March 1994 was $ 92.7 billion. However, the relatively high grant element in India's external debt translates into downsizing the nominal value of the debt by about one-third in 'present value' (PV) terms to $ 60.5 billion (see *Economic Survey 1995-96*, Government of India, p. 102). With interest payments on the external debt being equal to the existing (unadjusted) foreign interest rate (i_f) times the stock of debt, using the actual nominal value of the external debt *per se* under these circumstances would have resulted in overestimating interest payments. Consequently, it is this PV estimate that is used as an approximate measure of the stock of external debt and its corresponding level for 1995–6 was $ 64.03 billion, that is $Fg^*(-1) = 64.03$. However, in order to avoid confusion between

this definition of the present value of debt and its existing definition in the literature which is inextricably linked to the concept of solvency, we shall refer to this downsized estimate of the nominal debt as the 'adjusted' external debt.

[15]Two points need to be made at this juncture regarding the accuracy of the forecasts: (i) The consolidated fiscal deficit, within the framework of the model, implies the sum of the gross fiscal deficit of the central, state, and local governments plus the quasi-fiscal deficit of the entire banking system (inclusive of the central bank, that is the Reserve Bank of India). As such, the predicted value of Rs 1638 billion for the fiscal deficit should not be considered as an overestimate; and (ii) Although the estimate of external debt in our model corresponds to its so-called 'present value' concept, its predicted annual increase of about \$ 2.1 billion corresponds to its average annual increase over the last 4 years. Thus, using the 'interest-adjusted' concept of the external debt does not distort its dynamics in any significant manner.

[16]While the impact of domestic credit expansion ($\Delta DC > 0$) on growth has been unambiguously positive in all versions of the model, it is only in this final fully integrated system, that the impact of an exchange rate depreciation ($e > 0$) on growth becomes negative. Thus, it is seen that unlike the standard IMF paradigm, output growth would be lower (at least, in the Indian context) after a depreciation rather than higher. Needless to say, however, the actual direction and magnitude of the exchange rate effects on growth would depend crucially upon the estimated parameters.

[17]Thus, it is seen that the equality between the number of instruments and the number of targets is a necessary but not a sufficient condition for the derivation of the programming mode of the model.

[18]This is a permissible procedure as we are operating on the reduced form of the model after the impacts of the lagged target variables have been imbedded into the intercept term. However, reducing the dimension of the system in this manner does not imply that the interest rate can be set *a priori*. It is still an endogenous variable and the procedure for determining its value will be illustrated in the next subsection.

REDISTRIBUTION, ADJUSTMENT, AND GROWTH

10

Redistributive Adjustment with Growth

10.1 INTRODUCTION

Until the 1960s, much of the focus of development economics was on capital accumulation and growth. However, several studies that highlighted the continuing and significant inequalities around the world and the failure of widespread economic growth to remedy the problem, which had been 'assumed away' by the 'trickle down' theories of the 1940s and 1950s, led to widespread disillusionment with the post-war economic progress—despite its impressive growth record—and, in that context, emerged a new professional interest in income distribution and its relationship with growth in the   mid-1970s.

However, unfortunately, distributional issues only had 'one brief shining moment' at centre stage before the second oil price shock of 1980 and the debt crisis of 1982 commanded most of the attention of the developing countries. Adjustment issues began to dominate and the balance of payments (BOP) became the determining factor in policy. Countries were forced to focus not only on getting their macroeconomics right, via appropriate monetary, fiscal, and exchange rate policies, but also on an entire spectrum of related issues—including financial sector reforms, trade reforms, external debt management policies, amongst others—which eventually 'crowded out' distributional concerns.

Growth—or rather its absence—became the recurrent theme and this led inevitably to the role of the state in guiding the development process. However, since the 1990s, the differences in the regional performances have been wider than at any other time in the post-war era. Africa and Latin America have stagnated while Asia has moved rapidly ahead.

Consequently, given the extent of global expansion today, the questions of income inequality and poverty, and what can be done to reduce them, once again command serious attention.

Section 10.2 initially highlights the UNICEF-related concept of 'adjustment with a human face' which is followed by a brief discussion on the quality of growth in Section 10.3. The current thinking on the state of the relationship between inequality, poverty, and growth is examined in Section 10.4. Empirical evidence in this regard, with respect to the Indian economy, is initially presented in Section 10.5. The model of the previous chapter is then extended by integrating income distribution into its framework. The concept of joint Bank–Fund– UNICEF equilibrium is then established. In the process, the impact of policy variables, used in a standard adjustment programme, on income inequality is empirically verified.

10.2 ADJUSTMENT WITH A HUMAN FACE: THE UNICEF APPROACH

Several organizations belonging to the United Nations system, to which the Bretton Woods institutions, that is the World Bank and the IMF, are formally attached, have over the past decade or so voiced an increasing concern over the design and implementation of orthodox stabilization and adjustment programmes in developing countries. Prominent amongst this group of institutions is the UNICEF which, in line with its institutional mandate and concerns with the situation of the world's children, has consistently argued that the adjustment experiences of most countries cannot be considered as unqualified successes.

Although it is readily recognized by the UNICEF that without some form of adjustment, the situation would often be far worse, nonetheless, it is held that standard adjustment policies have aggravated poverty and caused social setbacks, especially amongst the vulnerable groups. Thus, it is felt that alternative adjustment policies, which take into account such negative social consequences and provide a basis for equitable growth, are required.

Accordingly, the UNICEF has called for 'adjustment with a human face', an expression originally coined by Cornia, Jolly, and Stewart (1987a,b). At the heart of their proposal is the notion that if adjustment is not people-oriented, it is wrongly conceived. Therefore, the human dimension must be made an integral aspect of all adjustment policies, rather than being ignored completely or treated as yet another welfare component to be incorporated residually into the structure of the model.

Under their framework, economic policies should seek to improve the productivity and incomes of the poor directly, and essential services and subsidies should be increased rather than reduced. Furthermore, since the social sectors are central to the formation of human capital, basic health and education should not be treated as consumer goods, but rather as capital goods which need to be augmented. For unless these are provided, the further ability to produce would be affected and, consequently, the future potential for productivity growth would be seriously impaired. This perspective contrasts starkly with the widespread reductions in social sector budgets which have often been a consequence of structural adjustment programmes.

While it is correct, as argued by the IMF and the World Bank, that many adjustment programmes are intended to move societies towards greater equality by reducing the prevailing urban bias, such expectations about positive distributional outcomes are neither analytically nor empirically grounded. Given this lacuna, there is, in fact, a *prima facie* case to infer that standard adjustment programmes could increase urban inequality, without alleviating rural poverty. This is because the dynamics of poverty and income inequality are far more complex than a simple urban–rural dichotomy seems to indicate.

However, distributive concerns are by no means a new topic within the field of development economics. The end of the first United Nations development decade (1960–70), as well as the decade of the 1970s, witnessed an upsurge in theoretical and policy literature about poverty, inequality, and unemployment; and the logical conclusion drawn by Seers (1969) was that if one or two of these indicators have worsened, and especially if all three have, it would be impossible to label the result as 'development', even if growth was very high.

The 'trickle down' theories of the 1940s and 1950s came under close scrutiny during this period, and the resulting empirical evidence led to widespread disillusionment with the progress made in the 1960s, despite its historically impressive growth record. Attention then switched to 'human capital' formation and, in the process, 'basic human needs' and 'redistribution with growth' soon acquired the status of paradigms in development economics and subsequently became cornerstones in the World Bank development approach of the 1970s (see Chenery *et al* 1974). The World Bank was in the forefront of much of the new thinking in these areas and, along with other organizations such as the International Labour Organization (ILO), fully supported the emphasis on equitable growth. In effect, the pendulum of mainstream development economics had by the early 1970s swung away from its exclusive emphasis on growth *per se*.

However, these broader perceptions and views did not retain their dominance in development theory and practice for very long and, by the early 1980s, distributive concerns somehow became submerged in the adjustment debate partly because the stabilization programmes of the IMF continued to focus only on the economic, and not the human, dimensions of adjustment; but mostly because, the World Bank, even after the stand it had taken during the 1970s, failed to consider a more perceptive view of the distributional consequences of development aid and, more importantly, was unable to ensure the success of projects which were being targeted towards poverty alleviation. This neglect of social issues was reinforced by the fact that the more delicate and decentralized process and sectoral details which are required during the formulation of an adjustment programme geared towards promoting equitable distribution were, by and large, overlooked in the 1980s.

Consequently, the UNICEF approach is a reminder of the distributive concerns and the development insights of the previous decades, and 'adjustment with a human face' therefore adds the poverty alleviation dimension to adjustment in much the same way as 'redistribution with growth' added the distribution dimension to growth. In such a context, 'adjustment with a human face' can be thought of as the 'basic needs approach to adjustment' and the importance of this dimension is even more significant now than during the growth experiences of the 1960s and 1970s since per capita incomes are stagnating, if not declining, in so many countries around the world.

The alternative UNICEF policy package which is geared towards the goal of a more satisfactory adjustment process comprises five key elements which can be briefly summarized as follows implicitly comparing them with a typical or orthodox IMF/World Bank-supported programme:

- More expansionary (that is, less austere) fiscal, monetary, and wage policies which are aimed at sustaining levels of production, employment, and basic needs over the adjustment period.
- Sectoral policies aimed at restructuring production to provide greater emphasis to income-generating and productive employment of the poorer sections of the society.
- Restructuring of social expenditures towards low-cost basic education and primary health care, with a view to improving equity as well as efficiency in service provision.

- Compensatory programmes that provide temporary, but additional and targeted, support for those affected by adjustment programmes, with a view to protecting basic health and nutritional standards.
- Appropriate 'meso' policies which combine macroeconomic instruments (such as government expenditure, taxation, and credit policy) with selectivity, such that distributional concerns are taken into account.

Improvements in the modalities of the adjustment design are also suggested. The extension of the time perspective of the adjustment (or gradualist strategies) as well as the mobilization of additionally required external resources (or reciprocal conditionality) are also some of the aspects of the UNICEF policy package. Such changes are perceived as necessary measures to focus sufficient attention on the human dimension of the adjustment process, as well as to identify and assess the effectiveness of adjustment programmes, so that they can be monitored and modified whenever required.

In summary, the UNICEF approach implies that adjustment policies are not merely intended only to reduce macroeconomic imbalances but are seen as an integral part of a longer-term development strategy. As such, the approach takes account of, both, the economic as well as the non-economic aspects of society. Focusing only on economic policy, to the exclusion of the 'human face', is, in the opinion of the UNICEF, a far too narrow approach, which would only endanger the future growth and development potential of the economy.

10.3 QUALITY OF GROWTH

In such a context, environmental quality is a key ingredient in the well-being of people. While some environmental changes have no bearing with human activities, most other forms of environmental degradation are directly related to economic expansion largely because most economic activities, by and large, require some form and amount of environmental inputs. This leads to the trade-off between the benefits of economic growth (as a result of depleting natural resources) and the costs of the ensuing environmental damage. However, the latter aspect, in view of the hidden costs involved, has been difficult to quantify largely because of our incomplete understanding of the complex relationship between environment damage, human activity, and economic growth.

In such a context, two polarized views have dominated the debate over environment and economic growth. The 'anti-growth' view that economic growth and development are essentially damaging to the environment because of the inevitable depletion of natural resources involved; and the 'pro-growth' view that economic growth will lead to an increase in per capita incomes which, in turn, will be more conducive for environmental protection. In between them is the 'green growth' hypothesis which contends that while, in the short term, growth could have an adverse impact on environmental resources, in the longer term, higher growth and per capita incomes will lead to sustainable economic development and growth. In addition, there is the 'environmental transition' hypothesis of Ruttan (1971) which states that growth is likely to be accompanied by environmental degradation at low income levels, but as income increases, the demand for environmental quality would also increase, thereby leading to sustainable economic development (see Antle and Heidebrink 1995).

The anti-growth view is based on the two-way association between growth and environmental degradation: in effect, there is a limit to the renewal rate of the environment and therefore rapid growth would eventually lead to a depletion of natural resources. The consequent environmental degradation, if untreated, would impose limits on future growth. Even if contained through stricter environmental regulations, these would raise costs and, by diverting investment away from production, would reduce growth. In this context, there is no doubt, as pointed out by the 1987 Brundtland Commission Report (World Commission on Environment and Development), that economic growth, especially in the industrial countries, by emphasizing needs rather than resource limitations, has exhausted a relatively high share of global resources.

However, at an empirical level, the anti-growth view finds very limited support. If growth does cause environmental depletion or damage, then the industrial countries should have exhibited a gradually declining trend in environmental quality and their environmental state should have been far inferior to that of the developing countries. However, the fact that this has not happened does not mean to imply that unfettered growth and economic development will be beneficial to the environment because enough examples abound regarding the harmful residual effects of growth on the environment.

Regardless of such evidence, or the lack of it, the growth–environment trade-off faced by countries during the process of development is yet to be fully understood. While in the short term, such a trade-off may be observed, in the longer term, even in a world in which environmental quality does not command a market price, economic growth may not necessarily lead to environmental degradation. This is because, with increasing economic growth and per capita incomes, the negative external effects of environmental degradation can be contained by policies which ensure that a larger share of the gross national product (GNP) is committed to environmental protection activities. Moreover, it has also been observed that as economies mature, there is a gradual shift away from environmentally degrading industries towards 'cleaner' technologies and services that are less environmentally demanding. For example, during the period 1986–91, on a per capita basis, the United States is estimated to have emitted ten times the carbon dioxide than that emitted by China (see World Bank 1995). However, the same data on greenhouse gas emissions, when examined relative to GNP, suggests that as a result of greater efficiency and changing economic structures from manufacturing to services based industries, the emissions in the richer countries have declined with increases in their GNP.

Considering that the observed income elasticity of demand for environmental quality is quite high, the above evidence implies that consumers in richer nations would be more willing than those in the developing countries to spend (or be taxed) a larger proportion of their incomes for environmental protection. Such environmental regulations are likely to increase resources expended on research and development which, in turn, may lead to technological innovations with a positive impact on environmental quality. Moreover, increases in investment costs due to forced compliance of environmental regulations could change the composition of the aggregate capital stock that could leave the long-term growth unaffected. To sum up, environmental regulations and policies could not only lead to 'green growth' but could also improve the quality and productivity of human capital and, therefore, raise the long-term growth rate.

10.4 INEQUALITY, POVERTY, AND GROWTH

10.4.1 *Redistribution and Growth*

Since the publication of *Redistribution with Growth* (Chenery *et al* 1974), the issue of the two-way relationship between income distribution and economic growth has been intensively investigated by development economists. The basis of the seminal approach was very simple. First, there was the tacit acceptance of the Kuznets insight, reinforced by new empirical analysis, that income distribution shows a natural tendency towards greater equality during the early as well as the later stages of development. Second, there was the firm insistence on a need for policy packages specifically targeted towards those below the poverty line. Third, there was the unshaken belief in the compatibility of growth and simultaneous efforts to improve income distribution: 'poverty-focused planning does not imply the abandonment of growth as an objective. It implies instead redistribution of the benefits of growth' (Chenery *et al* 1974, p. xviii).

Against such a two-decade old background, the increased, but still largely static, information on income distribution presently accumulated does, however, permit more careful analysis of the simple ∩-hypothesis initially advanced by Kuznets (1955). That concept—which states that both low-income and high-income countries would have lower inequality because of the greater homogeneity of their respective labour forces— has been subject to careful re-examination in recent years.

The key result so far—characteristic of recent works by Persson and Tabellini (1994) and Alesina and Rodrik (1994)—is that inequality is negatively related to growth. These results have been confirmed by Chen, Datt, and Ravallion (1994) and Ravallion (1995) who found no support for the Kuznets hypothesis when allowing for fixed effects. It is thus possible that in most of the earlier studies confirming the ∩- shaped curve between income inequality and per capita incomes, the country level determinants of inequality could have been correlated with income levels, thereby leading to biased estimates. Moreover, studies by Li, Squire, and Zou (1995), who used 464 observations on Gini indices covering 42 countries for the period 1950–90, and by Ravallion and Datt (1995), who used time-series data on the Indian economy (33 observations on Gini indices for the period 1951–92), have revealed that while there could be substantial variability in inequality across countries, there was relative stability within countries over time. For India, the results suggest that there is little evidence to indicate that higher growth rates put any upward pressure on the Gini index.

Although the postulated inverted-U relationship between income and inequality is not borne out in most of the recent studies, Fishlow (1995) contends that the problem exposed by such types of analysis has less to do with the inherent inconsistency of the Kuznets hypothesis than with the reality of substantial intervention in the economic system. He suggests that a slightly more complex relationship obtained by introducing an additional variable—participation in secondary education—allows a partial revival of the Kuznets hypothesis. However, this claim is rather difficult to accept because, although the ensuing results signal the correct parabolic shape, the coefficients of both income as well as its square are extremely insignificant for the set of developing countries.

Equally, if not more, important, the cited studies by Persson and Tabellini (1994), as well as by Alesina and Rodrik (1994), strongly indicate that the effects of equality on growth are not only statistically significant but also quantitatively important. In both cases, a one standard deviation reduction in the independent variable (income share of the middle quintile in the former study; and the Gini coefficient in the latter) increases the growth rate by between half and one percentage point, thus strongly supporting the notion that policies which are geared towards reducing income inequalities may yield higher rates of growth. The reasoning behind this is attributed to the fact that high income inequalities either motivate populist policies which are inimical to the higher rates of investment required to assure adequate growth (Sachs 1990) or tend to increase political instability thereby reducing private investment (Alesina and Perotti 1993). This is an important conclusion for policy makers who have long adhered to the conventional paradigm that policies which reduce income inequality can adversely affect growth because: (i) redistributive programmes often redirect funds away from more productive uses towards less productive ones (such as investment in human capital) and (ii) transfers and taxes used to redistribute wealth and incomes may adversely affect high-income groups who have a larger propensity to save, thereby decreasing savings and, thus, investment and growth. The fundamental conclusion that emanates from the above studies, including Clark (1995), is that income distribution and growth are related in a positive self-reinforcing manner with high growth reducing income inequality which, in turn, increases growth still further, although the extent of feedback is largely determined by initial conditions.

10.4.2 *Poverty Alleviation*

It is estimated that about 1.1 billion people around the world still live in absolute poverty by earning less than US $ 1 a day (World Bank 1993b). Although in certain high-growth economies of East Asia, growth promoting policies and programmes have brought about significant reductions in poverty, in most other developing countries of the world, especially those in Africa and Latin America, the number of poor (or those subsisting below the poverty line) has increased approximately at the same rate as population growth.

Consequently, much of the current attention of policy makers is slowly turning away from dealing directly with income distribution to the task of reducing poverty. These are not the same objectives, because it has four implications. First, such a shift implies more concern with those who are the worst off, the poorest of the poor. Second, it suggests directing attention away from Asia, which has a more skewed income distribution, to Africa, where incomes are much lower; in effect, changing the geographic focus. Third, it means directing attention to the rural sector, where the poverty burden is much larger. Finally, it helps reduce the perceived tension (if any) between the simultaneous objectives of improving the distribution of income and accelerating growth, because incomes *per se* at the bottom quintile of the income distribution can more easily be increased with greater production—even though the distribution of income could remain as unequal as it had been or become even more unequal. Thus, trickle-down effects, long discarded as a means to achieving an equitable distribution of income, could still be invoked to eliminate some poverty. However, if distribution is assumed to remain constant, then growth should reduce absolute poverty. In 17 of the 20 countries for which extensive data is available for the 1980s and 1990s, the mean as well as the proportion of people living below a 'dollar a day' revealed a concomitant improvement along with growth, thereby testifying to the important fact that, both, poverty as well as income distribution are not growth neutral.

A leading part in the initial efforts launched more than 15 years ago to direct attention on poverty was played by the basic needs approach which focused on the importance of separating generalized increases in income from the more significant attainments in the quest for a permanent reduction in poverty, such as improvements in health, regular access to nutritious food, more education, and better as well as affordable shelter. Basically, two arguments were advanced to support this view. First, many poor people are not themselves producers, but are part of the dependent population. Second, there is no guarantee that increased income will be spent on essential services.

However, in the end, 'basic needs' vanished as a tracking device, mainly because of the difficulties of aggregating this concept. But the attention that the concept directed, both, to the poor as well as to the policies required to improved their lot, has persisted. The United Nations Development Programme (UNDP) *Human Development Report 1993* (see UNDP 1993) is illustrative in this regard: 'The purpose of development is to widen the range of people's choices. Income is one of these choices—but it is not the sum-total of human life' (p. 3). To put it differently, even if one (still) believes in a negative correlation between per capita income and income distribution, this does not negate the relevance of public policies directed towards increasing the incomes of the poor and thereby improving income distribution.

One important consequence of the failure of aggregating the concept of 'basic needs' is the renewed focus on developing robust measures of poverty. For example, in the early 1970s, the usual method of measuring poverty was a simple headcount measure that used an arbitrary poverty line based on expenditures and incomes. Recently developed measures, such as the poverty gap index, are more sensitive to the depth of poverty as well as to inequalities among the poor. Moreover, multi-faceted measures of poverty that assess the concept of the overall quality of life are now being used by economists to address the complex problem of poverty.

Using such revised poverty measures on the Indian economy over the period 1951–92, Ravallion and Datt (1995, 1996) and Datt and Ravallion (1996a, 1996b) show that it is the service sector, followed closely by the agricultural sector, that has by far delivered the most gains to India's poor, while industrial growth has brought no discernible gains to either the urban or rural poor. The generalization that follows from these findings is that agricultural growth is crucial for reducing poverty (both rural as well as urban), while the service sector has to be encouraged to further bring about reductions in poverty.

As a result of these and other research efforts, much greater attention is being paid to the importance of social safety nets (SSNs) to ensure the welfare of the poor. However, SSNs are not the only requirement. The World Bank adds two more essential requirements (see World Bank 1990c): attention to labour-intensive growth, especially in agriculture (which may also boost exports), and an emphasis on primary education and health.

But a further dimension—recently emphasized by Bardhan (1994) and stated explicitly in the *Human Development Report 1993*—merits some discussion. The literature on poverty alleviation suggests two opposing views in this regard. On the one side is the market-oriented approach, with its provision for SSNs only for those who fail to be absorbed in productive employment. And on the other side is the basic needs emphasis on public intervention on a large scale to meet the unsatisfied needs of the poor for a wide range of essential services. In such a context, Bardhan suggests a third alternative, relying on 'local self-governing institutions and community involvement to improve the material conditions and autonomy of the poor' (p. 3).

However, the issue this raises is the capability of the poor to organize their demands effectively and continuously. Equally important, such emphasis calls for a different role from the state—an activist one nonetheless but through effective decentralization. Such a restructuring would involve important changes, especially with regards to the unequal concentration of public expenditures at the national level.

Finally, community groups, assisted by non-government organizations (NGOs), have been an important force to reckon with in the expansion of local authority. They have been much favoured by bilateral assistance programmes, largely in view of the capacity of NGOs to reach low-income groups, especially in the rural areas (they now reach an estimated 250 million people). Although still considerably short of total coverage, the more than doubling of their reach in the past decade has been quite impressive. However, in the end the issue comes back to the ability of the central government to initiate, reinforce, and sustain decentralization. The first decade of this millennium should test that capability.

10.5 INCOME DISTRIBUTION IN A FINANCIAL PROGRAMMING FRAMEWORK

10.5.1 *Inflation, Growth, and Income Distribution*

The empirical results in this section are based on a World Bank research project, led by Martin Ravallion and Gaurav Datt, that collated all the available data on income distribution for the Indian economy over the period 1951–92 during which time the Government of India undertook 34 surveys relating to the measurement of income inequality under the auspices of the National Sample Survey Organization (NSSO). The preliminary results of the latest survey (NSS 48th Round) for 1993–4 which concluded in July 1996 have not been considered. Nonetheless, it is for the first time that such a unique data set, containing time series estimates on Gini coefficients (30 annual observations over a 42 year period), is available for researchers, and this should provide them with an opportunity to undertake exhaustive empirical analyses on poverty, income distribution, and growth for the Indian economy, in particular, and for developing economies, in general, because India is one of the few developing countries for which such a long and reliable time series measure of income distribution has been constructed.

The purpose of the ensuing analysis was to determine the extent of the correlation between the Gini index (*GI*) and, both, inflation (π) as well as growth (*g*), based upon the basic premise that while inflation should naturally increase the Gini index (worsen income distribution), growth should, following the lead of Alesina and Rodrik (1994), amongst others, decrease the Gini index (improve income distribution). From the viewpoint of rigour, we were interested in explaining the change in the Gini index (ΔGI), rather than its level. As such, we were constrained to use only the time series estimates over the 7-year period 1986–93, as this was the latest available data on a continuous basis.

The estimated equation, corrected for first-order serial correlation, is given below (where the figures in parentheses indicate *t*-statistics, S.E.R. stands for the standard error of regression and D.W. refers to the Durbin–Watson statistic):

$$\Delta GI = 13.4681\pi - 25.6143g,$$
$$(4.2) \qquad (-4.5)$$
$$R^2 = 0.84; \quad \text{S.E.R.} = 0.66; \quad \text{D.W.} = 2.6. \qquad \qquad ...(10.1)$$

The results vindicate the hypothesis that growth (inflation) reduces (increases) income disparities in the Indian economy. Both the regressors are highly significant which testifies to the robustness of the estimated relationship considering that we were explaining the change in the Gini index.

Based upon the above estimated equation, and using existing data on actual inflation and growth rates, we predicted the Gini index through 1995–6. Doing so indicates that the Gini index in 1995–6 was 31.55 which represents a considerable improvement *vis-à-vis* its level of 32.53 in 1991–2, that is the year in which the Indian economy implemented a structural adjustment programme in the aftermath of the foreign exchange crisis. However, the results also indicate that despite five years of adjustment, the Gini index has still not yet returned to its pre-reform level of 29.69 in 1990–1, implying that just because inflation (growth) has stabilized (resumed), there should be no let-up by policy makers in their quest to secure a more equitable income distribution.

10.5.2 *Joint Fund–Bank–UNICEF Equilibrium*

Before integrating (eqn 10.1) into the formal framework of the model developed in the previous chapter, we carry out a brief preliminary analysis into the concept of policy coordination measures, between the Fund and the Bank, that are essential to ensure an equitable income distribution.

To do so, we initially set $\Delta GI = 0$ in (eqn 10.1) above, yielding an 'iso-Gini line', and solve the resultant in terms of the growth rate obtaining:

$$g = 0.5258\pi. \tag{10.2}$$

(Eqn 10.2) which traces out a positively-sloped locus in $\pi - g$ space, denoted by UU in Figure 10.1, thus denotes all combinations of inflation rates and growth rates at which the income distribution remains unchanged. It indicates that for every percentage point increase in the rate of inflation (π), the growth rate (g) must rise by at least 0.526 percentage points to ensure a *status quo* as far as the income distribution is concerned. This yields the following generalization for the Indian economy: As long as the ratio between growth and inflation is 1:2, the income distribution will remain unchanged. If, however, the inflation–growth ratio exceeds (falls short of) two, then income distribution would worsen (improve).

Considering that the above equation lies at the very heart of the UNICEF argument regarding 'adjustment with a human face', we have termed it as the UNICEF equilibrium in Figure 10.1 which also depicts the Fund equilibrium, (eqn 6.36), and the Bank equilibrium, (eqn 6.37), determined in Chapter 6.

We thus have the three equilibrium relationships:

Fund equilibrium: $g = 0.1379 - \pi;$
Bank equilibrium: $g = 0.0514 + 0.0869\pi;$
UNICEF equilibrium: $g = 0.5258\pi;$

and it is these lines which are plotted in Figure 10.1, denoting, respectively, Fund equilibrium (FF), Bank equilibrium (BB), and UNICEF equilibrium (UU).

Figure 10.1 lends itself easily to some very important comparative-static analysis. As the intersection of the FF and BB lines occurs at E which is above the UU line, this would improve income distribution. However, from (eqn 6.30), it is evident that the FF line shifts outward with, say, a devaluation which, given the slope of the BB line, implies that the equilibrium point (E) could move to the zone below UU signifying a worsening of income distribution. However, this can be pre-empted if, along with devaluation, adequate supply-side policies to stimulate savings are put into effect. This would imply that, although the FF line shifts outwards, the BB line would now move upwards, as well as swivel in a counter-clockwise direction, and therefore their intersection (E) could still remain above the UU line. The analysis therefore clearly highlights the need for Fund–Bank policy coordination in order to ensure that adjustment programmes have a distributional perspective automatically inbuilt into it; in effect, that it is an 'adjustment with a human face'.

10.5.3 Growth with Redistribution

In order to formally incorporate income distribution into the integrated model, referred to as the Representative Model—Version 7 (RM7), we initially rewrite (eqn 10.1) as follows:

$$GI = GI(-1) + \psi(1)\pi - \psi(2)\pi, \qquad (10.3)$$

where $\psi(1) = 13.4681$ and $\psi(2) = 25.6143$.

Substituting (eqn 10.3) into (eqn 9.38) yields the structure of the fully integrated Representative Model—Version 7 (RM7) which is set out below:

$$
\begin{bmatrix}
1 & -\alpha(1) & -\alpha(2) & 0 & 0 & 0 & 0 \\
1 & \beta(1) & \beta(2) & 0 & 0 & -1 & 0 \\
\gamma(1) & \gamma(2) & \gamma(3) & -\gamma(7) & \gamma(10) & -\gamma(5) & 0 \\
0 & -\delta(4) & -\delta(2) & 1 & 0 & 0 & 0 \\
0 & -\varepsilon(1) & -\varepsilon(2) & -\varepsilon(3) & \varepsilon(4) & 0 & 0 \\
-\phi(1) & \phi(2) & \phi(3) & -\phi(4) & 0 & \phi(5) & 0 \\
0 & -\psi(1) & \psi(2) & 0 & 0 & 0 & 1
\end{bmatrix}
\begin{bmatrix}
\Delta R^* \\
\pi \\
g \\
i \\
FD \\
Fg^* \\
GI
\end{bmatrix}
=
$$

$$
\begin{bmatrix}
0 & 0 & 0 & 0 & 0 & 0 & 0 \\
0 & 0 & 0 & 0 & 0 & -1 & 0 \\
0 & 0 & 0 & -\gamma(8) & 0 & -\gamma(5) & 0 \\
0 & 0 & 0 & \delta(5) & 0 & 0 & 0 \\
0 & 0 & 0 & 0 & 0 & \varepsilon(5) & 0 \\
0 & 0 & 0 & 0 & 0 & \phi(6) & 0 \\
0 & 0 & 0 & 0 & 0 & 0 & 1
\end{bmatrix}
\begin{bmatrix}
\Delta R^*(-1) \\
\pi(-1) \\
g(-1) \\
i(-1) \\
FD(-1) \\
Fg^*(-1) \\
GI(-1)
\end{bmatrix}
$$

$$
+
\begin{bmatrix}
-\alpha(3) & -\alpha(3) & -\alpha(4) & 0 & 0 & 0 \\
0 & 0 & \beta(3) & 0 & 0 & 0 \\
0 & 0 & \gamma(4) & \gamma(9) & \gamma(11) & 0 \\
0 & 0 & \delta(1) & 0 & 0 & 0 \\
0 & 0 & 0 & -\varepsilon(6) & \varepsilon(7) & 0 \\
0 & \phi(7) & \phi(8) & -\phi(9) & \phi(10) & -\phi(11) \\
0 & 0 & 0 & 0 & 0 & 0
\end{bmatrix}
\begin{bmatrix}
\Delta DCg \\
\Delta DCp \\
e \\
\tau \\
Ig \\
\Gamma
\end{bmatrix}
+
\begin{bmatrix}
0 \\
\beta^*(4) \\
\gamma(6) \\
\delta(6) \\
\varepsilon(8) \\
\phi(12) \\
0
\end{bmatrix}
$$

$$...(10.4)$$

which, as before, can be solved in terms of x as follows:

$$x = Ax(-1) + Bu + z, \qquad (10.5)$$

where: $x = [\Delta R^* \; \pi \; g \; i \; FD \; Fg^* \; GI]'$ is a (7×1) target vector; and
$u = [\Delta DCg \; \Delta DCp \; e \; \tau \; Ig \; \Gamma]'$ is a (6×1) instrument vector.
Substituting the values of the composite parameters, provided in
Table 9.4, along with $\psi(1) = 13.4681$ and $\psi(2) = 25.6143$, into (eqn
10.4) yields the following estimated form of (eqn 10.5):

$$
\begin{bmatrix} \Delta R^* \\ \pi \\ g \\ i \\ FD \\ Fg^* \\ GI \end{bmatrix} =
\begin{bmatrix}
0 & 0 & 0 & 52.2743 & 0 & 0.063844 & 0 \\
0 & 0 & 0 & 0.5510 & 0 & 0.000513 & 0 \\
0 & 0 & 0 & -0.1488 & 0 & -0.000022 & 0 \\
0 & 0 & 0 & 0.3569 & 0 & 0.000015 & 0 \\
0 & 0 & 0 & 1937.04 & 0 & 2.851490 & 0 \\
0 & 0 & 0 & 57.9950 & 0 & 1.085353 & 0 \\
0 & 0 & 0 & 11.2325 & 0 & 0.007457 & 1
\end{bmatrix}
\begin{bmatrix} \Delta R^*(-1) \\ \pi(-1) \\ g(-1) \\ i(-1) \\ FD(-1) \\ Fg^*(-1) \\ GI(-1) \end{bmatrix}
$$

$$
+\begin{bmatrix}
-0.03 & 0.00253 & 37.1633 & -57.7864 & 0.03247 & -218.12 \\
0 & 0.00023 & 0.4222 & -0.44594 & 0.00023 & -1.5414 \\
0 & 0.00002 & -0.0051 & 0.00135 & 0.00002 & -0.1367 \\
0 & 0.00004 & 0.0781 & -0.02932 & 0.00004 & -0.2347 \\
0 & 0.54449 & 978.933 & -2635.25 & 1.54449 & -3658.1 \\
-0.03 & 0.01630 & -34.720 & -78.8993 & 0.04624 & -310.67 \\
0 & 0.00257 & 5.81815 & -6.04043 & 0.00257 & -17.258
\end{bmatrix}
\begin{bmatrix} \Delta DCg \\ \Delta DCp \\ e \\ \tau \\ Ig \\ \Gamma \end{bmatrix}
$$

$$
+\begin{bmatrix}
-4.9362 \\
-0.1067 \\
0.0687 \\
0.0613 \\
56.577 \\
0.6883 \\
-3.1958
\end{bmatrix}. \qquad \qquad ...(10.6)
$$

The forecasts of the targets for 1996–7 were obtained by setting: (i)
the lagged interest rate, the lagged value of the external debt, and the
lagged Gini index at their actual levels for 1995–6: $i(-1) = 0.12$, $Fg^*(-1) = 64.03$, and $GI(-1) = 31.55$; and (ii) the instruments at their
predicted levels for 1996–7: $\Delta DCg = 300$, $\Delta DCp = 350$, $e = 0.1061$,
$\tau = 0.1350$, $Ig = 1150$, and $\Gamma = 0.15$. This yielded: $\Delta R^* = -1.91$, $\pi = 0.0898$, $g = 0.0591$, $i = 0.1266$, $FD = 1637.73$, $Fg^* = 66.11$, and $GI = 31.25$ implying a reserve drawdown of \$ 1.9 billion, an inflation rate
of 9.0 per cent, a growth rate of 5.9 per cent, an (equilibrium) interest
rate of 12.7 per cent, a consolidated fiscal deficit of Rs 1638 billion,
an external debt of \$ 66.1 billion and a Gini index of 31.3.

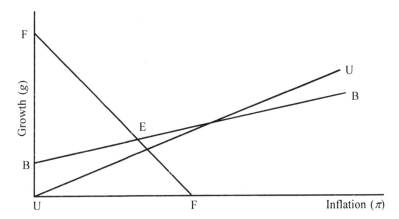

FIGURE 10.1   JOINT FUND–BANK–UNICEF EQUILIBRIUM:
INDIAN ECONOMY (1995–6)

It is thus seen that because the Gini index is added recursively into the model, the forecasts for the other variables remain unchanged *vis-à-vis* those obtained for them in the previous chapter. However, the results indicate that there would be an improvement in income distribution in 1996–7, although the Gini index would still be above its pre-reform level.

More importantly, the reduced form of the model, as presented above, yields information on the impact multipliers of all the six policy variables with regard to the Gini index. As this could provide invaluable guidelines for designing 'growth-oriented redistributive adjustment programmes', they are briefly summarized in Table 10.1 wherein we have estimated the change in the Gini index for either a given percentage or an absolute increase in the concerned policy variable.

The results unequivocally prove that exchange rate adjustments have serious repercussions on income distribution: in effect, a 10 per cent devaluation is seen to increase the Gini index by almost 0.6. While an expansion in domestic credit to the public sector has no impact on the Gini index, it is seen that a similar expansion in credit to the private sector or an increase in public sector investment worsen income distribution, albeit very marginally. It is also seen that increases in tax revenues or domestic borrowings reduce income disparities considerably, the latter being a particularly potent instrument in this regard. By way of illustration, it is seen that a 10 per cent devaluation along with a 10 per cent increase in tax revenues would leave income distribution

TABLE 10.1　Effects of Increases in Policy Variables
on Income Distribution

Variable changed	Type of change	Amount of change	Effect on Gini index
ΔDCp	absolute	+Rs 1 billion	+0.0026
e	percentage	+10 per cent	+0.5818
τ	percentage	+10 per cent	−0.6040
Ig	absolute	+Rs 1 billion	+0.0026
Γ	percentage	+10 per cent	−1.7258

practically unchanged. The results thus broadly indicate how policy coordination measures, to ensure an equitable income distribution, can be implemented whenever adjustment programmes are being contemplated.

10.6 Conclusions

The UNICEF concern about the human dimensions of development is a most pertinent reminder that structural adjustment programmes should be people-centred and that social issues cannot be treated as residual components while formulating stabilization packages. The UNICEF call has met with considerable success, judging by the way that both the IMF and the World Bank have now seemed to accept the need for targeting poverty and income distribution, and recent policy framework papers (PFPs) make explicit reference to these issues.

However, rather than actually integrating distributional concerns into the formal modelling framework, the IMF and the World Bank have concentrated on adding compensatory measures, specifically targeted towards the poor, to existing programmes, in a manner that leaves their basic modelling design unaltered. Apart from the fact that this would involve practical follow-up at the field level which could prove difficult, if not impossible, it also implies that formal trade-offs between stabilization and distributional concerns are yet to be fully evaluated or explored by these institutions. However, to the extent that the integration of such objectives into programme design is proving to be difficult because differences still persist on how distributional issues need to be perceived and modelled, the methodology spelt out in this chapter should help in formalizing some of the more relevant issues and concerns involved in designing growth-oriented redistributive adjustment programmes.

11

Alternative Approaches to Adjustment and Growth

11.1 INTRODUCTION

Subsequent to the review of the macroeconomic framework and adjustment policies in Chapters 2 and 3, emphasis was initially placed on the models of the IMF and the World Bank; and subsequently on the much needed extensions of these models in order to fully understand the theory underlying stabilization and adjustment programmes which have, after all, occupied the centre stage in much of what is currently transpiring in many developing countries.

However, needless to say, the mounting importance of the IMF/ World Bank approaches to macroeconomic adjustment, which is evident in the large number of such programmes being currently implemented in many developing countries, has not gone unchallenged. While certain non-orthodox critiques were discussed in the previous chapter, no attempt was made to present a more coherent analysis of some of the existing alternative approaches, especially with regard to the 'structuralist' school of thought which is presented in the literature as a challenge to the more orthodox approaches discussed hitherto.

While this chapter is meant to redress the balance, it needs to be stressed right at the outset that what is intended here is not a detailed and comprehensive review but rather a succinct, but consistent, outline of the main routes of thought that attempt to set up a counterpoint to the orthodox approaches that are evident in the Fund/Bank models and adjustment programmes.

To this end, Section 11.2 initially discusses the structuralist approach to development with special reference to the rules governing alternative model closures. Based upon these rules, a structuralist model is then presented and, subsequently, the three-gap model is integrated into it to explain the factors determining growth and inflation. Section 11.3 highlights the orthodox twin-deficits approach to growth which, by strengthening the structuralist arguments in certain respects, accentuates some of the fundamental complementarities that exist, but are largely ignored in the literature, between these two rival schools of thought. In doing so, a more balanced approach to the macroeconomics of developing economies is presented. Increases in nominal wages and/or imported inflation have kept domestic inflation stubbornly high in many developing countries, and the failure of orthodox measures in this regard has been a key argument for adopting heterodox stabilization programmes. To explain this phenomena, the underlying concept of inertial inflation is discussed in Section 11.4. Many economists have been extremely vocal in stating that the external community has not been very forthcoming in providing aid or even conditional finances to many developing countries and, in this context, the concept of reciprocal conditionality is presented in Section 11.5 which reworks the two-gap model from the viewpoint of determining the extent of external financing that countries undertaking reforms actually need.

11.2 STRUCTURALIST-INSPIRED VIEWS AND MODELS

Since the inception of development economics as a separate branch of economics in the 1940s, orthodox neoclassical economic theory has, with the possible exception of the 1980s, been on the defensive in this terrain (see Chenery and Srinivasan 1988). Seers (1963) even went to the extent of suggesting that the greater the ability to absorb the neoclassical doctrine, the greater will be the difficulty in adapting to the study of development issues.

While this is, admittedly, a very extreme position, it, nevertheless, suggests that the neoclassical assumptions of perfect competition, well-functioning markets with flexible prices, and the mobility of factors and products are the exception rather than the rule in most developing economies. Under the circumstances, many development economists have focused their attention on trying to identify and formalize non-neoclassical behavioural relationships, including macroeconomic imbalances and institutional rigidities, that are thought to better reflect the characteristics of Third World economies. In this context, a series of influential books by Lance Taylor (1983, 1988, 1989, 1991) has attempted to provide a systematic analytical treatment of the 'structuralist' approach to macroeconomics which is presented as a challenge to 'orthodox' neoclassical economics.

Despite the common perception of the restricted usefulness of orthodox economics, such structuralist-inspired views on development and adjustment do not form one consolidated body of theory and policy advice. As pointed out by Taylor (1990), structuralism is more a programme of research and policy formulation than a well-defined set of rules for putting models together. It is therefore impossible to provide an overview that would satisfactorily cover all the different lines of structuralist macroeconomic analysis which is essential in order to place the IMF and World Bank approaches to stabilization and adjustment programmes into a proper perspective.

Nevertheless, one can, by going across the structuralist spectrum, trace out a distinct analytical approach to stabilization and adjustment issues amongst a group of political economists. Leaving out the views more adequately covered under the heading of 'dependency theory', they take as a starting point the existence of disequilibria that work through macroeconomic mechanisms, but whose causes are thought to be embedded in the underlying economic, social, and political characteristics of society.

This school of thought, at times called 'Latin American structuralism', includes Lance Taylor and Edmar Bacha as prominent members and it is indisputable that the distinct political economy nature of this approach is shared with the early structuralist writers; in fact, the focus on political and social conflicts over distribution and the attempt to identify the fundamental roots of macroeconomic disequilibria rather than their more immediate and apparent causes and effects are the same. Nevertheless, these original ideas have since been revised considerably, and the macro-structuralist nature of this newer body of analysis can be traced to the post-Keynesian academics at Cambridge, including Kalecki and Kaldor (see Eshag 1983). Consequently, it seems more appropriate, as suggested by FitzGerald (1988), to perceive this approach as 'analytical structuralism' or use the label 'neo-structuralism' in accordance with Taylor (1989).

11.2.1 *Alternative Model Closure Rules*
Much of the macroeconomic debate, inspired by neo-structuralists over the past decade or so, has been carried out under the heading of

'alternate closure rules' of economy-wide models. When aggregate demand and supply are out of balance *ex ante*, economic adjustments must take place since balance is established via the sectoral budget constraints *ex post*. The key problem, therefore, before any appropriate policy conclusions can be drawn, is to identify the causal factors driving the system towards a balance. The adjustment mechanisms must be specified and the equilibrating variables identified in the models that are formulated to capture the essence of the economy.

The structuralists are generally unsatisfied with the kind of assumptions underlying the IMF financial programming and World Bank RMSM models. The IMF model is based on a stable money demand function with model closure being applied by assuming that money demand will always equal money supply. The World Bank model is 'investment driven' since consumption is adjusted, so that model closure is applied by assuming that necessary savings will always equal the desired level of investment. Due to the nature of these closure rules, there is no scope for variations in output and employment levels, and the focus is, with the exception of the foreign exchange constraint in the RMSM, turned away from structural constraints in the economy. Furthermore, in the IMF/World Bank models, the domestic sector is assumed to react in a stable manner. Thus, when external or internal disequilibria appear and persist, the logical conclusion is that the cause must necessarily lie in monetary or fiscal mismanagement. Yet the behaviour of the private sector is not specified precisely. The analysis remains, therefore, in the formulation of FitzGerald (1988), *ex hypothesi*.

It is against this background that the structuralists try to emphasize the institutional context in their models, which have a focus on practical and socially relevant policy problems. Strong links between the real and monetary sectors are generally postulated, and there is a preference to work within multi-sectoral frameworks with at least some prices fixed. Two equilibrating mechanisms are common in their writings. The first is a Keynesian multiplier effect by which changes in aggregate demand lead to changes in aggregate supply. This mechanism is possible when supply constraints are absent. The model therefore becomes demand-driven, since the required changes in savings to close any *ex ante* gaps are generated by increased incomes.

The second typical structuralist closure rule involves 'forced savings' as a result of inflation (inflation tax revenue), which occurs when output is constrained on the supply side. In such a case, the economy cannot be driven by demand, and output prices are likely to be market clearing.

To this, the structuralists add the key observation that the 'forced savings' process of closing the savings–investment gap would result in changes in the functional distribution of income rather than changes in the allocation of resources along neoclassical lines. Savings rates are assumed to differ amongst social classes, so that the necessary changes in aggregate savings are related to the efforts of various social classes to increase their respective income shares. The reduced consumption, essential to close the savings–investment gap, is, in other words, a result of conflict, and is borne by particular social groups rather than spread out smoothly across the economy as a whole. In practice, however, overall model closure will involve a little bit of both mechanisms.

11.2.2 *A Structural Model of Inflation and Growth*

Based upon the above closure rules, we now specify the key behavioural assumptions put forward by Taylor (1989) to illustrate the macro-structuralist reasoning on adjustment problems, and the perceived linkages between nominal macroeconomic aggregates and real output and employment.

Following Kalecki (1971), the class analysis is modelled in terms of wage-earners (workers) versus profit recipients (capitalists). However, by disaggregating production costs into the wage bill, profits, and costs of imported inputs, a third class, 'foreigners', can be implicitly introduced into the analysis. In the tradition of Kalecki, it is assumed that: (i) commodity output is not limited by available capital stock or capacity; (ii) final goods prices are determined from variable costs by a mark-up rule defined over the prime cost of labour and imported intermediates, (iii) interest rates and tax rates can be incorporated into the analysis and these will drive up the price level, (iv) the nominal wage rate is fixed at any time and is the outcome of a history of bargaining and class struggle; and (v) firms operate under oligopolistic conditions and, hence, the mark-up rule.

The first behavioural equation is a distinctive structuralist fixed-price rule in which prices are directly related to the production process itself. More specifically, the overall price level (P) is determined using a mark-up (h) defined over the prime cost of labour and imported intermediates. Prime cost per unit of output (B) can be broken down as follows:

$$B = Wb + EP_f a, \qquad (11.1)$$

where W is the money wage rate, b is the labour–output ratio, E is the (fixed) nominal exchange rate, P_f is the price (in foreign currency units) of imported intermediate inputs, and 'a' is the input–output coefficient of such intermediates (that is foreign inputs per unit of domestic output). Thus, Wb is the wage bill per unit of output, while $EP_f a$ is the cost of imported intermediates, per unit of output, in domestic currency units.

It is assumed that W is fixed through wage-bargaining processes, and the mark-up rate responds to social conflicts over distribution as well as to past inflation experiences. A nominal devaluation (an increase in E) will raise the domestic currency costs of imported inputs and, consequently, prime costs which, in turn, will drive up the overall domestic price level given by:

$$P = (1 + h)B, \tag{11.2}$$

which indicates that the price level is obtained by adding the mark-up rate to the per unit prime costs. Substituting (eqn 11.1) into (eqn 11.2) and solving in terms of the real wage rate ($w = W/P$) yields:

$$w = W/P = (1/b)[(1/1 + h) - a(EP_f/P)], \tag{11.3}$$

which implies *ceteris paribus* a negative relationship between the real wage rate (W/P) and the real exchange rate (EP_f/P). Thus, wage earners, who will try to counteract the fall in the real wage rate as a result of a nominal devaluation, will contribute to additional inflationary pressures.

To take account of the impact of the indirect tax rate (t) on the prices of final goods, as well as the cost of financing working capital, the price determination equation needs to be modified. This can be done as follows:

$$P = (1 + t)(1 + h)(1 + i\omega)B, \tag{11.2a}$$

where h now represents the mark-up over interest-inclusive costs, i is the nominal rate of interest, and ω is the time period over which prime inputs must be financed as working capital. These modifications imply that any monetary restraint that drives up the interest rate will contribute towards increasing inflation, and the same applies for increased tax rates.

By measuring economic activity by the output–capital ratio (k), used as a proxy for capacity utilization, the mark-up behaviour can be stated as follows:

$$\Delta h = \alpha(k - k^*), \tag{11.4}$$

where k^* is the level of activity when the mark-up is held constant by 'satisfied' firms. The sign of α is assumed to be positive under the assumption that profit income is positively associated with economic expansion.

Solving the above set of equations provides the reduced forms for price inflation ($\Delta P/P$) and the growth in real wages ($\Delta w/w$). A nominal devaluation will contribute to inflation both through the cost increase in imported inputs, as well as the upward pressure on nominal wages. Such a phenomenon is called 'wage inflation'. In practice, this is recognized by the IMF and the World Bank, which often include wage controls as a common anti-inflationary measure in their adjustment programmes in order to dilute the wage–price feedback. However, such a restrictive wage policy leads to increasing inequality in favour of the capitalists (profit earners), which results in further skewing the income distribution between these two classes. Hence, such attempts to curb inflation via wage controls do nothing to ease the underlying social conflicts, which is why social classes are explicitly identified and modelled in structuralist models, because it makes it possible to decompose production costs and analyse the effect of changes in income distribution on the economy.

Substituting (eqn 11.1) into (eqn 11.2a) and multiplying the result throughout by real output (y) yields:

$$Py = Wby + EP_f ay + h(1 + i\omega)By + i\omega By + t(1 + h)(1 + i\omega)By, \tag{11.5}$$

which indicates that nominal output ($Y = Py$) is equal to the sum of the wage bill, intermediate import costs, mark-up (profit) income, interest on working capital, and value-added (indirect) taxes.

The decomposition of the demand side of the economy follows directly from Chapter 2. It is merely the national balance, (eqn 2.2), which is modified as:

$$Y = Py = P[Cp + Cg + \Theta I + (X - Z)], \tag{11.6}$$

where Cp and Cg are real private and public consumption, I is real investment, $(X - Z)$ is exports net of competitive imports, and Θ is the share of investment that is produced domestically with the balance, ($1 - \Theta$), being imported.

The next step in the structuralist approach is to specify behavioural rules for private consumption (Cp), gross investment (I) and the trade balance $(X - Z)$ in (eqn 11.6), with public consumption (Cg) being treated as a policy variable. This yields reduced forms for internal as well as external balances which are referred to as the savings and trade gaps, respectively, which will be dealt with separately in the next section. Savings rates are differentiated by social classes to allow the investigation of the long-run growth effects of alternative distributional outcomes associated with the 'forced savings' (inflation tax) mechanism. Investment is financed by borrowing from either the banking system or the public and hence it is assumed to depend inversely on the rate of interest (i). Finally, an independent equation is added for the determination of the interest rate by assuming that loan markets clear. Savings and investment decisions are thus carried out independently of each other in a characteristic structuralist/Keynesian manner.

The above summary implies that the total model can be reduced to a 4-equation system in the four unknown variables: inflation $(\Delta P/P)$, capacity utilization (k), the trade surplus $(X - Z)$ and the interest rate (i). These four interacting variables which are relevant in the short-run analysis of all structuralist models can then be used for analytical purposes to understand the workings of the economy and assess the impact of shocks and policy actions. While a wide range of conclusions can be derived from the disaggregated versions of the above model, the following short-run structuralist results regarding the effects of monetary and exchange rate policies can be derived from this basic version: (i) Monetary restraint is contractionary because, by driving up the rate of interest, it has a negative effect on investment and, therefore, growth; as well as inflationary through the price rule mechanism; (ii) Devaluations are inflationary because they contribute to increasing costs and nominal wage pressures; and (iii) Financial liberalization, implying interest rate increases, leads to rising prices in a similar manner.

Capacity utilization is the key closure mechanism behind the classic structuralist short-run adjustments, and the above output adjustments do indeed appear reasonable when typical stabilization measures are applied in an unduly harsh manner. With these caveats in mind, structuralists are more inclined to suggest less austere adjustment packages with relatively more monetary and fiscal flexibility than those implied by the IMF and World Bank approaches. It is also held that selective policy interventions directed by the state in a conscious manner often make sense. For example, the use of import quotas is often proposed as an alternative to avoid the potentially unfavourable economy-wide effects of a devaluation. However, if the capacity limits are reached, thereby eliminating capacity utilization as an adjusting variable, then a 'forced savings' mode of adjustment sets in, implying that only inflation can bring about internal balance. Under the circumstances, demand is affected in various ways by changes in the inflation rate, and the consequences for long-term growth will depend upon the resulting distributional outcomes.

While the above model is complete by itself, the fact that the trade constraint, if binding, can be relaxed in many ways, including reduced public spending, has led the structuralists to model the mounting evidence that growth prospects have become increasingly impaired by fiscal constraints. In doing so, they have specifically incorporated the fiscal gap into their models, thereby extending the two-gap version into its current three-gap framework.

11.2.3 *The Three-gap Framework*
Since the 1980s, with the advent of fiscal adjustment programmes, the government budgets of most developing countries have been tightened. This has squeezed out public expenditures, with the result that public investment programmes and recurrent expenditures towards maintenance of essential infrastructure have been drastically reduced. As a result, the government budget constraint (GBC) has become the main constraint to growth, a situation which has been further exacerbated because of the possible 'crowding-in' effects of public on private investment. In response, structuralist economists, including Bacha (1990) and Taylor (1994), have noted that a third fiscal gap should be added to the savings and foreign exchange gaps of the two-gap models. Their three-gap formulations, which are based on flow-of-funds identities, carry a considerable potential for becoming relevant in the analysis of growth and adjustment issues.

In the two-gap model, if domestic savings plus foreign savings (or the current account deficit) is less than or equal to investment requirements, then the savings gap is said to be the binding constraint. On the other hand, if the flow of foreign resources is not adequate to fill the gap between imports and exports, then foreign exchange is said to be the binding constraint. In such a framework, in order to understand the three-gap model, we initially rewrite the savings–investment constraint, given by (eqn 2.26), as follows:

$$I = Sp + (T - G) + (Z - X), \tag{11.7}$$

where I is nominal investment, $(Z - X)$ is the CAD defined as the difference between imports (Z) and exports (X), Sp is private sector savings, and, following (eqn 2.9), government savings (Sg) have been equated to the difference between total government revenue $(T = Yg)$ and expenditure $(G = CEXPg)$.

The external sector budget constraint, see (eqn 2.19), is given by:

$$Z - X = \Delta F - \Delta R, \tag{11.8}$$

where ΔF is net foreign borrowings and ΔR is the change in foreign reserves.

Substituting (eqn 11.8) into (eqn 11.7) and rewriting the result in constraint notation yields:

$$I \leq [Sp + (T - G) - \Delta R] + \Delta F, \tag{11.9}$$

which states that total investment (I) is constrained by the sum of private savings (Sp), public savings $(Sg = T - G)$, and net foreign borrowings from abroad (ΔF) less the change in international reserves (ΔR). In $\Delta F - I$ space, this so-called 'savings gap' has a slope of unity.

Under the assumption that imports (Z) are a linear function of income (Y) and investment (I), we have:

$$Z = \Theta I + mY, \tag{11.10}$$

where $0 \leq \Theta \leq 1$ is the import content of investment and m is the marginal propensity to import out of income.

Substituting (eqn 11.10) into (eqn 11.8) above, and rewriting the result in terms of I in constraint notation yields:

$$I \leq [(1/\Theta)X - (\mu/\Theta)Y - (1/\Theta)\Delta R] + (1/\Theta)\Delta F, \tag{11.11}$$

which states that total investment (I) is basically constrained by a shortage of exports (X) and foreign borrowings (ΔF), for given levels of income (Y) and reserve changes (ΔR). In the $\Delta F - I$ space, this so-called 'foreign exchange' constraint has a slope of $1/\Theta > 1$, implying that foreign borrowings (or capital inflows) have a larger impact on the growth rate in foreign-exchange constrained economies.

Beginning with the external debt crises in the early 1980s and as a result of the more recent tight budgetary situations in several Western countries, external borrowings by the governments of developing countries have been curtailed. Given that domestic capital markets are still at an incipient stage in several developing countries, most governments are unable to raise resources from the domestic economy through the sale of government bonds and securities. Under the circumstances, and to prevent the government budget constraint from becoming an impediment to growth, governments generally resort to the inflation tax (or forced savings) to capture from the excess savings $(Sp - Ip)$ of the private sector. Based upon (eqn 8.10), we know that inflation tax revenue is given by πm where π is the rate of inflation and m denotes the stock of real money balances $(m = M/P)$. Therefore, we have:

$$Sp - Ip = \pi m. \tag{11.12}$$

In addition, let public investment (Ig) be complementary to private investment (Ip) which is the 'crowding-in' hypothesis according to which public sector investment, especially in the infrastructural sector, attracts supporting private sector investment. This implies that:

$$Ip = \alpha Ig, \tag{11.13}$$

where $\alpha > 0$. Therefore, total investment (I) is given by:

$$I = Ig + Ip = (1 + \alpha)Ig. \tag{11.14}$$

Rewriting (eqn 11.7) in terms of public sector investment (Ig) yields:

$$Ig = (Sp - Ip) + (T - G) + (Z - X). \tag{11.15}$$

Substituting (eqn 11.8) and (eqn 11.12) into (eqn 11.15), and the resultant into (eqn 11.14), yields the following expression for total investment (I) in terms of constraint notation:

$$I \leq (1 + \alpha)\,[\pi m + (T - G) - \Delta R] + (1 + \alpha)\Delta F, \tag{11.16}$$

which states that total investment is constrained by a shortage of forced savings (πm), public sector savings $(T - G)$ and foreign borrowings (ΔF), for given levels of reserve changes (ΔR). In the $\Delta F - I$ space, this so-called 'fiscal constraint' has a slope of $(1 + \alpha) > 1$; and the relative magnitudes of $(1/\Theta)$ and $(1 + \alpha)$ would determine whether foreign borrowings have a larger impact on the growth rate in foreign exchange constrained or in fiscal constrained economies.

If the fiscal gap is binding, apart from the fact that public investment is automatically lower, because of the complementarity assumption, private investment will also be reduced, thereby adversely affecting overall investment and growth. Hence, in order to relax the constraint, governments invariably resort to inflationary financing of public investment because, under the complementarity assumption, maximization of public sector investment implies maximization of total (public and private) investment. However, a better option would be that governments generate an adequate budget surplus in order to leverage domestic private investment. In this context, external debt relief, including debt forgiveness, by lowering the debt service costs would enable governments to reduce budget deficits. In addition, there is a need for governments to facilitate the development of capital markets in order to channel private savings for public investment purposes.

From the savings and fiscal constraints, (eqn 11.9) and (eqn 11.16), it can be seen that if there is a reduction in foreign transfers (ΔF), for whatever reason, the domestic economy should be in a position to generate additional savings (either from the private or public sectors) in order to maintain the existing level of investment. However, since the fiscal budget of most developing and transition economies is usually in deficit (implying negative public sector savings), if orthodox policies to generate additional private savings are not successful, then investment would need to be reduced unless the government resorts to inflationary financing of public investment. If, however, the government is averse to raising the inflation rate deliberately, it has the final option of using international reserves until they are exhausted, at which stage public sector investment has to be finally reduced. However, it is fairly certain that long before this stage is reached, most governments would have imposed strict foreign exchange controls to prevent further reserve erosion.

(Eqn 11.16) also provides a clue as to why there is a greater likelihood of an economy facing a fiscal constraint after a devaluation. Not only is the fiscal deficit worsened after a devaluation as it raises the domestic currency value of interest payments on the external debt, but reserve accumulation is increased. The widening of the fiscal gap is exacerbated, if the public sector also imports (as is usually the case), for the domestic currency value of these imports would also have increased. In order to keep the budget deficit within reasonable limits, the government is thus locked into a position of cutting back on its expenditures (especially investment). Moreover, devaluation raises the price of imported capital goods and, because it is often a large component of investment in most developing countries, this raises the price of investment, as well. Thus, total investment in real terms could decline, especially if credit in nominal terms to the private and public sectors is kept constant. This situation of declining real investment could be further compounded by rising interest rates as a result of monetary contraction.

In summary, therefore, the three-gap structural model of economic growth is a 5-equation system in the five unknown variables: inflation, capacity utilization, the trade surplus, the interest rate, and investment. Its solution procedure would primarily involve deriving the binding constraint and the minimum level of investment before attempting to solve for the remaining four variables. This represents a considerable improvement over the existing Bank approach where, despite using the two-gap model, the solution is usually obtained by solving the model in its one-gap (either savings or trade) mode.

11.3 THE TWIN DEFICITS APPROACH TO GROWTH

While the structuralist approach to macroeconomics is often presented as a challenge to 'orthodox' macroeconomics, there are many areas in which the orthodox thinking has provided much insight and, ironically, even strengthened structuralist arguments. This is especially true as regards the links suggested by these two approaches between the twin (fiscal and trade) deficits and growth, which demonstrate the fundamental complementarities that often exist between these two rival schools of thought. The 'orthodox' framework developed below (see Fischer and Easterly 1990) shows how fiscal sustainability, external viability, and growth are interrelated and indicates some of the trade-offs involved in alternative strategies of financing fiscal and trade deficits with special reference to their implications for growth.

Following the logic of the three-gap approach, the savings–investment constraint, given by (eqn 11.7), can be rewritten as:

$$I = Sp - BD + CAD, \qquad (11.17)$$

which states that total investment (I) is equal to national savings, given by the sum of private sector savings (Sp) and public sector dissavings ($BD = G - T$), plus external savings given by the current account deficit ($CAD = Z - X$).

Following the logic set out in Chapters 8 and 9, the mode of financing these fiscal and trade deficits is useful in understanding how the deficit–debt dynamics relates with total investment and, thus, real economic growth.

From the mode of financing the budget deficit (BD), given by (eqn 8.5), we have the following relationship:

$$BD = D + iB = \Delta M + \Delta B, \qquad (11.18)$$

where D is the primary deficit, i is the domestic interest rate, B is the stock of internal debt, iB refers to interest payments on internal debt, and ΔM and ΔB are the amounts of money-financing and debt-financing, respectively, needed to finance the budget deficit (exclusive of public investment).

From the mode of financing the current account deficit (CAD), given by (eqn 9.1), we have the following relationship (where, as before, $\Delta R = 0$):

$$CAD = NICA + i_f EF^* = E\Delta F^*, \tag{11.19}$$

where $NICA$ is the non-interest current account deficit, i_f is the foreign interest rate, E is the nominal exchange rate, F^* is the stock of external debt (in foreign-currency units), $i_f EF^*$ refers to interest payments on the external debt (in domestic currency units), and ΔF^* is the amount of foreign borrowing (in foreign currency units) needed to finance the current account deficit.

Substituting (eqn 11.18) and (eqn 11.19) into (eqn 11.17) yields:

$$I = S - D + NICA, \tag{11.20}$$

where: $\qquad S = Sp - iB + i_f EF^*$. $\qquad\qquad\qquad$ (11.21)

However, from (eqn 11.18), we also have:

$$D = \Delta M + \Delta B - iB. \tag{11.22}$$

Substituting this expression into (eqn 11.20) and dividing throughout by nominal income ($Y = Py$) yields:

$$I/Y = s - (\Delta M/Py) - (\Delta B/Py) + ib + n, \tag{11.23}$$

where s ($= S/Y$) is the propensity to save of the private sector; b ($= B/Py$) is the nominal debt–income ratio; and n ($= NICA/Y$) is the ratio of the non-interest current account to nominal income.

From (eqn 8.23), it is seen that:

$$\Delta M/Py = \Delta m + (\pi + g)m, \tag{11.24a}$$
$$\Delta B/Py = \Delta b + (\pi + g)b, \tag{11.24b}$$

where m ($= M/Py$) denotes real money balances as a fraction of real output, and π and g are the inflation rate and real growth rate, respectively.

Similarly, from (eqn 9.4), we have:

$$n = \Delta f^* + (g - r_f - e)f^*, \tag{11.25}$$

where f^* $(= EF^*/Y)$ is the external debt-income ratio, $r_f (= i_f - \pi)$ is the real rate of interest on foreign debt, and e $(= \Delta E/E)$ is the rate of depreciation of the nominal exchange rate.

Substituting (eqn 11.24) and (eqn 11.25) into (eqn 11.23) yields:

$$I/Y = s - \Delta m - (\pi + g)m - \Delta b + (r - g)b + \Delta f^* + (g - r_f - e)f^*, \tag{11.26}$$

where r $(= i - \pi)$ is the real rate of interest on domestic debt.

Thus, it is seen that the investment–income ratio is determined not only by the private savings rate, but also by the evolution of total (public and external) debt which, in turn, is determined by the twin (fiscal and trade) deficits as well as their modes of financing. (Eqn 11.26) states that while net external capital inflows ($\Delta f^* - r_f f^*$) complement the domestic private savings rate (s), additional domestic public debt (Δb) can be viewed as a transfer of resources from private savings to the public sector. In a similar vein, increased money-financing via seignorage revenue [$\Delta m + (\pi + g)m$] transfers resources to the public sector through the 'forced savings' mechanism.

With the eruption of the debt crisis in the 1980s, external borrowing was severely curtailed. This, coupled to the fact that in many developing countries, especially in sub-Saharan Africa and, to some extent, Latin America, domestic bond markets were not fully developed, led governments to resort to inflationary financing of their fiscal deficits. The result was either complete seignorage financing [$\Delta m + (\pi + g)m$] of the budget deficit, or quasi-seignorage financing via the inflation tax (πm), both of which resulted in considerably higher rates of inflation.

Given that the real growth rate (g) is related to the incremental capital–output ratio (ICOR) and the investment rate in the following manner:

$$gv = I/Y, \tag{11.27}$$

where v is the ICOR, and I/Y is the ratio of investment to GDP in real (assumed equal to nominal) terms. Substituting (eqn 11.27) into (eqn 11.26) above and solving uniquely in terms of the growth rate yields:

$$g = k(s - \Delta m - \pi m - \Delta b + rb + \Delta f^* - r_f f^* - ef^*), \tag{11.28}$$

where: $k = 1/(v + m + b - f^*)$. \tag{11.29}

(Eqn 11.28) states that long-term economic growth, apart from being influenced by the savings rate (s) and the ICOR (v) in the traditional

Harrod–Domar fashion, is positively related to fresh capital inflows (Δf^*) and inversely related to the stock of outstanding domestic obligations ($m + b$). Other things remaining the same, the real growth rate will increase if injections into private savings in the form of external capital inflows (Δf^*) and real interest payments on the domestic debt (rb) are greater than leakages from private savings in the form of government borrowings (Δb), real interest payments on the external debt ($r_f f^*$), capital losses on the external debt as a result of depreciation (ef^*), and, of course, inflationary financing in the form of seignorage revenue ($\Delta m + \pi m$).

The adverse impact of inflationary financing on the real growth rate is obvious. However, policy makers continue to resort to it for as Keynes (1923, p. 41) pointed out, 'Inflationary tax is a form of taxation which the public finds hardest to evade and even the weakest government can enforce, when it can enforce nothing else.' If domestic debt financing is used as an alternative, then private investment, through a reduction in private savings, is crowded out. If distortionary taxes, such as trade taxes, are used to finance the deficit, then the efficiency of investment would be lower and, thus, the rate of growth would also be lower. On the other hand, an increase in corporate taxation or taxes on capital goods would lower private investment directly. Thus, the last alternative, that is, external borrowing, seems to be the only solution, at least in the short term, although this could have severe repercussions in the long run in terms of an increasing interest burden.

The following is a summary of the results based on the growth equation:

- the higher the average savings rate, the higher would be the growth rate, for a given level of the ICOR
- additional public debt and increases in seignorage revenue which are used to transfer resources away from private savings in order to finance public sector expenditures reduce the real growth rate
- external resource flows complement private sector savings and thereby increase real economic growth in the short run; although the rising burden of interest payments on these external borrowings, coupled to possible increases in real foreign interest rates, would reduce net external capital inflows in the future, and thus adversely affect the long-run real growth rate
- the larger the burden of interest payments on external debt, the more will be the leakage of resources from the domestic economy, resulting

in lower, and perhaps even negative, growth rates. This situation is particularly applicable to the heavily indebted countries (HICs) where the external debt to GDP ratios are relatively much higher and, consequently, so are the debt-servicing costs. As such, debt relief measures proposed under the Brady Plan could go a long way in enhancing economic growth

- sustainable economic growth requires external financing accompanied, sooner or later, by some debt relief such that there is a net inflow of external resources
- an increase in domestic debt (including monetary obligations) would increase interest payments on the domestic debt and thereby transfer resources to the private sector. However, the rise in the domestic debt ratio would more than offset the increase in interest payments on the domestic debt, and therefore the net result would be to lower the real growth rate
- increasing the efficiency of investment will enhance the growth rate.

The Brady initiative correctly linked additional external borrowings with growth inducing policies. Furthermore, the Bush administration's emphasis on more multilateral lending to the private sector (rather than directly to the government sector) of developing countries is also on the right track because such loans will complement the average private savings rate and thereby positively impact itself upon the real gross domestic product (GDP) growth rate. However, this emphasis on private sector lending for stimulating economic growth in the developing countries is not without pitfalls. In most cases, the governments of the developing world are reluctant to cut public expenditures because they are genuinely interested in satisfying social demands through increased government spending, particularly in the areas of education, health, and infrastructure. In such a situation, the government, when faced with reduced external assistance on account of most foreign capital being directly earmarked for the private sector, can be justified in raising taxes on the private sector (including income and profit taxes) and/or resorting to seignorage revenue in order to finance their already high fiscal deficits. Alternatively, the governments may coerce the private sector to buy government-issued bonds as a *quid pro quo* for various public services, in which case the domestic debt to GDP ratio cannot be stabilized. All these factors may lead to an uncertain macroeconomic environment with no clear rules of the game, thus thwarting private investment of its legitimate role in economic development. Therefore, lending to the developing world by international financial institutions should contain a proper mix between loans to the private and public sectors. In summary, sustainable long-run economic growth in developing countries would, within the framework developed above, require a combination of moderate external financing (accompanied by some debt relief), a higher savings rate, and, above all, an increase in the efficiency of investment.

The above 'orthodox' results which clearly highlight the expansionary (contractionary) role of debt relief (devaluation), apart from strengthening the 'structuralist' arguments in these respects, demonstrate the fundamental complementarities that exist between these alternative viewpoints, thereby suggesting the need for a balanced approach to development macroeconomics.

11.4 INERTIAL INFLATION, HETERODOX PROGRAMMES, AND GROWTH

Two explanations are possible for accelerating inflation. The first is the 'orthodox' one, suggested above, which is obtained by linking inflation to the mode of financing fiscal deficits. In such a context, money financing and the inflation tax provide a direct link between fiscal deficits and high inflation. On the other hand, there is also the explanation based upon 'inertial' inflation. Several countries in Latin America during their high and chronic inflationary phase in the 1980s had nominal wages and other payments indexed to inflation and the resulting staggered wage contracts contributed to such an inertia. Moreover, inflation in most open developing countries is partly due to 'imported inflation' as it depends upon the cost of imported consumer, intermediate, and capital goods which play a major role in the functioning of the domestic economy. Therefore, the 'heterodox' approach attempts to link inflation with the rate of growth in unit costs of production, the rate of devaluation of the local currency, imported inflation, and the excess demand (or slack) in the goods market.

Under the circumstances, the rate of inflation (π) is given by:

$$\pi = \alpha(\Delta W/W) + \beta(\Delta E/E + \pi_f) + \gamma(y/y^*), \tag{11.30}$$

where $\Delta W/W$ is the rate of wage-inflation (that is the rate of growth of nominal wages), $\Delta E/E$ is the rate of depreciation of the nominal exchange rate, π_f is the foreign inflation rate which is a proxy for imported inflation, y is actual real output, and y^* is capacity (potential) output, such that the ratio (y/y^*) provides an estimate of the degree of excess demand $(y > y^*)$ or slack $(y < y^*)$ in the goods market. If there is neither $(y = y^*)$, then it is assumed that output is close to its full employment level, implying that $y/y^* = 1$.

In most high inflation economies, such as the now reforming transition economies, the rate of wage inflation $(\Delta W/W)$ is indexed to inflation in the past period, implying that:

$$\Delta W/W = \Theta(1)\ \pi(-1),\ 0 < \Theta(1) < 1. \tag{11.31}$$

Similarly, the nominal exchange rate is also indexed to inflation under a crawling-peg system or under a managed floating exchange rate regime so as to prevent an appreciation of the real exchange rate. Therefore, we have:

$$\Delta E/E = \Theta(2)\ \pi(-1),\ 0 < \Theta(2) < 1. \tag{11.32}$$

Substituting (eqn 11.31) and (eqn 11.32) into (eqn 11.30) above yields:

$$\pi = \Theta\ \pi(-1) + \beta\pi_f + \gamma(y/y^*), \tag{11.33}$$

where we have replaced $[\alpha\Theta(1) + \beta\Theta(2)]$ by Θ. Thus, it is seen that the inflation rate is not dependent upon either money supply growth or the fiscal deficit and has an intrinsic inertia of its own especially when $\Theta > 1$, which is usually the case. For example, Jamaica, during 1994–6, despite consistently generating adequate fiscal surpluses, just could not lower inflation because of such an inertial component between past and present inflation, exacerbated by nominal wage increases and exchange rate changes, combined with low real GDP growth.

The heterodox programmes, such as the Austral Plan in Argentina in 1985–6 and the Cruzado Plan in Brazil in 1986, consisted basically of nominal exchange rate targeting and wage controls either by government fiat or a pact with trade unions. However, as shown above, such a stabilization programme puts continuous pressure on the nominal exchange rate to depreciate, thereby fueling further inflation. Therefore, under the circumstances, active government intervention in the form of an incomes policy and/or price controls is needed to slow down the rate of wage inflation for any heterodox programme to be successful. It has often been suggested that because of inertial inflation, which is a structural feature of some Latin American countries, orthodox stabilization programmes, based upon tight fiscal and monetary policies, are not successful in bringing down the inflation rate rapidly. This is, however, not exactly true because in order to keep the nominal exchange rate constant, monetary policy must be willing (and able) to offset rising expectations of further devaluation by raising domestic interest rates through a tight money policy. As this would imply a rising interest burden, the logical corollary is that fiscal policy also has to be tightened in order to reduce domestic borrowings.

11.5 RECIPROCAL CONDITIONALITY AND GROWTH

The debate over the policy prescriptions of the Fund and the Bank in stabilization and adjustment programmes has provided new concepts such as 'asymmetric adjustment' and 'asymmetric conditionality'. Among other arguments, the critics of the Bank–Fund programmes contend that the frequency of failed reform efforts is high largely because of underfunding by the lenders: in effect, the burden of adjustment is unfairly imposed upon the borrowers (developing countries) while the lenders (developed countries and international financial institutions) are not accountable for the disbursement of funds already committed at the time of loan agreements. In other words, borrowers should have the right to impose a reciprocal conditionality on the lenders in an attempt to monitor and rank their performance.

Bacha (1987) showed how a simple manipulation of the identities derived in Chapter 2 provides a framework for not only estimating the requirements of foreign resources (as in the two-gap model of Chapter 5), but also for imposing this reciprocity on foreign creditors. Bacha contends that if this reciprocity condition is not satisfied, then the borrowing country should be automatically entitled to an increase in drawings from the international financial institutions, failing which interest payments due on outstanding external debt should be capitalized, thus ensuring that the required foreign exchange is available during the reform process.

In order to highlight the concept of reciprocal conditionality, we initially use the growth equation, given by (eqn 6.21), which is repeated below for convenience:

$$g = \frac{k[I / Y(-1)]}{(1 + \pi)} - d, \tag{11.34}$$

where g and π are the real growth rate and inflation rate, respectively; k is the output–capital ratio, d is the rate of capital stock depreciation, I is nominal investment, and $Y(-1)$ is nominal income in the previous period.

From the investment equation, given by (eqn 6.7), we have:

$$I = S + \Delta F - \Delta R, \tag{11.35}$$

where S is nominal savings, ΔF is the change in foreign borrowings, and ΔR is the change in foreign exchange reserves.

Substituting (eqn 11.35) into (eqn 11.34) and solving the resulting expression in terms of ΔF yields:

$$\Delta F = (g/k)\ Y(-1) - S + \Delta R + (d/k)\ Y(-1) + (d\pi/k)\ Y(-1). \tag{11.36}$$

This equation provides an estimate of foreign resources (ΔF) needed to achieve a targeted real growth rate (g), for a given inflation rate (π), after considering the level of domestic savings (S) and reserve accumulation (ΔR), on the assumption that the ICOR ($= 1/k$) as well as the depreciation rate (d) are provided exogenously (or can be calculated from historical data).

From the equation of 'foreign transfers', given by (eqn 2.19), we have:

$$Z - X = \Delta F - \Delta R, \tag{11.37}$$

where Z and X are nominal imports and exports, respectively.

Assuming, for simplicity, that nominal imports (Z) are a linear function of nominal income (Y), we have:

$$Z = mY, \tag{11.38}$$

where m is the marginal propensity to import out of income.

From (eqn 4.16), we have the following definitional identity:

$$Y = Y(-1) + (g + \pi)\ Y(-1). \tag{11.39}$$

Substituting (eqn 11.38) and (eqn 11.39) into (eqn 11.37) and solving the resulting expression in terms of ΔF yields:

$$\Delta F = mY(-1) + m(g + \pi)\ Y(-1) - X + \Delta R. \tag{11.40}$$

This equation provides an estimate of the requirement of foreign resources (ΔF) needed to achieve a targeted real growth rate (g), for a given inflation rate (π), after taking into consideration the desired levels of exports (X) and reserve accumulation (ΔR), on the assumption that the marginal propensity to import (m) is provided exogenously. Thus, (eqn 11.36) and (eqn 11.40) provide two estimates of foreign borrowings required to sustain a targeted GDP growth rate and it is suggested that the higher of these two values be incorporated as an additional variable into the financial programming exercises of the Fund. This maximum value of foreign resource needs will serve as a 'performance criteria for foreign creditors, the violation of which would entitle the programme country to an automatic increase in its drawings either from the IMF or the World Bank, if not to an automatic capitalization of the interest due on its outstanding external debt' (Bacha 1987, pp. 1464–5).

11.6 CONCLUSIONS

The alternative concepts and perspectives reviewed above illuminate some of the shortcomings of the standard IMF and World Bank approaches to stabilization and structural adjustment. The policy elements of the UNICEF 'basic needs' approach, discussed in the previous chapter, are in line with some of the recommendations emanating from a number of country studies carried out by structuralist researchers. This reflects the evolutionary relationship between the basic needs and the structuralist paradigms of development although differences between these two approaches still remain (see Taylor 1988).

The analytical structuralist framework makes it possible to pose some questions not considered in conventional IMF/World Bank models. The policy recommendations emanating from such an approach differ in certain fundamental respects from the orthodox approach. While the latter kind of programmes have been widely tested over the past 15 years or so with varying degrees of success, it is now clear that stabilization and adjustment packages with a greater basic needs and structuralist views are beginning to be formulated.

However, it needs to be noted that the structuralist model should be used with care. The model must, first of all, be considerably disaggregated and must take into account that most developing economies are small primary product exporters, critically short of foreign exchange. Hence, the maintenance and expansion of domestic activity in manufacturing sectors would require crucial imported inputs. In addition, since financial markets are usually small in such economies, fiscal and monetary policy would be closely related. Hence, model closure by invoking typical Keynesian changes in capacity utilization is not advisable. If financial markets are completely absent, then, strictly speaking, only two types of adjustment mechanisms present themselves: the first involving government management, and the other 'forced' savings through inflation.

Under extreme circumstances, fixed-price rules will be transformed into flex-price behaviour, a characteristic which is normally reserved for the food sector in the structuralist models. Key prices may be set by the government and even if they are out of line with economic realities, this is largely irrelevant since economic transactions will then drift outside the control of the state into the flourishing unofficial parallel markets. Monetary and fiscal policy cannot then be considered as irrelevant. On the contrary, orthodox policy approaches may appear almost ideal for inflation stabilization. Yet eliminating the inertial component of inflation would not remove structural bottlenecks, and binding constraints would be satisfied in many ways. Thus, structuralist theory would continue to be useful in providing guidelines which might otherwise be overlooked. The recent contribution in this regard is the focus on a possible third gap which needs to be added to the traditional savings and foreign exchange gaps of the two-gap formulation of the World Bank. In fact, the three-gap model seems to be a feasible supplement to the RMSM and the IMF financial programming models, although it is not as simple as the proposed synthesis reviewed in this study. In summary, one reason why the structuralist approach retains its relevance is its insistence on putting development issues at the centre stage, and the clear recognition of the importance of institutional factors. These not only shape the environment in which stabilization and adjustment policies are implemented, but also influence the decision as to the kind of adjustment to be opted for.

LESSONS OF ADJUSTMENT
EXPERIENCE

12

Financial Policies and Growth

12.1 INTRODUCTION

The financial crisis that engulfed East Asia—seriously derailing the economies of Indonesia, Korea, Malaysia, the Philippines, and Thailand—in the second half of 1997 was the latest and probably the worst in a series of such episodes, which include the 1992–3 exchange rate management (ERM) crisis in Europe and the 1994–5 'tequila' crisis in Latin America, that have plagued many economies in various regions across the world in the 1990s. These crises have been costly in varying degrees, and particularly so when banking sector problems have been involved, both in terms of lost output as well as in terms of the fiscal and quasi-fiscal outlays needed to shore up the fragile financial sectors. Also, in a number of cases, they have required considerable international financial assistance in order to limit their severity and costs, and to contain their contagious spread and spillovers to other countries.

However, financial crises are not unique to current financial systems and history is replete with banking and exchange rate crises (see Kindleberger 1978). In the second half of this century, for instance, there were the sterling and French franc crises of the 1960s, the breakdown of the Bretton Woods system in the early 1970s, and the debt crisis of the 1980s. Earlier periods, too, have had their share of financial crises, with the two notable examples being the Barings crisis of 1890—which bears a striking resemblance to the Mexican crisis of 1994–5—and the US exchange rate crisis of 1894–6, which was a speculative attack on the United States' adherence to the gold standard and an early example of the effectiveness of official borrowings of international reserves to stem a currency crisis (see Grilli 1990). Indeed, it was largely in response to various such crises that modern institutions and international financial arrangements—especially the IMF—were established.

Thus, not only are financial crises a recurring phenomenon with a distant past, they seem to be characterized by almost similar forces which have often been at work in different crises. However, financial innovations and the increased integration of global financial markets over the past two decades appear to have introduced some new elements and concerns. In particular, the spillover effects and the contagious spread of crises in recent years seem to have become more pronounced and far reaching. Thus, a key concern of policy makers and financial markets currently is to identify the causes of crises and develop an early warning system based upon which it would be possible to design and implement appropriate financial policies which can either pre-empt or mitigate such crises.

In such a context, Section 12.2 initially discusses the characteristics of financial crises with special reference to the types, origins, identification, and signals of crises. A brief overview about some of the stylized facts pertaining to the Asian crisis, in particular, contagion effects as well as the balance sheet and transfer problems, is taken up in Section 12.3. Based upon this, a theoretical model of financial crisis is then set out in Section 12.4 which also highlights some appropriate crisis management policies. Finally, in Section 12.5, we develop an analytical framework for assessing a given policy stance which, in Section 12.6, is used to empirically illustrate some of the important issues involved in designing appropriate policy coordination measures which are capable of pre-empting currency crises.

12.2 FINANCIAL CRISES

12.2.1 *Types of Crises*
A number of broad types of financial crises can be distinguished in the literature. A *currency crisis* may be said to occur when a speculative attack on the domestic currency results in its devaluation (or sharp depreciation), or forces the central bank to defend the currency by expending large volumes of foreign exchange reserves or by sharply raising interest rates. A *banking crisis* refers to a situation in which actual or potential bank runs or failures either induce banks to suspend

the internal convertibility of their liabilities or compel the government to intervene by extending assistance on a large scale. Broadly speaking, when defining a banking crisis, a distinction is made between financial distress and financial panic which refer, respectively, to situations of insolvency and illiquidity in the banking system. The former occurs when 'a significant fraction of the banking sector is insolvent but remains open'; while the latter occurs when 'bank debt holders suddenly demand that banks' convert their debt claims into cash to such an extent that banks are forced to suspend the convertibility of their debts into cash'. Finally, a *debt crisis* is a situation in which a country cannot service its foreign debt, whether sovereign or private.

Crises of all types have often had common origins in the build-up of unsustainable economic imbalances and misalignments in asset prices or exchange rates, often in a context of financial sector distortions and structural rigidities. Thus, a crisis may be triggered off by a loss of confidence in the currency or banking system, often prompted by developments such as a sudden correction in asset prices or by a disruption to credit or external financing flows, that expose the underlying economic and financial fragilities. The ensuing crises may then involve sharp declines in asset prices, and failures of financial institutions and non-financial corporations. However, not all corrections of imbalances entail a crisis. Whether or not they do depends, apart from the magnitude of the imbalances themselves, on the credibility of policies designed to correct the imbalances as well as on the inherent robustness of the country's financial system to economic shocks.

At times, elements of currency, banking, and debt crises may be present simultaneously as in the recent East Asian crisis. This close association was initially noticed by Diaz-Alejandro (1985) who suggested that the bailout of the banking sector in Chile was the cause of inconsistency between its monetary and exchange rate policy and a possible explanation for the speculative attack on the Chilean peso in the early 1980s. Since then, several other channels have been proposed to explain the close timing of these events. In particular, banking problems, by resulting in an excess supply of money or by causing a sudden downward shift in the money demand function, may cause or precipitate a currency crisis. On the other hand, a currency crisis may cause a banking crisis either by deteriorating the net worth of the banking system or by inducing a withdrawal of deposits. However, as is very often the case, the fact that one type of crisis precedes another does not necessarily imply causality. This is because banking sector difficulties may not always be very apparent, especially in poorly supervised and inadequately regulated systems or in situations where lending booms and asset price inflation mask banking problems, until a correction in asset prices exposes the fragility of the financial system. The same is true for corporate sector indebtedness. In these situations, the actual weakness of the banking system or the corporate sector may be fully revealed only after a run on the currency has precipitated speculative attacks that exacerbate banking and debt problems. This has been a feature of the recent East Asian crisis, as illustrated most clearly in the case of Indonesia.

12.2.2 *Origins of Crises*

The factors that underlie the emergence of imbalances that render an economy vulnerable to financial crises may be grouped under the following headings: unsustainable macroeconomic policies, global financial conditions, exchange rate misalignments, weaknesses in financial structure, and political instability. Macroeconomic insfeasibility has been one of the most important underlying factors in many financial crises. Very often, overly expansionary monetary and fiscal policies have spurred lending booms, excessive debt accumulation, and over-investment in real assets, which have driven up equity and real estate prices to unsustainable levels. The eventual tightening of policies to contain inflation and promote external sector adjustment, and the inevitable correction of asset prices that have followed as a result, have then led to economic recession, debt-servicing difficulties, declining collateral values and net worth, and rising levels of non-performing loans that have threatened the solvency of the banking system (see Eichengreen and Rose 1998).

In addition to domestic macroeconomic policies, external conditions have also played a role in precipitating financial crises, especially in the emerging market economies. Most notable have been the sudden large shifts in the terms of trade and in world interest rates. Movements in interest rates in the major industrial countries have become increasingly important to emerging market economies worldwide, reflecting the increasing integration of world capital markets and the globalization of investment (see Calvo, Leiderman and Reinhart 1993, 1996). An abrupt rise in world interest rates can drastically reduce the flow of foreign financing to the emerging markets, raising the cost to domestic banks of funding themselves offshore, thereby increasing adverse selection and moral hazard problems and the fragility of the financial system. The composition of capital inflows has also been considered an important factor in a number of currency crises in emerging markets. In both the recent crisis in Thailand and in the 1994–5 Mexican crisis, the reliance on short-term borrowing to finance large current account deficits was a crucial ingredient in precipitating the crisis.

Another lesson of the recent crises is that currency mismatches in private sector balance sheets (of either financial institutions or corporations) may be more of a problem in countries with inflexible exchange rates, since an exchange rate peg may encourage borrowers to ignore exchange rate risks which are implicit in any crawling-peg regime, especially if the rate of depreciation of the so-called 'shadow floating exchange rate'[1] is higher than the crawl rate. Experience suggests that in such cases of unsustainable crawl rates, countries with foreign-currency-denominated debt or foreign debt intermediated through domestic financial institutions are particularly vulnerable to financial crises.

Financial sector distortions, in conjunction with macroeconomic volatility, form another group of factors behind many banking crises. Often these distortions arise in times of rapid financial liberalization and innovation in countries with weak supervisory and regulatory policies or where the government intervenes directly in the allocation or pricing of credit. Insufficiently stringent regulatory regimes in more liberalized financial environments have created moral hazard by encouraging financial institutions with low capital ratios to assume imprudent risks thereby worsening the quality of their asset portfolios. And deficiencies in accounting, disclosure, and legal frameworks add to the problem by allowing financial institutions to disguise the extent of their difficulties. Finally, to all this must be added the frequent failure of governments, primarily because of political instability, to take prompt corrective action when problems initially emerge, with the result that when they finally do so because of external compulsions, it becomes a case of too little, too late.

12.2.3 *Identifying Crises*
A currency crisis could be identified simply as a substantial nominal currency devaluation. This criterion, however, would exclude instances where a currency came under severe pressure but the authorities successfully defended it by intervening heavily in the foreign exchange market, or by raising interest rates sharply, or by other means. Thus, an alternative approach is to construct an index of speculative pressure that

takes into account not only exchange rate changes, but also movements in international reserves or interest rates that absorb such pressure and thus serve to moderate exchange rate variations (see Eichengreen, Rose, and Wyplosz 1996).

Banking crises are more difficult to identify empirically, partly because of the nature of the problem and partly because of the lack of relevant data. Although data on bank deposits are readily available for most countries, and thus could easily be used to identify crises associated with runs on banks, most major banking crises in recent years have not originated from the liabilities side of banks' balance sheets, that is they have not been associated with runs on deposits. However, whenever such runs on deposits have occurred—such as during the recent financial crisis in Indonesia—they have tended to follow the disclosure of difficulties on the assets side or widespread uncertainty about the future value of the currency. Similarly, a failure to roll over inter-bank deposits, as in Korea recently, can have results similar to those of a run on banks. Thus, in general, runs on banks have been the result rather than the cause of banking problems.

Banking crises, which generally stem from the assets side of banks' balance sheets, are basically due to a protracted deterioration in asset quality. This suggests that variables such as the share of non-performing assets (NPAs) in banks' portfolios, large fluctuations in real estate and stock market prices, and indicators of business failures could be used to identify banking crises episodes. The difficulty is that data on such variables are rarely available in many developing countries or are incomplete. In cases where central banks have detailed information on NPAs, it is usually laxity in the follow-up action in response to such data that allows the situation to deteriorate to a point of crisis. Given such limitations, banking crises have usually been dated by researchers on the basis of a combination of events such as forced closure, merger, or government takeover of financial institutions, runs on banks, or the extension of government assistance to financial institutions.

Using some of the above criteria, 116 currency crises and 42 banking crises were identified by the IMF (1998) for a group of 31 developing countries for the period 1975–97 (see Table 12.1). In 42 of the currency crises, the exchange rate component of the index (of speculative pressure) accounted for more than 75 per cent of its overall value and these episodes were termed as 'currency crashes'. Cases in which more than one country was affected by a crisis, either because of a common shock or because of contagion effects, were counted as more than one crisis.

For instance, the recent East Asian financial crises comprised five currency crises.[2] Several interesting points emerge from the data.

On the basis of the operational criteria used by the IMF, currency crises were seen to be relatively more prevalent during 1975–86. The number of currency crises was particularly high in the mid-1970s (a period of large external shocks to many countries) and in the early to mid-1980s (Latin American debt crises). Banking crises, in contrast, were somewhat more prevalent during 1987–97, probably reflecting the increasing incidence of financial sector liberalization that occurred in many emerging market economies during this period.

Given that the two types of crises often have common origins, or that one type of crisis often induces the other, it is not surprising that countries appear to have banking and currency crises at around the same time. In these instances, banking crises have preceded currency crises more often than the other way around (see Kaminsky and Reinhart 1996). However, since the late 1980s, currency and banking crises seem to have become more contemporaneous. This evidence, while suggestive, should be interpreted with caution in view of some of the aforementioned difficulties in dating the genesis of banking crises.

Financial crises can be very costly, both in terms of the direct fiscal and quasi-fiscal costs of restructuring the financial sector, as well as in terms of the indirect effects on economic activity on account of the inability of financial markets to function effectively. Resolution costs for banking crises have in certain cases reached to over 40 per cent of GDP (for example, in Chile and Argentina in the early 1980s), while NPAs have exceeded 30 per cent of total bank assets (for example, in Malaysia during 1988 and Sri Lanka during the early 1990s). In addition to their fiscal and quasi-fiscal costs, banking and currency crises have also led to misallocation and underutilization of resources, thereby resulting in real output losses.

As seen in Table 12.1, for currency crises, on average, output growth returned to trend in about one and a half years, while the cumulative loss in output growth per crisis was slightly under 5 percentage points (relative to trend). For currency crashes, the average recovery time and cumulative loss of output growth increased to almost 2 years and 8 percentage points, respectively. Banking crises, not surprisingly, were more pronounced and more costly than currency crises: on average, it took almost 3 years for output growth to return to trend, and the cumulative loss in output growth was 12 percentage points. When banking crises occurred within a year of currency crises, the losses were substantially larger, amounting to almost 13.5 percentage points on average. The study also reveals an interesting feature: for both currency and banking crises, the recovery time is shorter in the emerging market economies than in the industrial countries, although the cumulative output losses are much higher.[3]

TABLE 12.1   CHARACTERISTICS OF FINANCIAL CRISES IN EMERGING MARKET ECONOMIES (1975–97)

	Number of Crises	Average Recovery Time[a] (in years)	Cumulative Loss of Output per Crisis[b] (in percentage points)
Currency Crises	116	1.5	4.8
Currency Crashes[c]	42	1.9	7.9
Banking Crises	42	2.8	12.1
Currency and Banking Crises[d]	26	2.6	13.6

Notes: [a] Average amount of time until GDP growth returned to trend.
[b] Calculated by summing the differences between trend growth and output growth after the crisis began until the time when annual output growth returned to its trend and by averaging over all crises.
[c] Currency 'crashes' are identified by crises where the currency component accounts for 75 per cent or more of the exchange market pressure index.
[d] Identified when a banking crisis occurred within a year of a currency crisis.
Source: World Economic Outlook (IMF 1998).

12.2.4 *Signals of Crises*

In view of the costly adjustment that economies undergo in the wake of financial crises, there has been considerable interest in identifying configurations of economic variables that can serve as early warning signals of crises (see Goldstein 1996). Such indicators of vulnerability could be used to identify situations in which an economy faces the risk of a financial crisis being triggered by changes in either world economic conditions, spillovers from crises in other countries, or other forces that are liable to cause a sudden shift in market sentiment if imbalances go unaddressed. A commonly used approach to constructing an 'early warning system' is to identify a set of variables whose behaviour prior to episodes of financial crises is systematically different from that during normal or tranquil periods. By closely monitoring these variables, it may be possible to detect behaviour patterns similar to those that, in the past, have preceded crises.

There are potentially a large number of variables that could serve as indicators of the vulnerability to currency and banking crises. The choice is ultimately determined by one's understanding of the causes and proximate determinants of crises. Considering that, by and large, currency crises have been caused by external sector problems, variables such as the real exchange rate, the imports-to-reserve ratio, the current account balance, changes in the terms of trade, the differential between foreign and domestic interest rates, and changes in the level and maturity structure of foreign capital inflows tend to feature prominently in the set of leading indicators (see Kaminsky, Lizondo, and Reinhart 1997). On the other hand, considering that banking crises have been largely due to weaknesses in the financial sector, exacerbated by the failures of prudential regulations to keep pace with advances in financial liberalization, variables such as domestic credit expansion, measures of financial liberalization (such as the M3-to-M1 ratio), the level of short-term foreign indebtedness of the banking system, the structure of domestic real interest rates, changes in the money multiplier and equity prices, and the quality of bank assets as measured by the extent of NPAs have been extensively used as indicators (see Demirguic-Kunt and Detragiache 1997).

However, unlike currency crises, where sharp changes in high-frequency variables such as international reserves, interest rates, and the exchange rate itself make the dating of crises relatively straightforward, the lack of such high-frequency data that could be used to consistently mark the onset of banking problems makes the construction of leading indicators of banking crises more difficult. As mentioned earlier, the dating of banking crises is much more approximate than that of currency crises because it depends on the occurrence of actual 'events' such as the closure or government takeover of financial institutions, bank runs, and the like. Therefore, there is always the risk of dating crises either 'too late'—since financial problems usually begin well before bank closures or runs actually occur—or 'too early' since the peak of a crisis is generally reached much later in many cases. Nevertheless, even with approximate dates for the onset of banking crises, an analysis of the behaviour of pertinent variables around the time of crises has been found to be useful in constructing an early warning system of vulnerability indicators.

Finally, considering the empirical evidence that currency and banking crises seem to have become more contemporaneous of late, as well as the fact that the causes of banking crises are very often similar to those of currency crises—in particular, loose monetary conditions, overheating of the economy, the bursting of asset price bubbles, and increasing financial integration—it is possible to assume that many of the leading indicators of both types of crises could be broadly similar.

Such an approach was used by the IMF (1998) to analyse the behaviour of a number of macroeconomic variables around the time of *currency crises* during the period 1975–97, for a group of 50 advanced and emerging market countries. In many instances, the behaviour of several key monetary, financial, and trade-related variables was found to be different in the months leading to a crisis from their corresponding behaviour during the tranquil periods. Unfortunately, several such differences were only suggestive and the concerned variables could not be used with any confidence as an early warning system of crises for three reasons. First, the statistical significance of the differences identified was not established. Second, a number of variables were unable to signal vulnerability until a crisis was just about to occur. Finally, information about the behaviour of many variables was available with a lag too long to make them useful as an indicator.

When these requirements were taken into account, only a handful of variables[4] could be considered to consistently provide information about such vulnerability—in the sense that, apart from correctly signalling crises a significant number of times (without sounding frequent false alarms), they provided such signals early enough for appropriate countermeasures to be taken. These variables were the real exchange rate, credit growth, and the M3-to-reserves ratio. Together they provide some useful information about the risks of a possible currency crisis. Specifically, if these variables have been consistently above their average levels during normal times, then a country would seem to be potentially vulnerable to a crisis in the event of any exogenous shock that adversely affects investor confidence (see Table 12.2).

The overvaluation of the real exchange rate was one of the earliest and most persistent signals of vulnerability. As early as 13 months before a crisis, a real appreciation of the domestic currency relative to its previous two-year average tended to signal a currency crisis. Moreover, this signal persisted throughout the buildup to the crisis. Other variables that displayed these properties were the growth of domestic credit and the M3-to-reserves ratio. Low domestic real interest rates, reflecting easy monetary conditions, and equity price declines significantly signalled currency crisis only for the industrial countries.[5] On the other hand, a terms of trade deterioration at around eight months prior to the crisis provided a strong signal only for the emerging market countries. Finally, and interestingly enough, the world interest rate was not a significant indicator—for both groups of countries—except at times that were very close (about 3 months prior) to a crisis.

TABLE 12.2 SIGNIFICANCE OF EARLY WARNING INDICATORS OF VULNERABILITY TO CURRENCY CRISES IN EMERGING MARKET ECONOMIES (1975–97)

Indicator	Months Prior to a Crisis		
	13	8	3
Real exchange rate appreciation	•	•	•
Domestic credit expansion		•	•
M3-to-reserves expansion	•	•	•
Terms of trade deterioration		•	
World real interest rate increase			•

Note: The table shows the results of a series of probit regressions of the binary crisis indicator on the previous 6-month lagged average value of each variable at 3, 8, and 13 months before the crisis date. Each regression included a dummy for the industrial countries and an interaction term of the dummy with the variable. A variable was deemed to be a significant predictor at the indicated lag if the appropriately estimated coefficients were significant at least at the 10 per cent level. A bullet denotes that the variable is significant at the indicated lag. The regressions were based on monthly data from January 1975 to November 1997 for a sample of 50 countries, which included 20 industrial countries. The results for the industrial countries—which are not too dissimilar—have, however, not been included in the above table.
Source: World Economic Outlook (IMF 1998).

However, it needs to be noted that in instances where a crisis in one country spills over or spreads contagiously to other countries—owing, say, to trade or financial linkages—these variables may not provide the best indicators for the non-originating countries. In such cases, a crisis in a closely linked economy, or in an economy perceived to have broadly similar characteristics, may be the most informative signal of all. Nevertheless, the above variables can serve as indicators of the vulnerability to spillovers. In the recent Asian currency crisis, although contagion effects were certainly evident in spreading the crisis, the affected economies, by and large, also displayed signs of macroeconomic vulnerability when measured against the yardstick of the above indicators.

The appreciation of the real exchange rate, the growth of real domestic credit, and the growth of unbacked domestic banking sector liabilities (the ratio of M3 to international reserves) were used to form an index of macroeconomic vulnerability to a currency crisis, which was calculated for six Asian and four Latin American countries.[6] The index indicated that, beginning in early 1997, vulnerability increased in almost all of the East Asian economies most affected by the recent turmoil: Thailand, Malaysia, and, to a lesser extent, Indonesia, and Korea were all vulnerable according to the index. A sustained buildup in macroeconomic imbalances was often followed by a sudden jump in the index of foreign exchange market pressure that was used to identify the eruption of a potential currency crisis. This was most evident in the cases of Thailand and Malaysia. Such a buildup was also present in the 1994–5 Mexican crisis. In the major emerging market countries that successfully resisted contagion and spillover effects from the East Asian crisis, there were no such signs of vulnerability. For instance, Argentina, Brazil, Chile, Mexico, and Singapore showed little signs of vulnerability. The rather short lead-up to the crisis in Thailand shown by the index, and the absence of vulnerability in some of the non-Asian emerging market economies that did actually experience contagion effects, suggests that other indicators, such as the 'shadow floating exchange rate', also need to be monitored.

However, it is unlikely that any single index is ever going to capture the complexity of developments leading up to a crisis, which usually includes significant elements of vulnerability coupled with economic disturbances, political events, or changes in investor sentiment associated with contagion effects. Indicators of vulnerability need to be supplemented with country-specific information in order to arrive at a judgment concerning a country's true vulnerability to a currency crisis. As noted earlier, the usefulness of the index as an early warning system depends also on the availability of timely information. If the relevant information is not available on a timely basis, the index merely serves to summarize certain elements of vulnerability after the event and is useful only as an analytical tool to study historical crises.

12.3 ANALYTICAL AFTERTHOUGHTS ON THE ASIAN CRISIS

The East Asian economic meltdown not only vindicated currency crisis theory but also demonstrated in a devastatingly thorough manner the importance of the subject; that in a world of high capital mobility, the threat of speculative attack becomes a central issue—indeed, for some countries the *only* issue—of macroeconomic policy. However, viewing the Asian crisis through the lens of conventional currency-crisis theory—which basically focuses attention on the relationship between fiscal, monetary, and exchange rate policies—seems to reveal the inadequacy of existing crisis models.

In order to explain this lacuna we have to, following Krugman (1999a), think in terms of the distinction between 'first-generation' and 'second-generation' crises models. The canonical first-generation crisis models, exemplified by Krugman (1979), in effect explain crises as the product of budget deficits: it is the ultimately uncontrollable need of the government for seignorage to cover its deficit that ensures the eventual collapse of a fixed exchange rate, and the efforts of investors to avoid suffering capital losses when that collapse occurs provoke a speculative attack on the currency when foreign exchange reserves fall below a critical level. The self-fulfilling multiple equilibria second-generation models, exemplified by Obstfeld (1994), instead explain crises as a result of a conflict between a fixed exchange rate and the desire to pursue a more expansionary monetary policy: when investors begin to suspect that the government will choose to let the parity go, the resulting pressure on interest rates can itself push the government over the edge, that is the crisis is a result of self-fulfilling outcomes. Both class of models have had considerable relevance to currency crises in the 1990s: for example, the sterling crisis of 1992 was driven by the (correct) perception that the UK government would, under pressure, choose domestic employment over exchange rate stability; while the Mexican crisis of 1994 was caused by the banking sector bailout which, by increasing the supply of money, hastened reserve depletion thereby precipitating a speculative attack.

Despite the usefulness of these models in making sense of many historical crises, it has become clear that they miss certain important aspects of the Asian crisis which seem to have differed from the standard story in several distinctive ways. To begin with, the Asian crisis arrived suddenly with little warning. By normal criteria, most of the macroeconomic indicators were in good shape, apart from the fact that current account deficits were large in Thailand and Malaysia. On the eve of the crisis, all the governments were more or less in fiscal balance; nor were they engaged in irresponsible credit creation or runaway monetary expansion. Indeed, right up to the summer of 1997, many observers echoed the conclusions of the now-discredited World Bank (1993a) report, *The East Asian Miracle*, that good macroeconomic and exchange-rate management was the key ingredient in the Asian recipe for success. Thus, none of the fundamentals that drive the first-generation crisis models seem to have been present in any of the afflicted Asian countries. Second, although there was some slowdown in growth in 1996, the Asian victims did not have any substantial unemployment problems when the crisis began, implying that there was no strong case for any of these countries to carry out a devaluation for competitive or macroeconomic reasons. In other words, there did not seem to be the kind of incentive to abandon the fixed exchange rate in order to pursue expansionary monetary policy that is generally held to be the cause of the 1992 ERM crisis in Europe. Thus, the Asian crisis was not brought about by macro-economic temptation as is usually the case in the second-generation models. Clearly something else was at work; implying the need for a 'third-generation' crisis model which approximates as closely as possible the stylized facts of actual experience. In such a context, it has been suggested that there are three essential aspects that such a model should attempt to capture.

12.3.1 *Contagion*

The first and most stunning aspect of the recent financial crisis has been the extent to and the speed by which instability in foreign exchange markets was transmitted across countries. The initial speculative attack on one currency (the Thai baht in June 1997) led to a contagious attack on another in a matter of weeks (the Philippines' peso in July 1997), spilled over to the currencies of two more countries (the Malaysian ringgit and Indonesian rupiah by September 1997), before spreading all the way over to the currency of another country with apparently sound fundamentals (the Korean won in December 1997). The fact that even South Korea succumbed to the contagion seems to suggest, as Krugman (1998) put it, that, '. . . "bahtulism" apparently mutated into an even more virulent strain by the time it reached northeast Asia'. The virus then attacked, albeit with less force and persistence, Hong Kong, Singapore, and Taiwan within the region, and finally before dying, in a highly attenuated form, it managed to affect a number of emerging market economies in other regions as well.

In such a context, it would be useful to distinguish three sets of reasons as to why currency crises tend to be clustered in time. One is that crises may stem from a common cause—for instance, major economic shifts in industrial countries that trigger crises in emerging markets—in what has been referred to as 'monsoonal effects.' The sharp increases in US interest rates in the early 1980s was an important factor in the Latin American debt crisis. Similarly, the large appreciation of the US dollar, especially versus the Japanese yen, between mid-1995 and 1997 contributed to the weakening of the external sector in several South East Asian countries. But while external events may contribute to or precipitate a crisis, a country's vulnerability to a crisis depends on domestic economic conditions and policies, such as overborrowing for unproductive purposes, a fragile financial sector, or an inflexible exchange rate system. A second reason why crises may be clustered is that a crisis in one country may affect the macroeconomic fundamentals in another country, either because of trade and capital market linkages (for example, a devaluation in one country adversely affects the international competitiveness of other countries) or because of interdependences in creditors' portfolios (for example, illiquidity in one market forces financial inter-mediaries to liquidate assets in other markets). Such 'spillovers' resulting from interdependences have been cited as contributing in important ways to the spread of the East Asian crisis. Finally, a third reason for clustering is that a crisis in one country may lead creditors to re-evaluate the fundamentals of other countries, even if these have not changed objectively, or may lead creditors to reduce the riskiness of their portfolios and 'flee to quality'. This is often associated with 'herding' by investors, resulting from bandwagon effects driven by asymmetric information or from incentives faced by fund managers. It is this third effect, specifically, that is sometimes referred to as contagion (or 'pure' contagion) which arises only if financial markets exhibit multiple equilibria and self-fulfilling speculative attacks (see Masson 1998).

The evolution of the East Asian crisis suggests that spillover and contagion effects played a role, although formal empirical evidence at this juncture is sketchy. However, it needs to be noted that such evidence on contagion can never be definitive because it is impossible to be certain that the estimated model incorporates the true fundamentals, or does so correctly. For instance, given the known difficulties involved in modelling the banking sector weaknesses, it may be impossible to graft this aspect formally into any of the various versions of the financial programming models developed in this study. As such, systematic empirical modelling of contagious financial crises can still be considered to be in its infancy, especially for emerging markets, although, as mentioned earlier, there have been important developments in the construction of early warning signals of the vulnerability to currency crisis.

12.3.2 Balance Sheet and Transfer Problems

Descriptive accounts, both, of the fundamentals of the crisis countries and of the policy discussions that led the crisis to be handled in the way it was, place extensive emphasis on the problems of firms' balance sheets. On the one side, the deterioration of these balance sheets played a key role in the crisis itself—notably, the explosion in the domestic currency value of the dollar debt had a disastrous effect on Indonesian firms, and the fear of corresponding balance sheet effects on other countries was the principal reason as to why the IMF was so overly concerned to avoid any further deterioration of the affected currencies. On the other side, the prospects for any rapid recovery are especially difficult because of the weakened financial conditions of firms, whose capital in many cases was all but wiped out by the combination of declining sales, high interest rates, and a depreciated currency.

Despite the fact that the role of balance-sheet problems in constraining firms has been the subject of some recent work in the macroeconomics literature, this issue has been neglected in the currency crisis literature. However, in the last year or so, a number of economists seem to have converged towards a view about the Asian crisis that might be described as 'open-economy Bernanke-Gertler' (see Krugman 1999b; Aghion, Bachetta, and Banerjee 1999). The key idea here is this: suppose that, as argued by Bernanke and Gertler (1989), investment is often wealth-constrained—that is, because firms face limits on their leverage, the level of investment is strongly affected by the net worth of their owners. And also suppose that for some reason, many firms have substantial debt denominated in foreign currency. Then two distinct possibilities can emerge. First, a loss of confidence by foreign investors can be self-justifying, because capital flight leads to a plunge in the currency, and the balance-sheet effects of this plunge leads to a collapse in domestic investment. Second, the normal response to recession—printing more money—becomes counter-productive because loose money reinforces the currency depreciation, and thereby worsens the balance-sheet crunch. And hence the Asian crisis: seemingly irrelevant events triggered off self-fulfilling collapses in confidence, and conventional macroeconomic remedies were of no avail.

And, finally, if there is a single statistic that captures the violence of the shock caused by the Asian financial crisis, it is the dramatic reversal in the current account of some of the afflicted economies. In the case of Thailand, for instance, the country was forced, on account of the reversal of capital flows, to convert a current account deficit of about 10 per cent of GDP in 1996 to a current account *surplus* of about 8 per cent by 1998, that is an 18 percentage point reduction in its current account over a two-year period. This desperate need to effect such a huge reduction in the current account represents what may be history's most spectacular example of the classic 'transfer problem' debated by Keynes and Ohlin in the 1920s.

Yet despite the evident centrality of the transfer problem—which was effected partly through massive real depreciation and partly through severe recession that produced a drastic compression of imports—to what actually happened in Asia, this issue has been conspicuously missing from all formal currency crisis models. Perhaps because the modellers have been more concerned with the behaviour of investors rather than with the real economy *per se*, all of the major models in this context have been one-good models in which domestic goods can be freely converted into foreign goods and vice versa without any movement in either the terms of trade or the real exchange rate. However, many economists are of the opinion that this is an unacceptable strategic simplification because the difficulty of affecting a transfer, and the need to achieve a current account counterpart of a reversal of capital flows, either via real depreciation or via recession, is the actual heart of the recent financial crisis.

12.4 A Theoretical Model of Financial Crisis

Based upon the above insights, Krugman (1999a) spelt out the framework for constructing a highly simplified crisis model which also has apparent implications for policy. It is based on the Mundell–Fleming framework which in its simplest version has three equations. First is an aggregate demand equation relating domestic spending to real income (y) and the interest rate (i), together with net exports (NX) that depend on the real exchange rate (EP_f/P), that is,

$$y = D(y, i) + NX(y, EP_f/P). \tag{12.1}$$

Second, is a demand function for real balances (M/P) given by:

$$M/P = L(y, i). \tag{12.2}$$

And, finally, in the simplest version, investors are assumed to be risk-neutral and have static expectations about the exchange rate, implying an interest-arbitrage equation given by:

$$i = i_f, \tag{12.3}$$

where i_f is the world interest rate.

Admittedly the model is simple; in particular, nobody believes in static expectations about the nominal exchange rate (E). However, under a crawling-peg exchange rate arrangement, with a pre-announced *fixed* rate of crawl, we can assume that once the exchange rate has been revised upwards given the existing rule, there would be no further expectations of an exchange rate depreciation during the current period, thereby yielding (eqn 12.3).

The above framework can be regarded as simultaneously determining both output (y) and the nominal exchange rate (E). The vertical line AA in Figure 12.1 shows all the points at which, given (eqn 12.2), the domestic and foreign interest rates are equal. Meanwhile, the line GG shows how output is determined given the exchange rate; it is upward-sloping because depreciation increases net exports and therefore stimulates the economy. The intersection of these two lines at E_0 indicates the equilibrium level of output and the exchange rate.

To convert this into a model that can yield crises, all we need to do is to add a strong open-economy Bernanke–Gertler effect. Assume, then, that many firms are highly leveraged, that a substantial portion of their debt is denominated in foreign currency, and that under some circumstances their investment will be constrained by their balance sheets. Then the aggregate demand equation will have to incorporate a direct dependence of domestic demand on the real exchange rate. Consequently, (eqn 12.1) will need to be modified as follows:

$$y = D(y, i, EP_f/P) + NX(y, EP_f/P). \tag{12.4}$$

Now at very favourable real exchange rates, few firms would be balance-sheet constrained; so at low EP_f/P, the direct positive effect of the real exchange rate on aggregate demand would prevail, and hence the curve GG would be upward-sloping. At very *unfavourable* real exchange rates, firms with foreign-currency debt would be practically bankrupt and unable to invest at all, and therefore once again the direct positive exchange-rate effect on aggregate demand would dominate. As such, the curve GG would also be upward-sloping in this region. However, over an intermediate range, the indirect negative balance-sheet effect of the real exchange rate on investment might overwhelm its direct positive effect on export competitiveness, so that over that range, depreciation of the currency would be contractionary rather than expansionary.

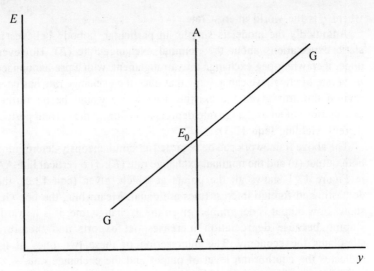

FIGURE 12.1   THE MUNDELL–FLEMING MODEL

In short, as pointed out by Aghion *et al* (1999), we might expect the GG curve to have a backward-bending segment, as in Figure 12.2. Hence, there could be multiple stable equilibria, one with a 'normal' exchange rate, such as E_0, and one with a hyperdepreciated exchange rate, such as E_2. We immediately have here a simplified version of an Asian-style financial crisis. Any event—a financial crisis in another country, political instability, economic sanctions, or deliberate market manipulation by big speculators—causes a sudden large currency depreciation; this depreciation creates havoc with balance sheets, and the economy plunges from normal equilibrium (E_0) into the crisis equilibrium (E_2).

In the above framework, it is clear that the application of fiscal austerity does *not* help prevent or cure an Asian-style financial crisis. As indicated in Figure 12.3, fiscal contraction shifts the GG curve to the *left* towards its new position G'G' and, consequently, both the normal and crisis equilibrium points shift up towards E_0' and E_2' implying a still greater depreciation in the currency. If these austerity measures are pushed hard enough, then the GG curve could shift so far to the left that the normal equilibrium could be eliminated altogether, leaving behind only an even more hyperdepreciated crisis equilibrium.

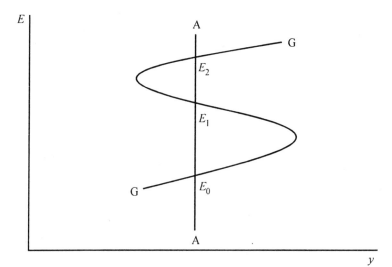

FIGURE 12.2   THE MODIFIED MUNDELL–FLEMING MODEL

Fiscal expansion, on the other hand, just about might work: it shifts GG to the right, and if undertaken on a sufficient scale can rule out the crisis equilibrium. The question is whether countries are able to undertake the requisite expansion. Deficit spending after all did strengthen the yen, just as Mundell–Fleming would predict, but it may not be a sustainable option for smaller countries that are debtors rather than creditors. Be that as it may, it is by now well known that although during the early stages of the Asian crisis the IMF imposed fiscal austerity, currently the recovery is being partly driven by deficit spending.

Finally, the above model provides a rationale for the principal, and much-disputed, tool in IMF stabilization programmes which is a temporary sharp tightening of monetary policy to support the exchange rate, followed by a gradual loosening once confidence has been restored. Consider Figure 12.4, and imagine that for some reason markets appear to have become convinced that the economy is heading for the crisis equilibrium (E_2)—a belief that, if unchecked, will become self-fulfilling. One way to pre-empt this is to drastically tighten monetary policy, shifting the AA curve so far to the left that it becomes A′A′—that is, far away to rule out the crisis equilibrium. Once investors are convinced that the exchange rate is not going to depreciate massively, this monetary contraction can be relaxed.

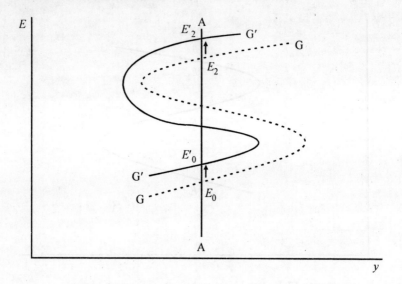

FIGURE 12.3   FISCAL POLICY IN THE MODIFIED MODEL

The problem, however, is that all along the way, from E_0 to E'_0 the economy faces a sharp and sustained contraction in real output which is a feature that is being currently witnessed in these Asian countries. However, it could be argued, based on the Korean experience, that this strategy—of imposing a temporary monetary contraction and hence a severe, but hopefully short-lived, real contraction—works in the end. By and large, the analysis indicates that a moderate fiscal (monetary) expansion (contraction) could serve to defuse the situation by dissipating the crisis equilibrium although, going by the government budget constraint specified in (eqn 2.11), it is immediately obvious, that this would—in the absence of official capital flows—entail an increase in private sector borrowings. This, in turn, could, given the private sector budget constraint specified in (eqn 2.15), crowd out private investment even in the normal equilibrium putting the economy into a different but equally unpleasant form of a low-level trap. All this implies that, because the stabilization policy options confronting the authorities during a crisis could be rather limited, they should be derived from a model which integrates the best ingredients of, both, the above analytical framework as well as the early warning signals of vulnerability discussed earlier.

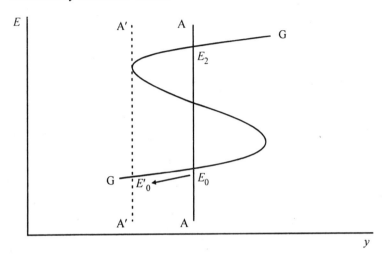

FIGURE 12.4   MONETARY POLICY IN THE MODIFIED MODEL

12.5 POLICY COORDINATION AND SUSTAINABILITY: AN ANALYTICAL FRAMEWORK

In such a context, we now set out a framework (see Rao 1997a, b; Rao and Singh 1998) for a currency crisis model which, as will be shown later using empirical illustrations for the Indian economy, has considerable policy implications.

Consider an open economy in which residents consume a single tradeable good, whose foreign currency price (that is the nominal exchange rate) is revised upwards at a constant pre-announced rate every period. The domestic inflation rate is a weighted average of excess money growth relative to real output growth (the quantity theory assumption) and nominal exchange rate variations (the purchasing power parity theory assumption). With complete financial openness, the domestic nominal interest rate is governed by the uncovered interest rate parity equation. There are no private banks, so that the money stock is equal to the sum of domestic credit issued by the central bank (which is assumed to expand at a constant rate) and the domestic currency value of foreign reserves held by the central bank. Finally, it is assumed that the output growth rate is positively influenced by the supply of real domestic credit (the credit availability effect) and real interest rates (the financial repression hypothesis), although very high real rates can reduce investment and thereby lower the growth rate (the crowding-out effect). The model is thus defined by the following equations:

$$M - p = C + \alpha y - \beta i, \tag{12.5}$$
$$M = \sigma_1 D + \sigma_2 R, \tag{12.6}$$
$$\Delta D = \mu, \tag{12.7}$$
$$\Delta e = \varepsilon, \tag{12.8}$$
$$\Delta p = \delta_1 (\Delta M - \Delta y) + (1 - \delta_1)\Delta e, \tag{12.9}$$
$$i = i_f + \Delta e, \tag{12.10}$$
$$\Delta y = \theta_0 + \theta_1(\Delta D - \Delta p) + \theta_2(i - \Delta p) - \theta_3(i - \Delta p)^2, \tag{12.11}$$

where M is the nominal money stock, D is domestic credit, R is the domestic currency value of foreign exchange reserves, e is the nominal exchange rate, p is the price level, y is real output, i is the domestic nominal interest rate, and i_f is the (exogenous) foreign interest rate. All variables, except interest rates, are measured in logarithms and, therefore, the change in the logarithmic value of these variables would denote their growth rates. As such, in all the ensuing derivations we shall set $\Delta p = \pi$ (inflation rate) and $\Delta y = g$ (real growth rate).

(Eqn 12.5) relates real money demand positively to real income and negatively to the nominal interest rate. (Eqn 12.6) is a log-linear approximation of the identity defining the money stock as the sum of domestic credit and reserves. (Eqn 12.7) specifies that domestic credit grows at a constant rate. (Eqn 12.8) specifies a crawling peg exchange rate arrangement with the nominal exchange rate being depreciated at a constant rate each period. (Eqn 12.9) indicates that the inflation rate is a weighted average of relative excess liquidity and the depreciation rate. (Eqn 12.10) provides the interest rate parity equation where the expected rate of depreciation is replaced by the actual rate under the assumption of a constant pre-announced rate of crawl. Finally, (eqn 12.11) indicates that the real growth rate of output is positively related to the growth rate of *real* domestic credit as well as the real rate of interest. The negative parabolic term is introduced on the assumption that once the real rate crosses a critical threshold, the resulting crowding out of investment would adversely affect growth.

12.5.1 *Iso-reserves Line*
Combining together the time-derivatives of (eqn 12.5), (eqn 12.6), and (eqn 12.10) yields:[7]

$$\sigma_1 \Delta D + \sigma_2 \Delta R - \pi = \alpha g - \beta \Delta i_f. \tag{12.12}$$

Substituting (eqn 12.9) into (eqn 12.12) above, and using (eqn 12.7) and (eqn 12.8), yields:

$$\sigma_1 \mu + \sigma_2 \Delta R - \delta_1 (\sigma_1 \mu + \sigma_2 \Delta R - g) - (1 - \delta_1)\varepsilon = \alpha g - \beta \Delta i_f. \tag{12.13}$$

Assuming $\alpha = 1$ yields the following equation for the rate of change of reserves:

$$\Delta R = [(g + \varepsilon - \sigma_1 \mu)/\sigma_2] - [\beta \Delta i_f / \sigma_2 (1 - \delta_1)]. \tag{12.14}$$

(Eqn 12.14) indicates that if domestic credit expansion exceeds the sum of the real growth rate and the crawl rate, reserves are depleted each period. Thus, any finite stock of reserves will be exhausted in a finite period of time. The equation also indicates that even if there is consistency between monetary and exchange rate policy in as much as $\varepsilon = \sigma_1 \mu - g$, so that the first term in parentheses on the right-hand-side of (eqn 12.14) vanishes, reserves can still be depleted if foreign interest rates are rising, that is $\Delta i_f > 0$, because this would lead to reserve depletion via capital outflows. To offset this, even higher crawl rates would automatically be required. Thus, exchange rate management, apart from necessarily being consistent with monetary policy, would also be subject to foreign influences.

We now assume an import demand function of the following form:[8]

$$z - e = \ln A + my - b(e - p), \tag{12.15}$$

where z is the logarithm of imports measured in domestic currency units. Thus, (eqn 12.15) implies that imports measured in foreign currency units, that is $z - e$, are positively related to real output and negatively to the real exchange rate; with m and b measuring their corresponding elasticities. If we assume that reserves should be some fixed fraction of imports, then regardless of the value of this constant, we have:

$$\Delta R = \Delta z = mg + (1 - b)\varepsilon + b\pi, \tag{12.16}$$

Linking up (eqn 12.14) and (eqn 12.16) and assuming that $\pi = \pi^*$ (the desired inflation rate) and $g = g^*$ (the desired growth rate) yields:[9]

$$mg^* + (1-b)\varepsilon + b\pi^* = [(g^* + \varepsilon - \sigma_1 \mu)/\sigma_2] - [\beta \Delta i_f / \sigma_2 (1 - \delta_1)]. \tag{12.17}$$

Rearranging terms, we obtain the iso-reserves line given by:

$$\sigma_1\mu = [(1 - \sigma_2 m)g^* - \sigma_2 b\pi^* - \beta\Delta i_f/\sigma_2(1 - \delta_1)] + [1 - \sigma_2(1 - b)]\varepsilon, \tag{12.18}$$

which is an upward sloping line in $\varepsilon - \mu$ space—depicted by the RR line in Figure 12.5—implying that higher domestic credit growth rates (which deplete reserves) would have to be compensated by rising crawl rates (which attract reserves) in order to maintain reserves at their desired level. All points lying above (below) the RR line indicate that the actual reserve accretion rate is lower (higher) than the desired target rate.

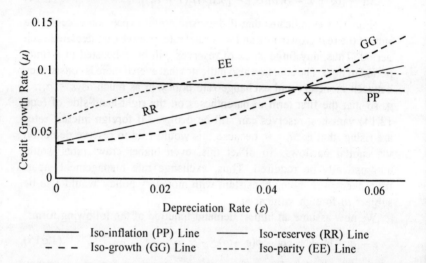

FIGURE 12.5   AN ANALYTICAL MODEL OF CURRENCY CRISIS

12.5.2 *Iso-Inflation Line*
Substituting the time derivative of (eqn 12.6) into (eqn 12.9) yields:

$$\pi = \delta_1(\sigma_1\mu + \sigma_2\Delta R - g) + (1 - \delta_1)\varepsilon, \tag{12.19}$$

which is obtained by invoking (eqn 12.7) and (eqn 12.8). Substituting (eqn 12.16) into (eqn 12.19) above and setting, as before, $\pi = \pi^*$ and $g = g^*$ yields the iso-inflation line given by:

$$\delta_1\sigma_1\mu = [\delta_1(1 - \sigma_2 m)g^* + (1 - \delta_1\sigma_2 b)\pi^*] \\ - [\delta_1\sigma_2(1 - b) + (1-\delta_1)]\varepsilon, \tag{12.20}$$

which is a downward sloping line in $\varepsilon - \mu$ space—the PP line in Figure 12.5—implying that high credit expansion rates (which increase inflation) would have to be offset by low crawl rates (which decrease inflation) to keep the inflation rate at its desired level. All points above (below) the PP line indicate that the actual inflation rate is higher (lower) than the target rate.

12.5.3 *Iso-growth Curve*

Substituting (eqn 12.10) into (eqn 12.11), setting $\pi = \pi^*$ as well as $g = g^*$, and using (eqn 12.7) and (eqn 12.8) yields the following iso-growth curve:

$$\theta_1 \mu = [g^* - \theta_0 + \theta_1 \pi^* - \theta_2(i_f - \pi^*) + \theta_3(i_f - \pi^*)^2]$$
$$- [\theta_2 - 2\theta_3(i_f - \pi^*)]\varepsilon + \theta_3 \varepsilon^2, \qquad \ldots(12.21)$$

which is a parabola in $\varepsilon - \mu$ space shown by the convex curve GG in Figure 12.5. As the real interest rate is given by $r (= i - \pi = i_f + \varepsilon - \pi)$, it implies that rising values of ε, by increasing the real rate, would be initially growth inducing, thereby requiring lesser rates of credit expansion. However, once ε exceeds a critical level, the ensuing high value of r would retard growth and therefore require a higher rate of credit expansion to offset this effect.

12.5.4 *Iso-parity Curve*

Assume that there exists a pre-announced minimum level of reserves (R_{min}) which, if reached, would compel the central bank to abandon the crawling peg exchange rate system, withdraw from the foreign exchange market, and allow the exchange rate to float freely. In such a situation, the speculative attack would occur at the point where the 'shadow floating exchange rate', which reflects market fundamentals, is equal to the prevailing crawling rate.

The shadow floating rate is the exchange rate that would prevail with the current credit stock if reserves had fallen to the minimum level and the exchange rate was allowed to float freely. As long as the official parity is more depreciated than the shadow floating rate, the existing exchange rate regime is viable; beyond that point, it is not sustainable. The reason is that if the shadow floating rate is below the official parity, speculators would not profit by driving down the central bank's stock of reserves to its pre-announced lower bound (R_{min}) thereby forcing an adoption of a floating rate regime, since they would experience an instantaneous capital loss on their purchases of foreign reserves. On the other hand, if the shadow floating rate is above the official parity, speculators would experience an instantaneous capital gain. As neither anticipated capital gains or losses are compatible with a perfect-foresight equilibrium, speculators will compete with each other to eliminate such opportunities. This type of behaviour incorporates the arbitrage condition that the pre-attack official parity must equal the post-attack floating rate at the exact time of the speculative attack.

The first step, therefore, is to find the expression for the money stock when reserves reach their lower bound (R_{min}). This is given by:

$$M = \sigma_1 D + \sigma_2 R_{min}. \tag{12.22}$$

Setting, as before, $\alpha = 1$, taking the rates of change of (eqn 12.5) and (eqn 12.22), using (eqn 12.7) and (eqn 12.9), and rewriting the resultant expression in terms of Δe, which has now to be interpreted as the rate of change of the shadow floating exchange rate, yields:

$$\Delta e = \sigma_1 \mu - g + \beta \Delta i_f / (1 - \delta_1). \tag{12.23}$$

(Eqn 12.23) indicates that the lower the credit growth rate, μ; or the higher the real growth rate, g; the slower will be the rate of depreciation of the shadow floating exchange rate. As far as the parameters are concerned, it is seen that the larger the proportion of domestic credit in the money stock, σ_1; or the greater the sensitivity of the inflation rate to excess money growth, δ_1; or the larger the value of β, the faster will be the rate of depreciation of the shadow floating rate.

Now, if the crawling exchange rate is above the shadow floating exchange rate to begin with (which is a necessary condition for the crawling-peg regime to be viable in the first place), and the rate of crawl is exactly equal to the rate at which the shadow floating rate is depreciating, then the shadow floating rate can never overtake the prevailing crawling rate. And as long as the crawling exchange rate is more depreciated than the shadow floating exchange rate, the crawling-peg regime is viable.

The optimal crawl rate is therefore obtained by equating the right-hand-side of (eqn 12.8)—which is the rate of change of the official parity—with the right-hand-side of (eqn 12.23)—which is the rate of change of the shadow floating rate Doing so yields:

$$\varepsilon = \sigma_1 \mu - g + \beta \Delta i_f / (1 - \delta_1), \tag{12.24}$$

which, from (eqn 12.14), is seen to be exactly equal to that rate of crawl for which $\Delta R = 0$. Thus, the results indicate that if the crawl rate is less than the rate at which the shadow floating rate is depreciating, sustained speculative attacks would result in reserve depletion.

Substituting (eqn 12.11) into (eqn 12.24) above and setting $\pi = \pi^*$ as before, yields the so-called iso-parity curve which is given by:

$$(\sigma_1-\theta_1)\mu = [\theta_0 - \theta_1\pi^* + \theta_2(i_f - \pi^*) - \theta_3(i_f - \pi^*)^2 - \beta\Delta i_f/(1 - \delta_1)]$$
$$+ [(1 + \theta_2) + 2\theta_3(i_f - \pi^*)]\varepsilon - \theta_3\varepsilon^2, \qquad (12.25)$$

which is a parabola in $\varepsilon - \mu$ space depicted by the concave curve EE in Figure 12.5. This iso-parity curve defines all combinations of μ and ε for which the rate of depreciation of the shadow floating exchange rate is exactly equal to the crawl rate. It needs to be noted that all points lying above the EE curve indicate combinations of μ and ε at which the shadow floating exchange rate would be depreciating faster than the official parity (whose depreciation rate is given by ε). This implies that the shadow exchange rate would eventually overtake the official parity, culminating in a speculative attack which would ultimately compel the abandonment of the official parity. Consequently, all points lying in this region indicate an unsustainable mismatch between monetary and exchange rate policy.

12.5.5 *Policy Implications*
Thus, all policy mixes can be categorized as follows: consistent and sustainable, inconsistent but sustainable, consistent but unsustainable, and inconsistent and unsustainable.

If, now, for a desired π_0 and g_0, the iso-reserves line (RR), the iso-inflation line (PP), and the iso-growth curve (GG) all intersect at a unique point below the iso-parity curve (EE)—such as the point X in Figure 12.5—it would imply that the policy mix is both consistent as well as sustainable. If, however, one targets over-ambitious inflation and growth rates, such as $\pi_1 < \pi_0$ and $g_1 > g_0$, then the resulting policy stance would imply a higher μ (to increase g) and a lower ε (to reduce π) and this pair could very well lie above the iso-parity curve implying unsustainability.

Equally true, an increase in the world interest rate (i_f) could push down the iso-parity curve to such an extent that, although there is no change in the original targets (π_0, g_0), the intersection of the PP and GG lines could still take place above the EE line rendering the policy stance unsustainable. This would imply that the desired growth (inflation) target would have to be revised downwards (upwards) until the iso-inflation and iso-growth lines once again intersect below the iso-parity line.

All this suggests that there is much more to policy coordination under complete financial openness than what is implied in the literature, because it entails a very high level of policy discipline and flexibility in order to rapidly adapt to changing circumstances.

12.6 ON THE DESIGN OF POLICY: SOME ILLUSTRATIVE EXAMPLES

12.6.1 *The Estimated Model*

In order to empirically apply the above theory in the Indian context, as we have been doing all along, we need numerical estimates of the parameters of the model. These were obtained by using annual time-series data on the Indian economy over the 12-year period 1986–7 to 1997–8 and then applying the Kalman filtering and smoothing recursion algorithms (see Rao 1997b) to this data set. The five estimated behavioural equations of the model were:

$$M - p = -0.3565 + y - 0.5335i, \tag{12.26}$$
$$M = 0.9547D + 0.0641R, \tag{12.27}$$
$$\pi = 0.8453(\Delta M - g) + 0.1547\Delta e, \tag{12.28}$$
$$g = 0.0378 + 0.4286(\mu - \pi) + 0.6576(i - \pi) - 8.3594(i - \pi)^2, \tag{12.29}$$
$$z = -15.6171 + 2.1328y - 0.2455e + 1.2455p. \tag{12.30}$$

(Eqn 12.26) was estimated by initially constraining α to be equal to unity following the analytical derivation. (Eqn 12.28) implies that about 85 per cent of the inflation rate is explained by excess money growth and the remaining 15 per cent by exchange rate variations. (Eqn 12.29), besides validating the 'credit availability hypothesis', indicates that, while growth rates would be stimulated at low real rates of interest, once real rates cross a threshold limit of about 4 per cent, growth rates would be adversely affected.[10] (Eqn 12.30) indicates that the elasticity of nominal imports with respect to the nominal exchange rate is about –0.25.

12.6.2 *Overambitious Targets and Unsustainable Policies*

Using the parameter values listed above in (eqn 12.26)–(eqn 12.30), we initially set the desired growth rate at 7 per cent, the desired inflation rate at 2 per cent, and the foreign interest rate at 9.3 per cent.[11] We thus obtained the following four curves in $\varepsilon - \mu$ space:

Iso-reserves: $\mu = 0.0616 + 1.0639\varepsilon,$ \hfill (12.31)
Iso-inflation: $\mu = 0.0864 - 0.1752\varepsilon,$ \hfill (12.32)

Iso-growth: $\mu = 0.0871 + 1.3133\varepsilon + 19.5040\varepsilon^2,$ (12.33)

Iso-parity: $\mu = 0.0621 + 0.8309\varepsilon - 15.8894\varepsilon^2.$ (12.34)

The intersection of the iso-inflation and iso-growth lines yields a domestic credit expansion rate of 8.7 per cent (that is $\mu = 0.087$) and a *fixed exchange rate* (that is $\varepsilon = 0.00$). However, these policy settings are unsustainable because the intersection of the PP and GG lines occurs above the iso-parity curve EE. The reason for this is with such a high world interest rate, both (eqn 12.14) and (eqn 12.24) indicate that the rate of credit expansion (exchange rate depreciation) should be decreased (increased) to ensure sustainability. However, the overambitious target levels do not permit these adjustments because that would imply a lower (higher) growth (inflation) rate. This implies that there is every likelihood of succumbing to a speculative attack because the optimal crawl rate necessary to realize the desired inflation rate—which in this case is zero per cent—is lower than the rate at which the shadow exchange rate is depreciating making it profitable for speculators to attack the currency eventually. Therefore, the results highlight the fact that an overheating economy, because it involves destabilizing increases in the shadow floating exchange rate, becomes increasingly vulnerable to external shocks. This could be one possible reason as to why, despite such strong economic fundamentals, some of the afflicted East Asian countries succumbed to the contagious speculative attack, because, by and large, the macroeconomic policies they pursued to achieve such overambitious targets were, in fact, unsustainable.

12.6.3 *Domestic Adjustment and Sustainability*

Repeated iterations indicated that a 4.3 per cent growth rate and a 5 per cent inflation rate would entail a sustainable policy mix at this high world interest rate of 9.3 per cent. Using these altered settings, we obtained the following four curves in $\varepsilon - \mu$ space (see Figure 12.5):

Iso-reserves: $\mu = 0.0347 + 1.0639\varepsilon,$ (12.35)

Iso-inflation: $\mu = 0.0967 - 0.1752\varepsilon,$ (12.36)

Iso-growth: $\mu = 0.0322 + 0.1430\varepsilon + 19.5040\varepsilon^2,$ (12.37)

Iso-parity: $\mu = 0.0555 + 1.7842\varepsilon - 15.8894\varepsilon^2.$ (12.38)

For these revised target values, the iso-inflation, iso-growth and iso-reserves lines all intersect at a unique point—which is denoted by the point X in Figure 12.5 that is *below* the iso-parity curve—indicating a domestic credit growth rate of 8.8 per cent and an exchange rate depreciation of 5 per cent. As the PP and GG lines intersect on the RR line, it implies that the instrument pair ($\mu^* = 0.088$, $\varepsilon^* = 0.05$) not only attains the corresponding target pair ($g^* = 0.043$, $\pi^* = 0.05$), but is also simultaneously compatible with the reserve accretion target. Thus, it is seen that consistency and sustainability have both been achieved, albeit at a considerable cost as it entails scaling down the growth rate besides allowing inflation to build up. This is broadly indicative of the extent of domestic adjustment that is necessary to accommodate external shocks of such a magnitude. Thus, it is noticed that the resulting strategy of imposing a drastic *real* monetary contraction[12] and hence a severe real contraction prevents the speculative attack and, analogous to the model discussed in Section 12.4, thereby rules out the crisis equilibrium.

12.7 CONCLUSIONS

The recent East Asian crisis and the 'tequila crisis' of 1994–5 are the latest in a series of financial crises witnessed over the past two decades. These crises have been extremely costly for the countries most directly affected: the countries where the crisis originated and the countries that, although perhaps vulnerable, might have escaped had it not been for the spillover and contagion effects. In view of these costs, a key concern of policy makers has been to identify the causes of the crisis in an effort to predict as well as to prevent them.

It is of course practically impossible to construct models that can predict crises reliably because any successful attempt to construct such a model would presumably affect the behaviour of policy makers and financial market participants alike, quickly rendering such a model obsolete. Under these circumstances, what is more feasible is to identify certain indicators of vulnerability to financial crisis, including contagion effects, in an effort to provide an early warning system which can alert policy makers about the impending possibility of a crisis, whether or not such a crisis actually materializes. However, it should be emphasized that most of the indicators developed in the literature are best suited for studying crises related to the buildup of overheating pressures and are not suitable for analysing other kinds of crises—for instance, those associated with macroeconomic policy inconsistencies or unsustainable policy stances which, if pursued long enough, can typically render economies, even with apparently sound fundamentals, highly vulnerable to financial crises.

In such a context, one of the most fundamental propositions of open-economy macroeconomics is that it is theoretically impossible for the government to simultaneously aim at stable exchange rates, financial openness, and monetary independence—the so-called 'impossible trinity'—and therefore the sustainability of any instrument–target mix under increasing capital mobility requires continuous policy coordination. Monetary policy would, thus, be subject to an exchange rate rule rather than to a monetary growth rule. Therefore, excessive domestic credit creation could lead to a gradual loss of foreign exchange reserves and, ultimately, to an abandonment of the existing exchange rate once the central bank becomes incapable of defending the parity any longer. Equally true, any central bank that is forced to tolerate a persistent balance of payments (BOP) deficit as a result of an exchange rate misalignment will eventually find itself unable to fix the exchange rate between domestic and foreign currency. If capital is internationally mobile, the collapse of the existing exchange rate is typically triggered off by a sudden BOP crisis in which speculators, fleeing from the domestic currency, acquire a large portion of the central bank's foreign exchange reserves. Faced with this reserve haemorrhage, the bank would have no other option other than withdrawing from the foreign exchange market and allowing the exchange rate to float as witnessed in East Asia.

As an illustrative application of the research in this area of monetary and exchange rate policy coordination, we set out an analytical framework for the Indian economy—based upon some of the early warning signals of vulnerability developed by the IMF as well as a theoretical financial crisis model—which has considerable policy implications. The empirical results indicate that a currency crisis, in the form of a speculative attack, can be prevented only if there exists substantial policy flexibility which enables the authorities to continuously respond and adjust to external shocks. However, while external events may contribute to or precipitate a crisis, the results also suggest that a country's vulnerability to a crisis could also be due to divergences in policy requirements owing to overambitious targets—the so-called overheating syndrome—which, by bringing about growing disparities between the official parity and the shadow floating exchange rate, eventually culminates in a speculative attack.

NOTES

[1]The shadow floating exchange rate, which differs from the equilibrium exchange rate, will be defined in Section 12.5.4.

[2]The five crises identified by the index were the crises in Indonesia, Korea, Malaysia, Philippines, and Thailand.

[3]The results, which are not shown separately in the table, indicate that for industrial countries, the average recovery time and cumulative output loss was 1.9 years and 3.1 percentage points for currency crises, respectively; while it was 4.1 years and 10.2 percentage points for banking crises, respectively.

[4]Some of these indicators of vulnerability will be used when we specify and construct an empirical model of currency crises in Sections 12.5 and 12.6.

[5]The only substantive differences in the case of industrial countries *vis-à-vis* the emerging market economies were: (i) equity price declines were significant predictors of currency crises right throughout the buildup to the crisis; and (ii) low domestic interest rates signaled currency crises at 13- and 8-month lags. Both these indicators were insignificant for emerging market economies.

[6]It needs to be noted that this index was used to identify vulnerabilities that give rise to a substantial risk of crises, and not to predict crises *per se*. This is because policy actions or a change in economic conditions can dissipate the risk of a crisis. Moreover, it is possible that crises can also occur even when there are no apparent vulnerabilities, owing to pure spillover or contagion effects.

[7]Under the assumption that the crawl rate ε is fixed, it implies that $\Delta i = \Delta i_f + \Delta \varepsilon = \Delta i_f$.

[8]This is directly obtained from (eqn 6.57)–(eqn 6.59) by setting $P_f = 1$.

[9]Strictly speaking, we should replace π and g by (eqn 12.9) and (eqn 12.11), respectively. However, the resulting expression then becomes very complicated for any meaningful interpretation. As such, we assume that with π and g fixed at their desired levels (π^* and g^*), the intersection of the PP line for ($\pi = \pi^*$) and the GG line (for $g = g^*$) would indicate the definitive policy settings which would then determine reserve accretion/depletion, as well as the possibility of a speculative attack.

[10]Differentiating (eqn 12.29) with respect to r ($= i - \pi$) and setting the resultant expression equal to zero yields $r = 0.0393$, that is about 4 per cent. The fact that r is currently well over this threshold limit could be one possible reason for the continuing industrial slowdown.

[11]This was the value of the LIBOR which prevailed in 1989–90.

[12]It is seen that the real domestic credit growth rate, defined as $\mu - \pi$, is drastically reduced by over forty per cent: from a 6.7 per cent growth rate in the previous experiment to just about 3.8 per cent in this one.

13

Economic Policies and Growth

13.1 INTRODUCTION

Until the 1970s, research in the developing countries was mainly concerned with long-run structural issues related to growth. With the harsh shocks of the early 1980s and the ensuing debt crisis in several countries throughout the world, attention has increasingly turned towards comparative studies of macroeconomic policies and its relation to the growth performance of countries. This is partly because the growth rates in many developing countries declined in the 1980s due to these macroeconomic problems (as was to be expected); but mainly because—as many have argued—of the perception that the adjustment policies that were subsequently adopted by these countries were basically responsible for their continued stagnation (which was indeed unexpected).

Although a large body of literature on this subject has accumulated over the years, most of it has dealt with the Latin American countries and has been primarily devoted to comparing the attempts at stabilizing inflation. To that extent, therefore, it has been rather unbalanced. In an effort to remedy the situation, more recently, several studies have been carried out to evaluate the experience of the developing countries in relation to the adjustment programmes and the macroeconomic policies that they implemented. By highlighting certain common elements, such lessons of experience, along with formal methods of reasoning, have often helped in isolating the likely policies and reforms, as well as economic and non-economic factors, which are most conducive to growth, thereby providing guidelines for the future.

The two main concerns of the literature on the sequencing of reforms are, first, to determine the optimal order for liberalization measures and, second, to determine how this order fits into the overall framework of macroeconomic stabilization and structural adjustment programmes. Section 13.2 is initially devoted to discussing these issues. It then presents the concept of the high-inflation trap and highlights related issues dealing with stabilization from high inflation. Section 13.3 discusses the political economy of stabilization and adjustment. It initially presents the observed relationship between the form of government and economic performance for a sample of countries; and then provides empirical evidence by estimating growth regressions by incorporating non-economic factors, related to the role of institutions, into the analysis. Finally, in Section 13.4 the lessons of experience are briefly summarized with reference to the lessons of political economy and economic policy lessons. It concludes with a few brief injunctions to policy makers in the form of specific economic policy guidelines.

13.2 LIBERALIZATION WITH STABILIZATION

13.2.1 *The Optimal Sequence of Liberalization Measures*

Financial and trade liberalization, with borrowing and lending at substantial real rates of interest made possible by a stable price level, is not easy and is full of potential pitfalls. Nevertheless, it remains the only game in town as far as successful economic development is concerned. [McKinnon 1989, p. 53].

The rich and growing literature on both the theory of liberalization and the experience of a number of countries which have embarked on such programmes of macroeconomic stabilization and structural adjustment seems to suggest that there is a clear need for reform of the financial system of many developing countries, both to increase the efficiency of existing financial markets and to develop new markets in order to enable the financial system to serve better the needs of the real economy. However, aside from the transitional problems that usually reform packages face, many economists have started questioning the very content of these packages and have argued that it may be misleading to view all forms of government intervention in financial markets as 'financial repression' calling for a policy of 'liberalization'. It is for this reason that Gibson and Tsakalotos (1994), in their comprehensive survey on the scope and limits of financial liberalization, suggest that

McKinnon's view (cited above) on financial liberalization being 'the only game in town' is unhelpful.

Under the circumstances, what is needed in developing countries is a better understanding of how financial markets work and in what way institutions are important, the aim being to develop and promote strategies which combine measures of financial liberalization with the development of old or the creation of new financial institutions. This is clearly an important issue since the liberalization of domestic financial markets has been the *leitmotif* of a number of developing economies of late, including India, all of whom seem to be motivated by a common goal: less government intervention. One reason for this motivation seems to be the widely held notion that government-led development policies in many LDCs have resulted only in 'shallow finance' rather than 'deepening finance' which, *inter alia*, is what really matters in promoting economic growth (Shaw 1973). If inflation occurs, although nominal finance rises, real finance does not rise by the same proportion since it is taxed away by inflation and this state is referred to as shallow finance. When finance is shallow as a proportion of income, real rates of return tend to be very low, even negative. When finance is deepening (one index of which is an increase in liquidity reserves), governments can tend to be less dependent on taxes and foreign savings, capital flight is reversed and real savings grow in financial rather than physical assets.

Thus, the policy prescription of domestic financial liberalization entails a move towards a more market-oriented system. The typical programme of liberalization comprises two main components. First, there is an attempt to allow interest rates to be market determined. Thus, controls on both deposit and lending rates are abolished or reduced. Second, liberalization involves reducing quantitative controls in an attempt to allow financial intermediaries greater control over the use of their liabilities subject to certain minimum controls required for prudential supervision.

However, most literature surveys on the set of policies carried out by many developing countries in the 1970s and 1980s seem to suggest that there could be certain theoretical limitations within the corpus of the financial liberalization literature which could have led to mistaken, or at least incomplete, policy programmes. Central to much of what is being said there is: (i) that the definition of financial repression is too broad, including as it does not only intervention which leads to genuine inefficiencies in financial markets but also intervention that can be seen as a response to market failure, and (ii) the need to take the design, operation, and sequencing of reforms much more seriously than it has been done hitherto.

While much of the focus of the discussion so far has been largely on the macroeconomic effects of specific reforms, the determination of the sequential order of specific policies as well as the appropriate pace of reform that policy makers should follow when implementing comprehensive reform programmes raises important practical and conceptual questions.

Most developing economies undertaking liberalization and stabilization programmes are open economies. Experience has shown that the question of exchange-rate policy is crucial to the success of liberalization, not least because it affects capital flows through its impact on the expected rate of depreciation. Usually liberalization leads to capital flows because it entails an increase in the domestic interest rate above world levels and, since stabilization programmes often involve a prior devaluation in the exchange rate, the resulting interest rate differential may not be offset by any further expected depreciation of the domestic currency. In addition, capital flows are likely because, since the marginal productivity of capital is usually higher in recently liberalized developing countries, firms can afford to borrow from abroad. However, such inflows could undermine the ability of the monetary authorities to control the monetary base, therefore putting the stabilization programme in jeopardy. Thus, the open economy extensions to the McKinnon–Shaw hypothesis and the issue of capital flows raise the general issue of the relationship between domestic financial liberalization and external liberalization. One way in which capital flows could be prevented would be to maintain controls on capital movements until domestic financial liberalization and the stabilization programme are completed. Another way would be sterilization of reserves to prevent an erosion of control over the monetary base.

All these possibilities raise the issue of the optimal order in which an economy should liberalize and these, and a host of related issues, form the two main concerns of the literature on the sequencing of reforms. The first one is to determine the optimal order for liberalizing the domestic real sector, the domestic financial sector, the external real sector, and the external financial sector. Should all these sectors be liberalized simultaneously or does the existence of 'adjustment costs' imply that there is an optimal path? The second concern is how the order of liberalization fits into the framework of macroeconomic stabilization and structural adjustment programmes. In particular, this is a major concern of much of McKinnon's later work (for example McKinnon 1991) where he seeks to determine whether there are any macroeconomic prerequisites to liberalization. Was he disenchanted by the experience of liberalization programmes in many developing countries or did he, in fact, finally succumb to the rather belated realization that there should exist a set of 'rules' before one can play the 'only game in town'?

Table 13.1, largely based on Gibson and Tsakalotos (1994), describes the kind of reforms which liberalization of each sector broadly entails and the numbers in each box suggest, by and large, the accepted order of the sequencing of reforms. It is generally agreed that domestic financial liberalization should come only after domestic real liberalization but before external financial liberalization. Assume, for example, that a country decides to liberalize the financial system before it has liberalized the domestic real sector. In such a scenario, credit is likely to flow only to industries which are considered profitable because relative prices are distorted.

The issue of whether domestic financial liberalization should come before or after external real liberalization is however not entirely clear. If, for example, a country liberalizes its domestic financial sector before it liberalizes its external real sector, then once again credit could flow to a tradeable sector which could be profitable because of the barriers to trade. Alternatively, if the sequence is reversed, then this would hamper the ability of the domestic industry to compete in the world markets. Finally, it is agreed that domestic financial liberalization should come before external financial liberalization. If external liberalization occurs while domestic interest rates are still below world levels, then a capital flight could take place. More generally, domestic banks would find it difficult to compete with foreign banks because they are still subject to a variety of controls and regulations which only serve to increase the cost of intermediation. Overall, this therefore leads to the conclusion that domestic financial liberalization should be second in the overall sequence of reforms.

What about the issues of macroeconomic control? McKinnon (1991) argues that there are two main macroeconomic prerequisites to successful liberalization. First, there is the need for fiscal control. Many of the regulations imposed on the domestic banks raise revenue which helps to finance the government deficit. Since liberalization involves the removal of many of these regulations, it is clear that other sources of revenue need to be tapped. Thus, this sets up a case for widening the tax base as well as developing a proper means of tax collection before liberalization. Second, there is a need for control over domestic banks for monetary policy purposes. Often financial liberalization is associated with a loss of control by the authorities over credit creation. Such arguments often warn against the removal of reserve requirements as a means of liberalization. The consensus view in this regard is that liberalization is more likely to be successful if controls on interest rates are removed gradually while the necessary preconditions of a strong and effective system of bank supervision are established.

TABLE 13.1　SEQUENCING OF ECONOMIC REFORMS

	Domestic	*External*
	1	**3**
Real	• Setting up a market-price system • Removal of subsidy • Tax base widening • Privatization	• Removal of trade barriers (current account), that is trade account convertibility
	2	**4**
Financial	• Raising domestic interest rates • Central Bank autonomy • Improving domestic capital markets	• Removal of capital controls, that is short-term capital account convertibility

The issue of financial liberalization is now seen as much more complex than what was originally envisaged. Because the needs of the real economy can be met only through liberalization, the literature still holds as its ultimate goal the full liberalization of the economy. However, the speed and sequencing of liberalization, the manner in which liberalization should be integrated into macroeconomic stabilization and structural adjustment programmes, and the prerequisites for the eventual success of liberalization are all still matters of ongoing concern. Much of the work on these transitional problems has arisen from the experience of liberalization in a number of developing countries and it is on such experiences that we must draw upon if we are to determine whether or not there might actually be limits to the liberalization process.

13.2.2 *The High-inflation Trap*

Many economies in the process of liberalization find themselves in serious internal or external macroeconomic imbalance. A double-digit, or even triple-digit, inflation is one indicator of such an imbalance. A balance of payments (BOP) crisis and a run on foreign exchange reserves are other indicators. Policies adopted to tackle one set of problems frequently exacerbate another set: for example, a devaluation may worsen inflation, whereas a temporary price freeze may accentuate a foreign exchange crisis. The liberalization process often begins at a time of simultaneous internal and external disequilibrium, and even if it does not, these problems are bound to arise at some stage or the other during the process unless appropriate stabilization measures are in place. 'One is thus invariably led to ponder the necessary links between the choice of stabilization policies and the maintenance of the liberalization process' (Bruno 1988, p. 239).

When an economy, in the course of opening up, encounters prolonged periods of inflation, the problem in most cases lies in the government budget deficit. A lack of a sufficiently broad tax base leads governments to rely on the inflation tax mechanism, and even if a broad tax base exists, high inflation, by causing fiscal erosion (via the Olivera–Tanzi effect), increases the budget deficit. In addition, if the capital account is opened up prematurely, as was the case of Israel in 1977 and Mexico in 1991, inflation is bound to accelerate because of the loss of control over the monetary base.

More importantly, the destabilizing effects of a budget deficit in an open economy are not confined to inflation alone. The budget deficit, which constitutes negative public sector savings, increases the current account deficit of the BOP (when it is viewed as the difference between domestic investment and savings). Thus, inflation and BOP crises often go hand in hand with budget deficits. It is thus a necessary condition for both stabilization as well as an orderly conduct of the liberalization process to close the government budget deficit as rapidly as possible.

However, the elimination of budget deficits is not a sufficient condition for rapid stabilization from an initially high-inflation trap because, although the source of prolonged inflationary pressures is in most cases a large budget deficit, elements of inertia in the dynamics of inflation often give inflation a life of its own after a certain period of high inflation has elapsed. Thus, inflation may accelerate in response to certain other factors, for example, external price shocks, even when the government budget deficit has been reduced or has not risen.

The dynamics of such a high-inflation process usually manifests itself in stepwise or discrete jumps in the inflation rate. The new enhanced rate may then persist in a more-or-less stable fashion for a considerable length of time before yet another (price) shock results in another stepwise jump in the inflation rate. The inflationary processes in Argentina, Brazil, and Israel in the 1970s and early 1980s are a good example of such high-inflation traps. While such inflation-rate jumps are influenced by the size of the budget deficit, they may not be directly correlated with it: in effect, an economy may be stuck at a high inflation equilibrium because of a given high budget deficit although, with the same budget deficit, it could have been at a lower rate.

Such a phenomenon was modelled by Bruno and Fischer (1990) who, in the process, highlighted the role of inflationary expectations and the potentially destabilizing effects of fiscal rigidities. To explain their model, we consider a closed economy with exogenous real output. Assume that the money demand function takes the Cagan semi-logarithmic form, with unitary income elasticity, similar to the one used in analysing inflationary financing in Chapter 8, that is

$$m = e^{-\beta\pi(e)}, \beta > 0, \tag{13.1}$$

where m ($= M/Py$) denotes real money balances (M/P) as a fraction of real output (y) and $\pi(e)$ is the expected rate of inflation. Assuming that the government cannot issue bonds to the public and runs a budget deficit (BD)—that is a constant proportion (d) of output—which is financed only through seignorage, then this financing rule implies (with a dot for the time derivative) that:

$$d = BD/Py = \dot{M}/Py = (\dot{M}/M)(M/Py) = \mu m = \mu e^{-\beta\pi(e)}, \tag{13.2}$$

where μ ($= \dot{M}/M$) is the growth rate of nominal money supply.

(Eqn 13.2) reveals how the budget deficit affects the equilibrium growth rate of money supply and, hence, the equilibrium inflation rate. However, to the extent that real money demand is non-linearly related to the expected rate of inflation, the possibility of multiple solutions to (eqn 13.2) arises which is in line with the existence of the so-called 'seignorage Laffer curve'.

(Eqn 13.2) is plotted in Figure 13.1, which is based on Bruno and Fischer (1990). The curve B_0D_0 represents all combinations of μ and $\pi(e)$ for which the budget deficit is constant at, say, $d(0)$: hence B_0D_0 represents an iso-deficit line. From (eqn 13.2), it is seen that $d(0) = \mu$ when $\pi(e) = 0$, and therefore the deficit is measured by the distance OB_0 from the origin to the intercept of the B_0D_0 curve on the μ-axis. The economy is always located on the B_0D_0 curve, since the government is arithmetically bound by its budget constraint.

Logarithmic differentiation of (eqn 13.1) with respect to time yields:

$$\dot{M}/M - \dot{P}/P - \dot{y}/y = \mu - \pi - g = -\beta\dot{\pi}(e), \tag{13.3}$$

where $\pi \, (= \dot{P}/P)$ is the inflation rate and $g \, (= \dot{y}/y)$ is the real growth rate.

In steady-state, therefore we have:

$$\pi = \pi(e) = \mu - g. \tag{13.4}$$

(Eqn 13.4) is represented by the 45° line EE in Figure 13.1, with intercept equal to $-g$ on the $\pi(e)$-axis. As depicted in the figure, the B_0D_0 curve and the EE line intersect twice, implying two potential steady-state equilibria: the low-inflation equilibria at L, and the high-inflation equilibria at H. The dual equilibria are a reflection of the seignorage Laffer curve; the same amount of seignorage can be obtained at either a low or high inflation rate.

The maximum steady state seignorage revenue is obtained by setting the inflation rate at: $\pi^* = \pi^*(e) = 1/\beta - g$; and the corres-ponding maximum seignorage revenue (d^*) is equal to: $d^* = (1/\beta)e^{(\beta g-1)}$.

Thus, depending upon the actual size of the deficit which the government wishes to finance, there may be zero, one, or two equilibria. Because the government cannot obtain more than d^* in steady state, there is no steady state solution if $d > d^*$ (as is the case with the curve B_1D_1). For $d = d^*$, there would be a unique steady state at M (as is the case with the curve B_2D_2). The existence of two steady state equilibria in the case of $d < d^*$ (as is the case with the original curve B_0D_0) thus suggests that an economy may find itself at a higher than necessary inflation rate over extended periods of time, that is, at the high inflation trap H, rather than at the low inflation equilibrium L. Whether this is likely to happen would depend upon the stability of the respective equilibrium points (see Rao 1994).

The following important question therefore immediately emerges in this context: Is the reduction of the budget deficit a sufficient condition

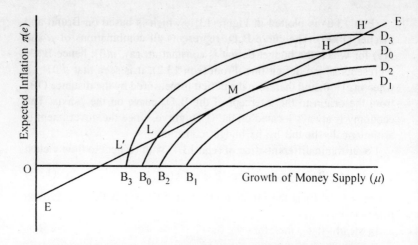

Source: Adapted from Bruno and Fischer (1990. p. 355).

FIGURE 13.1   THE HIGH-INFLATION TRAP

for stabilization to a lower level of inflation. The answer is a qualified negative. For example, in Figure 13.1, reducing the deficit from $d(0)$ to, say, $d(3) < d(0)$, that is shifting the original curve $B_0 D_0$ to its new position $B_3 D_3$ which is closer to the origin with $OB_3 = d(3) < OB_0 = d(0)$, could switch the economy on to a still higher inflation rate given by $H' > H$, if this high-inflation trap is a stable one compared to the lower inflation rate $L' < L$. Thus, as stated earlier, while the source of an inflation could be a large budget deficit, the dynamics of inflation may be such that it could refuse to respond to budget cuts unless accompanied by special stabilization measures.

13.2.3 *Stabilization from High Inflation*

The stability of the high-inflation trap largely depends on the degree of accommodation to the price level of the various nominal (domestic-currency denominated) magnitudes, such as monetary aggregates, the exchange rate, and the wage rate. Such an accommodation is either built in endogenously (the wage–price spiral) or through policy design (the crawling-peg exchange rate system), both of which contribute to the dynamics of inertial inflation. However, as a result of such accommodation, once inflation starts accelerating, the economy loses its nominal anchor, and there is nothing left to hold down prices.

Some economists believe that as the link between the budget deficit and inflation is indirect, the inflationary process is nothing more than a bubble reflecting expectations. According to such a view, a temporary freeze on wages, exchange rates, and prices is sufficient to explode the bubble. However, if the source of internal and external disequilibria emanating from the budget deficit is not eliminated, such temporary freezes would inevitably lead to renewed inflationary expectations and therefore a still higher inflationary trap.

Another mistaken belief is that a gradual reduction in the rate of devaluation would reduce the rate of inflation. This strategy was followed in several Latin American countries in the 1970s, in the form of pre-announced 'tablitas' which specified the actual devaluation strategy that the government would be implementing in the future. However, such attempts at gradualism failed not only because they were not accompanied by contractionary fiscal measures, but also because the various nominal magnitudes were not synchronized to the process of disinflation. Even when a slowdown in the rate of devaluation reduces the rate of inflation, as long as there is an adjustment lag, there will be a real appreciation, with negative consequences for the BOP. Likewise, if prices come down faster than nominal wages, real wages will rise with an adverse effect on economic activity and international competitiveness.

Thus, any stabilization programme directed at steering the economy away from a high-inflation trap must comprise the following measures (Bruno 1988):

• The primary sources of imbalance in the economy, usually the budget and current account deficits, must be tackled first with appropriate orthodox measures.
• There should be a simultaneous and synchronized disinflation of all nominal magnitudes; in particular, the indexation of wages to past prices must be suspended at least temporarily. However, forward indexation, that is obtaining workers' support for a temporary wage freeze in return for future compensation if prices are not stabilized as a result of the programme, need not be excluded.

The above measures should, with any luck, ensure that the high-level inflation trap becomes unstable. However, in order to simultaneously ensure that the newly-established low inflation equilibrium (the point L' in Figure 13.1) will be stable, the programme should include a system of price controls (which are needed to support a wage freeze as well as break the bubble of inflationary expectations). However, for such a price freeze to be sustainable, the government must also announce and incorporate a clearly defined method of gradual price decontrol, once relative stability has been achieved. In addition, a credible set of new nominal anchors need to be established (see Bruno 1991).

There is also a need for a strong and independent central bank so that it can target key monetary aggregates (such as money supply or domestic credit) as part of the stabilization programme. Under the circumstances, greater flexibility could be allowed on nominal exchange rate adjustments. Typically, however, in an inflation-prone economy, exchange rate targeting may be more effective if it is accompanied by a clearly defined wage policy.

Finally, sharp disinflation may, in fact, be preferable to a gradualist strategy. The logic of this course of action is partly based on the dynamics of the model presented above which clearly indicate that it is prone to sudden stepwise increases (or decreases) in the inflation rate: in effect, a gradual reduction in inflation is ruled out. In such a context, although the potential for an increase in unemployment has often been used as an argument to justify a gradualist approach to inflation control, the same arguments can be switched around in favour of rapid disinflation. The sharper and more comprehensive the stabilization package, the more credible are the government's intentions and consequently the faster the reduction in inflationary expectations. Moreover, a sharp disinflation requires a shorter period of credit restraint and, consequently, economic slowdown. On the other hand, because a gradualist disinflation strategy requires prolonged contractionary and fiscal policy which could entail substantial cumulative unemployment, both political and social considerations make it a less advisable course to follow.

These disinflation strategies have been followed successfully by several semi-industrialized countries, including Argentina, Brazil, and Israel, who, in the process of opening up their economies, found themselves confronted by a stepwise acceleration of inflation rates. One will, however, need to examine the stabilization-from-high-inflation experiences of more countries, especially developing ones, before passing any judgment on the general applicability of the model although the evidence so far does seem to be in its favour.

13.3 THE POLITICAL ECONOMY OF STABILIZATION AND ADJUSTMENT

Although the integrated macroeconomic framework developed in this book is fairly robust, cross-country differences in growth cannot be completely explained either by it or by the other factors specified above. Recent developments in mainstream macroeconomics as well as recent research on stabilization and structural adjustment programmes have attempted to seek the residual explanation elsewhere.

First, policy makers may not actually seek the desired macroeconomic objectives, despite this almost universal commitment attributed to them. Rather, their foremost concern may be the nation's political stability.

Second, although policy makers may wish to attain these objectives, they cannot do so because of uncooperative interest groups, or because of the inability of the public to endure these policies long enough for them to work.

Finally, despite well-meaning decisions and implementation, the economy may be structured in such a way that the 'orthodox' policy prescriptions to achieve these objectives may not work, as has been persistently argued by the structuralists; alternatively, well-intentioned and implemented policies following 'heterodox' lines may fail to work because the economy is structured along more conventional lines.

Having dealt with the structuralist critique in the Chapter 11, here, we briefly deal with the first two of these explanations: political factors that either inhibit or prevent the attainment of economic objectives.

13.3.1 *The Form of Government*

It has often been suggested that authoritarian governments are better able to manage economies in developing countries than democratic governments since the former have the ability to push through harsh adjustment programmes. Moreover, it is also alleged that over the longer term such governments, in view of their perceived stability, are better able to carry out a coherent programme for economic development. In contrast, democracies, in view of their rather fragile nature, are often assumed to have difficulties maintaining a focused policy over time as they constantly need to defer to special interests groups whose appeasement is not always most conducive to long-run growth.

To examine this hypothesis, Little *et al* (1993) used comparable data on a set of developing countries over the 17-year period 1973–90 and categorized them in terms of two characteristics (see Barro 1991): (i) economic performance (either good or poor) and (ii) political climate (either stable or unstable). The interest group dimension was introduced by using the political rights and civil liberties index compiled by Freedom House (see Gastil 1987, Rao and Karnik 1994) on the assumption that greater the freedom, the greater is the influence of special interest groups on economic policy making, and hence the poorer is the economic performance in terms of growth rates (see Kormendi and Meguire 1985, Grier and Tullock 1989). Averaging the Freedom House scores over the period 1973–85 produced comparable rankings for these countries which were then divided into two groups (either free or less free) on the basis of the mean score.

The results of this classification are provided in Table 13.2 and it is seen that no clear-cut pattern emerges. A roughly equal number of stable governments performed well and poorly, as was the case for unstable governments. Moreover, countries with a greater degree of freedom, India and Sri Lanka, can be found among the good economic performers; while authoritarian regimes, both stable (such as Cameroon) and unstable (such as Nigeria), are among the poor economic performers. As a matter of fact, countries with a greater degree of freedom can be found in all four categories and therefore the role of interest groups in deliberately steering long-run economic growth away from its optimal is questionable. Thus, it can be inferred that neither the form of government nor the degree of political stability seem to have any significant bearing on economic performance, and therefore simple

TABLE 13.2   POLITICAL REGIMES, HUMAN RIGHTS AND ECONOMIC GROWTH

Economic Performance	Political Regime			
	Stable		Unstable	
Good	* India	3.0	* Thailand	5.3
	Indonesia	3.3	* Turkey	2.9
	Pakistan	2.9		
	South Korea	7.2		
	* Sri Lanka	2.6		
Poor	* Brazil	0.2	* Argentina	−1.5
	Cameroon	−0.8	Nigeria	−1.3
	* Costa Rica	0.6		
	Côte d'Ivoire	−3.2		
	Kenya	0.4		
	* Mexico	−1.0		

Notes: (i) Countries marked with an asterisk (*) before them are in the upper half of the Freedom House list;
(ii) Trend annual growth rate in GDP per capita over the period 1980–90 follows each country.
Source: Little, Cooper, Corden, and Rajapatirana (1993).

generalizations about the effectiveness of various political systems in recording good economic performances do not seem to hold up. Perhaps an authoritarian government does have some edge when it comes to adopting difficult albeit desirable policies, but clearly many authoritarian governments are unable or unwilling to do so. The cases of India and Sri Lanka also serve to demonstrate that democratic governments in developing countries can also successfully implement policies of macroeconomic adjustment in response to adverse external shocks.

13.3.2 *The Role of Institutions*
As is well recognized, in most developing countries, there often exists a considerable gap between the desire to establish a properly framed adjustment programme and the ability to implement it. One of the most important factors needed to close this gap is the quality of the institutional framework.

Several economists, notably Olson (1982) and North (1990), amongst others, have stressed the role of institutions in economic performance. In this context, several aspects have been emphasized in the many studies which have highlighted the importance of institutions. These include political instability (Barro 1991), property rights and security of contracts (Tornell and Velasco 1992), and rent-seeking behaviour (Rama 1993), amongst others. Some of these have used proxy variables to model institutional characteristics although these proxies have either not been fully developed or, being qualitative, have been essentially subjective. Moreover, many of the independent variables used in the studies have been themselves sensitive to economic growth and, as such, it has been possible to hypothesize a reverse causality.

However, there is no doubt that institutions that protect property rights are crucial for private investment and environmental protection and, therefore, economic growth and the quality of life, respectively. In order to test this hypothesis, Knack and Keefer (1995) experimented with variables that included expropriation risk, corruption in the government, quality of bureaucracy, and contractual enforceability by the government, amongst others, and found that institutions were almost as important to economic growth as human capital.

The results of the growth regressions are presented in Table 13.3. The cross-section sample consisted of the same set of countries examined by Knack and Keefer (1995). In all the three equations, (Eqn a)–(eqn c), the dependent variable was the average real GDP growth rate over the sample period, that is 1980–93.

The independent variables were: (i) the average investment–GDP ratio over the sample period (I/Y); (ii) the average schooling (in years) of the labour force ($EDUC$); (iii) the average annual inflation rate over the sample period ($INFL$); (iv) the average external debt–GNP ratio at the beginning of the adjustment process in 1980 (D/Y); (v) the real per capita income in 1980 (PCI); (vi) corruption in the government ($CORR$); (vii) the quality of bureaucracy ($QUAL$); and (viii) the risk of expropriation ($RISK$). The data on the last three variables were based on Knack and Keefer (1995).

TABLE 13.3   SOME CROSS-COUNTRY GROWTH REGRESSIONS (1980–93)

Eqn No.	Variable							R^2
	I/Y	$EDUC$	$INFL$	D/Y	PCI			
a	0.09	0.64	−0.006	−0.02	−1.89	−0.41	CORR	0.48
	(1.9)	(2.3)	(−2.4)	(−1.7)	(−2.9)	(−1.5)		
b	0.09	0.64	−0.006	−0.02	−2.10	−0.42	QUAL	0.46
	(2.0)	(2.3)	(−2.3)	(−1.7)	(−3.0)	(−1.3)		
c	0.09	0.64	−0.006	−0.02	−2.07	−0.36	RISK	0.45
	(1.9)	(2.3)	(−2.3)	(−1.7)	(−2.9)	(−1.4)		

Note: Figures in parentheses indicate *t*-statistics.
Source: Author's calculations based on data from World Bank (1996); Knack and Keefer (1995).

The results of the exercise indicate that the main determinants, that is investment, educational attainment, inflation, external debt and the initial conditions, influence long-run growth significantly. As far as the other three variables are concerned, while they are negatively associated with the growth rate as would be expected, they are not as significant as the main determinants. However, these institutional variables do add to the explanatory power of the regressions and, by and large, it is found that, in descending order of importance, government corruption, lack of bureaucratic quality, risk of property appropriation and debt repudiation, and law and order (not reported) help to explain variations in growth rates across the sample of countries.

13.3.3 *Political Lessons of Economic Reforms*
Political scientists have presented several hypotheses to try and explain the implementation of economic reforms: for example, reforms are

successful only under authoritarian regimes, reforms take place only after a crises has occurred, reforms are undertaken only by new governments, reforms are not possible in transitional economies, reforms are possible only with solid legislative support or, alternatively, in the face of weak opposition, reforms need a social consensus, and successful reforms are possible only under visionary leaders, amongst others.

The most quoted hypothesis is that authoritarian regimes are better at economic management in developing countries than are democratic governments since repressive regimes can blunt opposition to economic reforms and implement a consistent and coherent programme of economic development. However, as was shown in the preceding section, there appears little association between economic reform and political regime. Despite this lack of evidence, political scientists have still pursued this hypothesis and, in doing so, have often suggested that a distinction needs to be made between 'weak' and 'strong' authoritarian states. However, when applied to economic policy, this distinction runs the risk of being almost tautologous, with weak authoritarianism being defined as those states that are unable to frame and execute a coherent and effective macroeconomic policy. Nevertheless, it is true that weak democratic institutions in Turkey, Brazil, and Peru in the 1980s did contribute to the stalling of badly-needed economic reform.

Similarly, it is often suggested that economic policy reforms are only undertaken after a crisis has emerged. However, while a crisis can play a significant role in stimulating reform, it is neither a necessary nor a sufficient condition to initiate reform. For example, crises played a major role in the reform efforts in Indonesia in 1965 and 1982, Chile in 1973 and 1982, South Korea in 1979, Turkey in 1980, Ghana in 1983, Poland in 1989, and India in 1991. However, there are cases such as Australia, Colombia, and Portugal in the 1980s, where a crisis does not appear to have played a role in the reform effort. Moreover, despite the debt crisis in 1982, Mexico initiated a belated response to it and did not embark on reforms until five years later in 1987.

It has also been suggested (see Haggard and Kaufman 1992) that the governments experiencing the greatest difficulty in introducing economic reforms are those in 'democratic transition', that is those countries in which an authoritarian government has yielded to a fledgling democracy. There have been many examples of this transformation such as Argentina (1983), Turkey (1983), Brazil (1985), Pakistan (1988), and Chile (1989), amongst others. Several reasons, including the need for building political coalitions, are cited as to why democratic transitions are most likely to lead to 'expansionist' economic policies. However, it needs to be noted that these governments are not the only ones to indulge in such policies because, in a sense, nearly all democratically elected governments seem to specialize in reconciling conflicting claims by various interest groups on resources by increasing public expenditures.

It is also suggested that new governments are more likely to make drastic changes in economic policy than are incumbent governments. Such changes were introduced by many democratically elected governments including Costa Rica (1982), Argentina (1989), Poland (1989), and India (1991), amongst others. The assumption here is that new governments can more easily break with the past and take the necessary steps to reduce the 'chaos' left by the earlier government. Turkey (1980) provides the exception because the military leadership, after overthrowing a democratically elected government, not only continued, but actually strengthened, the economic reforms of their predecessors. The Hawke administration in Australia, the Gonzalez government in Spain, and the Barco administration in Colombia, on the other hand, are examples where successful reforms were implemented at the middle or end of their respective tenures.

A solid legislative support is another factor suggested as a prerequisite for reform. This hypothesis appears to be consistent with the democratically elected governments in Australia, Colombia, New Zealand, Portugal, India, Spain, and Turkey. However, in Poland, the Solidarity government had to be supported by smaller parties in the parliament. On the other hand, Chile, Indonesia, South Korea, and Turkey are cases where the opposition was suppressed before reforms were implemented; while Russia is an example of reforms in the face of weak opposition. While social consensus was important in the reform efforts in Australia, Mexico, Poland, Portugal, and Spain; Brazil and Peru are cases where there was no consensus; and Chile and Turkey are examples of intense opposition to reforms being converted into widespread endorsement as the programme yielded positive results.

Therefore, the evidence suggests no simple answers although a strong political leadership, not necessarily authoritarian in style, backed by a competent economic team is likely to improve the chances of successful reforms.

13.4 THE LESSONS OF EXPERIENCE

The period from the early 1980s onwards has been an especially turbulent one for most of the developing countries around the world.

Such a turbulence has posed several fundamental challenges to macroeconomic management, and this study has attempted to put together an integrated framework which is capable of analysing some of the underlying factors responsible for it, as well as suggesting remedies in order to reduce it. Despite the complexity of the issues involved in this regard, a number of common strands have emerged.

The most important is that macroeconomic policies are often as important as external shocks in determining the course of the economy. Indeed, the size of the external shock seems to have little bearing on subsequent economic difficulties because while some countries have adjusted well to large shocks, others have adapted poorly even to small ones. In such a context, although very often a poor economic performance is attributed to external disturbances, countries cannot eschew responsibility for coping badly with such shocks because so many economies have indeed coped well with them. All this implies that it may not always be possible to disentangle the effects of bad policies from those of adverse external shocks because eventually both would lead to almost identical consequences. This is important because although the genesis of most structural reforms can be traced to crisis situations, very often such crises are merely a reflection of past unsound policies rather than the outcome of adverse external shocks.

13.4.1 *Macroeconomic Policy and Growth*

The primary conclusion of this study is that macroeconomic stability, which is often synonymous with reduced inflation and improvements in the BOP, is essential for long-run growth. Therefore, more than anything else, macroeconomic policies should be designed to stabilize real output in the face of exogenous disturbances. Few countries— South Korea being amongst them—have systematically followed macroeconomic policies that have tended to stabilize output growth around its trend; and even fewer still—India notably being amongst them—have attempted to adopt macroeconomic policies that have actually increased the trend rate of growth in the face of such shocks.

While the formal model developed in this study indicated that nearly all the determinants of growth, notably the deficit–debt dynamics, act through the investment rate, it is nevertheless true that some of the other important factors include human capital as well as the efficiency of investment. However, as our formal modelling efforts did not include any work on the derivation of the quality-adjusted labour force or on the factors influencing the apparent efficiency of investment (by 'apparent efficiency', we mean the growth rate divided by the investment rate), we were forced to limit ourselves only to the macroeconomic effects of policy on the investment rate *per se*.

Most importantly, we showed that inflation is both a symptom as well as a cause for instability and it is capable of substantially reducing the growth rate of output. This finding clearly suggests that inflation always carries a price tag and therefore there is no such thing as a 'free' inflation. To sum it up, growth is largely a decreasing function of inflation.

13.4.2 *The Lessons of Political Economy*

It is seen that the form of government—democratic or authoritarian—does not determine the success or failure of macroeconomic policy. It is true that some of the most successful economies, notably South Korea and Indonesia, have been authoritarian, but then again, so have been some of the least successful. Democratic transitions may create or intensify macroeconomic problems, as in Argentina and Brazil, although this was not true in the case of Chile. Equally true, large democracies, like India, can successfully implement reform programmes. Thus, there are no simple lessons here, other than the one stressed before, namely that sound macroeconomic policies can be pursued under many forms of government.

Tradition, history and the role of institutions can influence the current attitude of the general public. In certain cases, things may have to get worse before they get better. The stabilization successes of Israel since 1985 and India since 1991 seem to bear out this hypothesis. However, there is no real policy lesson here, since one is unlikely to advocate creating hyperinflation (the case of Israel) or running down reserves (the case of India) in order to stress the need for macroeconomic discipline. The conclusion that one derives is rather elementary: those who are responsible for determining macroeconomic policy must be convinced of its consistency, sustainability, and correctness.

In a democracy, the relevant group may be the larger community or a limited elite, while in an authoritarian state, it may just be one or a few individuals. However, regardless of 'where the buck stops', if high inflation is to be avoided, they must first of all believe, very firmly, that inflation is undesirable. Secondly, they must understand the dynamics of inflation and realize that whether budget deficits are financed through monetization or through continuous debt financing, eventually it must lead to inflation. To sum it up, they must appreciate the need for financial control.

It thus goes without saying that formulating and implementing good policy depends, to a large extent, on a cadre of technically competent officials who have the ability to recognize and analyse problems skilfully. In authoritarian states, the personal views of individuals—such as Park of South Korea, Suharto of Indonesia and Pinochet of Chile—have obviously been crucial. In more liberal countries, there often have been strong and visionary leaders who have been able to generate adequate consensus and implement reforms successfully as for example, Salinas in Mexico, Hawke in Australia, Walesa in Poland, Silva in Portugal, Gonzalez in Spain, and Ozal in Turkey.

In several other countries where macroeconomic policies have on the whole been a success, there usually have been particularly well-qualified individuals who have been elevated to high political positions—above all the Ministry of Finance—and who have been able to carry weight with the ultimate decision makers, thus being able to propose courses of action to steer the economy as desired. In recent years, these have often been professional economists with political backing, the so-called 'technopols'. They have been the actual makers and implementers of policy. For example, Poland had Leszek Balcerowicz during 1989–91, Argentina had Domingo Cavallo during 1991–6, Czechoslovakia had Vaclav Klaus during 1990–2, Russia had Yaiger Gaider during 1992–4, Mexico had Carlos Salinas during 1991–5, and India had Manmohan Singh during 1991–6.

13.4.3 *Economic Policy Lessons*
We can sum up the policy lessons of economic reform, derived from our findings in this study, in the form of the following propositions:

- Long-run economic growth is a very gradual process and needs sustained stabilization, a competitive real exchange rate to promote exports, a high rate of savings, and adequate supply-side policies to increase the productivity of investment. However, attention has also to be paid to the quality of growth which has often proved to be immiserizing. In such a context, 'green growth' that improves both environmental as well as distributive well-being is far more preferable as it is conducive to the quality of life.
- Institutional developments, with special reference to the central bank and the banking system, financial and capital markets, as well as regulatory and supervisory agencies, are crucial for sustained long-run growth.

- Most of the determinants of growth act through the investment rate. However, two of the most important factors which influence the efficiency of investment include human capital as well as income distribution. As such, the pursuit of sound educational and redistributive policies should normally help to increase the long-run trend rate of growth of output.

- The key is, by and large, to avoid building rigidities into the economy in the form of persistent import controls, widespread wage indexation, and extensive term structure of administered interest rates. In such a context, a flexible policy stance which is quickly capable of adapting to changing circumstances as well as to past mistakes is crucial to ensure success.

- Policy responses should also be sound and prompt. The adjustment programme itself should be comprehensive but could be phased in gradually, except in certain exceptional circumstances, such as controlling a hyperinflation or, as in the case of the transitional economies, during times of extraordinary developments. However, a shock therapy, in retrospect, is proving to be a far less risky and more viable option than originally envisaged.

- Prudent economic management entails that aggregate national spending be restricted to the level of the country's permanent income. Transitory income from a positive external shock should be channelled towards investment in economic infrastructure which is complementary to private investment. A useful rule-of-thumb in such a context is that all positive shocks should be treated as if they were transitory and all negative shocks as if they were permanent.

- Inflation is both a symptom as well as a cause for instability and it is capable of substantially reducing the growth rate of output. Thus, there is no such thing as a little inflation being good for the economy because growth is largely a decreasing function of inflation.

- Overvaluation of the real exchange rate as well as volatility in the nominal exchange rate should be avoided. As far as possible, the exchange rate should not be used as a nominal anchor. This implies that it is generally better to have a flexible exchange rate regime, with adjustments. However, these adjustments have to be backed by demand-management policies.

13.4.4 *Economic Policy Guidelines*

We can sum up the policy guidelines of economic reform, derived from our findings in this study, in the form of the following injunctions:

- Beware of the 'unpleasant fiscal arithmetic': namely, the future implications of both domestic as well as external government debt. Implicit in the above dictum is that fiscal restraint is the cornerstone of sound macroeconomic management and that fiscal balance is one of the best indicators of macroeconomic health. Thus, credit-worthiness has to maintained at all costs.
- While liberalization is essential in the medium term, the sequencing of economic reforms is critical in the short-run. In effect, the domestic real sector has to be liberalized first. While some controversy still persists regarding which sector, the domestic financial or the external real, ought to be liberalized at the next stage, there is no doubt that external financial liberalization involving capital account convertibility must come last and that too only after an appropriate institutional framework has been properly established.
- Financial liberalization is associated with removing controls on (the term structure of) interest rates. Considering that private savings are often interest-sensitive, there is a usually a strong case for increasing interest rates. However, this step has to be examined in a fuller perspective, especially with regard to the possible reduction in private sector investment which could be offset by a probable rise in the apparent productivity of investment, the likely burgeoning of interest payments on the existing domestic debt, and the definite increase in the cost of future government borrowings.
- Regardless of whatever other sacrifices the economy is compelled to make in the process of adjustment, there should be no reductions in government expenditures on education. Moreover, if the situation allows, these should be increased in order to take full advantage of the positive feedback that exists between education, income distribution, and long-run growth.
- Excessive reserve accumulation should be avoided. The optimal level of reserves should basically reflect projected import requirements, along with a strategic 'reserve' component earmarked for handling adverse external shocks, which could include defending a desired nominal exchange rate in the face of speculative attacks that could cause a run on reserves. Excess reserves should then be used for increasing investment.
- The pursuit of an external debt management policy in the above context suggests that external borrowings should not be used for merely augmenting reserves, but primarily for promoting investment and, thereby, growth. However, these borrowings have to be consistent with sustained creditworthiness.

- The adverse effects of a retrogressive tax structure on growth has to be corrected in the medium term. In the short-run, however, the tax system has to be made more buoyant so that collection lags are reduced and the impact of fiscal erosion on real tax revenues is minimized. A consistency between the design of monetary policy reform (with respect to increasing interest rates) and that of fiscal policy reform (with respect to increasing tax revenues) has to be maintained at all times.

13.5 EPILOGUE

The primary aim of this study has been to provide an integrated macroeconomic framework and model to try and answer certain relevant questions regarding stabilization and growth-oriented adjustment programmes. Such an integration was primarily carried out by merging the Fund and Bank models together, thereby endogenizing inflation, growth, and the BOP. This merged model was subsequently expanded by sequentially integrating the financial, fiscal, and external sectors into the framework in a logical and coherent manner, thereby endogenizing the interest rate, the fiscal deficit, as well as the external debt into the analysis. In doing so, it has revealed both the unity of the ensuing framework as well as the diversity of policy options emanating from such an integrated approach.

However, regardless of the fairly robust and plausible empirical scenarios that the integrated framework seems to generate, caution needs to be exercised in drawing widespread generalizations from these results, partly because various aspects of the economy have not been completely incorporated into the model and partly because very often generalizations are subject to important qualifications and exceptions. Furthermore, some very important concepts, like human capital and income distribution, which were briefly dealt with, would require to be more completely integrated into such a (class of) model. We have in mind, particularly, the need for a more comprehensive framework for equilibrating growth, inflation, and income distribution on the lines briefly outlined in Chapter 10. Our limited work in this area does suggest substantial scope for improvements and refinements, particularly with regard to the effects of macroeconomic policies, especially in terms of their coordination, on the dynamics of such a concept.

History and tradition are extremely important in determining what the people expect, and these have a considerable effect on the public's willingness to accept short-run hardships for the sake of desired long-term objectives which it believes that the government is genuinely pursuing. While a full explanation of these factors is still awaited, the important point in such a context is that the ability of the government to successfully implement a structural adjustment programme depends not only on the actual economic policies formally adopted, but also on the convictions of the leaders and, most importantly, the people with regard to the desirability as well as the ultimate attainability of these targeted outcomes.

In conclusion, we would like to stress that macroeconomic policies can explain only a certain part of a country's economic performance. A well-planned stabilization and growth-oriented structural adjustment programme will provide a solid foundation for the continuing success of government policies. However, evidence suggests that regardless of the soundness of such a framework, if complementary policies are poor, or if the dynamism of the private sector is inhibited by political uncertainty, a country can still experience a low growth rate. Yet, when something goes wrong on the macroeconomic front, as it clearly did for many developing countries in the 1980s and India in the early 1990s, concern with macroeconomic policy dominates everything else. History may never repeat itself again, but even if it does, it would have provided many valuable lessons for the future. For when formal models by themselves fail to provide guidelines for the conduct and implementation of policy, it is such lessons alone that will help make the final diagnosis.

References

Addison, D. (1989), 'The World Bank Revised Minimum Standard Model: Concepts and Issues', PPR Working Paper No. WPS 231, The World Bank, Washington, DC.

Adelman, I. and S. Robinson (1988), 'Income Distribution and Development', in H.B. Chenery and T.N. Srinivasan (eds), *Handbook of Development Economics,* North Holland, Amsterdam.

Agenor, P.R. and P.J. Montiel (1996), *Development Macroeconomics,* Princeton University Press, Princeton, New Jersey.

Aghion, P. and G. Saint-Paul (1993), 'Uncovering Some Causal Relationships Between Productivity Growth and the Structure of Economic Fluctuations: A Tentative Survey', NBER Working Paper No. 4603, National Bureau of Economic Research, Cambridge, MA.

Aghion, P. and P. Howitt (1992), 'A Model of Growth Through Creative Destruction', *Econometrica,* 60.

Aghion, P., P. Bacchetta, and A. Banerjee (1999), 'A Simple Model of Monetary Policy and Currency Crises', Unpublished, National Bureau of Economic Research, Cambridge, MA.

Alesina, A. (1995), 'The Political Economy of Macroeconomic Stabilization and Income Inequality: Myths and Reality', Paper presented at the Conference on Income Distribution and Sustainable Growth, June, Washington, DC.

Alesina, A. and R. Perotti (1993), 'Income Distribution, Political Instability and Investment', NBER Working Paper No. 4486, National Bureau of Economic Research, Cambridge, MA.

Alesina, A. and R. Perotti (1996), 'Budget Deficits and Budget Institutions', IMF Working Paper No. 96/52, International Monetary Fund, Washington, DC.

Alesina, A. and D. Rodrik (1994), 'Distributive Politics and Economic Growth', *Quarterly Journal of Economics*, 109.

Alexander, S.S. (1951), 'Devaluation Versus Import Restriction as an Instrument for Improving Foreign Trade Balance', *IMF Staff Papers*, 1.

Alexander, S.S. (1952), 'Effects of a Devaluation on a Trade Balance', *IMF Staff Papers*, 2.

Alogoskoufis, G.S. and N. Christodoulakis (1990), 'Fiscal Deficits, Seignorage and External Debt: The Case for Greece', CEPR Discussion Paper No. 468, Centre for Economic Policy Research, London.

Amsden, A., J. Kochanowicz, and L. Taylor (1994), *The Market Meets its Match: Restructuring the Economies of Eastern Europe*, Harvard University Press, Cambridge, MA.

Anand, R., R. Rocha, and S. van Wijnbergen (1988), 'Inflation, External Debt and Financial Sector Reform: A Quantitative Approach to Consistent Fiscal Policy With an Application to Turkey', NBER Working Paper No. 2731, National Bureau of Economic Research, Cambridge, MA.

Anand, S. and R. Kanbur (1993), 'The Kuznets Process and the Inequality–Development Relationship', *Journal of Development Economics*, 40.

Antle, J. and G. Heidebrink (1995), 'Environment and Development: Theory and International Evidence', *Economic Development and Cultural Change*, 43.

Bacha, E.L. (1987), 'IMF Conditionality: Conceptual Problems and Policy Alternatives', *World Development*, 15.

Bacha, E.L. (1990), 'A Three-Gap Model of Foreign Transfers and the GDP Growth Rate in Developing Countries', *Journal of Development Economics*, 32.

Bain, A.D. (1973), 'Flow of Funds Analysis: A Survey', *Economic Journal*, 83.

Balassa, B. (1989), 'A Conceptual Framework for Adjustment Policies', PPR Working Paper No. WPS 139, The World Bank, Washington, DC.

Balcerowicz, L. and A. Gelb (1994), 'Macropolicies in Transition to a Market Economy: A Three-Year Perspective', in M. Bruno and

B. Pleskovic (eds), *Proceedings of the World Bank Annual Conference on Development Economics,* The World Bank, Washington, DC.

Bardhan, P. (1994), 'Poverty Alleviation', ODC Occasional Paper No. 1, Overseas Development Council, Washington, DC.

Barro, R.J. (1974), 'Are Government Bonds Net Wealth?', *Journal of Political Economy,* 82.

Barro, R.J. (1990), 'Government Spending in a Simple Model of Endogenous Growth', *Journal of Political Economy,* 98.

Barro, R.J. (1991), 'Economic Growth in a Cross Section of Countries', *Quarterly Journal of Economics,* 106.

Barro, R.J. (1996), *Getting it Right: Markets and Choices in a Free Society,* MIT Press, Cambridge, MA.

Barro, R.J. and J-W. Lee (1993), 'International Comparisons of Educational Attainment', *Journal of Monetary Economics,* 32.

Barro, R.J. and X. Sala-i-Martin (1992), 'Public Finance in Models of Economic Growth', *Review of Economic Studies,* 59.

Barro, R.J. and X. Sala-i-Martin (1995), *Economic Growth,* McGraw Hill, New York.

Bartelmus, P. (1989), 'Environmental Accounting and the System of National Accounts', in Y.J. Ahmad, S. El Serafy and E. Lutz (eds), *Environmental Accounting for Sustainable Development,* UNEP–World Bank Symposium, The World Bank, Washington, DC.

Bernanke, B. and M. Gertler (1989), 'Agency Costs, Net Worth and Economic Fluctuations', *American Economic Review,* 79.

Bhagwati, J.N. (1983), *International Trade and Development Theory,* Columbia University Press, New York.

Bhagwati, J.N. (1987), 'Outward Versus Inward Policies', in V. Corbo, M. Goldstein and M. Khan (eds), *Growth-oriented Adjustment Programs,* IMF–World Bank, Washington, DC.

Birdsall, N., D. Ross, and R. Sabot (1995), 'Inequality and Growth Reconsidered: Lessons from East Asia', *The World Bank Economic Review,* 9.

Blades, D.W. (1989), 'Measuring Pollution Within the Framework of the National Accounts', in Y.J. Ahmad, S. El Serafy, and E. Lutz (eds), *Environmental Accounting for Sustainable Development,* UNEP–World Bank Symposium, The World Bank, Washington, DC.

Blanchard, O.J. and S. Fischer (1989), *Lectures on Macroeconomics,* MIT Press, Cambridge, MA.

Blejer M.I. and A. Cheasty, eds (1993), *How to Measure the Fiscal Deficit*, International Monetary Fund, Washington, DC.

Blejer, M.I. and M.S. Khan (1984), 'Private Investment in Developing Countries', *IMF Staff Papers*, 31.

Blejer, M.I., M.S. Khan, and P.R. Masson (1995), 'Early Contributions of *Staff Papers* to International Economics', *IMF Staff Papers*, 42.

Blitzer, C.R., P.B. Clark, and L. Taylor, eds (1975), *Economy-Wide Models and Development Planning*, Oxford University Press, London.

Bourgignon, F. and C. Morrison (1990), 'Income Distribution, Development and Foreign Trade: A Cross-Sectional Analysis', *European Economic Review*, 34.

Bruno, M. (1988), 'Opening Up: Liberalization with Stabilization', in R. Dornbusch and F.L.C.H. Helmers (eds), *The Open Economy: Tools for Policymakers in Developing Countries*, Oxford University Press, New York.

Bruno, M. (1989), 'Econometrics and the Design of Economic Reform', *Econometrica*, 57.

Bruno, M. (1991), *High Inflation and the Nominal Anchors of an Open Economy*, Princeton University Press, Princeton, New Jersey.

Bruno, M. (1993), 'Inflation and Growth: An Integrated Approach', in P.B. Kenen (ed.), *Understanding Interdependence: The Macroeconomics of the Open Economy*, Princeton University Press, Princeton.

Bruno, M. (1995), 'Inflation, Growth and Monetary Control: Nonlinear Lessons from Crisis and Recovery', Paolo Baffi Lectures on Money and Finance, Banca d'Italia, Rome.

Bruno, M. and W. Easterly (1995), 'Inflation Crisis and Long-Run Growth', NBER Working Paper No. 5209, National Bureau of Economic Research, Cambridge, MA.

Bruno, M. and S. Fischer (1990), 'Seignorage, Operating Rules and High-Inflation Traps', *Quarterly Journal of Economics*, 105.

Bruno, M., M. Ravallion, and L. Squire (1995), 'Equity and Growth in Developing Countries: Old and New Perspectives on the Policy Issues', Paper presented at the Conference on Income Distribution and Sustainable Growth, June, Washington, DC.

Buffie, E.F. (1992), 'Short- and Long-Run Effects of Fiscal Policy', *World Bank Economic Review*, 6.

Buiter, W.H. (1985), 'A Guide to Public Sector Debt and Deficits', *Economic Policy*, 1.

Buiter, W.H. (1988), 'Some Thoughts on the Role of Fiscal Policy in Stabilization and Structural Adjustment in Developing Countries', NBER Working Paper No. 2603, National Bureau of Economic Research, Cambridge, MA.

Buiter, W.H. (1989), 'Some Thoughts on the Role of Fiscal Policy in Stabilization and Structural Adjustment in Developing Countries', in W.H. Buiter (ed.), *Principles of Budgetary and Financial Policy*, MIT Press, Cambridge, MA.

Buiter, W.H. and U.R. Patel (1992), 'Debt, Deficits and Inflation: An Application to the Public Finances of India', *Journal of Public Economics*, 47.

Burdekin, R.C.K. and F.K. Langdana (1992), *Budget Deficits and Economic Performance*, Routledge, London.

Burki, S.J. and S. Edwards (1996), *Dismantling the Populist State: The Unfinished Revolution in Latin America*, Viewpoints, The World Bank, Washington, DC.

Calvo, G. (1995), 'Varieties of Capital Market Crises', Unpublished Working Paper, University of Maryland.

Calvo, G. (1996), 'Capital Flows and Macroeconomic Management: Tequila Lessons', Unpublished Working Paper, University of Maryland.

Calvo, G., L. Leiderman, and C.M. Reinhart (1993), 'Capital Inflows and Real Exchange Rate Appreciation in Latin America: The Role of External Factors', *IMF Staff Papers*, 40.

Calvo, G., L. Leiderman and C.M. Reinhart (1996), 'Inflows of Capital to Developing Countries in the 1990s', *Journal of Economic Perspectives*, 10.

Camdessus, M. (1989), 'The Role of the IMF in a Challenging World Economy', *Nationalokonomisk Tidsskrift*, 127.

Chand, S.K. (1987), 'Towards a Growth-Oriented Model of Financial Programming', IMF Working Paper WP/87/10, International Monetary Fund, Washington, DC.

Chen, S., G. Datt, and M. Ravallion (1994), 'Is Poverty Increasing or Decreasing in the Developing World', *Review of Income and Wealth*, 40.

Chenery, H.B. (1975), 'Structural Approach to Development Policy', *American Economic Review*, 65.

Chenery, H.B. and M. Bruno (1962), 'Development Alternatives in an Open Economy: The Case of Israel', *Economic Journal,* 72.

Chenery, H.B. and T.N. Srinivasan, eds (1988), *Handbook of Development Economics: Volume 1,* North Holland, Amsterdam.

Chenery, H.B. and T.N. Srinivasan, eds (1989), *Handbook of Development Economics: Volume 2,* North Holland, Amsterdam.

Chenery, H.B. and A.M. Strout (1966), 'Foreign Assistance and Economic Development', *American Economic Review,* 56.

Chenery, H.B., M.S. Ahluwalia, C. Bell, J. Duloy, and R. Jolly (1974), *Redistribution With Growth,* Oxford University Press, New York.

Choudhry, N.N. (1991), 'Collection Lags, Fiscal Revenue and Inflationary Financing: Empirical Evidence and Analysis', Working Paper No. 91/41, International Monetary Fund, Washington, DC.

Christ, C.F. (1969), 'A Model of Monetary and Fiscal Policy Effects on the Money Stock, Price Level and Real Output', *Journal of Money, Credit and Banking,* 1.

Clark, G. (1995), 'More Evidence on Income Distribution and Growth', *Journal of Development Economics,* 47.

Coe, D.T. and E. Helpman (1993), 'International R & D Spillovers', NBER Working Paper No. 4444, National Bureau of Economic Research, Cambridge, MA.

Cohen, D. (1988), 'External and Domestic Debt Constraints of LDCs: A Theory with Numerical Applications to Brazil and Mexico', *World Bank Economic Review,* 2.

Corbo, V., M. Goldstein, and M.S. Khan, eds (1987), *Growth Oriented Adjustment Programs,* IMF and World Bank, Washington, DC.

Corden, M. (1990), 'Macroeconomic Policy and Growth: Some Lessons of Experience', in S. Fischer, D. de Tray, and S. Shah (eds), *Proceedings of the World Bank Annual Conference on Development Economics,* Washington, DC.

Cornia, G.A., R. Jolly, and F. Stewart (1987a), *Adjustment with a Human Face: Volume I—Protecting the Vulnerable and Promoting Growth,* Clarendon Press, Oxford.

Cornia, G.A., R. Jolly, and F. Stewart (1987b), *Adjustment with a Human Face: Volume II—Ten Country Cases,* Clarendon Press, Oxford.

Crockett, A.D. (1981), 'Stabilization Policies in Developing Countries: Some Policy Considerations', *IMF Staff Papers,* 28.

Cumby, R. and S. van Wijnbergen (1989), 'Financial Policy and Speculative Runs with a Crawling Peg: Argentina 1979–81', *Journal of International Economics,* 27.

Daly, H.E. (1989), 'Towards a Measure of Sustainable Social Net National Product', in Y.J. Ahmad, S. El Serafy, and E. Lutz (eds), *Environmental Accounting for Sustainable Development,* UNEP–World Bank Symposium, The World Bank, Washington, DC.

Darby, M.R. (1975), 'The Financial and Tax Effects of Monetary Policy on Interest Rates', *Economic Inquiry,* 13.

Datt, G. and M. Ravallion (1992), 'Growth and Redistribution Components of Changes in Poverty Measures: A Decomposition with Applications to Brazil and India in the 1980s', *Journal of Development Economics,* 38.

Datt, G. and M. Ravallion (1996a), 'What was the Impact on Poverty of India's Macroeconomic Crisis and Stabilization?', Unpublished Report, Policy Research Department, The World Bank, Washington, DC.

Datt, G. and M. Ravallion (1996b), 'Why have Some States of India Performed Better than Others in Reducing Absolute Poverty?', Policy Research Working Paper No. 1594, The World Bank, Washington, DC.

Deininger, J. and L. Squire (1995), 'Income Distribution and Development', Unpublished Working Paper, Policy Research Department, The World Bank, Washington, DC.

de Gregorio, J. (1992), 'The Effects of Inflation on Economic Growth', *European Economic Review,* 36.

De Melo, M., C. Denizer, and A. Gelb (1996), 'From Plan to Market: Patterns of Transition', World Bank Working Paper: World Development Report 1996, The World Bank, Washington, DC.

Demirguic-Kunt, A. and R. Levine (1996), 'Stock Market Development and Financial Intermediaries: Stylized Facts', *The World Bank Economic Review,* 10.

Demirguic-Kunt, A. and E. Detragiache (1997), 'The Determinants of Banking Crises: Evidence from Developing and Developed Countries', Working Paper 97/106, International Monetary Fund, Washington, DC.

Diamond, P. (1965), 'National Debt in a Neoclassical Growth Model', *American Economic Review,* 55.

Diaz-Alejandro, C. (1985), 'Good-bye Financial Repression, Hello Financial Crash', *Journal of Development Economics,* 19.

Domar, E.D. (1946), 'Capital Expansion, Rate of Growth and Employment', *Econometrica*, 14.

Dornbusch, R. (1975), 'Exchange Rates and Fiscal Policy in a Popular Model of International Trade', *American Economic Review*, 65.

Dornbusch, R. (1977), 'Inflation, Capital and Deficit Finance', *Journal of Money, Credit and Banking*, 9.

Dornbusch, R. (1981), *Open Economy Macroeconomics*, Basic Books, New York.

Dornbusch, R. (1988), 'Balance of Payments Issues', in R. Dornbusch and F.L.C.H. Helmers (eds), *The Open Economy: Tools for Policy Makers in Developing Countries*, Oxford University Press, New York.

Dornbusch, R. and S. Edwards, eds (1991), *The Macroeconomics of Populism in Latin America*, University of Chicago Press, Chicago.

Dornbusch, R. and F.L.C.H. Helmers, eds (1988), *The Open Economy: Tools for Policy Makers in Developing Countries*, Oxford University Press, New York.

Drazen, A.H. and E. Helpman (1987), 'Stabilization with Exchange Rate Management', *Quarterly Journal of Economics*, 102.

Drazen, A.H. and E. Helpman (1990), 'Inflationary Consequences of Anticipated Macroeconomic Policies', *Review of Economic Studies*, 57.

Easterly, W. (1989), 'A Consistency Framework for Macroeconomic Analysis', Working Paper Series No. 234, The World Bank, Washington, DC.

Easterly, W. (1993), 'How Much do Distortions Affect Growth?', *Journal of Monetary Economics*, 32.

Easterly, W. and S. Rebelo (1993), 'Fiscal Policy and Economic Growth: An Empirical Investigation', *Journal of Monetary Economics*, 32.

Easterly, W. and K. Schmidt-Hebbel (1994), 'Fiscal Adjustment and Macroeconomic Performance: A Synthesis', in W. Easterly, C.A. Rodriguez, and K. Schmidt-Hebbel (eds), *Public Sector Deficits and Macroeconomic Performance*, Oxford University Press, New York.

Easterly, W., C.A. Rodriguez, and K. Schmidt-Hebbel, eds (1994), *Public Sector Deficits and Macroeconomic Performance*, Oxford University Press, New York.

Easterly, W., M. Kremer, L. Pritchett, and L.H. Summers (1993), 'Good Policy or Good Luck?: Country Growth Performance and Temporary Shocks', *Journal of Monetary Economics*, 32.

Edwards, S. (1988), *Exchange Rate Misalignment in Developing Countries,* The Johns Hopkins University Press, Baltimore.

Edwards, S. (1991), *Real Exchange Rates, Devaluation and Adjustment: Exchange Rate Policies in Developing Countries,* MIT Press, Cambridge, MA.

Edwards, S. and M.S. Khan (1985), 'Interest Rate Determination in Developing Countries: A Conceptual Framework', *IMF Staff Papers,* 32.

Eichengreen, B. and A.K. Rose (1998), 'Staying Afloat When the Wind Shifts: External Factors and Emerging-Market Banking Crises', NBER Working Paper No. 6370, National Bureau of Economic Research, Cambridge, MA.

Eichengreen, B., A.K. Rose, and C. Wyplosz (1996), 'Contagious Currency Crises: First Tests', *Scandinavian Journal of Economics,* 98.

Elias, V.J. (1990), *Sources of Growth: A Study of Seven Latin American Economies,* ICS Press, San Francisco.

El Serafy, S. (1989), 'The Proper Calculation of Income from Depletable Natural Resources', in Y.J. Ahmad, S. El Serafy, and E. Lutz (eds), *Environmental Accounting for Sustainable Development,* UNEP–World Bank Symposium, The World Bank, Washington, DC.

Eshag, D. (1983), *Fiscal and Monetary Policies and Problems in Developing Countries,* Cambridge University Press, Cambridge, MA.

Everaert, L., F. Garcia-Pinto, and J. Ventura (1989), 'An RMSM-X for Turkey', CECMG Manuscript, The World Bank, Washington, DC.

Fankhauser, S. (1994), 'The Social Costs of Greenhouse Gas Emissions: An Expected Value Approach', *The Energy Journal,* 15.

Feldstein, M. and C. Horioka (1982), 'Domestic Savings and International Capital Flows', *Economic Journal,* 92.

Findlay, R. (1971), 'The Foreign Exchange Gap and Growth in Developing Economies', in J.N. Bhagwati, R.W. Jones, R. Mundell, and J. Vanek (eds), *Trade, Balance of Payments and Growth,* North Holland, Amsterdam.

Fischer, S. (1991), 'Growth, Macroeconomics and Development', NBER Working Paper No. 3702, National Bureau of Economic Research, Cambridge, MA.

Fischer, S. (1993), 'Macroeconomic Factors in Growth', Paper presented at the Conference on *How Do National Policies Affect Long-Run Growth?,* July, Washington, DC.

Fischer, S. and W. Easterly (1990), 'The Economics of the Government Budget Constraint', *World Bank Research Observer,* 5.

Fishlow, A. (1995), 'Inequality, Poverty and Growth: Where Do We Stand?', in M. Bruno and B. Pleskovic (eds), *Annual World Bank Conference on Development Economics,* The World Bank, Washington, DC.

FitzGerald, E.V.K. (1988), 'The Analytics of Stabilization Policy in the Small Semi-Industrialized Economy', Development Economics Seminar Paper No. 7, Institute of Social Studies, The Hague.

Frenkel, J.A. and H.G. Johnson, eds (1976), *The Monetary Approach to the Balance of Payments,* George Allen & Unwin, London.

Friedman, M. (1968), 'The Role of Monetary Policy', *American Economic Review,* 58.

Friedman, M. (1970), 'A Theoretical Framework for Monetary Analysis', *Journal of Political Economy,* 78.

Friedman, B. (1978), 'Crowding Out or Crowding In? The Economic Consequences of Financing Government Fiscal Deficits', *Brookings Papers on Economic Activity,* 3.

Fry, M.J. (1988), *Money, Interest and Banking in Economic Development,* Johns Hopkins University Press, Baltimore.

Fry, M.J. (1993), 'Financial Repression and Economic Growth', Working Paper No. 93-07, University of Birmingham.

Gastil, R.D. (1987), *Freedom in the World,* Greenwood Press, Westport.

Gelb, A. (1989), 'Financial Policies, Growth and Efficiency', Working Paper WPS 202, The World Bank, Washington, DC.

Gibson, H.D. and E. Tsakaiotos (1994), 'The Scope and Limits of Financial Liberalization in Developing Countries: A Critical Survey', *Journal of Development Economics,* 30.

Goldschmidt-Clermont, L. (1982), *Unpaid Work in the Household,* International Labour Organization, Geneva.

Goldstein, M. (1986), 'Global Effects of Fund-Supported Adjustment Programs', IMF Occasional Papers No. 42, International Monetary Fund, Washington. DC.

Goldstein, M. (1996), 'Presumptive Indicators/Early Warning Signals of Vulnerability to Financial Crises in Emerging Market Economies', Unpublished, Institute of International Economics, Washington, DC.

Grier, K. and G. Tullock (1989), 'An Empirical Analysis of Cross-National Economic Growth: 1951–80', *Journal of Monetary Economics,* 28.

Grilli, V. (1990), 'Managing Exchange Rate Crises: Evidence from the 1890s', *Journal of International Money and Finance*, 9.

Guitian, M. (1981), 'Fund Conditionality: Evolution of Principles and Practices', IMF Pamphlet Series No. 38, International Monetary Fund, Washington, DC.

Gunning, J.W. (1983), 'Rationing in an Open Economy: Fix-Price Equilibrium and Two-Gap Models', *European Economic Review*, 23.

Haan, J. and D. Zelhorst (1990), 'The Impact of Government Deficits on Money Growth in Developing Countries', *Journal of International Money and Finance*, 9.

Haggard, S. and R. Kaufman, eds (1992), *The Politics of Economic Adjustment*, Princeton University Press, Princeton, New Jersey.

Hamilton, K. (1995), 'Genuine Savings in Developing Countries', CSERGE, University of East Anglia and University College, London.

Haque, N.U. and P.J. Montiel (1994), 'The Macroeconomics of Public Sector Deficits: The Case of Pakistan', in W. Easterly, C.A. Rodriguez and K. Schmidt-Hebbel (eds), *Public Sector Deficits and Macroeconomic Performance*, Oxford University Press, New York.

Harberger, A.C. (1963), 'The Dynamics of Inflation in Chile', in C.F. Christ (ed.), *Measurement in Economics: Studies in Mathematical Economics and Econometrics in Memory of Yehuda Gruenfeld*, Stanford University Press, Stanford.

Harberger, A.C. (1986), 'Economic Adjustment and the Real Exchange Rate', in S. Edwards, and L. Ahmed (eds), *Economic Adjustment and Exchange Rates in Developing Countries*, University of Chicago Press, Chicago.

Harrod, R.F. (1939), 'An Essay in Dynamic Theory', *Economic Journal*, 49.

Havrylyshyn, O. (1976), 'The Value of Household Services: A Survey of Empirical Estimates', *Review of Income and Wealth*, 22.

Hemmings, R. and J. Daniel (1995), 'When is a Fiscal Surplus Appropriate?', Papers on Policy Analysis and Assessment, No. 95/2, International Monetary Fund, Washington, DC.

International Monetary Fund (1977), *The Monetary Approach to the Balance of Payments*, IMF, Washington, DC.

International Monetary Fund (1985), *Fund-Supported Adjustment Programs and Economic Growth*, IMF, Washington. DC.

International Monetary Fund (1987), *Theoretical Aspects of the Design of Fund-Supported Adjustment Programs,* Occasional Paper No. 55, IMF, Washington, DC.

International Monetary Fund (1995), *Guidelines for Fiscal Adjustment,* Pamphlet Series No. 49, IMF, Washington. DC.

International Monetary Fund (1998), *World Economic Outlook,* IMF, Washington, DC.

Ize, A. and G. Ortiz (1987), 'Fiscal Rigidities, Public Debt and Capital Flight', *IMF Staff Papers,* 34.

Johnson, G.G. (1985), 'Formulation of Exchange Rate Policies in Adjustment Programs', IMF Occasional Papers, No. 36, International Monetary Fund, Washington, DC.

Johnson, H.G. (1958), *International Trade and Economic Growth,* George Allen & Unwin, London.

Johnson, H.G. (1977), 'The Monetary Approach to the Balance of Payments', *Journal of International Economics,* 7.

Jung, J. (1992), 'Personal Income Distribution in Korea, 1962–86: A Human Capital Approach', *Journal of Asian Economics,* 3.

Kalecki, M. (1971), *Selected Essays on the Dynamics of the Capitalist Economy,* Cambridge University Press, New York.

Kaminsky, G.L. and C.M. Reinhart (1996), 'The Twin Crises: The Causes of Banking and Balance-of-Payments Problems', International Finance Discussion Paper No. 544, Board of Governors of the Federal Reserve System, Washington, DC.

Kaminsky, G.L., S. Lizondo and C.M. Reinhart (1997), 'Leading Indicators of Currency Crises', Working Paper No. 97/79, International Monetary Fund, Washington, DC.

Kelley, M.R. (1982), 'Fiscal Adjustment and Fund-Supported Programs', *IMF Staff Papers,* 29.

Keynes, J.M. (1923), *A Tract on Monetary Reform,* MacMillan Press, London.

Keynes, J.M. (1936), *The General Theory of Employment, Interest and Money,* MacMillan Press, London.

Khan, M.S. (1981), 'Macroeconomic Adjustment in Developing Countries: A Policy Perspective', *World Bank Research Observer,* 2.

Khan, M.S. and M.D. Knight (1981), 'Stabilization Programs in Developing Countries: A Formal Framework', *IMF Staff Papers,* 28.

Khan, M.S. and M.D. Knight (1982), 'Some Theoretical and Empirical Issues Relating to Economic Stabilization in Developing Countries', *World Development,* 10.

Khan, M.S. and M.D. Knight (1985), 'Fund-Supported Adjustment Programs and Economic Growth', *IMF Occasional Papers*, No. 41, International Monetary Fund, Washington, DC.

Khan, M.S. and P.J. Montiel (1989), 'Growth-Oriented Adjustment Programs: A Conceptual Framework', *IMF Staff Papers*, 36.

Khan, M.S. and P.J. Montiel (1990), 'A Marriage Between Fund and Bank Models: A Reply to Polak', *IMF Staff Papers*, 37.

Khan, M.S. and D. Villanueva (1991), 'Macroeconomic Policies and Long-Term Growth: A Conceptual and Empirical Review', IMF Working Paper, WP/91/28, International Monetary Fund, Washington, DC.

Khan, M.S., P.J. Montiel, and N.U. Haque (1990), 'Adjustment With Growth: Relating the Analytical Approaches of the IMF and the World Bank', *Journal of Development Economics*, 32.

Khan, M.S., P.J. Montiel, and N.U. Haque, eds (1991), *Macroeconomic Models for Adjustment in Developing Countries*, International Monetary Fund, Washington, DC.

Kindleberger, C.P. (1978), *Manias, Panics and Crashes: A History of Financial Crises*, Basic Books, New York.

Kletzer, K. (1988), 'External Borrowings by LDCs: A Survey of Some Theoretical Issues', in G. Ranis and P.T. Schultz (eds), *The State of Development Economics*, Basil Blackwell, New York.

Knack, S. and P. Keefer (1995), 'Institutions and Economic Performance', *Economics and Politics*, 7.

Kormendi, R.C. and P.G. Meguire (1985), 'Macroeconomic Determinants of Growth: Cross-Country Evidence', *Journal of Monetary Economics*, 24.

Kragh, B. (1970), *Financial Programming*, Publication No. 27 (143), OECD, Paris.

Krugman, P. (1979), 'A Model of Balance of Payments Crises', *Journal of Money, Credit and Banking*, 11.

Krugman, P. (1988), 'External Shocks and Domestic Policy Responses', in R. Dornbusch and F.L.C.H. Helmers (eds), *The Open Economy: Tools for Policymakers in Developing Countries*, Oxford University Press, New York.

Krugman, P. (1998), 'Bubbles, Boom and Crash: Theoretical Notes on Asia's Crises', Unpublished, Massachusetts Institute of Technology, Cambridge, MA.

Krugman, P. (1999a), 'Analytical Afterthoughts on the Asian Crises', Unpublished, Massachusetts Institute of Technology, Cambridge, MA.

Krugman, P. (1999b), 'Balance Sheets, the Transfer Problem and Financial Crises', in *Festschrift in Honour of Robert Flood,* MIT Press, Cambridge, MA.

Krugman, P. and L. Taylor (1978), 'Contractionary Effects of Devaluation', *Journal of International Economics,* 8.

Kunte, A. (1996), 'Estimating a Nation's Wealth: Methodology and Preliminary Results', Information Paper, Pollution and Environmental Economics Division, The World Bank, Washington, DC.

Kuznets, S. (1955), 'Economic Growth and Income Inequality', *American Economic Review,* 45.

Kuznets, S. (1966), *Modern Economic Growth,* Yale University Press, New Haven.

Lal, D. (2000), *The Poverty of 'Development Economics',* Oxford University Press, Delhi.

Leipert, C. (1985), 'Social Costs as a Factor of Economic Growth', in P. Ekins (ed.), *The Living Economy: A New Economics in the Making,* Routledge and Kegan, London.

Levine, R. and D. Renalt (1992), 'A Sensitivity Analysis of Cross-Country Growth Regressions', *American Economic Review,* 82.

Levine, R. and S.J. Zervos (1996), 'Stock Market Development and Long-Run Growth', *World Bank Economic Review,* 10.

Li, H., L. Squire, and H. Zou (1995), 'Income Inequality, Human Capital Accumulation and Political Economy', Mimeograph, The World Bank, Washington, DC.

Little, I.M.D., R. Cooper, M. Corden, and S. Rajapatirana (1993), *Boom, Crisis and Adjustment: The Macroeconomic Experience of Developing Countries,* Oxford University Press, New York.

Lucas. R.E., Jr. (1972), 'Expectations and the Neutrality of Money', *Journal of Economic Theory,* 4.

Lucas, R.E., Jr. (1986), 'Principles of Fiscal and Monetary Policies', *Journal of Monetary Economics,* 25.

Lucas, R.E., Jr. (1988), 'On the Mechanism of Economic Development', *Journal of Monetary Economics,* 27.

Lutz, E., ed. (1993), *Toward Improved Accounting for the Environment,* UNSTAT-World Bank Symposium, World Bank, Washington, DC.

Mankiw, G.N. (1995), 'The Growth of Nations', *Brookings Papers on Economic Activity,* 20.

Mankiw, N.G., D.H. Romer, and D.S. Weil (1992), 'A Contribution to the Empirics of Economic Growth', *Quarterly Journal of Economics,* 107.

Masson, P.R. (1998), 'Contagion: Monsoonal Effects, Spillovers, and Jumps Between Multiple Equilibria', Unpublished, International Monetary Fund, Washington, DC.

McKinnon, R.I. (1964), 'Foreign Exchange Constraints in Economic Development', *Economic Journal,* 74.

McKinnon, R.I. (1973), *Money and Capital in Economic Development,* Brookings Institution, Washington, DC.

McKinnon, R.I. (1989), 'Financial Liberalization and Economic Development: A Re-assessment of Interest Rate Policies in Asia and Latin America', *Oxford Review of Economic Policy,* 5.

McKinnon, R.I. (1991), *The Order of Economic Liberalization,* Johns Hopkins University Press, New York.

Meade, J. (1951), *The Balance of Payments. Volume I: The Theory of International Economic Policy,* Oxford University Press, Oxford.

Mills, C.A. and R. Nallari (1992), *Analytical Approaches to Stabilization and Adjustment Programs*, EDI Seminar Paper, No. 44, The World Bank, Washington, DC.

Montiel, P.J. (1990), 'Orthodox Models for Adjustment and Growth', *Ricerche Economiche,* XLIV.

Mosley, P. (1989), 'Effective Stabilization Policy in Less Developed Countries', *Journal of International Development,* 1.

Mundell, R.A. (1963), 'Inflation and Real Interest', *Journal of Political Economy,* 71.

Mundell, R.A. (1968), *International Economics,* MacMillan, New York.

Murphy, M. (1980), 'The Measurement and Valuation of Non-Market Economic Activities', in C. Hefferan (ed.), *The Household As Producer: A Look Beyond The Market,* American Home Economics Association, Washington, DC.

Musgrave, R.M. (1959), *The Theory of Public Finance: A Study in Public Economics,* McGraw Hill, New York.

Nordhaus, W. and J. Tobin (1972), 'Is Growth Obsolete?', in *Economic Growth,* NBER General Series 96, New York.

North, D.C. (1990), *Institutions, Institutional Change and Economic Performance,* Cambridge University Press, Cambridge, MA.

Obstfeld, M. (1994), 'The Logic of Currency Crises', *Cahiers Economiques et Monetaires,* 43.

Olivera, J.H. (1967), 'Money, Prices and Fiscal Lags: A Note on the Dynamics of Inflation', *Banca Nazionale del Lavoro Quarterly Review,* 20.

Olson, M. (1982), *The Rise and Decline of Nations: Economic Growth, Stagflation and Social Rigidities,* Yale University Press, New Haven.

Orsmund, D. (1990), 'The Size of Government and Economic Growth: A Methodological Review', Unpublished, International Monetary Fund, Washington, DC.

Pagano, M. (1993), 'Financial Markets and Growth: An Overview', *European Economic Review,* 37.

Papanek, G. and O. Kyn (1986), 'The Effect on Income Distribution of Development, the Growth Rate and Economic Strategy', *Journal of Development Economics,* 23.

Park, Y.C. (1991), 'Financial Repression and Liberalization', in L.B. Krause and K. Kihwan (eds), *Liberalization in the Process of Economic Development,* University of California Press, Berkeley.

Persson, T. and G. Tabellini (1994), 'Is Inequality Harmful for Growth? Theory and Evidence', *American Economic Review,* 84.

Phelps, E.S. (1973), 'Inflation in the Theory of Public Finance', *Swedish Journal of Economics,* 75.

Phylaktis, K. and M.P. Taylor (1992), 'Monetary Dynamics of Sustained High Inflation: Taiwan, 1945-1949', *Southern Economic Journal,* 58.

Phylaktis, K. and M.P. Taylor (1993), 'Money Demand, the Cagan Model and the Inflation Tax: Some Latin American Evidence', *Review of Economics and Statistics,* 75.

Polak, J.J. (1957), 'Monetary Analysis of Income Formation and Payments Problems', *IMF Staff Papers,* 4.

Polak, J.J. (1990), 'A Marriage Between Fund and Bank Models?', *IMF Staff Papers,* 37.

Polak, J.J. and V. Argy (1971), 'Credit Policy and the Balance of Payments', *IMF Staff Papers,* 18.

Quirk, P.J., B.C. Christensen, K-M. Huh, and T. Sasaki (1987), 'Floating Exchange Rates in Developing Countries', *IMF Occasional Paper No 53,* International Monetary Fund, Washington, DC.

Rama, M. (1993), 'Empirical Investment Equations in Developing Countries', in L. Serven and A. Solimano (eds), *Striving for Growth After Adjustment,* The World Bank, Washington, DC.

Rao, M.J.M. (1987), *Filtering and Control of Macroeconomic Systems,* North Holland, Amsterdam.

Rao, M.J.M. (1992a), *Money, Deficits and Inflation,* Monograph Series, Indian Economic Association Trust for Research and Development, Interest Publications, New Delhi.

Rao, M.J.M. (1992b), 'Operating Procedures for Conducting Monetary Policy', *Indian Economic Journal,* 39.

Rao, M.J.M. (1994), 'The Explosive Dynamics of Hyperinflation: A Study in Pitchfork Bifurcations', Paper presented at the *Twelfth European Meeting on Cybernetics and Systems Research,* April, Vienna.

Rao, M.J.M. (1997a), 'Financial Openness, Shadow Floating Exchange Rates and Speculative Attacks', *Economic and Political Weekly,* XXXII (46).

Rao, M.J.M. (1997b), 'The Macroeconomics of Capital Account Convertibility', *Economic and Political Weekly,* XXXII (51).

Rao, M.J.M. and S. Bhogle (1990), 'The Chaotic Dynamics of Hyperinflation', Project Document DU 9004, *National Aerospace Laboratories,* Bangalore.

Rao, M.J.M. and A.V. Karnik (1994), 'Economic Systems, Political Structures and Human Rights', *Bulletin of Economic Research,* 46.

Rao, M.J.M. and S.M. Rao (1998), 'Interest Rate Targeting: The Critical Role of the Fiscal Stance', *Economic and Political Weekly,* XXXIII (29–30).

Rao, M.J.M. and B. Singh (1995), *Analytical Foundations of Financial Programming and Growth-oriented Adjustment,* DRG Study No. 10, Reserve Bank of India, RBI Press, Bombay.

Rao, M.J.M. and B. Singh (1996), 'Designing Growth-oriented Structural Adjustment Programmes: A Financial Programming Approach for the Indian Economy', Paper presented at the International Seminar on Development Planning: Relevance and Approaches, March, New Delhi.

Rao, M.J.M. and B. Singh (1998), 'Optimizing the Pace of Capital Account Convertibility', *Economic and Political Weekly,* XXXIII (21).

Rao, M.J.M., A.P. Samant, and N.L. Asher (1999), 'Macroeconomic Database in a Consistency Accounting Framework (1950–51 – 1997–98) – I: Identifying Sectoral and Economy-Wide Budget Constraints', *Economic and Political Weekly,* XXXIV (32).

Ravallion, M. (1995), 'Growth and Poverty: Evidence for the Developing World', *Economics Letters,* 63.

Ravallion, M. and G. Datt (1995), 'Growth and Poverty in Rural India', Policy Research Department Working Paper No. 1405, The World Bank, Washington, DC.

Ravallion, M. and G. Datt (1996), 'How Important to India's Poor is the Sectoral Composition of Growth?', *World Bank Economic Review*, 10.

Rebelo, S. (1991), 'Long Run Analysis and Long Run Growth', *Journal of Political Economy*, 99.

Reinhart, C.M. (1991), 'A Model of Adjustment and Growth: An Empirical Analysis', in M.S. Khan, P.J. Montiel, and N.U. Haque (eds), *Macroeconomic Models for Adjustment in Developing Countries*, International Monetary Fund, Washington, DC.

Robichek, E.W. (1967), 'Financial Programming Exercises of the International Monetary Fund in Latin America', Address to a Seminar of Brazilian Professors of Economics, September, Rio de Janeiro.

Robichek, E.W. (1971), 'Financial Programming: Stand-By Arrangements and Stabilization Programs', Mimeograph, International Monetary Fund, Washington, DC.

Robichek, E.W. (1985), 'Financial Programming as Practiced by the IMF', Mimeograph, The World Bank, Washington, DC.

Romer, P.M. (1986), 'Increasing Return and Long-Run Growth', *Journal of Political Economy*, 94.

Romer, P.M. (1990), 'Endogenous Technological Change', *Journal of Political Economy*, 98.

Ruttan, V. (1971), 'Technology and the Environment', *American Journal of Agricultural Economics*, 53.

Sachs, J. (1990), 'Social Conflict and Populist Policies in Latin America', Occasional Papers No. 9, International Center for Economic Growth, San Francisco.

Sachs, J. (1996), 'Economic Transition and the Exchange Rate Regime', *American Economic Review* Papers and Proceedings, 86.

Sachs, J., A. Tornell, and A. Velasco (1995), 'The Collapse of the Mexican Peso: What Have We Learned?', Harvard Institute of Economic Research, Discussion Paper No. 1724, Harvard University, Cambridge, MA.

Sachs, J., A. Tornell, and A. Velasco (1996), 'Financial Crisis in Emerging Markets: The Lessons From 1995', NBER Working Paper No. 5576, National Bureau of Economic Research, Cambridge, MA.

Saint-Paul, G. (1992), 'Fiscal Policy in an Endogenous Growth Model', *Quarterly Journal of Economics,* 107.

Sargent, T.J. (1985), 'Reaganomics and Credibility', in A. Ando, H. Eguchi, R. Farmer, and Y. Suzuki (eds), *Monetary Policy in Our Times,* MIT Press, Cambridge, MA.

Sargent, T.J. and N. Wallace (1975), 'Rational Expectations, the Optimum Monetary Instrument and the Optimal Money Supply Rule', *Journal of Political Economy,* 83.

Sargent, T.J. and N. Wallace (1981), 'Some Unpleasant Monetarist Arithmetic', *Federal Reserve Bank of Minneapolis Quarterly Review,* 5.

Seers, D. (1963), 'The Limitations of the Special Case', *Oxford Bulletin of Economics and Statistics,* 25.

Seers, D. (1969), 'The Meaning of Development', *International Development Review,* 11.

Serageldin, I. (1996), 'Sustainability and the Wealth of Nations: First Steps in an Ongoing Journey', Environmentally Sustainable Development Studies and Monographs Series, No. 5, The World Bank, Washington, DC.

Serven, L. and J. Ventura (1989), 'The Structure and Closure of a Macroeconomic Model', CECMG Manuscript, The World Bank, Washington, DC.

Shaw, E.S (1973), *Financial Deepening in Economic Development,* Oxford University Press, New York.

Solow, R.M. (1956), 'A Contribution to the Theory of Economic Growth', *Quarterly Journal of Economics,* 70.

Standaert, S. (1985), 'The Foreign Exchange Constraint, Suppression of the Trade Deficit and the Shadow Price of Foreign Exchange in a Fix-Price Economy', *Journal of Development Economics,* 18.

Summers. L. and L. Pritchet (1993), 'The Structural Adjustment Debate', *American Economic Review Papers and Proceedings,* 83.

Tanzi, V. (1976), 'Inflation, Indexation and Interest Income Taxation', *Quarterly Review,* 116.

Tanzi, V. (1978), 'Inflation, Real Tax Revenue and the Case for Inflationary Finance: Theory with an Application to Argentina', *IMF Staff Papers,* 25.

Tanzi, V. (1988), 'Lags in Tax Collection and the Case for Inflationary Finance: Theory with Simulations', in M.I. Blejer and K.Y. Chu (eds), *Fiscal Policy, Stabilization and Growth in Developing Countries,* International Monetary Fund, Washington, DC.

Tanzi, V., ed. (1993), *Transition to Market: Studies in Fiscal Reform,* International Monetary Fund, Washington, DC.

Tarp, F. (1993), *Stabilization and Structural Adjustment,* Routledge, London.

Taylor, L. (1983), *Structuralist Macroeconomics: Applicable Models for the Third World,* Basic Books, New York.

Taylor, L. (1987), 'IMF Conditionality: Incomplete Theory, Policy Malpractice', in R.J. Myers (ed.), *The Political Morality of the International Monetary Fund,* Transactions Books, New Jersey.

Taylor, L. (1988), *Varieties of Stabilization Experience: Towards Sensible Macroeconomics in the Third World,* Clarendon Press, Oxford.

Taylor, L. (1989), *Stabilization and Growth in Developing Countries: A Structuralist Approach,* Harwood Academic, New York.

Taylor, L., ed. (1990), *Socially Relevant Policy Analysis: Structuralist Computable General Equilibrium Models for the Developing World,* MIT Press, Cambridge, MA.

Taylor, L. (1991), *Income Distribution, Inflation and Growth: Lectures on Structuralist Macroeconomic Theory,* MIT Press, Cambridge, MA.

Taylor, L. (1993), 'The Rocky Road to Reform: Trade, Industrial, Financial and Agricultural Strategies', *World Development,* 21.

Taylor, L. (1994), 'Gap Models', *Journal of Development Economics,* 45.

Taylor, L. and P. Arida (1989), 'Long-Run Macroeconomics', in H.B. Chenery and T.N. Srinivasan (eds), *Handbook of Development Economics,* North Holland, Amsterdam..

Taylor, L. and U. Pieper (1995), 'Reconciling Economic Reform and Sustainable Human Development: Social Consequences of Neo-Liberalism', Discussion Paper Series, Office of Development Studies, UNDP, New York.

Tornell, A. and A. Velasco (1992), 'Tragedy of the Commons and Economic Growth: Why Does Capital Flow from Poor to Rich Countries', *Journal of Political Economy,* 100.

Turnovsky, S.J. (1977), *Macroeconomic Analysis and Stabilization Policy,* Cambridge University Press, Cambridge, MA.

Turnovsky, S.J. (1995), *Methods of Macroeconomic Dynamics,* MIT Press, Cambridge, MA.

United Nations Development Programme (1993), *Human Development Report 1993,* Oxford University Press, New York.

Waelbroeck, J. (1984), 'Capital, Foreign Exchange and Growth: The Two-Gap and Labor-Income-Flow Views', in M. Syrquin, L. Taylor, and L. Westphal (eds), *Economic Structure and Performance*, Academic Press, Orlando.

Warford, J.J., W. Cruz, and S. Hansen (1994), 'The Evolution of Environmental Concerns in Adjustment Lending: A Review', Environmental Department Working Paper No. 65, The World Bank, Washington, DC.

Weingast, B.R. (1994), 'Political Impediments to Economic Reform: Political Risk and Enduring Gridlock', IPR Working Paper Series No. IPR68, Institute for Policy Reform, Washington, DC.

Whalley, J. (1984), 'A Review of Numerical Modelling Activity at the World Bank', Unpublished Report, The World Bank, Washington, DC.

van Wijnbergen, S. (1986), 'Macroeconomic Aspects of the Effectiveness of Foreign Aid: On the Two-Gap Model, Home Goods Disequilibrium and the Real Exchange Rate Misalignment', *Journal of International Economics*, 21.

van Wijnbergen, S. (1991), 'Fiscal Deficits, Exchange Rate Crisis and Inflation', *Review of Economic Studies*, 58.

van Wijnbergen, S., R. Anand, A. Chhibber, and R. Rocha (1992), *External Debt, Fiscal Policy and Sustainable Growth in Turkey*, Johns Hopkins University Press, Baltimore.

Williamson, J., ed. (1990), *Latin American Adjustment: How Much Has Happened?*, Institute of International Economics, Washington, DC.

Williamson, J., ed. (1994), *The Political Economy of Policy Reform*, Institute of International Economics, Washington, DC.

World Bank (1989), 'Adjustment Lending: An Evaluation of Ten Years of Experience', Policy and Research Series Paper 1, The World Bank, Washington, DC.

World Bank (1990a), 'The Third Report on Adjustment Lending ', Policy and Research Series Paper 12, The World Bank, Washington, DC.

World Bank (1990b), 'Adjustment Lending for Sustainable Growth', Policy and Research Series Paper 14, The World Bank, Washington, DC.

World Bank (1990c), *World Development Report 1990*, The World Bank, Washington DC.

World Bank (1993a), *The East Asian Miracle*, Oxford University Press, New York.

World Bank (1993b), *World Development Report 1993,* The World Bank, Washington DC.

World Bank (1995), 'Monitoring Environmental Progress', Environmentally Sustainable Development, The World Bank, Washington, DC.

World Bank (1996), *World Development Report 1996,* The World Bank, Washington, DC.

Young, A. (1995), 'The Tyranny of Numbers: Confronting the Statistical Realities of the East Asian Growth Experience', *Quarterly Journal of Economics,* 110.

Name Index

Subject Index

Adjustment, *see* growth, macroeconomic, structural adjustment, stabilization
alternatives to orthodox models/programmes of 253–75
asymmetric conditionality and 272
costs (high) of delayed 57, 210
deficit growth and fiscal 166–98
domestic credit expansion in *see* credit, 45
financial programming and growth-oriented 116–41
fiscal deficit and failure of 163
getting the exchange rate 'right' in 57–9
growth programming and 100–15
guidelines for fiscal 51–7
interest rate determination in 148–53
long term 42,56, 239, 309
policy coordination in 191, 193, 209–10
programmes 42–3, 55–7, 60, 91–4
short-run 61, 260
(and) stagnation 309

'with a human face' 236–9
agriculture, gains to poor from 245
sector reforms 4
assets, acquisition 34–5; (financing of) 31; (and savings) 23–4, 39
domestic/foreign 148
foreign exchange 34, 67,147
money and capital 146
state owned 6
asymmetric information 290

balance of payments (BOP) 2, 15, 25, 41, 43, 63, 69, 235, 307
disequilibria in 105, 116
forecasts 126
IMF and monetary approach to (MABP) 17, 37, 45, 47, 74–9; (Chicago version) 75–7; (money demand in) 79
Polack model in analysis of 72–4
surplus as inflationary 49
balances (in national accounts), *see* growth models
external 71–2, 119, 206
monetary 119, 150
national 101
savings–investment 37–9, 43, 52, 71, 101, 119